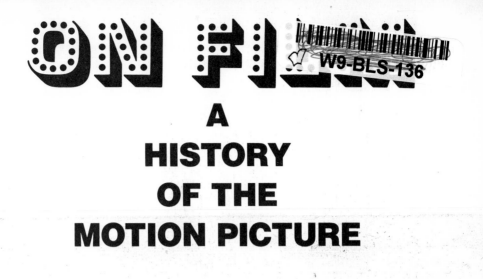

ON FILM

A
HISTORY
OF THE
MOTION PICTURE

ON FILM

A
HISTORY
OF THE
MOTION PICTURE

Frank E. Beaver
The University of Michigan

McGraw-Hill Book Company

New York   St. Louis   San Francisco   Auckland
Bogotá   Hamburg   Johannesburg   London   Madrid
Mexico   Montreal   New Delhi   Panama   Paris
São Paulo   Singapore   Sydney   Tokyo   Toronto

To my wife, Gail,
and
my parents,
John and Louise Beaver

ON FILM: A HISTORY OF THE MOTION PICTURE

Copyright © 1983 by McGraw-Hill, Inc. All rights reserved.
Printed in the United States of America. Except as permitted under the
United States Copyright Act of 1976, no part of this publication may be
reproduced or distributed in any form or by any means, or stored in a data
base or retrieval system, without the prior written permission of the
publisher.

1234567890 DODO 898765432

ISBN 0-07-004213-6 SC
ISBN 0-07-004219-5 HC

Library of Congress Cataloging in Publication Data

Beaver, Frank Eugene.
On film.

Includes bibliographies and index.
1. Moving-pictures.   2. Cinematography.
3. Moving-pictures—History.   I. Title.
PN1994.B39   791.43'09   82-196
ISBN 0-07-004213-6 (pbk)   AACR2
ISBN 0-07-004219-5

This book was set in Baskerville by Black Dot, Inc. (ECU).
The editors were Phillip A. Butcher and David Dunham;
the designer was Joan E. O'Connor; the production supervisor was Phil Galea.
The cover photograph was taken by Demarco/Tomaccio Studio.
R. R. Donnelley & Sons Company was printer and binder.

PHOTO CREDITS

Photographic stills of *The Great Train Robbery* chase and of the Magic
Lantern were provided by the George Eastman House International
Museum of Photography, Rochester, N.Y. All additional photographs
are the courtesy of the Museum of Modern Art Stills Library and the
University of Michigan Photographic Services Laboratory. The author
wishes to thank Columbia Pictures, MGM, Paramount, Warner Brothers, RKO, Twentieth Century-Fox, United Artists, and Universal Studios
for their cooperation in making stills available for this history of film.

CONTENTS

Part 5 NEW DEVELOPMENTS IN AMERICA AND EUROPE

PREFACE

The intention of *On Film* is to trace the development and progress of an art form that was born of technological innovation, nurtured by commercial enterprise, and brought to full stature by a host of international visionaries: directors, producers, studio chieftains, cinematographers, editors, performers, and writers.

The book's primary focus is on the aesthetic and stylistic contributions made to a unique medium of artistic expression by both pioneering filmmakers and mature practitioners, particularly those who helped discover the language and syntax of cinema and those who along the way have stood apart as important individualists.

They are men and women who have "mastered" the medium: sometimes through revolutionary methods, at other times through the forceful presentation of startling ideas; sometimes in a large body of film work, frequently in quite limited but still important effort.

In no way does this history pretend to have included every important filmmaker or to have singled out every innovative motion picture. Rather it has sought to provide a representative sampling, hopefully extensive, of people, films, and events that have affected the course of the cinema.

In recording the evolution and progress of film art, this history has taken into account in addition to the achievements of individual filmmakers those aesthetic and stylistic innovations resulting from aggregate interests and from the impact of political and cultural events. A group of avant-garde artists, for example, living in Paris in the 1920s, sees the rhythmic possibilities of the motion picture as opportunities for further experimentation with abstract methods of expression; Metro-Goldwyn-

Mayer under the strict guidance of Louis B. Mayer emphasizes glamorous stars and studio production values for a highly romantic film style during the thirties and forties; an embittered Italy at the conclusion of World War II turns to documentarylike, neorealistic methods of storytelling to expose forcefully the impact of social injustices within the country; the arrival of television in the late forties acts along with other social changes to impel the American film industry toward more sensational content and technologically inspired motion-picture experiences.

The unique personality of nations, of production organizations, of special-interest groups, and of the times in which films are made have also helped to shape motion-picture art. These influences and their impact on the cinema have been integrated into this aesthetic history of the medium.

ACKNOWLEDGMENTS

The realization of this book would not have been possible without the inspiration and assistance of a number of people and, hence, many thanks are in order. First, I want to express my gratitude to Julie, John, and Johanna, to Wayne Beaver, Nancy Spivey, Pat Chafin, John Place, Josephine Place, and Miriam Stephan. Their constant love, encouragement, and interest in this project carried me through to the end.

I owe thanks, too, to Kathryn Notestine, who typed the manuscript, and to David Zuppke, who served as my research assistant. Their help and criticism were inestimable.

I am also indebted to the group of perceptive reviewers who read the text in the early and later stages of its preparation and offered me their good advice: John Wellman, Northern Illinois University; David Yellin, Memphis State University; and Robert Holkeboer, Eastern Michigan University. I am especially grateful to Bob Holkeboer for his painstaking examination of my work. His constructive criticism made a major contribution to this book. Any errors that may still exist, however, are solely my own.

Carlos Clarens and Mary Corliss at the Museum of Modern Art and George Pratt at the George Eastman House Museum of Photography helped me to secure the stills used throughout the text. To them I also owe thanks.

And finally, special gratitude for support and advice must go to my sponsoring editor, Phillip Butcher, and to my development editor, David Dunham. I could not have had better, closer, or more tactful assistance than that provided by these two fine editors at McGraw-Hill. They made the long task of completing this film history a rewarding experience. I am truly grateful to them and to all those generous people listed above.

Frank E. Beaver

PART 1

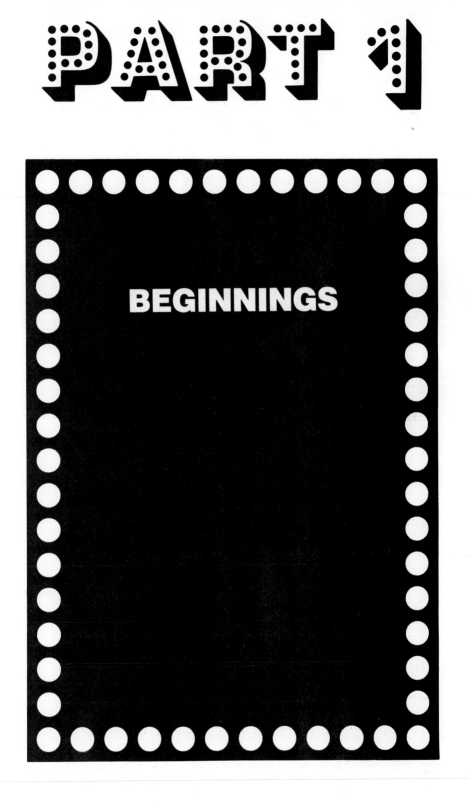

BEGINNINGS

SCIENCE PRODUCES
A NEW ART

Lumière's Cinématographe created a decided sensation here last week. It was fully described in last week's *Mirror,* and it is only necessary to add that the audiences were very enthusiastic over the new discovery. The depot picture with its stirring arrival of an express train, and the charge of the French hussars were wildly applauded and each of the pictures came in for its share of approval. A new picture was shown which represented the noon-hour at the factory of the Messrs. Lumière in Lyons, France. As the whistle blew, the factory doors were thrown open and men, women and children came trooping out. Several of the employees had bicycles, which they mounted outside the gate, and rode off. A carryall, which the Lumières keep to transport those who live at a distance from the factory, came dashing out in the most natural manner imaginable. A lecturer was employed to explain the pictures as they were shown, but he was hardly necessary, as the views speak for themselves.

A reporter writing for *The New York Dramatic Mirror,* July 11, 1896, p. 1.

Lumière workers leaving factory.

Through the combined achievements of scientists and artists from many different countries a workable moving-picture camera was realized near the end of the nineteenth century. The development of the motion picture had involved centuries of technological innovation by individuals who were curiously attracted to exploring various means of creating and projecting moving images.

THE *CAMERA OBSCURA*

As early as the eleventh century scientists had discovered the possibility of projecting light through a small hole so that a part of the exterior scene would appear on an interior surface. Astronomers at that time used the projections to study the heavens in greater detail.

In the sixteenth century the Italian artist-inventor Leonardo da Vinci outlined the concept of the *camera obscura* or "darkroom." Da Vinci observed that a ray of light, permitted to pass through a hole into a totally dark enclosure, would project an inverted and laterally reversed image of the outside scene onto the darkened wall. The image, if so desired, could be traced by an artist to achieve greater realism and dimensionality in artistic renderings. Da Vinci's *camera obscura* provided the basic principle on which all photographic cameras would operate: the projection of a collected image onto a surface for the purpose of preservation.

Another Italian, Giambattista Della Porta, in the mid-sixteenth century, took da Vinci's theories of the *camera obscura* and put them to work in demonstrating the concept. With the device Della Porta presented short scenic illustrations for the amusement of his friends.

THE MAGIC LANTERN

Athanasius Kircher, a German priest-scientist who lived during the seventeenth century, began to experiment with the creation of projection devices which could be transported and which did not depend on natural light. Using mirrors and candlelight Kircher cast images onto a wall from an apparatus which he called a "magic lantern." Eventually Kircher added a lens to the projector so that the images, usually drawn on slides, could be focused. Inspired by the artistic potential of the magic lantern, Kircher produced a treatise on the subject titled *Ars Magna Lucis et Umbrae* or *The Great Art of Light and Shadow*, published in 1649 and again in 1671. Magic lanterns were popular sources of visual entertainment in Europe during the seventeenth, eighteenth, and nineteenth centuries, and numerous variations of Kircher's invention were developed, some permitting the presentation of highly sophisticated slide programs.

A magic lantern.

PERSISTENCE OF VISION

The theoretical possibility of projecting a series of individual images so that they would appear to connect in continuous movement was articulated by the English thesaurist, Peter Mark Rôget, in 1824. On Christmas Eve of that year, Rôget read a paper to the Royal Society of London titled "The Law of Persistence of Vision with Regard to Moving Objects." The thesis of Rôget's paper stated that a physiological phenomenon permits the human eye to retain for a fraction of a second longer than it appears any image which moves before the eye. Through the "persistence of vision" phenomenon it is possible to pass individual images rapidly before the eye so that they overlap one another and produce a continuous visual impression. If the individual images depict a progressive action, either through a series of photographs or hand-drawings, the rapid projection of the series gives the illusion of "moving" pictures.

ANIMATING DEVICES

Almost simultaneously with Rôget's scholarly pronouncement of the theory of persistence of vision other curious minds of the nineteenth century were turning out gadgets which tested and proved the phenomenon. The Thaumatrope, popularly called a "wonder turner," was

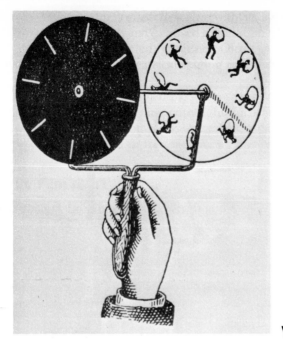

Von Stampfer's Stroboscope.

invented in 1826 by Dr. John Ayrton Paris and became a favorite parlor toy for the amusement of children and adults alike. In the simplest applications of Rôget's theory two separate images, one on each side of a circular card, were drawn on the Thaumatrope device. When the card was spun by attached strings, the two images blended to become one. A bird on one side of the card seemed to be sitting inside an empty wire cage which was on the opposite side.

More sophisticated applications of the potential of persistence of vision soon appeared in an assortment of inventions. The Phenakistoscope was a disclike device produced in the early 1830s by Joseph Plateau, a Belgian scientist. This "magic disc" contained a series of images of a figure in the progressive stages of a simple movement. The images were drawn in a circular pattern near the outside edge of the disc. A series of slits appeared at the very edge of the card. By spinning the disc, which was mounted on a handle, and by peering through the slits toward a reflected image of the Phenakistiscope in a mirror one could see the action series in continuous motion.

A similar device was invented in Germany in 1832 by Simon Ritter von Stampfer. This device, the Stroboscope, added a second disc which contained a series of slitted holes. The slitted disc could be rotated rapidly in front of the imaged disc: as the viewer looked through the slits toward the drawn images on the second disc the appearance of continuous motion was achieved. The slits acted as a shutter effect and prevented the action sequence from blurring.

A later version of this type of animating device known as the Zöotrope, or "wheel of life," placed the series of images on the inside of a cylindrical drum. The slitted holes were cut into the side of the drum so that, as the device was rotated like a carousel, the viewer could peep through the holes to see the semblance of movement. The invention of the Zöotrope has been attributed to William George Horner.

Eventually successful efforts were made at combining the projection capabilities of the magic lantern machines with the revolving animation devices. By casting artificial candlelight or torch light from behind Phenakistiscope-like discs, inventors such as Baron Franz von Uchatius of Austria were able by the mid-1850s to project animated sequences onto a wall.

These experiments in simple animation, often occurring simultaneously in various parts of the world, suggested an urgency to produce devices which would allow the recording and projection of movement taken from everyday life. The groundwork had been laid. Leonardo da Vinci had demonstrated the *camera obscura* process of gathering an image and projecting it onto a surface within an enclosed area. The knowledge of this basic photographic principle led scientists of the nineteenth century to seek a means of permanently retaining the collected image.

The Zöotrope, or wheel of life.

STILL PHOTOGRAPHY

It was in France through the efforts of Joseph Nicéphore Niepce and Louis J. M. Daguerre that still photography became a realization. These two men are credited with the discovery of technical processes which permitted through chemical action the retention of photographic images on metal plates. Both Daguerre and Niepce were naturalistic painters who almost simultaneously became interested in the possibility of a mechanical method of reproducing scenes of the natural world. In the 1820s Niepce was experimenting with the reproduction of images on lithographic stone. Daguerre heard of the efforts and the two entered into a partnership in 1829. Together the men worked on improving Niepce's earlier processes which had resulted in only a degree of success in the production of photographic images. Niepce's images had lacked sharp definition and therefore were unsatisfactory,

Although Niepce died in 1833, the achievement of an acceptable photographic process was imminent. By the end of the 1830s Daguerre was producing sharp, clear "daguerreotypes," as he called his permanent photographic images. Using the *camera obscura* process (now camera size) Daguerre "exposed" his subjects for several minutes until a latent image was fixed on a sheet of copper plated with silver. After exposure, for further fixing of the image, the silverplate was left in the camera for five to fifteen minutes, depending upon the room or outdoor temperature. The plate was then removed and the latent image developed through the use of liquid mercury.

In January 1839 Daguerre displayed examples of the daguerreotype in Paris, thus revealing to the world the startling discovery of still photography. It is interesting to note that while Daguerre's achievement was in the reproduction of static images, his early interest in a photographic process grew out of his work with moving images. Before becoming involved with photography, he had earned his living by painting dioramas, lengthy pieces of cloth, containing a series of individual scenes which could be moved vertically or horizontally before a viewing audience. Daguerre began his search for a photographic means of scenic reproduction in order to speed the process of turning out dioramas. Once more the fascination with moving imagery had been the inspiration for scientific invention which further advanced the possibilities of a complete motion-picture recording system.

TRANSPARENCIES

There were other advancements in the methods of still photography which also helped to advance a workable motion-picture system. In the 1840s two Englishmen, William Henry Fox Talbot and Sir John Herschel, were successful in producing photographic images on paper and in developing the images through a negative-positive process. In 1841 Talbot patented a process for making transparent prints. This patent was purchased a few years later by the Langenheim brothers of Philadelphia who were successful in refining Talbot's process. In 1849 the Langenheims introduced positive photographic images on paper and on glass plates. The glass plate transparencies made the projection of photographs possible.

So, by the middle of the nineteenth century scientific theory and innovation had acted together to provide the foundation for moving pictures. The persistence of vision theory had been widely illustrated in a variety of animating and projecting devices. A means of mechanically and permanently recording views of the natural world had been revealed with the introduction of the daguerreotype in 1839. Paper printing processes, introduced shortly thereafter, led to the production of image transparencies which with a strong light source could be projected onto a screen.

What yet remained to be done to advance the completion of moving pictures were (1) the development of a camera that would produce a series of individual photographs of an action and (2) a means of rapidly projecting the series of photographs.

EADWEARD MUYBRIDGE

The efforts of a still photographer, Eadweard Muybridge (1830–1904), helped to provide the final stimulus for a motion-picture recording device. Muybridge, like many other nineteenth-century innovators before him, had become keenly interested in the nature of motion.

While working as a still photographer in San Francisco, Muybridge earned a reputation for his studies of human and animal locomotion. In 1872 he was engaged by the former governor of California, Leland Stanford, to conduct a study of galloping horses. Stanford, who owned a large farm where he bred race horses, was curious about the way artists had drawn the gaits of running horses. He hired Muybridge to photo-

A Muybridge animal locomotion study.

Muybridge's trotting horse.

graph his horses to see if the depictions were accurate. In particular, Stanford was interested in determining if a running horse ever had all four feet off the ground at the same time.

Because of his locomotion studies, Eadweard Muybridge was a logical choice for Stanford's study. Also, Muybridge had been one of the first photographers in the United States to use a spring-activated shutter. Using this mechanism and other camera refinements, Muybridge had significantly improved the quality of photographs of moving figures.

Despite his expertise, Muybridge's first attempts to acquire satisfactory photographs of a galloping horse were unsuccessful. The unusually rapid movement of a horse caused the arrested images to blur. In 1872 the wet plate photographic materials on which exposures were made were not yet "fast" enough to produce sharp, clearly defined images of rapidly moving objects. (A fast photographic material is one which has a high sensitivity to light. The combination of a fast film and a rapid shutter aid in the acceptable photographing of rapidly moving objects.)

Muybridge continued to work on a camera system which would produce satisfactory results. In 1877, after enlisting the assistance of an engineer named John Isaacs, Muybridge proved successful in his efforts. Using an improved shutter exposure time of approximately 2/1000 of a second and employing a battery of twelve cameras which were aligned side by side and triggered by trip-wires running across the racetrack, Muybridge was able to acquire twelve distinct, although largely silhouetted, photographs of a passing horse. Eventually the battery of cameras was expanded to eighteen, then twenty-four, and an electrical circuit was added to trigger the shutters.

Not only was Muybridge able to show that Stanford's horse did indeed have all four feet off the ground simultaneously when galloping, he was also successful in acquiring in approximately a second's time a brief action sequence. The series of individual photographs, had they appeared on a continuous strip of material, would have constituted the first instantly recorded motion-picture sequence.

During the 1870s Muybridge produced an encyclopedic collection of photographic sequences of figures in motion. These studies were widely published with the individual photographs printed in sequential order and "read" like words on a printed page. By 1880 Muybridge had developed a projector patterned after the Zöotrope, at first called a zoogyroscope (and later the zoopraxiscope). The perfected zoogyroscope allowed him to cast his brief action sequences onto a screen. Muybridge toured the world with his amazing displays of actual movement that had been lifted from life.

THE PHOTOGRAPHIC GUN

Among the curious who came to hear Muybridge lecture when he appeared in Paris in 1881 and to see the action illustrations was a French physiologist, Etienne-Jules Marey. Marey also had developed an interest in animal locomotion and in wildlife photography. To better photograph birds in flight, a particular fascination for Marey, the physiologist was stimulated by Muybridge to invent in 1882 a gunlike camera. The camera made twelve rapid exposures on a circular glass plate which revolved like a bullet cylinder.

With the availability in France of Kodak rolls which George Eastman had first put on the market in 1884, Marey began in 1887 to employ paper film in his photographic gun. By 1888 he was using an electric motor to advance and halt the film for fifteen exposures per second.

THOMAS EDISON: INVENTOR AND ENTREPRENEUR

Marey's innovations had proved the possibility of a single camera mechanism for photographing action sequences. However, it was Thomas Alva Edison (1837–1931), the American inventor-entrepreneur, who took up the possibility and who was able to produce in his New Jersey laboratories the first workable motion-picture camera.

In 1877 Edison applied for a patent for the phonograph sound recorder. Some ten years later, after hearing Eadweard Muybridge lecture in Orange, New Jersey, Edison and his assistant, W. K. L. Dickson, became intrigued with the possibility of inventing a companion machine for the phonograph which would record images for the eye. Edison's inspiration from the start was to produce sound motion pictures.

Edison perforated film, circa 1889–1890.

In 1888 Dickson began working with a cylindrical device which could make pin-head size images on a strip of photographic paper. The paper was wound around the cylinder and the pictures were taken through a microscopic lens. Although the size of the cylinder was eventually increased to enlarge the size of the recorded images, the microphotographs lacked visual sharpness and the drum procedure was abandoned.

In 1889 the Edison laboratories developed the Kinetograph strip camera which permitted the use of perforated roll film manufactured by George Eastman. A film emulsion set on a transparent celluloid base had been patented by Eastman in 1888. With the use of this flexible celluloid material, manufactured in 200-foot strips, Edison was able to perforate one side of the film for use in the Kinetograph camera. As the strip passed laterally through the camera, images were recorded side by side in a horizontal position on the film.

Initially Edison had to manually perforate the celluloid strips by running them through a perforating machine produced in his laboratory. Before the end of 1889 the Eastman Dry Plate and Film Company in Rochester, New York, was manufacturing an improved cellulose base film which was also preperforated. Eastman entered into a business arrangement at this time to manufacture 35-mm film for Edison's newly developed camera.

The Kinetograph camera was far from perfect. The machine weighed nearly a ton and therefore could not be easily moved. But the device did allow Dickson to make short moving pictures which were at first of the simplest type: a close-up of a man sneezing, a person dancing. The Kinetograph also permitted the projection of these films which were often accompanied by sound recordings on the phonograph.

The Kinetoscope

Rather than project motion pictures to group audiences, Edison built and patented a single-viewer, peep-show machine, the Kinetoscope, in 1891. The Kinetoscope was later equipped to be coin-operated and permitted the showing of films of about a minute's length. A battery-powered motor carried a continuous loop of film, 25 to 50 feet long, past a viewing slot on the top of the boxlike apparatus. Electric light illuminated the images and a revolving shutter prevented the passing images from blurring.

The Black Maria: The First Motion-Picture Studio

In 1892 Edison decided to display the Kinetoscope publicly at the Chicago World's Fair scheduled for the following year. Realizing that it was necessary to create a space that was more suited to the photograph-

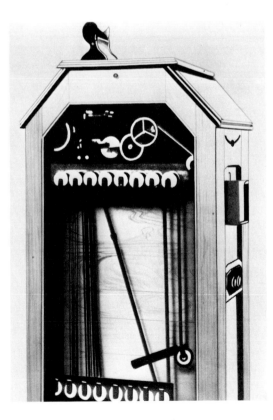

An inside view of Edison's Kinetoscope.

The Black Maria.

ing of motion pictures than that provided by the laboratory, Edison instructed Dickson to design and build on the West Orange property a small studio.

For less than $700 Dickson completed the building in early 1893. The modest structure contained two rooms. One at the end of the building housed the bulky Kinetograph camera. The other room, toward which the camera lens was directed, provided studio space for staging action vignettes. The entire structure was mounted on a revolving turntable with a skylight window on the roof. It was thus possible to rotate the studio and to regulate the amount of available light needed for satisfactory filming.

Dickson had discovered that the quality of images could also be improved when subjects were photographed in bold relief against dark backgrounds. For this reason the inside studio walls were painted black and the outside was covered with a tar paper material.

Because this simple structure was built for the production of film loops to be used in the Kinetoscope, the studio was officially named the Kinetoscope Theatre. In time, however, Edison's employees began to call the studio the "Black Maria," after they decided its black walls and funny shape caused the building to resemble a policewagon of that time also popularly called a Black Maria.

The early films made at the studio were simple in concept. Trained animals from circus acts, boxers, acrobatic performers, dancers, and theatrical celebrities were typical subjects filmed at the Edison studio. Occasionally singing groups were hired to appear in the minute-long Kinetoscope films; a phonograph recording would sometimes be made simultaneously for sound pictures. Some Kinetoscopes were equipped so that they could reproduce the sound recordings to accompany the moving pictures.

It is important to note that these first American films, although largely unmemorable except as museum items, suggest a strong inclination toward theatricality. In the sixty or so Kinetoscope films produced at the Black Maria in its first year, the list of titles is dominated by theatrical celebrities and theatrical events. Throughout its history the American film has shown a strong attraction for melodrama, sensationalism, and purely escapist entertainment. This tendency manifested itself in the earliest films made available for public display.

Two boxers, Jim Corbett and Peter Courtney, prepare to spar in front of the Kinetograph camera.

An early Kinetoscope parlor in San Francisco (1899).

Peep-Show Parlors

The sensation of seeing moving pictures led to the opening of Kinetoscope parlors or, as they were popularly called, "peep-show parlors." It was on April 14, 1894, that the first Kinetoscope parlor officially opened in New York City at 1155 Broadway. For 25 cents per showing peep show viewers could see a variety of Edison's short films.

Edison, who was principally interested in selling his machine, not marketing the films, had sold the concession rights to the Kinetoscope to a group of East Coast businessmen. Other investors soon followed and peep-show parlors sprang up in New York and in most major cities throughout the country. The novelty of the Kinetoscope and its attraction for drawing customers also caught the attention of other types of businesses: department stores, vaudeville houses, hotels, and night spots.

Response to Edison's films was enormous. Rapidly, the motion picture, although only five years old, was becoming a major new industry and a thrilling new mass entertainment medium.

PROJECTION

One of the earliest reviews of motion pictures appeared in *The Critic* magazine in 1894. The reviewer noted the pleasing effects of Thomas

Edison's Kinetoscope films, while also anticipating the future addition of color, screen projection, and sound.

> A number of instantaneous photographs illustrating all the important phases of a single action or series of actions are set on a wheel which is made to revolve very rapidly by a small electric motor, which also supplies the light by which they are seen, the whole thing being enclosed in a dark box. By this means the action which is analyzed in the series of photographs is reconstituted, and stage performers dance or go through their contortions, Sandow's muscles swell and relax, fighting cocks fight, and the organgrinder's monkey snatches off the small boy's hat. The element of color, only, is needed to complete the illusion, and it is possible that that may be supplied. As it stands, the machine should be of great service to artists and others in studying action. . . . If the figures were thrown upon a screen there would be many advantages in working from them rather than from a tired model. It is possible that we may yet see this done, and with the assistance of the perfected phonograph that we may witness and hear shadowplays in which the only real performer will be the electromagnetic motor behind the scene. [*The Critic,* May 12, 1894.]

Of the three future technical innovations visualized in this review—color, projection, and perfected sound—projection was the most imminent. In France, in England, and in the United States, inventors were working to produce projectors which would allow the viewing of motion pictures by groups of people rather than by the single-viewer Kinetoscope method.

Edison's staff itself had been actively engaged in attempting to perfect a workable projection system. At first Edison had resisted out of deference to the Kinetoscope, but eventually agreed to allow his staff to work on a projector device which was to be called a Kinetophone.

The Cinématographe

Before Edison could perfect his system, two brothers from Lyons, France, Auguste and Louis Lumière, were successful in projecting motion pictures publicly in Paris on December 28, 1895. The Lumière brothers, photographers and manufacturers of photographic materials, had devised a portable camera-projector machine early in 1895 which they called the Cinématographe. This machine employed an intermittent registration system in moving the film through the camera-projector. Each image on the film, which moved at a rate of sixteen frames per second, could be registered momentarily behind a lens and in front of a strong light source for clear, sharp projection on a screen.

Because of the portability of the Cinématographe, the Lumières were able to take their camera-projector outdoors. Appropriately, one of their first films, made in 1895, was *Workers Leaving the Lumière Factory,* a brief actualité or documentarylike film which set the precedent for the Lumière brothers' style of filmmaking. Within a year's time the Lum-

The Lumière brothers and their Cinématographe camera-projector.

ières had recorded hundreds of short domestic scenes of everyday life with such simple literal titles as *The Baby's Meal, Charge of the French Hussars, Train Arriving at the Station,* and *Boat Leaving the Harbor.*

The Vitascope

Urged on by the success of the Cinématographe in France, Thomas Edison stepped up his efforts to manufacture a similar machine in the United States. His own device, the Kinetophone, had proved unsatisfactory at projection. Early in 1896 Edison began negotiations with Thomas Armat, a young inventor from Washington, D.C., who the year before had been able to produce a projector which operated on the same principle as the Cinématographe. Armat's projector used a loop procedure which had been invented by Woodville Latham in New York. Two small loops in the film, one above and one below the projector aperture, permitted the film to be moved intermittently by sprocket without tearing. The Latham loop procedure of easing film tension is still a standard feature on most professional motion-picture projectors.

Armat, who had invented his projector with the assistance of C. Francis Jenkins, agreed to allow Edison's prestigious company to manufacture and promote projecting equipment which used Armat's sprocket and loop features. The machine was introduced as the "Edison Vitascope."

THE EDISON PROGRAMS

The first public demonstration of Vitascope projection occurred on April 23, 1896, in New York City at Koster and Bial's Music Hall. A short program of Edison's films was included as an additional "act" in that day's collection of vaudeville presentations. The films were all brief, a minute to a minute and one half in length, but the audience was thrilled by the life-sized views of the world in motion. A newspaper headline on the following day reported: "Edison's Achievement to Reproduce a Play Made Pictorially a Perfect Success."

A reviewer from *The New York Dramatic Mirror,* who attended the premiere program, described the experience this way:

> The first picture shown was the Leigh Sisters in their umbrella dance. The effect was the same as if the girls were on the stage; all of their smiles and kicks and bows were seen. The second picture represented the breaking of waves on the seashore. Wave after wave came tumbling on the sand and, as they struck, broke into tiny floods just like the real thing. Some of the people in the front rows seemed to be afraid they were going to get wet, and looked about to see where they could run to, in case the waves came too close. The third picture showed a burlesque boxing match between Walton and Mayon, the long and short comedians. Then followed in quick succession a scene from Hoyt's *The Milk White Flag* in which a couple of dozen people appeared; a serpentine dance with all the colored calcium effects, and an amusing picture showing an argument between John Bull and Uncle Sam.
>
> The Vitascope is a big success, and Mr. Edison is to be congratulated for his splendid contribution to the people's pleasure. [*The New York Dramatic Mirror*, May 2, 1896.]

Edison's selection of films for this first program consisted primarily of short burlesques and theatrical vignettes. These types of films obviously were considered appropriate for presentation in a vaudeville music hall. Yet, it was the documentarylike view of waves breaking on a seashore which apparently caused the greatest sensation. The introduction of pictorial naturalism into a theatrical environment was unique and startling. The pleasure provided by the motion-picture camera's ability to make drama of nature in the raw was apparent even to the naive audience at Koster and Bial's on April 23, 1896.

With the success of this premiere showing, Edison continued to provide films to Koster and Bial's vaudeville theater. Many more of the films were hand-tinted (as had been the "serpentine dance" in the first program) to add to the sensation of watching projected moving pictures. In time the film programs became longer and more varied in content.

A poster advertising the Lumière program of short films.

THE LUMIÈRE PROGRAMS

In June 1896, two months after Edison began projecting films at Koster and Bial's, a collection of Lumière films arrived in New York for showing at Keith's Union Square Theatre. This program displayed more fully than Edison's collections the realistic, documentary possibilities of the motion-picture camera as numerous actualities were shown.

The Lumière showing, however, was not without its contrivances. In the short film *The Sprinkler Sprinkled (Watering the Gardener)* audiences saw one of the first demonstrations of screen slapstick. A gardener is shown watering a lawn with a hose; a young boy walks up behind him and places his foot on the hose, stopping the water's flow. The gardener is enticed into looking into the end of the hose, at which point the lad raises his foot to sprinkle the man in the face. This act of harmless cruelty and surprise antedated the many silent-screen comedies which later would employ the same slapstick elements for laughs.

By July 1896 a half dozen theaters and vaudeville houses in New

York were regularly showing motion-picture programs. Soon projectors were being shipped to other large cities throughout the country as the "miracle" of motion-picture entertainment rapidly spread. On the West Coast Thomas Tally opened the first "Vitascope Parlor" in Los Angeles in August 1896.

THE GROWTH OF A NEW INDUSTRY

The majority of films made in the first years of motion-picture projection continued for the most part to be simple, unedited vignettes lifted from existing theatrical presentations or short action scenes taken of nature and everyday life. Nevertheless, a major new industry was emerging in the production, distribution, and exhibition of motion pictures. Syndicates were created to market projectors and to promote film programs. The K.M.C.D. Syndicate, named for its founders Koopman, Marvin, Casler, and Dickson, was formed in 1895. The

Following his mischievous act in *The Sprinkler Sprinkled,* the lad is apprehended and spanked.

American Mutoscope and Biograph Company was another early organization founded for the purpose of promoting motion-picture machines. The Biograph Company had developed its own peep-show device, called a Mutoscope, and shortly after the introduction of the Vitascope projector produced the Biograph projector which was superior to Edison's machines.

New film production companies also appeared to compete with Edison in the making of the movies, including Biograph, Essanay, and Vitagraph in the United States. In France Pathé Frères (the Pathé brothers) by 1900 had developed an impressive international system of film production and distribution. Other big companies soon set up production units and offices in the major cities of the world.

STORE THEATERS

Investors, aware of the enormous appeal of motion pictures, began to see the financial potential of film exhibition. "Store Theaters," as the first movie houses were commonly called, rapidly increased in number in the early 1900s.

The first fully equipped, specially decorated motion-picture theater in the United States was opened in 1905 by Harry Davis and John P. Harris in Pittsburgh, Pennsylvania. The theater, called the "Nickelodeon," contained nearly a hundred seats and presented regularly scheduled film showings throughout the day and evening. A piano player

An early nickelodeon.

provided musical accompaniment for the films. The Nickelodeon brought in hundreds of dollars every week, a figure which indicated that despite the simple nature of the films of that time the new motion-picture medium was more than a passing fancy. More and more businessmen made note of that fact. By the end of 1906 there were nearly a thousand nickelodeons in the United States. In a single decade, the motion picture had progressed from a novelty of scientific innovation to a major new mass entertainment medium.

Industrial growth, however, had outdistanced artistic refinement during the first ten years of motion-picture projection. The miracle of moving pictures cast onto a screen was apparently satisfaction enough for early film audiences. One critic of the time, after observing audience reaction in a nickelodeon, described the motion-picture experience as "an innocent amusement and a rather wholesome delirium." Even film reviewers and reporters at first did not expect a more sophisticated type of expression from filmmakers. Action and realism were sufficient at the time for a sensational, mechanically produced experience that cost only a nickel.

The work of enterprising photographers, inventors, and businessmen during the latter part of the nineteenth century resulted in the successful realization of moving pictures and, simultaneously, an important new industry. Efforts by Rôget, Talbot, and Herschel in England, Daguerre, Niepce, Marey and the Lumière brothers in France, Muybridge, Dickson, and Edison in the United States had made the birth of motion pictures a truly international event. Similarly, the discovery and exploitation of film aesthetics would also be the result of international enterprise. It is that story which follows.

SUGGESTED READINGS

Ceram, C. W. *Archaeology of the Cinema*. New York: Harcourt, 1965.

Dickinson, Thorold. *A Discovery of Cinema*. New York: Oxford University Press, 1971.

Dickson, W. K. L., and Antonia Dickson. *A History of the Kinetograph, Kinetoscope, and Kinetophonograph*. New York: Arno, 1970.

Edison, Thomas A. *The Diary and Sundry Observations of Thomas Alva Edison*. Edited by Dagobert D. Runes. New York: Philosophical Library, 1948.

Fielding, Raymond. *A Technological History of Motion Pictures and Television*. Berkeley: University of California Press, 1967.

Haas, Robert Bartlett. *Muybridge: Man in Motion*. Berkeley: University of California Press, 1976.

Muybridge, Eadweard. *Animals in Motion*. Edited by Lewis S. Brown. New York: Dover, 1957.

Newhall, Beaumont. *The History of Photography*. New York: Museum of Modern Art, 1964.

North, Joseph H. *The Early Development of the Motion Picture, 1887–1909*. New York: Arno, 1973.

ARTISTIC AND
NARRATIVE PROGRESS

Today a consistent plot is demanded. There must be, as in the drama, exposition, development, climax and denouement. . . . One studio manager said: "The people want a story. We run to comics generally; they seem to take best. So-and-so, however, lean more to melodrama. When we started we used to give just flashes—an engine chasing to a fire, a baserunner sliding home, a charge of cavalry. Now, for instance, if we want to work in a horse race it has to be as a scene in the life of the jockey, who is the hero of the piece—we've got to give them a story; they won't take anything else—a story with plenty of action. You can't show large conversation, you know on the screen. More story, larger story, better story with plenty of action—that is our tendency."

Joseph Medill Patterson, describing in 1907 what audiences of the time expected from film producers (*The Saturday Evening Post, November 23, 1907*).

The Great Train Robbery (1903).

The fact that the artistic development of the motion picture occurred at a slower pace than the industrial growth of the film industry can be attributed in large part to the creation of a new medium of expression whose full range of possibilities was not immediately apparent to filmmakers. Early film producers tended to respond to the new medium in one of two ways: (1) they saw the possibilities of the motion picture as an extension of the photograph, or (2) they saw the medium as a mechanical extension of theater.

THE PHOTOGRAPHIC RESPONSE

The motion picture was born into an intense climate of public curiosity for the photograph. Moving-picture machines offered an even more sensational means of looking at pictures. It is logical, then, that the natural impulse of early filmmakers was in large part photographic, approaching their subject matter simply as pictures in motion. The literalness of the Lumière brothers' actualities can probably be attributed more to their previous background as still photographers than to an avowed preference for film realism.

Even Thomas Edison's bent for photographing the theatrical event was counterbalanced by numerous documentary views of familiar scenes and places. In 1896 Edison's staff produced films with such titles as *Morning Bath, Feeding the Doves,* and *Burning Stable.* Many other films were made of New York street scenes.

Scenic Films

The major appeal of these early films was the same as the appeal of the photograph: an enjoyment of pictorial accuracy in the rendering of a scene with the added attraction of movement. Also, moving pictures provided opportunities for discovering and rediscovering reality, including the rhythms of life.

One of the earliest Edison films shows a single-angle view of a New York street scene, but includes within the scene a passing oyster cart which enters from screen left and an El train which passes across the top of the screen moving toward screen right. Other vehicles can be seen moving through the streets far in the background. While this short film lacks what we would call dramatic value as such, viewers at the time were impressed with the different movements and varied levels of activity within the film frame.

Many of the street films of the 1890s soon included people who passed across the frame in the foreground while trolley cars and automobiles crossed in the background. The addition of people person-

A New York street scene with several levels of passing action.

An early street scene that captures an embarrassing moment—titled for Kinetoscope viewers "What Happened on 23rd Street."

alized the scene while their presence in the foreground also gave a feeling of depth to the film frame.

A short film, *Fifth Avenue at Easter-Time*, concentrated entirely on the crowds of people who had gathered on Fifth Avenue on Easter Sunday. Early film viewers were given a newsreellike opportunity to discover New York fashion styles.

Camera Movement and Angles The camera, at first immobile, did not remain stationary for long. Scenic filmmakers for Essanay, Edison, and Biograph soon discovered that a moving camera added to the sensation of the movement of people and objects within the film frame.

A film made in San Francisco in the late 1890s was photographed from the front of a trolley car; as the vehicle moved through the streets other vehicles and pedestrians crisscrossed in the path of the approaching camera. An illusion of depth and the simple sensation of moving through space are achieved in the film. The effect for audiences at the time was similar in intention to the roller-coaster ride included in *This Is Cinerama* in 1952, and in the runaway car sequence in Alfred Hitchcock's *Family Plot* (1976).

An even more dramatic use of the moving camera appears in an Edison film photographed about 1898, *Fire Fighters*. The film includes three brief shots. The first shows a long view of a firehouse as three horse-drawn fire wagons dramatically charge out of the station on their way to a fire; in this shot the camera is stationary. A second shot, also taken from a stationary position, shows the fire wagons as they approach the scene of the fire; for a third shot, taken at close range, the camera is mounted on what would seem to be the lead fire wagon, the camera looking back at the wagon which follows. In this shot with its candid, *cinema-verité*-like realism the viewer is placed in the middle of the action.

The sensational effect of filming a moving vehicle from a camera position on another moving vehicle has remained a popular device with filmmakers, e.g., *Bullitt* (1968) and *Foul Play* (1977). The moving camera was an important early step in furthering the unique possibilities of the film medium.

A Romance of the Rails With the production of longer films containing narrative elements, dramatic angles as well as moving camera shots were incorporated whenever possible to aid the story. In 1902 Edwin S. Porter, a photographer for the Edison Company, directed a four-minute film titled *A Romance of the Rails*. The film was produced as a tourist promotion for the Lackawanna Railroad.

To get across the message of the pleasures of train rides a man and a woman meet at a station platform where they board a Lackawanna passenger train. The train moves slowly through the countryside while the couple sit at the rear of the car and observe the passing scene. A sharp angling of the camera by Porter allows the film viewer to see both the couple and the landscape.

In three shots an Edison photographer catches the rush of a fire wagon on an urgent mission. Shot number three puts the viewer, in *cinema verité* fashion, in the middle of the action.

Porter's couple observe the passing landscape.

Contained in this brief scenic film are many of the rudimentary elements of film expression as they existed at the time. The first element is the *photographic:* the principal interest in *A Romance of the Rails* is a pictorial display of a passing landscape.

A second expressive element in the film is the *moving camera shot.* By mounting the camera on an unseen platform car attached to the back of the train, the scenic view is constantly changing in a moving shot which lasts for more than a minute.

Another artistic element in Porter's film is that of varying *camera angles.* As the couple board the train the camera lens is angled toward the right of the film scene; the moving shot of the scenic landscape is angled toward the left side of the frame. Another shot, taken of the couple as they are married at the conclusion of the train ride, is composed in a straight-on, formal view. This formally balanced composition is an appropriate choice for the wedding ceremony. The angles serve to provide both visual variety and expressive qualities.

Editing The art of film editing is also advanced in *A Romance of the Rails.* The film consists of six separate shots, one including a special effect in

A formally balanced composition completes *A Romance of the Rails* !

which stop action is used to allow two hobos to disembark from beneath the train after it reaches its destination. The fragmentation of the train trip into several shots so that the travelogue includes a beginning, a middle, and an end was a simple step toward *narrative film editing.*

A Romance of the Rails, while traditionally intent on satisfying the scenic, photographic pleasures of the motion picture, nevertheless gave indication of a growing awareness of the cinematic devices of:

1   The moving camera
2   Expressive camera angles
3   Film editing
4   Narrative story construction
5   Special effect photography

Film Portraits

At the same time that the nineteenth century's curiosity for scenic realism was being extended into motion pictures, a similar curiosity occurred for moving-picture portraits. Thousands of famous public

Madame Curie at work in her lab.

figures, theatrical celebrities, and unusual personalities were photographed on motion-picture film in the late 1890s and early 1900s. Often the figures barely moved, and when they did it was frequently only an awkward reaction of embarrassment at the process of posing for moving pictures.

Among the innumerable famous people who appeared in these portrait motion pictures were the actress Sarah Bernhardt, the vaudeville comedian John Bunny, Alexander Graham Bell, his wife, and grandchild in a group portrait, the scientist Marie Curie, Teddy Roosevelt, Woodrow Wilson, and Thomas Edison.

Many of the short films of famous personalities were simple portraits taken of the subjects in familiar surroundings. Madame Curie was shown working in her laboratory, posed in a profile shot as though reluctant to look at the camera. John Bunny was photographed as he donned his costume for a theatrical performance. Thomas Edison sat in the backseat of his open-top automobile holding a flower.

In an effort to expand these studies of public figures the filmmaker soon began to include a scenic view of an event that involved the personality. This shot was then followed by a medium-length close-up of the subject. A portrait of Teddy Roosevelt, awkwardly stuffing his hands into his jacket pockets, was preceded by two long shot views of his "Heroic Rough Riders." A long shot of the crowds gathered for a parade in which Sarah Bernhardt was appearing immediately preceded the close-up of the actress in her parade car.

Portrait studies provided the most personal type of early film experience. The opportunity to see famous people in motion, while still essentially a photographic experience, permitted an act of discovery that went beyond the sensations of scenic motion. With the expansion of these films to include both scenic and portrait shots, filmmakers began to both personalize and objectify events. This was a simple step toward the reconstruction of reality through the editing process, a process which anticipated the art of the motion-picture newsreel as well as the traditional documentary film.

The Brighton School Other artistic possibilities resulting from a photographic, portrait response to early motion pictures occurred at the turn of the century in the work of a group of still photographers in Brighton, England. The group, known as the Brighton School, was headed by G. A. Smith (1864–1959), an established portrait photographer who had built a motion-picture camera in 1896.

In 1897 Smith began making short trick films. These early films included special effects which were achieved through stop-action photography and double exposures. The titles of his films during the eighteen-nineties suggest their nature: *X-Rays* (1897); *The Haunted Castle* (1897); *Photographing a Ghost* (1898); *The Haunted Picture Gallery* (1899); *Aladdin and the Wonderful Lamp* (1899).

In 1900 Smith joined with J. A. Williamson and several other still photography portraitists at Brighton for the purpose of experimenting with new ways of using the motion-picture camera. The Brighton School members were especially interested in utilizing their previous experience as portrait photographers.

In a group of films made between 1900 and 1905, Smith and his colleagues positioned the motion-picture camera close to actors' faces in order to record subtle changes in emotion through facial expression. These close-up shots were then incorporated into brief films which also contained shots of longer scope. The long shots usually depicted the actions of a simple story while the close-ups provided a view of a character's emotional response to a situation.

Smith's work suggested a significant advancement in the expressive possibilities of the motion picture. Filmmakers who earlier had photographed personalities in close-up had failed to go beyond the portrait concept, except to occasionally show the personality as a part of a newsreellike event. In the Brighton School films the close-ups depicted characters responding to events in a cause-and-effect relationship.

In a 1902 film, *Mary Jane's Mishap,* the Brighton School illustrated the expressive nature of close shot–long shot interaction. The simple story is that of a foolish young maid who pours gasoline into a stove after she is unable to start a fire. An explosion follows. This scene is immediately replaced by a scene in a cemetery, thus suggesting the fatal result of Mary Jane's act. As a group of maids reflect on Mary Jane's mishap beside her tombstone, the dead girl's ghost appears through the use of a double-exposure shot. The frightened maids scamper away.

Mary Jane's Mishap employs the close-up as an integral element in developing a film story. The film opens with a close view of Mary Jane's frustrated face. Then the viewer sees in a long shot the maid attempting to start a stove fire. By joining the two shots for a cause-effect relationship Smith arranges the close-up and the long shot so that the effect (frustration) is visible before the cause (unlit fire). The character's emotion is experienced before the situation. This approach to film construction simultaneously seizes attention and personalizes the event. The action of the event no longer exists merely for action's sake but becomes a part of reality that is related to human endeavor.

A cause-effect process is also achieved in *Mary Jane's Mishap* by advancing the story to the cemetery after the explosion of the stove. The immediate juxtaposition of the two shots (explosion and cemetery) cues the maid's death. This linkage of shots provides unstated narrative information which is easily understood.

The Brighton School's contributions to the development of film art grew out of their experimentation with the contextual value of film shots:

1 The close-up and the long shot in interaction to convey emotional responses to events and to involve the filmgoer
2 The linkage of shots through editing to convey unstated information

The tendency of early filmmakers to react to the motion picture in its formative years as an extension of the photograph was a natural response. Many of the innate possibilities and pleasures of still photography resided also in the motion picture. The early photographic films, however limited in artistic vision, nevertheless *suggested* a new medium that almost at once began gravitating toward its own peculiarities. Scenic views of New York anticipated the ever-popular "street film" with its unlimited opportunities for action and its sense of unstaged reality. Portrait films antedated the newsreel and the documentary film. The added dynamics of moving camera shots, varied camera angles, the contextual and emotional value of the close-up, the expressive possibilities of narrative editing, and the linkage of shots—all these cinematic techniques began to evolve as a part of the syntax of the motion picture at a time when audiences expected little more than the miracle of "seeing."

THEATRICAL TENDENCIES

While early filmmakers were extending the appeals of the photograph into the new medium of moving pictures, a simultaneous early response linked the new medium with the theater.

Theatrical tendencies of the nineteenth century had anticipated the expressive possibilities of the motion picture visually and structurally. Intense realism in stage design and in stage effects had become an obsession with many theater producers during the century; in form, the popular stage play became more active and more episodic in nature. Spectacle, romance, and melodrama gained in popularity as types of theatrical fare. Theater historian Nicholas Vardac has noted in his book *From Stage to Screen* that these developments constituted a movement toward dramatic expression which could be more easily supplied by the motion-picture medium.

The arrival of the motion picture in the 1890s did in fact constitute an event which often placed the new film medium and the theater of the time in strikingly similar points of aesthetic departure. The theater's progress toward realistic expression was matched immediately by the moving picture's innate capability for achieving that stylistic objective.

THEATRICAL FILMS

The early motion-picture director, however, did not immediately take full advantage of the naturalistic possibilities of the medium. Because the filming of existing plays was the simplest way of producing dramatic stories, pioneering filmmakers borrowed freely from the stage, not always recognizing that what was regarded as theatrical realism was not necessarily cinematic realism. Most early filmmakers who photographed parts of stage plays merely recorded the event.

In an early Edison film titled *Streetcar Chivalry* (1901), a brief vaudeville sketch was acted out for the motion-picture camera. In the comic sketch a group of men are seen riding on a subway car. They are seated along the side of the car facing the camera lens. As the men talk and read their newspapers, an attractive young woman enters the frame from the right. The men tip their hats and hurriedly make room for the woman to sit down. When a second woman of considerable size enters from the same direction, the men take up their newspapers and hide behind them as if not to notice the standing woman. She is forced to ride the subway car while holding on to a ceiling hand strap. When the car jolts, the woman lands in the laps of two of the men who then jump up and flee.

The comedy in *Streetcar Chivalry* develops from the contrasting of character types, a comedic element which was common in vaudeville and

The single-angled view of the comic interplay in *Streetcar Chivalry* (1901).

which also would become a familiar element of silent screen comedy. Aesthetically, however, the film is little more than a recording of a theatrical event. The subway car is suggested by a flat, painted backdrop. The camera is positioned straight onto the scene for a single uninterrupted filming of the sketch. A long shot view of the scene, in which all the actors are fully visible, gives the film the appearance of a play being acted out within a proscenium frame. No change of camera angle or closer views of the action occur. An angling of the camera would have resulted in overshooting the edges of the theatrical set.

The tendency of the early narrative filmmakers to remain bound to theatrical traditions resulted in the use of the terms "the silent stage," "photoplay," and "canned drama" to describe early theatrical film adaptations.

During the first decade of the twentieth century literally hundreds of short motion pictures were made from popular stage plays. A 1903 version of *Uncle Tom's Cabin*, directed by Edwin S. Porter, closely resembles the theatrical manner of producing the play on the stage at the turn of the century. The methods of changing scenery and location utilize stage machinery rather than the editing devices of the motion picture.

A theatrical *mise-en-scène* dominates Olcott's *Ben Hur* (1907).

Ben Hur

A one-reel version of the popular stage play·*Ben Hur* was produced on film in 1907 by the Kalem Company. The adaptation illustrates how even at this late date the motion picture was still struggling to break away from its ties with the theater.

Ben Hur displays a theatrical *mise-en-scène* and plot structure. The scenery backdrops are massive in size and have been painted to give the illusion of dimension. Action takes place in different areas of the set and on upper and lower levels. Large numbers of people are used in the crowd scenes to enhance the effect of realism. Actual horses are used for the chariot race.

Yet the effect of *Ben Hur* is not that of cinematic realism. The scenery is obviously constructed of canvas. Actors move and gesture with the stylized precision of stage performers. The crowds are posed in standard stage groupings designed to emphasize the principal players. One action replaces another through the entrances and departures of characters. The pace of the story is theatrical. During the chariot race the horse-drawn vehicles exit out the left side of the frame and make a full circle behind the set backdrop before reappearing at the right side of the frame. The race is without suspense altogether.

This production of *Ben Hur* with its spectacular settings and live horses would surely have caused a sensation in 1907 on the stage. Yet the film which was directed by Sidney Olcott is little more than an artifact which displays the theatrical staging practices in use at the beginning of the twentieth century.

As a side note, Olcott's screen version of *Ben Hur* in 1907 was produced without gaining copyright permission from the owners of the play. The Kalem Company was taken to court and fined $25,000, an important decision in the pirating of story material.

Le Film d'Art

In 1908 Le Film d'Art, a production company, was formed in France with the intention of putting onto film the majority of plays produced by French National theater companies. Le Film d'Art directors also recorded short segments from ballet performances.

Sarah Bernhardt emotes grandly in *Queen Elizabeth* (1912).

The goal of Film d'Art was to make available for the masses the best examples of dance and theater. The efforts were, quite literally, examples of "canned drama." Actors employed the same movements and gestures as those used on the stage, even speaking their lines of dialogue although their words could not be heard.

In 1912 Film d'Art earned the distinction of producing a four-reel, fifty-minute version of the stage play *Queen Elizabeth* with Sarah Bernhardt. This too was a simple recording of the theatrical event. But the length of the film and the prestige of Bernhardt constituted a significant moment in motion-picture history.

The failure to explore the full potential of the motion picture led writers of the time who evaluated early dramatic films to continue to view the new medium in theatrical terms. Walter Prichard Eaton, an American theater critic of the early twentieth century, responded to the motion picture as though the medium were a lower form of theater. In 1909 Eaton outlined his aesthetic and cultural expectations for motion pictures.

> If canned dramas are to retain their present extraordinary hold over the public, they can do it after the novelty has worn off by being genuine dramas, well planned and well played. When they are well planned and well played it is quite possible that they can always fill a useful function, in leading the lower strata of society up toward an appreciation of true dramatic art, which is, after all, only brought to flower on the stage of a true theater where actual men and women speak with the voices God gave them. [*American Magazine*, September 1909.]

This paternal response to dramatic films in 1909 by a prominent critic is a telling one. Eaton noted only the *silence* of the motion picture as a characteristic which distinguished film expression from theater expression.

Some critics were astute enough to recognize in film the potential of a new unique medium of expression with its own set of aesthetic standards, but they had difficulty determining what the aesthetics were. In 1910, a reporter for *Independent Magazine* wrote of the frustrations being experienced by critics in their attempt to accurately assess motion pictures as a medium separate from theater.

> The disadvantages of the cinematograph in comparison with the ordinary drama cannot be well discussed at present because we do not know which of them are inherent and which remedial. [*Independent,* September 1910.]

These critical reactions indicate the limited public awareness of the artistic potential for motion pictures in their first fifteen years of projection.

EARLY INNOVATORS

There were among the early filmmakers a number of individuals who earned important places in the annals of film history for their roles in suggesting the art of the narrative motion picture. Georges Méliès in France, Edwin S. Porter in the United States, and Cecil M. Hepworth and Robert W. Paul in England were innovative filmmakers who in the first decade of the motion picture's existence began to explore the expressive possibilities of the film camera and the expository potential of film editing. Together these men helped to advance the art of a new, unique method of story-telling.

Georges Méliès

Georges Méliès (1861–1938) stands prominently among early filmmakers as the first creative film artist. Numerous historians have also labeled this Frenchman "the father of the narrative film."

Méliès' most important contributions to cinema art and to the narrative film reside in his successful exploration of the optical possibilities of the motion picture for creating film fantasy. Although G. A. Smith in England began about the same time as Méliès to produce trick films, it was Méliès who delighted the world with hundreds of short films of a fantastical nature.

Georges Méliès was born in Paris in 1861 and as a young man enjoyed giving amateur magic shows. These interests eventually led him to leave work at his father's shoe factory and enter into a career as a theatrical producer whose specialty lay in creating stage spectacles which displayed all sorts of theatrical illusions.

In 1888 Méliès bought the Théâtre Robert Houdin in Paris where he developed stage machinery and invented theatrical devices that would enhance the production of fantasy. Among the already-existing devices incorporated into Méliès' presentations at the Théâtre Robert Houdin was a magic lantern.

In April 1896 Méliès also began to show short motion pictures as a part of his programs. These films had been produced by an English filmmaker-inventor, Robert W. Paul, and purchased along with Paul's Bioscope projector. The Bioscope had been put on the market by Paul in 1896.

Using his own experience as an inventor, Méliès studied the mechanical operation of the Bioscope and soon built a motion-picture camera that was patterned after Paul's projector. With this camera Méliès began photographing short trick films outdoors with such titles as *Conjuror Making 10 Hats.* Later in 1896 Méliès further developed his interest in trick films with *The Mysterious Indian Fakir, The Vanishing Lady, One Terrible Night,* and *The Haunted Castle.* That year he also founded his own production organization, the Star Film Company, and in 1897 he built a well-equipped studio at Montreuil-sous-Bois where he was able to produce a variety of different types of motion-picture stories.

In 1899 Méliès directed an important nonfantasy film, *The Dreyfus Affair*. This motion picture was notable for its probing treatment of the spy trial of Captain Alfred Dreyfus and for its story length. *The Dreyfus Affair* consisted of 650 feet of film—a projection time of more than twenty minutes. Other narrative films by Méliès also drew on historical events, among them *Joan of Arc* (1900), *Bluebeard* (1901), and *Benvenuto Cellini* (1904).

In these films Georges Méliès proved his ability to utilize the motion-picture medium for reconstructing events based on factual material. But it was in the area of make-believe that the French magician was most innovative.

Although primitive in comparision with more recent special effects films such as *2001: A Space Odyssey* (1968) and *Star Wars* (1977), Méliès established the motion picture's ability to move beyond its recording capability and to create films that were born entirely in the filmmaker's imagination. With his achievements Méliès stood at stylistic odds with the Lumière actualities: the Lumière brothers visualized the familiar; Méliès visualized the unfamiliar.

In total effort, Méliès produced more than 500 motion pictures. Among his most memorable fantasies were *Cinderella,* produced in 1899, and *A Trip to the Moon* (1902), a film which brought Méliès temporary wealth and international fame.

Cinderella *Cinderella* was adapted from the popular fairy tale in a film that consisted of twenty separate scenes. The production was staged for the motion-picture camera with spectacular settings and costumes and was enhanced by hand-tinted frames which added fantastic color to the various scenes. In the development of plot, changes are made from one scene to the next by winding the exposed film at the end of one scene back in the camera a few feet and then photographing the beginning of the new scene over the already-exposed film. The reexposure creates a crude dissolve as the end of one scene temporarily appears with the beginning of the next.

The magical metamorphosis of one object into another is achieved through stop-action photography. A pumpkin suddenly becomes an ornate riding carriage by first filming the pumpkin, then stopping the camera, replacing the pumpkin with a carriage, and resuming filming. When projected, the change of image from pumpkin to carriage occurs instantaneously. The ghostlike appearance of the fairy godmother is made possible through the double exposure of two separate images.

A Trip to the Moon In his most famous work, *A Trip to the Moon,* Méliès' cinematic imagination proved to be both ingeniously clever and prophetic. In a story told in Jules Verne fashion, the plot follows the efforts

A progressive view of the action in *A Trip to the Moon* (1902).

of a Scientific Congress to send explorers to the moon. Plans are laid, the explorers chosen, and the projectile built and launched. The spaceship is visualized approaching the moon and landing directly in the eye of "the man in the moon," after which the story follows the incredible discoveries of the explorers. The scientists encounter a volcanic eruption, a snow storm, and an assortment of moon creatures.

After being taken prisoners, the explorers are able to escape and flee to the moon's edge where the space capsule awaits. One of the scientists pulls the capsule over the edge while another figure clings to the outside. The space projectile falls to the Earth where its landing is made in the ocean surface. The film concludes when a ship hastens to rescue the returned explorers.

Altogether Méliès incorporates thirty separate scenes in *A Trip to the Moon,* and this variety in scenic locations is itself an impressive accomplishment. In addition to the episodic nature of the narrative, Méliès thoroughly amuses audiences with his combination of theatricality and filmic trick effects. Chorus girls from the Théâtre Robert Houdin move the space capsule into the launching rocket, after which they turn and wave with innocent delight to the motion-picture camera. Later the chorus girls appear as curious faces inside star beams, hovering above the moon.

When the space projectile lands in the eye of the man in the moon, the man's face (a real one) grimaces with displeasure. For scenes filmed on the moon, set pieces are raised and lowered so that in the background the planet Earth is shown rising slowly into space. Through double exposure and animation the explorers in their dreams imagine comets, meteors, and star beams passing over them.

Utilizing stop-action photography a mushroom grows into gigantic proportions and moon creatures explode and disappear. Through the use of double-exposure photography, the space capsule after returning to Earth is seen beneath the ocean surface. By filming one of the two images through an aquarium, and reexposing it over a painted view of the fallen capsule, fish are visible swimming about the projectile and marine plants waver in the foreground.

A Trip to the Moon offered audiences film spectacle and illusion in a type of narrative film which suggested the unlimited possibilities of the motion-picture medium for inventing worlds that do not exist. Surprisingly, Méliès' fantastic journey to the moon in 1902 contained in its visualization elements which would later bear striking similarities with actual space exploration of the 1960s and 1970s. The capsule splashdown and recovery procedures, in particular, had been prophetically anticipated. It is a tribute to Méliès' ingenuity that on December 24, 1968 when American astronauts were first circling the moon, *CBS Evening News* concluded its broadcast that day with an excerpt from *A Trip to the Moon.*

Georges Méliès advanced the creative and narrative possibilities of motion-picture storytelling. Yet, like most early dramatic filmmakers he was unable to break entirely from the practices of theater arts. Each of the individual scenes in *A Trip to the Moon* was photographed from a single straight-on camera position, giving each scene the look of a proscenium stage picture. The use of stage machinery and painted settings also added to the theatrical appearance. Incongruous music hall elements such as chorus girls and vaudevillelike costumes were incorporated freely into the fantasies. Méliès' intention first and foremost was to entertain in as spectacular a manner as possible through the magic of whatever visual means were available to him.

But by taking his entertainment into the new medium of film, Méliès earned credit for a number of significant accomplishments: the expansion of the narrative film; the creation of the nonrealistic film story; the extensive use of optical effects as story elements—dissolves, double- and multiple-exposure shots, stop-action photography tricks, and animation.

With Méliès' work in the motion picture the medium was freed from its scientific, photographic compulsions and the imagination was given free rein. Every filmmaker thereafter who would be drawn to the magical possibilities of the motion picture would pay homage directly to Méliès. Indeed, shortly after the success of *A Trip to the Moon*, other filmmakers began illegally to make duplicate prints of Méliès' films and to copy his ideas. Unable to control the pirating of his efforts and unable to improve upon the artistic achievements of his earlier films, The Star Film Company was bankrupt by 1918.

Despite these personal failures Georges Méliès had stimulated filmmakers and filmgoers to see the narrative possiblities of the motion-picture medium. The task of drawing the film story entirely away from its identification with the theater and of developing the unique editing possibilities of film expression fell to other innovators.

Edwin S. Porter

If Georges Méliès can be properly called the father of the film narrative, then Edwin S. Porter (1869–1941) can be appropriately designated as the father of film editing.

As noted earlier, G. A. Smith and the Brighton School at the turn of the century had experimented with long shot–close shot interaction and had recognized the symbolic value of two juxtaposed scenes. But the Brighton film experiments were short-lived and for the most part had gone unnoticed by the general public.

It was Edwin S. Porter, an American cinematographer-filmmaker, who brought to the public attention the unique possibilities of motion-picture story construction.

Porter was born in Pittsburgh, Pennsylvania. As a young man he embarked on a series of careers as an electrician, plumber, and theater manager. After a brief time in the Navy, Porter became a film salesman and an organizer of short advertising films. In 1897 he was hired by Thomas Edison as a mechanic and eventually became a newsreel cinematographer, filming short scenes of public events for use in the Edison Vitascope programs. Porter photographed boat races, presidential parades, funeral corteges, and other such newsworthy actualities.

In 1901 and 1902, while still working for Edison, Porter began to

Edwin S. Porter.

direct short comic films with such titles as *The Old Maid Having Her Picture Taken* (1901), *Happy Hooligan Surprised* (1901), *Happy Hooligan April-Fooled* (1901), and *Happy Hooligan Turns Burglar* (1902).

Porter's venture into the narrative film with the *Happy Hooligan* series led him to study films being made in Europe and to take note of their narrative construction. Among the films apparently examined by Porter was a short work titled *Fire!*, directed in 1901 by J. A. Williamson of the Brighton School. Williamson's staged drama about a fire rescue was notable for its melodramatic action.

The Life of an American Fireman The exciting nature of Williamson's *Fire!* inspired Porter to make a similar type of narrative film in 1903 which he titled *The Life of an American Fireman*.

Drawing on his expertise as a newsreel cinemaphotographer, Porter first filmed actual scenes of firemen and fire wagons leaving their stations in New York and New Jersey. These documentary scenes were incorporated into a simple melodrama of firemen who are summoned to rescue a woman and her child who have been trapped by fire in a house.

Altogether the film contains eight separate scenes. *Scene one* shows a fire chief sleeping at his desk and nervously dreaming of a mother putting her baby to bed. This dream is visible in a projected "balloon"

The sequence of events in *The Life of an American Fireman* (1903).

image set on the wall behind the fireman. *Scene two* includes a close-up view of a fire alarm box as an anonymous figure, who is only partially seen, pulls the lever that triggers the alarm. In *Scene three* Porter inserts a documentary view of sleeping firemen in their quarters being suddenly awakened by the sound of an alarm; they quickly dress and disappear down the fire station pole. *Scene four* shows another documentary view of the firemen as they hastily hitch their horses to the fire wagons and exit the station. *Scenes five and six* move to an exterior view of the horses and fire wagons as they charge out the station doors.

The final scenes of *The Life of an American Fireman* show the fire wagons rushing through the streets and arriving at the scene of the fire. An interior studio shot appears of the mother pacing desperately about the bedroom in which she is trapped. Just before being overcome by smoke the woman throws open a window and appeals for help. Shortly thereafter, the mother and child are rescued by the firemen and taken safely to the ground below.

The Life of an American Fireman explored the development of film narrative through the contextual relationship of its various scenes. The "dream" shot of the mother putting her child to bed is followed by shots of the alarm box and the awakened firemen. By joining these three shots in succession it must be assumed that the firemen have been alerted to rescue the mother and child. This contextually derived information resembles the methods employed by the Brighton School in *Mary Jane's Mishap* when a cut was made from the stove explosion to a cemetery tombstone.

In *The Life of an American Fireman* Porter also utilizes the logical order of sequential scenes to create increasing excitement. The four successive shots of the firemen on their way to the rescue (quickly dressing, hitching their wagons, charging out of the station door, and speeding down a street toward the fire) illustrate the accelerated pacing of action available to the motion picture through the relationship of movement in the frame with the length of the shot.

While Porter had suggested an intuitive awareness of the dramatic and symbolic possibilities of film editing, he failed, however, at this point to take the editing a step further and to crosscut between the speeding fire wagons and the frantic mother for greater excitement and tension.

The Great Train Robbery The creative possibilities of parallel editing were realized by Porter in his landmark film, *The Great Train Robbery*. In this western story, which was photographed in New Jersey and released in December 1903, Porter pushed the motion-picture narrative even further away from a rigid, theatrical ordering of events.

The opening scene of the film shows the interior of a railroad telegraph office. Almost immediately, masked robbers enter and force the telegraph operator to stop an approaching train which is visible through the station window. The appearance of the train is achieved through a rear-screen image projected onto the window frame of the set wall. After the operator is bound and gagged, the robbers hasten to catch the train.

This opening scene is followed by an exterior view of the train as it is taking on water at a water tank. The robbers stealthily climb aboard. The scene changes to an express car where a mail clerk goes about his business as the train continues on its journey. It is possible to see the passing landscape through the open car door; again the effect is achieved by rear-screen projection. The robbers enter, shoot the clerk, and blow up the mail-car safe with dynamite.

Next the robbers are seen approaching along the top of the train's engine where they knock out the fireman and toss him off the car. After the train engineer is forced to stop the locomotive, the passengers are

The robbers in *The Great Train Robbery* head for their hideout. Porter, using a crude pan-tilt of the camera, followed the three men as they ran from the locomotive and down an embankment.

made to disembark and then are robbed. One passenger is shot and killed as he tries to flee. The robbers make their escape on the uncoupled engine of the train, forcing the engineer to take them to a hideout location several miles away in the mountains. As the robbers disembark from the train, the camera pans over and tilts down with the men as they mount their waiting horses. Although the camera movement appears rough and unplanned, Porter's use of the pan-tilt to follow action is one of the earliest examples of these techniques in a narrative film.

It is at this point that the plotting structure of *The Great Train Robbery* employs parallel editing to pick up story elements which have occurred simultaneously with the actions of the robbers. The story returns to the telegraph station where the operator remains bound and gagged. He is struggling to free himself when his daughter enters with a lunch pail. After she cuts the ropes and revives her father with a glass of water, he rushes out to seek help. Another scene change occurs, this time to a log cabin dance hall in which a large group of people are dancing a lively quadrille; the telegraph operator suddenly staggers in with the news of the holdup and the men in the dance party grab their guns and leave.

George Barnes concludes *The Great Train Robbery* by aiming directly at the camera lens and firing. In some prints of the film Porter's symbolic shot of Barnes both introduced and closed the work.

The Great Train Robbery concludes with the posse in pursuit of the robbers; one of the bandits is killed and the other three are taken by surprise as they examine their stolen goods in a clearing of a woods. In an innovative use of frame composition, the robbers are visible in the foreground, dividing their loot, while the posse appears in the frame behind them. As the posse sneaks forward toward the robbers, the film viewer is permitted to enjoy several privileged moments of anticipation as a result of the in-depth composition of foreground-background action.

The final shot of *The Great Train Robbery* possesses an unusual symbolic quality. An actor (George Barnes) appears in a medium close shot and, looking directly into the camera lens, aims his gun as though toward the viewer and fires it. Some critics said that this act of firing point blank at the camera served to associate the viewer with the story which had gone before. Whatever its intention, its very directness provided an exciting concluding moment for film audiences who were viewing, for that time, a truly sensational motion picture.

Porter's Achievements *The Great Train Robbery's* innovations were manifold. Artistically Porter's work provided excitement through story-telling methods that were uniquely cinematic. Parallel structuring of events and the pull of the story forward by action provided new awareness of the narrative possiblities of the motion picture. In a story-line that was fragmented rather than chronological in time, the action in each scene combined to form a unified whole as the plot progressed toward its dramatic climax. Porter's editing illustrated the unusual ability of the motion-picture story to move about freely in time and location and still make perfect sense to the viewer.

With *The Great Train Robbery* the new motion-picture medium also discovered the inherent appeal of the western story. The western story had grown in popularity with fiction readers in the latter half of the nineteenth century. Characterized by adventuresome pioneers who struggled at the edge of civilization to make a decent life for themselves, the western novel provided simple action plots that titillated the imagination with conflicts between good and evil.

A mythology of western life on the frontier emerged in this popular fiction. Bad men were depicted as taking advantage of the unformed rules of conduct on the rough frontier, robbing and killing at will if they so chose. Fearless sheriffs and strong-willed citizens on the side of law and order would rise up against the bad men and, temporarily at least, restore peace. The primary symbols in the western myth were guns, horses, and the open spaces of the frontier landscape.

The Great Train Robbery employed these familiar symbols in its simple tale of a train holdup. What was especially exciting to viewers was the intensified action of the one-reel film, including the free use of guns and a posse chase. The ability of the motion picture to follow complex action as indicated in the posse's pursuit suggested to filmmakers one of the medium's unique possibilities, and helped to establish the chase as a standard ingredient of the western film. Also, *The Great Train Robbery* with its almost casual treatment of violence hinted at the prominent role which guns and bloodshed would play in the American film melodrama throughout the twentieth century.

The sensational nature of *The Great Train Robbery* caused this motion picture to remain the most popular film in the United States for at least a half-dozen years after its release.

Limitations Porter's later work as a film director was unremarkable, and he retired from filmmaking in 1915 without significantly improving on the apparent limitations of *The Great Train Robbery*. Even with its many innovations Porter's film falls short of exploring the full possibilities of film story construction. Each individual scene consists of a single take of the action without a change of camera position. Except for the final symbolic shot of Barnes no close-ups appear in the film. Porter does employ diagonal camera angles for scenes filmed outdoors; interior shots, however, of the telegraph office and the log cabin are photographed from a straight-on position. The backdrops are obviously painted canvas flats.

Other theatrical elements are evident in the film, particularly in the overwrought performances of several of the actors. On seeing her father, the telegraph operator's daughter emotes with broad theatrical gestures that are unintentionally comical. The shooting deaths of the express car clerk and the passenger who attempts to flee are melodramatic rather than realistic. It is likely that these broadly projected actions were permitted as a compensation for the silence of the story, but they appear decidedly theatrical in a medium which demands naturalistic performances.

There are other directorial flaws in *The Great Train Robbery* which detract from the film's realism. One robber struggles to mount his horse—an obvious novice from the East. The tossing of the train fireman from the locomotive is easily detectable as a trick of stop-action photography in which a cloth-stuffed dummy has been substituted for the actor.

Porter's failure to achieve absolute realism does not diminish *The Great Train Robbery's* significance as a unique film narrative which suggested the importance of editing in motion-picture art. Furthermore, the film's lasting popularity aided the development of the emerging motion-picture industry and produced one of the first film stars in William Aronson who appeared in several different roles in *The Great Train Robbery*. Aronson later changed his name to Bronco Billy Anderson and embarked on a successful career as a screen cowboy.

As primitive an effort as Porter's western film was, *The Great Train Robbery*, in form and in content, signaled a critical point of departure for cinematic expression.

Robert W. Paul and Cecil M. Hepworth

In England two film pioneers, Robert W. Paul and Cecil M. Hepworth, are noteworthy for innovations which parallel the efforts of Georges Méliès and Edwin S. Porter.

Paul Robert William Paul (1870–1943) earned the distinction of becoming England's first significant film entrepreneur. Between 1895 and 1910 he produced and promoted a variety of short actualities, comedies, and trick films. In addition he patented the Bioscope projector, a machine which he placed on the market in 1896 for £5. It was this machine that Georges Méliès purchased the same year along with a collection of Paul's trick films—works which inspired the French magician to venture into filmmaking himself.

In 1897 Paul built a motion-picture studio, Paul's Animatograph Works. At this London studio he and his principal director, Walter Booth, created films with many of the same magical qualities that characterized the efforts of Georges Méliès, including *The Haunted Curiosity Shop* (1900), *Lilliputians in a London Restaurant* (1902), and *The Magic Sword* (1903).

Paul's trick films never achieved the spectacular dimensions of those by his French counterpart, primarily because of the more diversified interests of the English producer. Yet it is important to observe that like the invention of the motion-picture camera and companion projector, the development of varying film styles also occurred simultaneously in different parts of the world.

Paul, who inspired Méliès with his trick films, may also have inspired J. A. Williamson's *Fire!* (1901), which in turn inspired Porter's *The Life of an American Fireman* (1903). In 1898, before either Williamson's or Porter's work, Paul produced his own fire rescue melodrama, *Plucked from Burning.*

Hepworth The other Englishman whose pioneering film efforts deserve notice is Cecil M. Hepworth (1874–1953), a director-producer who entered the motion-picture business after assisting his father in the presentation of magic lantern programs. In 1896 Hepworth went to work in film as an assistant to Birt Acres who was one of England's early prominent cinematographers. Before becoming a cinematographer himself in 1898, Hepworth published a book in 1897 entitled *Animated Photography* and patented an improved method of developing and printing motion-picture celluloid.

Hepworth produced and processed a number of significant films at a laboratory which he founded in 1899 at Walton-on-Thames. Among his early works were *Express Trains* (1898), *Two Fools in a Canoe* (1898), *The Explosion of a Motor Car* (1900), *How the Burglar Tricked the Bobby* (1901), and, not surprisingly, in 1903 *Fireman to the Rescue,* by then apparently an obligatory plot for any ambitious filmmaker.

RESCUED BY ROVER As his film titles suggest, Hepworth explored, among other interests, the motion picture's capability for action stories. In 1905 he produced his most famous work, *Rescued by Rover,* an action film suggested by his wife.

In many ways this story about the kidnapping of a baby by a gypsy woman and the child's rescue by the family dog surpasses the editing achievements of Edwin S. Porter. Hepworth's narrative employs many of the standard continuity procedures necessary for the logical progression of rapidly changing film action.

In *Rescued by Rover* the frantic nurse who was tending the stolen child informs the family of the kidnapping; Rover, an observant collie, leaps through the window and runs through a variety of locations to the house where the baby is being held. Rover then returns home and by barking indicates to the father that he knows the whereabouts of the child. The father follows the dog to the hiding place and the child is rescued.

In this forerunner to numerous *Lassie* films and other such action stories involving the intervention of animals, Hepworth utilizes the possibilities of story continuity that can be derived from the editing

Rover leads the way for his master and the man's child is rescued.

together of shots in which established patterns of screen movement remain consistent. As Rover heads for the hideaway, running through streets and swimming across a stream, the dog always appears in each separate shot moving from the left side of the screen toward the right. On the return journey home, a reversal of pattern occurs as Rover proceeds from screen right toward screen left.

Through this technique of screen direction continuity, the consistent patterns of movement allow Hepworth to rapidly advance the action of the story as the dog travelled through each location. The forward movement in each shot creates the semblance of a continuous journey, when in fact no such journey had actually occurred.

Rescued by Rover introduced a facet of film editing which would eventually serve all filmmakers who were required to arrange the movement of screen characters or vehicles through scenic locations without a loss of viewer orientation.

Even more creative possiblities for joining together shots of characters in patterns of screen movement would be explored by the Russian filmmaker Lev Kuleshov in the early 1920s. Kuleshov, like Hepworth, proved that carefully edited movement patterns can create their own fiction.

Georges Méliès, Edwin S. Porter, Robert W. Paul, and Cecil M. Hepworth together laid the foundation for the construction of narrative motion pictures. In idea, in form, and in style these men suggested the unique possibilities of a new and not readily understood medium of expression. Georges Méliès, inspired by Robert Paul, invented imaginary worlds through the optical magic of the motion-picture camera and helped to generate audiences for the infant medium of film. Edwin Porter and Cecil Hepworth tested and proved the unique possibilities of editing in the construction of motion-picture stories. Porter's parallel development of story-line revealed that the motion picture enjoys unusual opportunities for manipulating space and time. Furthermore, he showed how the action of carefully arranged shots can pull together the film narrative without explanation as the story progresses rapidly from location to location. In addition to these innovations in film editing, Porter introduced to film audiences the western genre with all the elements of this uniquely American type of film clearly intact. Cecil Hepworth further advanced the art of film editing and the action story by establishing the aesthetics of screen direction continuity. With these procedures Hepworth showed how it is possible to evoke a sense of geographic and narrative realities through screen direction and shot arrangement.

Even as a great number of filmmakers remained in easy alliance with the theater these rudimentary innovations between 1896 and 1910 demonstrated that the art of the motion picture was slowly but clearly emerging. Total separation from theatrical leanings and refinement of technique seemed within the grasp of filmmakers of larger artistic vision. David Wark Griffith would prove to be one of those visionaries.

SUGGESTED READINGS

Bessy, Maurice, and Lo Duca. *Georges Méliès, Mage; et "Mes Mémoires" par Méliès*. Paris. Prisma, 1945.

Betts, Ernest. *The Film Business: A History of the British Cinema 1896–1972*. New York: Pitman, 1973.

Frazer, John. *Artificially Arranged Scenes: The Films of Georges Méliès*. Boston: Hall, 1980.

Hampton, Benjamin. *History of the American Film Industry from Its Beginnings to 1931*. New York: Dover, 1970.

Jacobs, Lewis. *The Rise of the American Film*. New York: Teachers College, 1968.

Pratt, George C. *Spellbound in Darkness: Readings in the History and Criticism of the Silent Film*. Rochester: N.Y.U. of Rochester Press, 1966.

Slide, Anthony. *Early American Cinema*. Cranbury, N.J.: Barnes, 1970.

Vardac, A. Nicholas. *Stage to Screen*. Cambridge: Harvard University Press, 1949.

Wagenknecht, Edward. *The Movies in the Age of Innocence*. Norman: University of Oklahoma Press, 1962.

PART 2

DEVELOPMENT
AND GROWTH
IN AMERICA

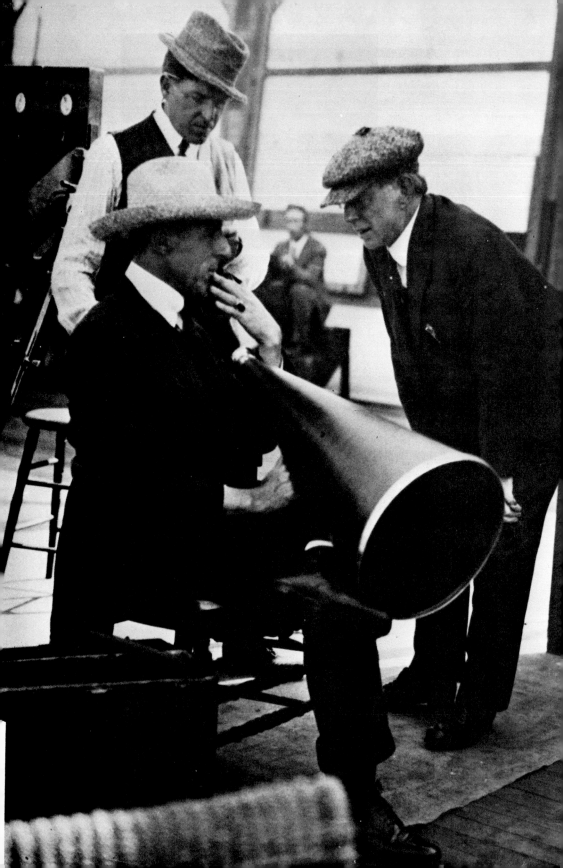

DAVID WARK GRIFFITH

It was the first movie without a chase. That was something, for those days, a movie without a chase was not a movie. How could a movie be made without a chase? How could there be suspense? How action? *After Many Years* was also the first picture to have a *dramatic* close-up—the first to have a cut-back. . . . When Mr. Griffith suggested a scene showing Annie Lee waiting for her husband's return to be followed by a scene of Enoch cast away on a desert island, it was altogether too distracting. How can you tell a story jumping about like that? The people won't know what it's about.

"Well," said Mr. Griffith, "doesn't Dickens write that way?"

> Mrs. D. W. Griffith describing
> Griffith's short adaptation of
> *Enoch Arden (After Many Years)*
> for Biograph in 1908. Cited in
> Mrs. Griffith's *When the Movies
> Were Young*, 1925.

D. W. Griffith.

$\mathbf{O}$f the early directors who played important roles in the development of film art, clearly David Wark Griffith was the most significant. Griffith, later known more familiarly as "D. W.," was born in Crestwood, Kentucky on January 23, 1875. He was the son of Jacob Griffith, a Kentucky state legislator and former colonel, who had served under Stonewall Jackson during the Civil War.

As a child D. W. adored listening to his father reminisce about the war and about his battle scars which were both real (he had been wounded five times) and psychological: there was a deeply felt bitterness in the father over the South's loss and over the fact that the Griffith family home had been burned to the ground in the early part of the civil conflict. Jacob Griffith communicated this bitterness and his fierce pride in being a Southerner to his son.

Although D. W. was only 10 when Jacob died in 1885, the two men by then were of the same emotional disposition when it came to reflecting on the Civil War. This disposition would later compel Griffith to make his most important motion picture, *The Birth of a Nation*.

WRITING ASPIRATIONS

As a young man D. W. Griffith first aspired to become a writer. He worked for a time as a correspondent for the *Baptist Weekly* in Kentucky and then as a newspaper reporter in Louisville. Eventually an avid interest in a theatrical career led him to give up his newspaper work, change his name to Lawrence Griffith, and join a touring stock company as an actor with the ultimate goal of becoming a "dramatist." The change more accurately suited Griffith's instincts and passions; as an actor he was able to continue his creative writing in the form of plays, although with little success. During this time Griffith also tried his hand at free-lance poetry (passionate and noticeably inspired by Walt Whitman in its use of natural imagery). He managed to sell some of these poems to respectable journals.

In 1906 Griffith and his actress-wife, Linda Arvidson, moved to New York City where Griffith hoped to launch his career as a playwright. To support themselves they auditioned for and received work in a play written by the Reverend Thomas Dixon, who at the time was enjoying great success as the author of a sensational, deeply biased Civil War novel, *The Clansman*. Later that year Griffith received word that his first stage script had been sold, so he turned his attention to tryouts in Washington, D.C. and Baltimore of his play, *A Fool and a Girl*. The play ran for two weeks.

These two events, the failure of *A Fool and a Girl* and the brief introduction to Thomas Dixon, would eventually prove to be of major significance in the life and career of D. W. Griffith. Together they led to

Griffith's introduction to the fledgling film industry and to the motion picture which would help establish the film medium as a great form of artistic expression and as a powerful social force.

FINDING THE MOVIES

After the failure of his play early in 1907, D. W. (Lawrence) Griffith sought work again as an actor and also attempted to interest the Edison Company in some of his scripts. When he went looking for a job as a film writer Griffith offered himself to a rapidly growing, competitive industry in which profits were the most important consideration.

Theater Expansion

Following the opening of the Nickelodeon Theater in Pittsburgh in 1905 the proliferation of similar types of motion-picture houses across the United States and abroad had been remarkable. In 1906 *The Billboard* magazine reported:

> In every town of sufficient size to support it there exists a theatre where moving shows are given exclusively. The admission is five or ten cents, and as many shows are given every day as warranted by the attendance. The larger towns support many institutions of this kind and dozens of new ones are being installed every week. . . . This evolution from the magic lantern is most remarkable when considered from a scientific standpoint, but it is even more wonderful from a business point of view. It amounts practically to a revolution; and yet those who are conversant with the inside workings of the business maintain that it is still in its infancy.
> What will it be in its prime? [*The Billboard,* September 15, 1906.]

Enterprising businessmen, many of whom would later become important film producers, had quickly recognized the potential profits in motion-picture exhibition. It is estimated that in 1907 there were more than 125 distribution exchanges in the United States which supplied films to these exhibitors.

Competition and Monopoly

The increased intensity of film exhibition led to the formation of the Motion Picture Patents Company in 1908. In a clearly monopolistic move to control the fledgling film industry, ten major movie production companies entered into an agreement which gave them exclusive rights to sixteen patents involving film stock, cameras, and projection devices. Included in the Patents Trust were the firms of Edison, Biograph, Vitagraph, Essanay, Kalem, Selig, Lubin, Pathé Frères, George Kleine, and Méliès. In addition to the exclusive rights by these companies to the use of certain patented cameras and Eastman Kodak film materials, the organization rented their films only to distributors and exhibitors who had licensed their projectors with the trust.

The impact of this monopoly on the film industry and on the developing art of the medium was felt in a number of ways. There ensued between the Patents organization and a group of feisty independents a war that lasted for years. Exhibitors such as William Fox and Carl Laemmle became impatient with the quality of films being provided them by the monopoly companies, and decided to produce their own motion pictures.

The Patents Organization, with no real threat of competition, was content to continue making one-reel films which simply repeated in unimaginative variations earlier film successes. Ten-minute versions of popular stage plays, such as Olcott's *Ben Hur* (1907), and stereotyped chase comedies of similar length dominated the market.

It was argued that the wide acceptance of cheaply made action films and screen adaptations of stage plays indicated the safest way to continue to realize large profits. It was also generally held by the production companies that audiences would not accept silent films longer than twelve minutes.

D. W. Griffith was aware of these artistic limitations when he first approached the film industry as a writer, particularly of the restriction of story length to one reel, a fact which provided little opportunity for development of character or theme. On seeing his first film in Chicago in 1905 Griffith had remarked "that any man enjoying such a thing should be shot."

Lawrence Griffith: Film Actor

But Griffith needed work and money, so in 1907 he took a script to Edwin S. Porter at the Edison Studios. Porter turned down Griffith's script (a version of *Tosca*) but offered him a role in an action story, *Rescued from an Eagle's Nest* (1907). This Porter film in which Griffith portrayed the hero was an early, crude attempt to create *Jaws*-like suspense on the screen by having a baby carried away by an eagle and rescued by the father.

Rescued from an Eagle's Nest In its attempt at special-effects realism *Rescued from an Eagle's Nest* is visually less credible than Porter's work in *The Great Train Robbery* four years earlier. An obvious conflict exists between exterior scenes which are painted on theatrical canvas and those which have been photographed in a natural environment.

This conflict of theatricality and realism is made even more apparent by twice juxtaposing shots in which geographic unity is intended. In the first instance, the mother—going for help after her baby has been snatched away (quite awkwardly by the eagle)—runs from the open area

Lawrence (D. W.) Griffith, the actor, is lowered down a real cliff in the concluding moments of *Rescued from an Eagle's Nest.* The shot which immediately follows, however, places him within a setting which is quite obviously hand-painted. A blurred eagle attacks the father.

outside the family's log cabin. She exits the right side of the screen. The scene changes to a location in the woods where the father (Griffith) and other men are felling trees. Almost immediately the mother enters frantically from screen left.

By use of screen pattern continuity (exit right, enter left) Porter was able to advance the mother rapidly from one location to the next; the woman, however, moves from a painted setting into a real one, producing a jolting contrast of scenic style.

The second stylistic contradiction occurs as the father is lowered by rope from the top of a cliff down to an aerie on the cliff's edge where the eagle has taken the child. The first shot of the father, as he disappears over the cliff, was photographed by Porter in an actual setting. The next shot taken from a longer view shows the man dropping to the cliff's edge which rests perilously close to a deep precipice.

This entire scenic representation of cliff's edge and distant mountains, unlike the previous scene, is one that has been painted on canvas backdrops. The matched editing of the two shots as the father is lowered into the scene suggests a spatial unity, but the effect again is belied by the conflict in the visual styles.

As the eagle attacks the father during the baby's rescue, Porter fails to employ any detail shots or closer views of the action. He is content to allow the illusion provided by the spectacular theatrical setting and the intended sensation of the eagle's attack to supply the film's dramatic climax.

Rescued from an Eagle's Nest, in spite of its limitations, illustrates the crude beginnings of screen melodrama in which special effects are a significant part of the story's reality. In time, and with more experience and improved technology, this kind of film story, as with Porter's work with the western genre, would develop as a standard type of American motion picture.

Except for his later fame as a director, D. W. Griffith's appearance in this 1907 melodrama would probably have had little significance. As was typical of many film actors of the day, he merely walked through his role. But from this acting job with the Edison Studios Griffith went on the next year to become a film actor and writer for one of Edison's major competitors, the Biograph Company. Before 1908 was over, Biograph, short on directors, put Griffith in directorial control of his first film, *The Adventures of Dollie.* Without fully realizing it, Griffith had once more changed careers, and again it was a career change for which he was aptly suited.

THE APPRENTICESHIP AT BIOGRAPH

D. W. Griffith's ability to direct movies was apparent from the beginning. *The Adventures of Dollie,* despite its brevity, told the rather complicated story of a kidnapping by a gypsy salesman (a throwback to *Rescued by Rover*), the search for the child, and the climactic rescue of the infant from a waterstream. This adventurous chain of events, involving several locations, flowed smoothly on the screen and Griffith's first directorial effort proved a big success.

Griffith's film apprenticeship at Biograph lasted from July 1908 until August 1913. During these five years he directed nearly 500 films for the company with a record 145 directorial assignments in 1909. In one eight-day period that year, between January 21 and January 28, Griffith held the reins for five separate motion-picture productions.

Among this huge number of Biograph films resides Griffith's

An advertisement offering Griffith's first film for distribution and exhibition.

emerging artistry. He experimented with unusual camera set-ups, beginning scenes with the action already in progress rather than having actors enter a scene as though the frame perimeters were a proscenium arch. He explored the possibilities of repeating actions and photographing them from different perspectives so that visual variety and closer views were possible in editing a continuous scene.

An examination of the Biograph films also shows Griffith's realization that a motion picture contains two types of rhythms: an *internal rhythm* provided by the movement of the actors in a scene and an *external rhythm* supplied by the film editor through the controlled length of shots and scenes. A series of short shots appears to accelerate the pace of a story. Accelerated editing combined with crosscutting became one of Griffith's favorite methods of effecting exciting last-minute screen rescues in films such as *The Lonely Villa* (1909) and *The Lonedale Operator* (1911).

The Lonely Villa

In *The Lonely Villa*, which was based on an actual newspaper story, Griffith gave indication of a well-developed, craftsmanlike understanding of motion-picture technique. The simple story involves a trio of robbers who employ a forged letter to entice a man away from the country manor where he lives with his wife and three young daughters. This ploy is intended to allow the robbers easy entry into the villa.

The film begins with a dramatic long shot of the house with the three conspirators in the lower left corner of the frame. Inside the villa, the husband, wife, and daughters are seen in a tableau (posed grouping) of domestic tranquility. One of the robbers appears at the door with a letter stating that the husband's mother, who is expected for a visit, is arriving earlier than originally planned. The husband departs for the train station.

In near academic illustration of screen direction continuity and crosscutting Griffith develops the story of the attempted robbery and last-minute rescue by the husband with exacting skill. *The Lonely Villa* utilizes fifty-two separate shots in its twelve-minute story. Length of shots varies from one minute (the shot of the father as he prepares to leave the house) to as short as three seconds. As the robbers force their way into the room where the mother and daughters have barricaded themselves, Griffith accelerates the drama by rapid crosscutting between the father's return trip home and the scene at the villa.

In an earlier series of shots involving crosscutting the husband is shown in the village inn talking to his wife on the telephone. This shot is followed by a cut to a dramatic low-angled view of one of the robbers on the roof-edge of the villa as he snips the phone line. In two following quick cuts the husband and then the wife are shown jiggling the phone receptacle as the line goes dead. This chain-of-events sequence displayed

The last-minute rescue begins in *The Lonely Villa* (1909) as the father, realizing from the phone call that his family is in immediate danger, rushes from the inn to return home.

the dramatic possibilities of simultaneously developing events through crosscutting.

The Lonely Villa also includes a lengthy camera pan as the husband leaves the village inn and crosses the street to a gypsy camp where he bargains for the use of a wagon. The smoothness of the panning movement by Billy Bitzer, Griffith's cinematographer, indicates a significant improvement in camera and camera-mount technology.

For the most part *The Lonely Villa* achieves scenic realism in its use of settings and locations. The living rooms of the villa possess a cramped, boxlike quality but the illusion of realism is maintained as the story moves from the exterior views of an actual house to interior views that appear to have been filmed in studio carrels.

Griffith's direction of his actors shows a marked interest in naturalistic screen performances. A hint of broad gesturing occurs in the actions of the mother and the principal robber, but the father and eldest daughter, portrayed by 16-year-old Mary Pickford in her second film role, are rather remarkable in their avoidance of projected acting styles.

A Corner in Wheat

As Griffith came in contact with many different types of stories at Biograph, his range of techniques and cinematic styles grew appreciably. Late in 1909 his stylistic diversity is sharply apparent in *A Corner in Wheat*. In a brief twelve minutes it tells the story of how the capitalistic greed of a wheat tycoon affects the poor. The film includes near the beginning of the story and as its final shot a poetic rendering of Jean François Millet's nineteenth-century painting, *The Sower*.

Between these poetic bookends, Griffith juxtaposes tableaux of common people waiting in line to buy bread with scenes showing the flamboyant life-style of the wheat tycoon. One tableau of the common people is so static it resembles a freeze-frame. The banquet scenes at the tycoon's home by contrast are alive with gaiety, and Billy Bitzer's camera compositions, deep into the frame, are remarkably like those used by Erich von Stroheim some fifteen years later in his realistic classic *Greed* (1924). (As a note of historical significance *A Corner in Wheat* was inspired by Frank Norris' story, *The Pit; Greed* was adapted from Norris' novel, *McTeague*.)

A Corner in Wheat's contrasting pictorial compositions, the opposing tenor of its action, and its symbolic-poetic imagery constitute an early effort at dialectical statement through methods that Sergei Eisenstein and other Russian socialist filmmakers in the 1920s would label "montage of collision." The Russians did, in fact, carefully study Griffith's works before they began making their own politically charged, theoretically based films.

In *A Corner in Wheat* (1909) a static shot of common workers waiting to purchase bread stands in vivid contrast to the extravagant lifestyle of the tycoon who has driven up the price of wheat.

The first Biograph stage in California, early 1910, located in Los Angeles at Washington Street and Grand Avenue. Griffith, his back to the camera, stands on the stage preparing to direct a scene.

Hollywood Is Discovered

During Griffith's apprenticeship at Biograph, regular clashes between the Motion Picture Patents Company and the independents continued, including police and hired-gun raids on unsanctioned studios and movie houses. To escape this violence and the frequent destruction of their production facilities, many independents in 1909 began to move west, most to southern California which was about as far away as one could get from the Trust strongholds of New York and New Jersey.

In California the independents enjoyed greater artistic freedom, a variety of outdoor settings, and a better climate for the year-round production of motion pictures. Most filmmakers settled on the edges of Los Angeles in a suburb which in 1913 would be named Hollywood—a name that in time would achieve a glamorous symbolic value unmatched in the world of mass entertainment. In the Los Angeles suburb make-shift studios and open-air sets without roofs or front walls were erected for the making of films under the usually bright sunshine of southern California.

In a brief time producers and directors for the Patents Trust also discovered the more ideal conditions in California and began taking their acting companies there for the winter season. In 1910 Griffith joined the winter exodus west. The stimulus of a new environment plus Griffith's own lofty ambitions would in the passage of a few years lead him to achieve unparalleled success as a motion-picture artist.

The Battle

In one of Griffith's California-made films, *The Battle* (1911), it is possible to see a hint of the spectacular realism which would later characterize his impressive and lengthy epics. Labeled by some film historians as the best one-reel motion picture ever made, *The Battle* narrates the story of a young woman (Blanche Sweet) and her soldier-lover whose cowardice causes him to flee a Civil War battle. The soldier loses the respect of his girlfriend but returns to his company to become a hero in the battle's victory.

In *The Battle* the crowds spill off the screen for an unstaged effect. The battle scenes are documentarylike in their realistic detail. And the film's rhythms, internal and external, are carefully regulated to intensify the action.

Griffith's achievement in *The Battle* is greater though than simple technical control and visual realism. In the scene in which the soldier rejoins his company, the boy—running backwards in the shot—slips undetected among a rush of soldiers as they dash across the screen in the fury of battle. The event is so fortuitously arranged that it has not the least bit of theatricality about it.

The Battle also managed to communicate the emotional feelings of Blanche Sweet as she responded to events around her. Her love, anger, fear, and final joy are fully realized by Griffith's careful direction and lingering camera. Griffith had discovered that a shot of a character left on the screen for a period of time will help convey inner meaning.

In addition to its splendid realism the film sought and won the empathetic involvement of the audience with the characters—an effect desired by all good drama. *The Battle* was proof of Griffith's intuitive understanding of the affective powers of the motion-picture medium. Yet it only hinted at what was to come.

EXPANDED PROJECTS

After the public and critical success of *The Battle* and the first American two-reeler, *Enoch Arden*, also made in 1911, Griffith considered himself to be the world's preeminent film director, and he continued to seek ways to prove this claim. In 1913, against the wishes of Biograph, Griffith produced *Judith of Bethulia*, a four-reel film of more than forty minutes in length.

THE BATTLE

An Influence that Makes the Hero

IN THE DAYS OF '61 how many of the brave soldiers were urged to deeds of valor and heroism by thoughts of "the girl he left behind". This story tells of the transforming of a pusillanimous coward into a lion-hearted hero by the derision of the girl he loved. The battle takes place outside her home, and he, panic-stricken, rushes in, trembling with fear, to hide. She laughs in scorn at his cowardice and commands him to go back and fight. Her fortitude inspires him and he manages to rejoin his company before his absence is noticed. Ammunition is low and somebody must take the hazardous journey to procure more from another regiment, which he volunteers to do. This undertaking cannot be adequately described, for the young man faces death at every turn. The most thrilling part of his experience is where the opposing forces build bonfires along the road to menace the powder-wagon. This, without question, is the most stirring war picture ever produced.

ⒶⒷ BIOGRAPH ⒶⒷ

Released Nov. 6, 1911

A Biograph trade journal describes the plot of *The Battle* (1911). A frame from the film depicts the heroic deed of the young soldier as he steers the ammunition wagon on its treacherous journey.

Two film events from abroad had given urgency to Griffith's aspirations of proving himself the world's top filmmaker. In 1912 the Film d'Art production of *Queen Elizabeth,* starring Sarah Bernhardt and directed by Louis Mercanton, was introduced to United States audiences by the American distributor Adolph Zukor. Early the next year *Quo Vadis?*, a lavish Italian spectacle, also enjoyed enormous popularity in the United States. Both *Queen Elizabeth* (four reels in length) and *Quo Vadis?* (nearly eight reels in length) commanded admission prices of $1.50 and each realized considerable profits.

Neither film, however, was a remarkable artistic achievement and Griffith was conscious of this fact. Thus, against the protests of Biograph's business managers, he was driven in 1913 to film *Judith of Bethulia* at an unheard-of cost of $36,000. Griffith's direction was impressive for its strong visual compositions, the superb handling of the actors and crowd scenes, and for its collective-story approach which anticipated Griffith's 1916 four-part epic *Intolerance.*

As a result of Biograph's resistance as well as his driving ambition for more prestige, Griffith completed the direction of *Judith of Bethulia* in California and severed his ties with Biograph. He went to work on the West Coast for Harry Aitken at the Mutual Film Corporation as head of the newly formed production subsidiary Reliance-Majestic. With him he took his close collaborator and cameraman, Billy Bitzer, as well as many of the actors and actresses to whom he had taught the art of intimate screen performance, including Blanche Sweet, Mae Marsh, Donald Crisp, and Dorothy and Lillian Gish. At Reliance-Majestic Griffith directed four films *(The Battle of the Sexes; The Escape; Home, Sweet Home;* and *The Avenging Conscience)* and supervised several others between October 1913 and late 1914, enjoying the financial means and artistic freedom he had sought. Still his ambitions had not been fully realized.

INSPIRATION

Griffith's wife, Linda Arvidson, in her book *When the Movies Were Young,* tells that it was Frank Woods, a former film critic for *The Dramatic Mirror* and a scenario writer, who first suggested the idea of a film version of Thomas Dixon's novel and play, *The Clansman.* Woods had already been involved as a writer in an abortive attempt in 1912 by the Kinemacolor Company of America to film Dixon's play. Woods believed Griffith was capable of getting the project done.

By April 1914 Harry Aitken and the Mutual Corporation had agreed to finance the picture under the newly formed company, Epoch. In his mind Griffith began to formulate the theme and plot for a film whose volatile content would be inextricably meshed with the mind of the Reverend Thomas Dixon, Jr.

Thomas Dixon, Jr.

Thomas Dixon, Jr.

Thomas Dixon, Jr. (1864–1946) usually receives only passing commentary as the Southern writer-minister on whose novel *The Birth of a Nation* was based. Yet Dixon was a prominent figure in his day (more so even than Griffith), influential, and highly successful, as well as being the root source of nearly every controversial idea in Griffith's film.

Dixon was born on January 11, 1864, near Shelby, North Carolina. Like Griffith, in his formative years Dixon had listened to tales of the Civil War while experiencing with his family the period of Southern Reconstruction. During Reconstruction Dixon's father had joined the Ku Klux Klan and his uncle, Colonel Leroy McAfee, also a member, had been a Grand Titan of the Western North Carolina Klans.

In the fall of 1879, Thomas Dixon, Jr., entered Wake Forest College in eastern North Carolina and upon graduation in 1883 was awarded a scholarship for graduate study in history at Johns Hopkins University. At Johns Hopkins he met Woodrow Wilson, a fellow student in one of his classes, and the two became close friends.

Like D. W. Griffith, Dixon's career followed several courses. Over the fifteen-year period between 1884 and 1899, he became a North Carolina legislator, a lawyer, an ordained minister, and one of the country's most successful public lecturers.

When he began to tire of his roles as minister and orator, Dixon turned to writing fiction inspired by his childhood memories of Reconstruction. In 1902 *The Leopard's Spots* was published and the degrading novel with its pro-Southern, pro-white thesis generated an enormous controversy.

The next year Dixon began work on an even more controversial sequel, *The Clansman*. This novel examined with romantic and biased fervor a chronology of events beginning with the last month of Abraham Lincoln's presidency and concluding with the emergence in the late 1860s of the Ku Klux Klan, an organization whose rise was cunningly justified in Dixon's book.

The Clansman became Thomas Dixon's most successful novel to date, ranking among the top five best-selling works of fiction published in 1905. The romantic, chivalrous nature of the novel, underscored by not-too-far removed historical events, was responsible for a large part of its popular appeal.

In 1905 Dixon combined plot elements from *The Leopard's Spots* and *The Clansman* to form a stage play which opened on September 22 in Norfolk, Virginia. The play version, like the novel, achieved public popularity despite being widely criticized for its incendiary nature. Many critics described it as "disgusting," "a riot breeder," and "obnoxious." Despite the criticism, two different theatrical companies toured throughout the United States with *The Clansman* for five years.

FILMING *THE CLANSMAN*

Near the end of 1913, after the abortive attempt to have *The Clansman* filmed, Dixon met with Harry Aitken of Mutual about full motion-picture rights to his novels (*The Leopard's Spots* would be included) and play version of *The Clansman*. Some accounts of the meeting claim that Dixon was offered $10,000 by Aitken (a $2,500 option with the remaining $7,500 to be paid later) but that a shortage of cash eventually forced Griffith and Aitken to forfeit the plan, and Dixon renegotiated for a 25 percent interest in the picture. Another account states that Dixon initially asked for the $10,000 but that Aitken offered instead the 25 percent arrangement, to which Dixon reluctantly agreed. Whichever, the contract would make Dixon a wealthy man as it turned out.

By April 1914 Mutual Production Company and Harry Aitken had committed themselves financially and artistically to D. W. Griffith's immense project. Lillian Gish, one of the stars of the film, speaks in her memoirs, *The Movies, Mr. Griffith, and Me,* of Griffith's determination in realizing the screen version of *The Clansman*. "I'm going to tell the truth about the War between the States. It hasn't been told accurately in history books. Only the winning side in a war gets to tell its story." This telling of the "truth" was the task Griffith set before himself.

The Birth of a Nation was filmed in and around Los Angeles (with several of the plantation scenes shot in Mexico) between July and

October 1914. Reports on the filming suggest that the production process involved meticulous research for Griffith while most of the others involved in the project went about their tasks without fully understanding what was happening around them.

Authenticity

To authenticate material in the first part of the story, which deals with the prewar and war periods (events not included in Dixon's books), Griffith consulted a variety of factual sources: Harper's *Pictorial History of the Civil War;* published volumes of Matthew Brady's *Civil War Photgraphs;* and biographies of Abraham Lincoln. These materials provided the visual data needed to duplicate important historical events and scenes from the Civil War. Sites for the filming of the battle scenes were chosen to resemble as much as possible the actual locations.

Griffith cast actors who resembled the major historical figures (Lee, Grant, Lincoln) so that he could copy the most familiar photographs of the war era: Lincoln's first call for volunteers, the surrender at Appomattox, the signing of the Emancipation Proclamation. In exacting facsimiles Griffith posed his actors in static positions, then brought these "photographs" to active life on the screen so that history could be seen in the making.

Griffith followed precisely the account of Lincoln's assassination as told in *Lincoln, A History* (written by Nicolay and Hay) so that the chronology of events in Ford's Theater on April 14, 1865, would be totally accurate. A set of Ford's Theater was built to match the original in size and detail. For scenes in the South Carolina legislature after the 1868 elections, Griffith also had sets copied from photographs of the legislative halls.

Settings, costumes, hairstyles, locations, all appeared authentic. By striving for visual authenticity and documentation of events, particularly impressive in the first part of the film, Griffith was putting onto film the first significant docudrama. Fact and fiction were being merged with great skill to achieve a powerful reinterpretation of history.

Forceful Drama

For the second part of the film Griffith relied almost entirely on the fiction of Thomas Dixon, Jr. Griffith concentrated his attention on dramatizing demoralizing events during Reconstruction in Piedmont, South Carolina, and particularly on the personalization of the story.

The cast of actors assembled for the film combined their own talents with Griffith's directorial skills to produce a drama of moving force. Lillian Gish, already well-trained by Griffith, portrayed Elsie Stoneman; Henry B. Walthall was Ben Cameron, the "Little Colonel"; Miriam Cooper was Margaret Cameron; Mae Marsh was the "Little Sister" Flora; Josephine Crowell and Spottiswoode Aiken were the Cameron

Two historical facsimiles in *The Birth of a Nation*.

Griffith inspects the set of Ford's Theater, being reconstructed for a six-minute scene depicting Lincoln's assassination.

mother and father; Ralph Lewis interpreted the role of Austin Stoneman; and the roles of Abraham Lincoln, Silas Lynch, and Gus were played by Joseph Henabery, George Seigmann, and Walter Long, respectively.

In directing the actors Griffith did not hesitate to combine naturalism with more flamboyant expression. At times Griffith would call to his cast to hold back emotion, to show no expression at all. At other times the actors were instructed to let the emotion pour forth. Griffith's goal was to make certain that the characters' emotions, subtle or overt, could be clearly understood in a complex film that was being made without the advantages of spoken dialogue.

The filming of *The Birth of a Nation* was almost halted midway when the production exceeded its original budget. However, a loan from William Clune, a California theater owner, allowed Griffith to finish. Lillian Gish reports that the film cost approximately $91,000 to make: $61,000 to produce the film and $30,000 to promote it. Tens of thousands of feet of film had been shot by Griffith. The task of editing this footage to a manageable length (13,000 feet) and providing a musical score consumed another four months before the film was ready to be shown to the public.

On February 8, 1915, D. W. Griffith's film, then still titled *The Clansman,* opened in Los Angeles at Clune's Auditorium.

AN ARTISTIC MASTERPIECE: *THE BIRTH OF A NATION*

The artistry within Griffith's labors was stunning. In an epic story nearly three hours in length Griffith utilized a full range of cinematic techniques and superb directorial control to achieve his aims. What audiences saw on the screen was an impressive account of supposedly truthful events as they acted to deeply affect the lives of the film's fully dimensioned fictional characters.

The Plot: Epic, Personal, and Political

The Birth of a Nation begins with two brief documentarylike scenes which depict the arrival of slaves in America and, much later in time, an Abolitionist meeting. This glib brush of events brings Griffith's story up to 1860 (five years earlier than the beginning of Dixon's novel) where he introduces the two families who prototypically represent North and South.

Austin Stoneman, a powerful member of Congress, and his three children are shown as Elsie is bidding farewell to her brothers who are about to leave to visit their prep-school chums—the Cameron boys—in Piedmont, South Carolina.

The story then shifts to Piedmont where the various members of the

Austin Stoneman (Ralph Lewis), the villain of *The Birth of a Nation*.

Cameron family are introduced as they interact on the columned porch of the family home. This scene of domestic bliss is briefly interrupted when Dr. Cameron drops a cat onto two puppies that lie at his feet. With a title reading simply "Hostilities" Griffith employs the animal imagery to suggest symbolically the impending war. Not coincidentally the Stoneman boys arrive shortly thereafter to visit their friends.

During the Stoneman boys' visit, they tour the Cameron plantation: the cotton fields, the slave quarters, the peaceful hills and valleys around Piedmont. In this setting a romance evolves between Phil Stoneman (Elmer Clifton) and Margaret Cameron. Likewise, Ben Cameron, admiring a photograph given to him of Elsie Stoneman, becomes attracted to his friends' sister from the North.

In an effort to characterize Austin Stoneman as the film's villain the Congressional leader is shown in angry debate in Washington with Senator Charles Sumner. Griffith's intention is to reveal Stoneman (a fictional version of Thaddeus Stevens) as a man of determined political ambition who is hostile toward the South.

The War In a sweeping progression of events, beginning with a photographic facsimile of Lincoln's first call for volunteers, Griffith advances the story toward an epic and moving treatment of the war. In the North, Elsie says good-bye to her brothers in a scene that is typical of Griffith's handling of emotions throughout the film. After giving the impression of a giddy, fully assured farewell to her war-departing brothers, Elsie runs, sobbing, to the small covered porch of the Stoneman home. Emotional moments such as this one are often marked by a combination of frivolity and sobriety to achieve an ironic, dimensioned edge.

In Piedmont, South Carolina, the departure of the Cameron boys follows an all-night dance and farewell parade. Recalling scenes from *The Battle*, the dance and parade are impressive in their spectacular realism.

Bitzer's camera work in the war scenes is both impressive in scope and intensely personal. Extreme long shots of the battlefields show as many as seven separate areas of action in a single frame. Within closer views battle action is staged in both foreground and background for greater realism. Masking devices and tracking shots are used to vary the compositions and intensify the action.

In what would later become a screen cliché, Griffith stages the simultaneous deaths of one of the Stoneman boys and one of the Cameron boys after the two come upon one another in battle. Turned from friends to enemies by war, the two die in each other's arms, friends once again.

The final battle of the war at Petersburg is spectacular and violent as Ben Cameron rallies the Confederate army in a last desperate assault against a unit of Union forces. The Union forces are under the command of Phil Stoneman. Extensive intercutting among long shots, medium shots, and close-ups heightens the fury of the battle. In one shot intended to convey the South's determination, the camera tracks rapidly ahead of Ben Cameron as he leads the charge.

The sequence concludes with an effective display of night photography as the battle rages on toward morning. At dawn, with the battle over and the North victorious, bodies of dead soldiers are visible in heaps. Griffith captures the stillness of "war's peace" in perfectly static shots of the scene. The tenor of these shots is in direct contrast to the fury of the battle scenes which have gone before and allow Griffith to achieve a powerful moment of reflection before proceeding with the personal aspects of the story.

The war's aftermath presents a sequence of concluding events. The Camerons receive news of the death of a second son and the wounding of Ben; a facsimile of Lee's surrender to Grant at Appomattox Courthouse is shown; Ben is seen recovering in a Washington hospital. There Elsie Stoneman, acting as a volunteer nurse, meets Ben for the first time. She also assists Mrs. Cameron in winning a pardon from Abraham Lincoln for Ben, who has been sentenced to be hanged as a traitor.

Intercutting of long shots, medium shots, and close-ups intensifies the documentary and personal effect of *The Birth of a Nation's* final war sequence.

The Homecoming Having sufficiently recovered and now fully enamored of Elsie, the Little Colonel departs for home. In the most humorous moments of the film, Griffith presents a hospital sentry who sighs with lovestruck awe at Elsie as she bids farewell to Ben.

The Little Colonel's homecoming is an exercise in emotional evocation through Griffith's control of setting, acting, and cinematic rhythm. The street outside the Cameron home in Piedmont is in ruins. Inside, the three Cameron women, dressed in simple unadorned clothing, giddily prepare to welcome Ben. Little Sister places raw cotton around the top of her dress to effect the look of ermine.

With slow, measured pacing, Ben enters the frame and limps to the gate of the house. His clothes are tattered; the look on his face is reflective and melancholic. At first Little Sister, always playful and animated, tries to control her excitement as she comes onto the porch to greet her brother. She points to the hole in Ben's hat while he plucks a piece of the raw cotton from her dress.

The two, saddened by the sequence of events which have brought them to these states, slowly turn and look directly into the camera. After several moments of hesitation, Little Sister, no longer able to control herself, flings her arms around Ben as she had done since a child and leads him to the door of the house. There the mother's arm reaches out, touches her son, and then goes around his neck to pull him into the house.

Griffith's use of the ravaged street scene outside the Cameron home, the controlled rhythms of Little Sister's welcome, the sustained, subjective moments of hesitation as the brother and sister directly address the camera, and capped by the economy of detail in the use of the mother's arm to greet her son, constitute a brilliantly directed scene full of emotional power.

The first half of *The Birth of a Nation* concludes with an exacting representation of Abraham Lincoln's assassination in Ford's Theater and the reactions to his death by Austin Stoneman in Washington and the Camerons in Piedmont.

Political Drama The second half of *The Birth of a Nation* presents Griffith's dramatic account of Southern Reconstruction with a twofold purpose: first, to depict Austin Stoneman as the source of the South's woes during the Reconstruction period; and, second, to justify the rise of the Ku Klux Klan as a force necessary for ending the inequities brought upon the South by the radical North.

Working without Dixon's overwrought and degrading rhetoric, Griffith develops through emotionally charged dramatic action a series of incidents which are designed to culminate in a conclusive justification of his points of view.

Austin Stoneman, too sick to oversee Reconstruction himself, sends Silas Lynch, a mulatto assistant, to Piedmont in his place. There Lynch is

Griffith's unique way of depicting a mother's "homecoming" welcome: Mrs. Cameron's arm reaches through the doorway to greet the "Little Colonel" (Henry B. Walthall).

Lincoln (Joseph Henabery) greets the audience at *Our American Cousin* minutes before his assassination.

shown calling freedmen away from their work while in the background a large sign promises every freedman 40 acres and a mule.

Nearby on the street in front of the Cameron home a unit of freed militiamen force Ben and his sister off the sidewalk as the soldiers march arrogantly by. Elsewhere a freedman is shown at the freedman's bureau being enrolled to vote in the forthcoming election.

In the first postwar election the freedmen and carpetbaggers "sweep the state" of South Carolina.

The nature and quality of the new government in South Carolina is assessed by Griffith in blatantly negative terms. During a legislative

The Klan assembles.

session many of the elected officials are shown eating, drinking, milling casually about, and taking off their shoes in the House chambers. Many wear garish clothing of mismatched stripes and plaids.

The idea for the formation of the Ku Klux Klan comes to Ben Cameron after this sequence of events. While sitting by a river bank "in agony of soul over the degradation of his people," Ben observes how four children are frightened away by other children who have thrown a sheet over their heads. The inspiration for a terrorizing organization causes him to leap up with excitement.

The scenes which follow show the Klan carrying out a series of intimidating acts in an effort "to restore order," and avenging the death of the youngest Cameron girl who dies while fleeing a militia captain.

In the sweeping climax of *The Birth of a Nation* the Klan completes its mission, its deeds done with unqualified cause and efficiency. With order restored, Margaret Cameron and Phil Stoneman along with Elsie Stoneman and Ben Cameron are seen in a symbolic double honeymoon by the sea's edge. Their marriages are meant to represent a movement toward the reunion of North and South. The final shots of the film depict a soldier on horseback beating his sword into a plowshare followed by a portrait of Christ. Both are superimposed over a Judean street scene. With these stylized images, apparently advocating unity and peace, *The Birth of a Nation* ends.

REACTIONS

When *The Clansman,* the original title given by Griffith to his film, opened at Clune's Auditorium in February 1915 in Los Angeles, a forty-piece orchestra and a chorus of singers accompanied the presentation. Joseph Carl Breil, a composer, had been commissioned by Griffith to arrange a special score for the film and as a result became the first musician to receive a film credit.

Breil's music included a series of lyric leitmotifs (identifying melodies) for the principal characters and stirring musical passages for the spectacular action of the battle and the Klan sequences. Rather than write an original score, Breil drew from existing pieces of popular, folk, and classical music. Lillian Gish's theme song was "The Sweetest Bunch of Lilacs," also known as "The Perfect Song." For Ben's homecoming the orchestra played "Home Sweet Home." The assembly of the Klan was accompanied by Wagner's "The Ride of the Valkyries," and during the triumphant march of the Klan the orchestra played Edvard Grieg's "In the Hall of the Mountain King." The pastiche score by Breil was an intricate one which provided Griffith's melodrama with an emotionally charged musical accompaniment that enriched the film's imagery and drew the audience more deeply into the story.

In addition to the enhancing element of music, Griffith had added tinted colors to many of the film's important scenes. For symbolic effect, a muted red color was supplied to the battle sequences; romantic scenes were tinted a soft blue; historical facsimiles were given the look of sepia-colored tintypes. Like the music, the use of tinting helped to set the mood for the varied parts of the story.

The impact of these accumulated effects in *The Clansman* resulted in standing ovations by audiences who saw the film during its initial run at Clune's Auditorium. Although many were angered by Griffith's political biases, it was impossible not to be deeply moved by *The Clansman's* spectacular, tragic view of war. The action, too, in the latter part of the film worked audiences into a frenzy as Griffith's meticulously developed protagonists and antagonists met head-on. No one could deny that the picture was a dramatic masterpiece.

It was a result of its dramatic impact and artistic achievement that opponents of the picture spoke up immediately and vociferously. Recognizing the enormous persuasive potential in so grand a film, concerned citizens encouraged the public to stay away and eventually attempted to suppress the picture altogether.

"Like Writing History with Lightning"

The Clansman was scheduled to open in New York City in early March. Several prominent Easterners who had heard of the controversial, degrading nature of Griffith's story were opposed to the film being shown in New York and Boston.

The Rev. Thomas Dixon, Jr., in a dramatic show of personal influence interceded on behalf of Griffith's seemingly doomed film. On February 18, 1915, ten days after *The Clansman* had opened in Los Angeles, Dixon went to Washington, D.C. with a print of the film where he persuaded his friend Woodrow Wilson, then President of the United States, to watch the motion picture.

After seeing *The Clansman* with his daughter Margaret and several members of his cabinet, Wilson is reported to have told Dixon: "It is like writing history with lightning. And my only regret is that it is all so terribly true." Through his secretary, Wilson would later deny making this remark.

The next day with the encouragement of Woodrow Wilson's praise Dixon offered a second showing of the picture in the ballroom of the Raleigh Hotel. In attendance were Chief Justice Edward Douglass White and other members of the Supreme Court along with members of the United States Senate and House of Representatives.

Dixon's shrewd act of winning the support of the nation's political elite helped squelch attempts in New York to bar the film. On March 3, 1915, the picture opened at the Liberty Theatre with sell-out crowds paying $2 a ticket for admission. The title of the film had been changed to *The Birth of a Nation* after Dixon had convinced Griffith that *The Clansman* was not depictive enough for such an epic story.

Many critics were lavish in their praise of the film's aesthetic qualities. Rupert Hughes, recognizing that with *The Birth of a Nation* Griffith had moved the art of the motion picture entirely away from its earlier theatrical tendencies, wrote: "It makes the most spectacular production of drama look like the work of village amateurs. It reduces to childishness the biggest things the theatre can do."

Hughes noted that audiences at the Liberty Theatre responded to the film with "an almost incessant murmur of approval and comment, roars of laughter, gasps of anxiety and outbursts of applause."

These responses of the time to *The Birth of a Nation* by politicians, critics, and filmgoers suggest the momentous impact that the film had on an audience that was yet naive to the social and dramatic potential of the motion-picture medium. In complexity of story structure, in technical assimilation, in mere magnitude, audiences had never been exposed to anything like it.

Not all reviews, however, were favorable. In his March 20, 1915, critique in *The New Republic* Francis Hackett wrote: "Whatever happened during Reconstruction, this film is aggressively vicious and defamatory. It is spiritual assassination."

Perhaps because of the dissension and controversy over Griffith's theme, public interest in *The Birth of a Nation* remained high for a number of years. It is estimated that in its first two years 25,000,000 people saw the film. At one time twenty-eight fully equipped road companies with orchestra and crew were touring the United States and abroad. According to Lillian Gish's memoirs, *The Birth of a Nation* in its first two months at the Liberty Theatre in New York fully recouped its total cost.

INTOLERANCE

After the release of *The Birth of a Nation* in 1915 Griffith began work on another epic motion picture which took nearly two years to complete. The new venture began with the working title "The Mother and the Law"; Griffith's intention was to develop the story of societal injustices

Lillian Gish portrays the rocker of the cradle, bearer of sorrow, in *Intolerance* (1916).

The massive settings for the Fall of Babylon sequence.

among factory workers in New York City at the beginning of the twentieth century.

As he worked on this facet of the story, the inspiration came to expand the idea of human cruelty into four separate stories which would span the course of history. Interwoven with the modern story set in the slums of New York would be an account of Huguenot persecution in sixteenth-century France, a "Judean story" which would recount the life and death of Christ, and a story set in ancient Babylon that would deal with the fall of that early kingdom.

Griffith titled his grand sermon *Intolerance*—a film which when released in 1916 was fourteen reels in length and ran for more than three hours playing time. The artistic significance of *Intolerance* in its original form resided in its imaginative structure and in the scope of Griffith's ambitions. By interweaving the four separate stories, each with its individual injustices, Griffith sought to achieve a larger abstract theme of intolerance. As many observers have speculated, Griffith's noble intentions must surely have been impelled in part by the desire to counter negative reactions to *The Birth of a Nation*.

The sophisticated structure of *Intolerance* included a poetic insert between elements of the stories in which a mother (Lillian Gish), dressed in white, is seen rocking a cradle. Introducing the shot was a title containing the lines by Walt Whitman; "Endlessly rocks the cradle, uniter of here and hereafter—Canter of Sorrows." This poetic cameo shot was conceived for the purpose of drawing together the separate stories through symbolic evocation. The mother was to be viewed as the unifying link of human progression and eternal bearer of human sorrow.

In addition to the original structure of *Intolerance* Griffith's grand use of scenic design, costumes, and crowds made the film one of the most impressive screen spectacles ever produced. Massive settings were erected for the picture's Babylonian sequences, including 100-foot high walls on which horse-drawn chariots were able to move along the tops. Total cost of *Intolerance* was estimated at $2,500,000—a staggering sum of money for a motion picture in 1916.

Despite the scope and originality of Griffith's work, *Intolerance* proved to be a commercial failure in its initial form. Because of the elaborate design of the narratives, filmgoers experienced difficulty understanding the meshed plots. Griffith's editing instincts in *Intolerance* would not be lost, however. They proved to be an inspiration to the Russian filmmakers of the 1920s who explored with intensity the expressive value of interrelated shots.

In order to recoup some of his financial losses, Griffith was forced to release in 1918 the modern story and the Babylonian sequence as two separate films under the titles *The Mother and the Law* and *The Fall of Babylon*. Each of these stories was able to stand alone as an engaging film narrative.

The Mother and the Law

The Mother and the Law was an effectively conceived and executed exercise in screen sentiment and social commentary—well-established Griffith trademarks. Its plot dealt with a young husband ("the Boy") and his wife ("the Dear One") who are the hapless victims of a tenement existence and of poor working conditions. The young man (Robert Harron) is convicted of a crime he did not commit and sent to prison. Claiming that the Dear One (Mae Marsh) is an unfit mother, social do-gooders place the couple's child in an institution. After returning from prison, the husband is falsely charged with the murder of the slum boss and is sentenced to be executed by hanging. *The Mother and the Law* concludes with an exciting last-minute rescue as the husband is saved from the gallows by the split-second arrival of the governor's pardon.

The Fall of Babylon

The Fall of Babylon, with its equally exciting climax, contained both a well-developed story and the grandeur of Griffith's crowd scenes and settings. The action spectacle tells the story of the overthrow of Babylon

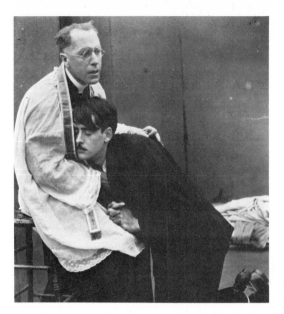

The Boy (Robert Harron) receives a final blessing in *The Mother and the Law*.

The Mountain Girl (Constance Talmadge) warns Belshazzar (Alfred Paget).

by Cyrus the Great (George Seigmann) in the sixth century, B.C. Romantic elements provide additional audience appeal as a heroic young Mountain Girl (Constance Talmadge) becomes involved in the intense battles and rushes to save her adored Prince Belshazzar (Alfred Paget). The film's climax includes a failed last-minute rescue attempt by the Mountain Girl. She dies in battle and the Prince takes his own life rather than surrender to Babylon's captors.

AFTER *INTOLERANCE*

In 1917 Griffith was invited by the government of England to make a film abroad dealing with World War I. He accepted and the result was *Hearts of the World.*

After touring the battlefields of Europe for locations, Griffith and Billy Bitzer shot a number of scenes in England and in France. Additional documentary footage was purchased from an Austrian officer for use with reenacted sequences. The story itself was a simple, personal account of the war's impact on the lives of several characters. Like so much of Griffith's work with screen characterization, emphasis was placed on sentiment and melodrama.

Hearts of the World, which opened at Clune's Auditorium in March 1918, is notable for several reasons. The picture, produced concurrently with the war, represented a propagandistic contribution to the war effort. Until the Armistice with Germany, the film was quite successful with audiences, inciting in many viewers intense hatred. Griffith's treatment of the Germans was one-dimensional and entirely negative.

After the war ended, Adolph Zukor, the film's distributor, insisted that the inflammatory scenes be deleted and reluctantly Griffith reedited *Hearts of the World* down from a twelve-reel story to an eight-reel version.

THE LILLIAN GISH FILMS

At this point in his career D. W. Griffith began to draw heavily on the talents of one of his leading actresses, Lillian Gish, who had been a principal player in *The Birth of a Nation* and in *Hearts of the World* as well as other Griffith efforts. In three important pictures made between 1919 and 1921 he used Gish as his star: *Broken Blossoms* (1919), *Way Down East* (1920), and *Orphans of the Storm* (1921).

Broken Blossoms: Studio Effects

Broken Blossoms was particularly notable for its studio effects and the atmospheric elements incorporated into the film's production design. The picture was based on a short story from Thomas Burke's book,

Lillian Gish.

The studio-controlled effects of poetic lighting and soft-focus photography enhance a moment of friendship in *Broken Blossoms*.

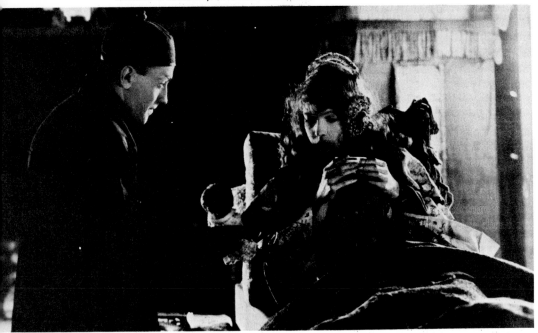

Limehouse Nights, in which a young abused English girl (Lillian Gish) finds solace through her friendship with a Chinese man (Richard Barthelmess). Griffith treats the girl's violent torture by her boxer father (Donald Crisp) in an open and shocking manner.

By contrast, the scenes in which the girl is befriended and comforted by the Chinese man are serene and poetic in visual quality. Fog effects, atmospheric lighting, and soft photography create an evocative mood for the melodramatic story. Griffith's expert handling of the atmospheric elements—possible only within the controlled environment of a studio—would inspire other filmmakers to move their productions indoors.

Because of the intense melodrama and evocative imagery, *Broken Blossoms* became both a popular and critical success. Lillian Gish was especially memorable as the sad-faced girl who could be made to smile only by the pressing of fingers to the corners of her mouth. This image of the forced smile remains one of the most haunting examples of Griffith's directorial penchant for screen sentiment.

Broken Blossoms also achieved significance as the first Griffith film to be distributed by the newly formed United Artists Corporation, a production-distribution organization which had been incorporated in January 1919 by Griffith, Mary Pickford, Charles Chaplin, and Douglas Fairbanks.

Between the completion of *Broken Blossoms* and his next important film, *Way Down East,* Griffith directed five pictures: *True Heart Susie* (1919), *Scarlet Days* (1919), *The Greatest Question* (1919), *The Idol Dancer* (1920), and *The Love Flower* (1920). All were fairly commonplace melodramas except for *Scarlet Days* which was a western story starring Walter Long and Richard Barthelmess. Lillian Gish appeared only in *True Heart Susie* and *The Greatest Question.*

The Greatest Question, The Idol Dancer, and *The Love Flower,* the last three in the series, were assignments taken on for First National Pictures as a means of raising money so that Griffith could finance his own films and complete the building of a production studio he had begun in Mamaroneck, New York. Griffith's ambition at this point in his career was to be totally free of all affiliations except the distribution arrangement with United Artists.

Way Down East: Creative Geography

Way Down East (1920) brought the Griffith-Lillian Gish team forcefully back to the screen in an adapted stage melodrama which showed the director and star at their best. The story, full of sentiment and action, was filmed at the Mamaroneck studio site with additional snow and ice scenes shot on location in Vermont and Connecticut. Gish portrayed an innocent young rural woman named Anna Moore who must bear the burdens of abandonment by a city cad, the birth and death of her child,

Lillian Gish is rescued from the ice floes by Richard Barthelmess in *Way Down East* (1920), one of Griffith's most daring exercises in screen melodrama.

and the hazards of a blizzard which leave the woman stranded on ice floes, moving toward certain death.

Way Down East was an enormous commercial success, principally because of Griffith's suspenseful editing of the last-minute rescue of the woman from the ice floes, the authentic location photography in scenes filmed during an actual blizzard, and the carefully shaped story in which sympathy builds for the innocent young woman who is played with considerable restraint by Gish.

An anonymous reviewer for *Exceptional Photoplays* praised Lillian Gish's performance in *Way Down East* and noted the results of the collaboration between her and Griffith:

> Mr. Griffith could be depended upon for bringing out the full pathos of Anna's tragedy. His genius for this sort of thing has always been great. And, as usual, he has had the advantage of Miss Lillian Gish's unlimited cooperation. It is a truly astonishing thing about the young artist that one can always say that her latest work is her best. One wonders how high she can still climb on the ladder of superb screen acting. Or perhaps it is a question of how far Mr. Griffith and Miss Gish can go together, for it is

often impossible to tell in their work where direction ends and interpretation begins. [*Exceptional Photoplays*, December 1920.]

The last-minute rescue in *Way Down East* remains exciting to this day because of the realism in filming the ice floe sequence. Lillian Gish and her rescuer, Richard Barthelmess, risked their lives in order to give Griffith the authenticity he sought in bringing the film to its dramatic climax. Only *The Birth of a Nation* earned more money for Griffith.

Orphans of the Storm: Historical Spectacle

Orphans of the Storm, which opened in Boston in late December 1921, was Griffith's last film with Lillian Gish and one of only two memorable motion pictures made after *Way Down East*. The story that became *Orphans of the Storm* was adapted from a popular stage melodrama, *The Two Orphans.*

Lillian Gish and her sister, Dorothy, another favorite Griffith actress, portray sisters on the screen who become involved in the tragedy of the French Revolution. Again Griffith's work was impressive for its sentiment and its spectacle. One of the sisters (Dorothy) is blind, a fact which further intensifies sympathy for the two innocent victims.

As in *Intolerance* grand-scale settings were constructed for *Orphans of the Storm,* settings which are even more realistic in detail than those built for the 1916 epic. The second half of the story recreates with considerable success the Revolution itself. Sensational crowd scenes, dramatic lighting effects, and Griffith's obligatory last-minute rescue of Lillian Gish from death at the guillotine produced an exciting motion-picture experience.

In many ways *Orphans of the Storm* represented the very essence of D. W. Griffith's screen career. His unmistakable film style was noted at the time by the critic for *Life,* Robert E. Sherwood:

> There is a definite Griffith tradition in the movies, and *Orphans of the Storm* lives up to this tradition in every respect. It contains the usual elements of pure, unsullied love as contrasted with base, degenerate passion, the usual suspense that is promoted by obvious but none the less efficacious tricks, the usual amount of strife, the usual railing against intolerance and oppression, the usual beauty, the usual note of sordid tragedy, and above all, the usual Ku Klux Klan climax. All these elements are to be found in every Griffith picture, from *The Birth of a Nation* to *Way Down East.* Pictorially and dramatically, *Orphans of the Storm* is better than any of them. [*Life*, February 2, 1922.]

This summary of Griffith's broad filmic style focuses on both the achievements and limitations of the early great master of motion-picture technique. By this time in his career Griffith could continue to impress audiences and critics with his powerful use of camera, scenic design, and

In *Orphans of the Storm* (1921) Lillian Gish must once more be saved from death in a last-minute rescue. The detailed realism of Griffith's settings is impressively evident in this dramatic shot.

editing. Yet the very nature of his stories—Victorian and moralistic in inspiration—were recognizable for their "obvious" repetitive elements and antiquated stance. Griffith's interests did not appear to be advancing beyond his desire for putting compelling sentiment and melodrama onto the screen. Subtlety would never become a Griffith characteristic and in time the flaw proved fatal to his career.

FINAL EFFORTS

In spite of its critical acclaim the expensive production design and costs of promotion for *Orphans of the Storm* prevented the film from realizing a profit. Subsequent efforts, *The White Rose* (1923) and *America* (1924), were also financial setbacks and Griffith's production studio was on the verge of bankruptcy.

In 1924, out of financial necessity, Griffith agreed to direct for Paramount Studios at a weekly salary of $6,000. Paramount was headed by Adolph Zukor who earlier as a film entrepreneur had handled the distribution of *Hearts of the World*.

Before going to work for Paramount Griffith went abroad to film *Isn't Life Wonderful* (1924) which would represent his last notable achievement as a film director. The story projected with sensitivity and documentarylike realism an account of refugees in Germany struggling to survive the degrading conditions that remained in the aftermath of World War I.

Isn't Life Wonderful was photographed on location in Germany where the authentic environment inspired Griffith and his actors to achieve an unusually naturalistic interpretation of the somber story. His inspiration for realist cinema cannot be overlooked. The bitterness and day-to-day struggle of the common people in *Isn't Life Wonderful* bear striking similarities with the theme and style of Vittorio De Sica's *The Bicycle Thief* (1948), a film also about common people who are struggling to survive in post-World War II Italy.

In 1931 after handling three run-of-the-mill assignments for Paramount and directing five unimpressive pictures for the Art Cinema Corporation, D. W. Griffith—disheartened and tired of working for others—retired from film directing. He died in Hollywood on July 23, 1948.

Griffith's career was a remarkable one with far-reaching ramifications for the artistic, social, and economic growth of the motion-picture medium. Through the refinement and assimilation of a full range of film techniques into his work, Griffith helped to bring cinema art to a sophisticated level of expression. The success of his screen melodramas and spectacles spurred the formation of United Artists and attracted the attention of enterprising film distributors such as Louis B. Mayer and Adolph Zukor. These distributors parlayed profits from Griffith's films into major production conglomerates of their own. The development of the Star System and the proliferation of movie palaces can also be attributed in part to the sensational public success of the Griffith films made between 1912 and 1922. His films inspired directors and producers to create screen epics, to explore the possibilities of both location shooting and studio filming, and to see the narrative, emotional, and abstract potential of editing. The ability of the motion picture to propagandize and persuade was well illustrated in Griffith's skillful docudrama approach in recreating history.

Pioneer, visionary, "father of film technique," primitive poet, social agitator, king of screen sentiment and melodrama—all are apt descriptions of David Wark Griffith, the first of the great film directors.

SUGGESTED READINGS

Arvidson, Linda [Mrs. D. W. Griffith]. *When the Movies Were Young.* New York: Dutton, 1925.

Bitzer, G. W. *Billy Bitzer: His Story.* New York: Farrar, Straus & Giroux, 1973.

Brown, Karl. *Adventures with D. W. Griffith.* New York: Farrar, Straus & Giroux, 1973.

Gish, Lillian. *The Movies, Mr. Griffith, and Me.* Englewood Cliffs, N.J.: Prentice-Hall, 1969.

Henderson, R. M. *D. W. Griffith: The Years at Biograph.* New York: Farrar, Straus & Giroux, 1970.

O'Dell, Paul, with Anthony Slide. *D. W. Griffith and the Rise of Hollywood.* New York: Barnes, 1971.

Silva, Fred, ed. *Focus on The Birth of a Nation.* Englewood Cliffs, N.J.: Prentice-Hall, 1971.

GRIFFITH'S CONTEMPORARIES (1910–1925)

The secret of Mack Sennett's success was his enthusiasm. He was a great audience and laughed genuinely at what he thought funny. He stood and giggled until his body began to shake. This encouraged me and I began to explain the character: "You know this fellow is many-sided, a tramp, a gentleman, a poet, a dreamer, a lonely fellow, always hopeful of romance and adventure. He would have you believe he is a scientist, a musician, a duke, a polo player. However, he is not above picking up cigarette butts or robbing a baby of its candy. And of course, if the occasion warrants it, he will kick a lady in the rear—but only in extreme anger."

Charles Chaplin, *My Autobiography,*
Simon & Schuster, 1964.

Chaplin's "Tramp."

$\mathbf{T}$he important contributions of D. W. Griffith to the development of film art occurred simultaneously with the innovations of other pioneering American directors and producers who had been similarly moved to increase the amount of time, money, and artistic energy put into the creation of motion-picture stories. Among these filmmakers were Thomas Ince, Cecil B. De Mille, Mack Sennett, Charles Chaplin, and Buster Keaton.

Like Griffith they too turned out potboilers along with more pretentious efforts, but within their silent-screen work there evolved other notable and influential techniques of cinematic expression.

THOMAS INCE: DIRECTOR-PRODUCER-DRAMATURGIST

Thomas Ince (1882–1924) was one of those pioneering motion-picture figures who in the early stages of his career engaged himself in all aspects of film production: acting, directing, writing, and producing. Like D. W. Griffith, Ince came reluctantly into motion pictures after working in the theater as an actor. Also like Griffith, Ince held a strong interest in dramatic writing—an aspiration which prompted both men, once committed, to indulge themselves fully in the tasks of making moving pictures.

Ince first earned a reputation as a skillful director and scenario writer—particularly of western films—and eventually came to be regarded as an efficient first-generation producer who insisted on supervising a film from the idea stage to its release for public consumption. In effect, Ince became Hollywood's first "executive producer."

The initial directorial effort by Thomas Ince (a collaborative assignment) was a picture titled *Little Nell's Tobacco* made in the east in 1911 for Carl Laemmle at International Motion Pictures (IMP). Later that year Ince left for the West Coast to head production in California for the New York Motion Picture Company. There he immediately began to pursue his avid interest in the western story which had been sparked by acting roles in western stage melodramas. He rented 18,000 acres of land on which to film westerns (eventually called "Inceville") and hired a popular group of rodeo performers to appear in the early pictures in California.

Between 1911 and 1924, the year of his death, Ince refined the elements of the western film which had been skeletally developed by Porter in *The Great Train Robbery*. Ince introduced the idea of the shooting script so that he and, later, the directors he supervised would have a precise blueprint for use during the process of filming. As a result, plots became more cohesive and Ince's films, although made for purely escapist purposes, were tightly crafted.

The shooting script also served as a guide for the editing of the film.

Thomas Ince on location, circa 1915.

This process facilitated the making of motion pictures at Inceville in an efficient, skillful manner. The practice was soon adopted at other production studios.

At first Ince produced, wrote, and directed films that were two reels in length, turning out nearly 200 pictures of wide diversity between 1911 and 1912. Late in 1913 Ince expanded story length to five reels with *The Battle of Gettysburg.* His reputation grew as a successful developer of film plots and as a director who supplied his pictures with strong pictorial qualities.

The Bargain, made in 1914 with the western star William S. Hart, was described by a critic of the time as "a model of what can be accomplished in a popular field of photoplay work." (*New York Dramatic Mirror,* November 18, 1914, p. 32.) The story is no more complex than that of a "two-gun" bandit who reforms after he meets and marries an innocent young girl. Yet the picture was praised for its "picturesque" photography, "remarkable set," and "story replete with action and suspense."

The critic Jean Mitry has written of Thomas Ince: "If Griffith was the first poet of an art whose basic syntax he created, one can say that Ince was its first dramaturgist."

By 1917 Ince had turned over production responsibilities to scenario writers and directors while he continued to serve as executive producer for the Triangle Film Corporation which he had formed in 1915 with D. W. Griffith and Mack Sennett. Among the directors who worked under Ince's guidance were Fred Niblo, Henry King, Frank Borzage, and Lambert Hillyer. Hillyer became well known as the director of the highly successful, hard-hitting western films which he made with William S. Hart for Triangle. Ince's final film, produced under his supervision for Associated Producers in 1923, was a highly praised adaptation of Eugene O'Neill's play, *Anna Christie*. Ince died unexpectedly in 1924 at the age of 42.

As a pioneer of motion-picture art it is often said that Ince was the only figure equal in stature to Griffith in the medium's formative years. Ince's pioneering contributions were not so much aesthetic as pragmatic. He saw the permanence of the motion-picture industry and set about devising an efficient system of creating quality films. His role in establishing the western film as a popular standard of the American screen added to Ince's long-lasting influence on American film.

CECIL B. De MILLE: DIRECTOR EXTRAORDINAIRE

Few names have been so frequently associated with Hollywood and the hypothetical "Hollywood picture" as that of Cecil B. De Mille's (1881–1959). To many the name De Mille is also synonymous with "film spectacle." Commonly held generalizations such as these have acted to

Cecil B. De Mille during the first phase of his long directorial career.

overshadow De Mille's significant position in early motion-picture history. His creativity, sophistication, and diversity, particularly evident during the medium's silent years, established De Mille as a pioneering film artist of considerable importance.

De Mille was born into a theatrical family in Ashfield, Massachusetts, on August 12, 1881. At the time his mother was an actress and his father an actor and playwright. With the intention of following the professional interests of his parents, at age 17 De Mille entered the New York Academy of Dramatic Arts to prepare for a career as a stage actor. After performing for a number of years in touring productions, he also turned to playwriting, and between 1906 and 1911 wrote a variety of plays in collaboration with his brother, William.

Through his mother, who had left acting to become a literary agent, De Mille met the theatrical producer Jesse L. Lasky in 1911. The two men began collaborating on the writing and producing of popular stage musicals. This association led to the formation in 1913 of Jesse L. Lasky Feature Plays—a theatrical producing organization which included De Mille, Lasky, Lasky's brother-in-law Samuel Goldfish (later Goldwyn), and a lawyer, Arthur S. Friend. De Mille was assigned the creative responsibility of stage director.

Entering Film: *The Squaw Man*

In 1914 the Lasky Company decided to broaden its producing activities and create dramas for the new medium of motion pictures. Rights were purchased that year to Edwin M. Royle's popular Broadway melodrama *The Squaw Man* for a screen adaptation that would be directed by De Mille.

The theme of *The Squaw Man* was that of self-sacrifice, developed through the episodic story of an English army officer (Dustin Farnum) who accepts responsibility for the embezzlement of money from a widow's trust fund. After taking blame for the theft in order to protect a British aristocrat, the officer flees England for New York where he remains until he learns that a detective is in pursuit. The officer changes his name, moves west, and settles on a ranch in Wyoming. There the hero is challenged by a character named Cash Hawkins. This standard western conflict comes to a climax when an Indian girl (Princess Redwing) kills Hawkins. A star-crossed marriage between the Indian girl and the ever-sacrificing officer follows, providing ample romance and sentiment.

The Squaw Man, a feature picture six reels in length, earned unexpected critical praise. De Mille's expertise showed in the cogency of the story, in the believable performances, and in the realistic action sequences.

The inclusion of location scenes in *The Squaw Man* was particularly impressive. De Mille had traveled to California to stage the studio work for the picture; after becoming caught up in the excitement of directing

The hero (Dustin Farnum) of *The Squaw Man* (1914) consoles Princess Redwing after she shoots Cash Hawkins.

a dramatic story outside a proscenium arch, he had the inspiration to include authentic western landscapes. He and his co-director Oscar Apfel left Hollywood and for two weeks filmed parts of the story in Wyoming. Careful studio work, combined with stark location scenes, significantly enhanced a commonplace story and led one critic of the time to declare *The Squaw Man* "one of the best visualizations of a stage play ever shown on the screen . . ." (*Moving Picture World*, February 28, 1914).

The critical and popular success of *The Squaw Man* resulted in De Mille's four-decade commitment to motion-picture direction and production.

The Cheat

During the early silent part of his career De Mille turned out an assortment of screen melodramas, comedies, westerns, and social dramas for the Lasky Company. Even in the midst of such diverse assignments, he displayed a keen sense of story-telling and an audacious approach in the treatment of subject matter. De Mille proved himself to be even more sophisticated than Ince or Griffith in the choosing and handling of story ideas. In 1915, a year in which he directed thirteen feature-length pictures, De Mille demonstrated his erudite approach to subject matter in *The Cheat.*

Consistent with the tone and moral stance of social dramas of the time, *The Cheat* told the story of a young woman (Fanny Ward) who misuses funds raised for charity. Rather than suffer the shame of public disclosure, the woman seeks to replace the squandered money by obtaining a loan from a wealthy Burmese ivory merchant (Sessue Hayakawa). The merchant attempts to take advantage of the woman's plight by forcing her into sexual bondage. In a fit of rage she shoots the merchant, an act for which her husband assumes blame. Following the merchant's recovery, a courtroom trial brings the story to a cathartic climax. A mob of spectators at the trial reacts with great fervor after the woman's confession of guilt and rises up to attack Hayakawa.

Sessue Hayakawa and Fannie Ward in *The Cheat* (1915). The brightly lit faces set against a dark background added an expressive dimension to the moralistic story.

The Cheat is regarded as an early masterpiece. The scenario, written by Hector Turnbull, gained from the inclusion of both impressionistic and realistic elements. For the scene in which Fanny Ward shoots Sessue Hayakawa, De Mille photographed the action through a transparent screen on which the shadowed silhouette of the ivory merchant appears. A stream of blood flows down the screen. This stylized approach conveyed a horror greater than that possible through open visualization. Special cameo-style lighting for *The Cheat* was arranged by De Mille's cinematographer, Alvin Wyckoff, so that a character's bright face often appeared against a totally dark background. The lighting contrasts (later labeled "Lasky lighting") added a psychological undercurrent to the story.

The courtroom scenes on the other hand were photographed in a bright naturalistic light and the control of the mob was handled with uncanny realism. This scene alone generated admiration for De Mille's creative powers as a film director. If one can ignore the East-West innuendo, *The Cheat* even today remains an engaging screen melodrama.

With its story of personal greed, self-sacrifice, violence, and sexual innuendo, *The Cheat* contained dramatic elements resembling those in *The Squaw Man*—although clearly raised to a more sophisticated level. These similarities suggest the development of characteristics which in time would become trademarks of De Mille's films. Consistently De Mille's directorial interests turned to motion-picture stories about human error, sin, and personal morality within a particular social climate. Eventually in both his historical spectacles, which he first introduced with *Joan the Woman* in 1917, and in his contemporary stories styled after *The Cheat*, De Mille openly presented on the screen "sinfulness" and free-living adults, although never without a concluding moralistic attitude.

The Swanson Era

Before turning almost entirely to historical and biblical spectacles in the late 1920s, De Mille issued a remarkable group of silent films which candidly explored sex and marriage. The sophistication and adult character of these films, made in an era of increasing censorship, established De Mille's work between 1916 and 1921 as bold and advanced. In *The Heart of Nora Flynn* (1916), *Old Wives for New* (1918), *Don't Change Your Husband* (1919), *Male and Female* (1919), *Why Change Your Wife?* (1920), and *The Affairs of Anatol* (1921) filmgoers were exposed to a candor the likes of which would not be seen again in American motion pictures until the 1960s.

Especially noteworthy among these "battle-of-the-sexes" films were those which had as their star Gloria Swanson. *Don't Change Your Husband, Why Change Your Wife?*, and *Male and Female* brought to the public a new image of the American woman.

Swanson, trained for the screen in Mack Sennett comedies, was at

**G**loria Swanson and Elliott Dexter in *Don't Change Your Husband* (1919).

once provocative, beautiful, sensuous, and independent in motion pictures which dealt with marital upheaval, displayed scanty costumes, and often contained scenes photographed in the bathroom. Swanson's performances received great praise from critics and these films were described in *Photoplay Magazine* of May 1919 as "vivid, timely, pulsating life-dramas." De Mille was lauded for his forward stance in character portrayal.

In time many of De Mille's domestic dramas and comedies, although always morally pointed, came into difficulty with film censors. Scenes had to be deleted from *Old Wives for New,* for example, to be acceptable to the Kansas Board of Censors. In other parts of the United States, rather than being viewed as timely, the material was often considered tasteless and unacceptable.

Beginning of Spectacle

With the impressive success of *The Ten Commandments* in 1923 and its near universal acceptance by the public, De Mille noted the saleability of spectacle which also included his standard themes of waywardness and

The Ten Commandments (1923).

repentance. Sinfulness and pagan sex, long before accepted as a part of the lessons of religious teaching, could be more easily condoned if implanted in costume spectacles of the past and if the sinners were punished and the virtuous rewarded. Numerous De Mille pictures after *The Ten Commandments* bore these morally compensating trademarks as well as the De Mille stamp of visual ostentation.

This visual style was characterized by opulent, meticulously detailed settings, extravagant costumes, huge casts that were carefully orchestrated for spectacular long shots, a precise control of lighting, and well-placed special effects such as "the parting of the Red Sea" in *The Ten Commandments,* now a legendary moment in motion-picture trickery. An ability to coordinate these elements in this film and in his later screen spectacles earned De Mille his unparalleled reputation for screen showmanship, and in the minds of many established him as Hollywood's director *extraordinaire.*

MACK SENNETT: "KING OF COMEDY"

Mack Sennett (1880–1960) who was born Michael Sinnott in Richmond, Canada, on January 17, nurtured the growth of more screen talent in the formative years of the American motion-picture industry than any other single individual. As director, producer, and inspired creator of silent film comedies Sennett helped shape the careers of Charles Chaplin, Mabel Normand, Mack Swain, Buster Keaton, Harry Langdon, Gloria Swanson, Louise Fazenda, Chester Conklin, Fatty Arbuckle, and Ford Sterling.

Sennett's involvement with motion pictures came after a brief theatrical stint in New York as a burlesque performer and occasional chorus member in Broadway musicals. Unhappy with the slow progress of his legitimate stage career, he left the theater in 1908 for acting jobs with the Biograph Company. At Biograph he appeared in numerous one-reelers, many directed by D. W. Griffith, while also working as a scenario writer who sketched out story plots for such films as *The Lonely Villa* (1909).

Compelled by his interest in burlesque, Sennett began directing short comedies at Biograph. Ford Sterling, Mabel Normand, and Sennett himself appeared as the stars of the first films: *Comrades, The Diving Girl, Snookie's Flirtation, A Victim of Circumstances,* and *When He Gave Up,* all released in 1911. In these one-reelers, which were created largely through improvisation, Sennett began to develop a zany, absurd brand of screen comedy where abnormality was the norm and caricature was a principal method of provoking laughter. Also apparent in these first films was a clear knowledge of motion-picture editing techniques which he learned from Griffith. Editing rhythms became as much a part of the Sennett style of comedy as caricatures and slapstick action. To Sennett, a motion picture, above all else, had to move.

Keystone

Sennett left Biograph in midyear 1912 to join the Keystone Film Company in Hollywood as the "director general" in charge of production. With him he took his principal players Ford Sterling, Fred Mace, and Mabel Normand, and with their assistance he began to cultivate a large troupe of Sennett-styled comedians. From this repertory group emerged the "Keystone Kops" and "Sennett's Bathing Beauties," series concepts which provided clever frameworks for Sennett's improvisational methods. Beautiful girls, inept authorities, harmless slapstick, grotesque-looking clowns, frenetic chases: these were the comic elements which evolved as the variants of Sennett's screen comedies.

A Hash House Fraud Each year Keystone turned out hundreds of comic shorts. *A Hash House Fraud,* produced in 1915, represents a typical farce comedy of Sennett inspiration and know-how. This one-reel comedy starred Louise Fazenda, Hugh Fay, Fritz Schade, and the Keystone Kops.

In the film's simple plot the owner-waiter (Hugh Fay) of the Busy Bee Restaurant becomes discouraged by a shortage of customers and

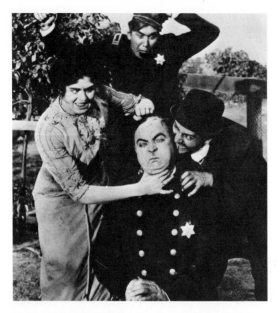

Murphy's *I.O.U.* (1913), an early Keystone Kops' comedy with Fred Mace as the beleaguered Kop.

Fritz Schade as the cook and Louise Fazenda as the cashier in *A Hash House Fraud* (1915).

takes to the street to find a "cash buyer" for the establishment. On seeing a prospective "sucker," several nonpaying customers are rounded up to make the Busy Bee look like a thriving business. The gimmick works, but the new owner soon discovers the fraud and a brawl ensues. He calls for help on the telephone, telling the police captain: "There's a riot, send the squad!"

This phone call sets the inept Keystone Kops into motion, but only after the police captain fires a bullet at the feet of the Kops who are asleep on the precinct floor. The Kops arrive at the scene of the riot just as Hugh Fay is escaping in an open-top automobile.

A fast-paced comic chase by automobile follows. Undercranked filming of the chase sequence and rapid cutting are employed to accelerate the action and heighten the visual gags. One of the two automobiles is continually turning around and passing the other. This repetition, a primary ingredient of Sennett's visual humor, becomes even funnier as a man who is pushing a vegetable cart attempts to cross the roadway. Each return of one of the automobiles forces the cart back off the road until finally the cart advances too far and is demolished. The cart driver's determination to cross the road, even after his narrow escapes, results in the desired comic effect.

Mack Sennett exploited this comic formula of foolish temptation, repetition, and slapstick surprise in film after film. The quick cutting and rapid pace of the filming heightened the moment of surprise.

However catastrophic and chaotic Sennett's screen world became, it was important that the slapstick violence be harmless and without serious consequence for the bumpkins who created it. It had to be clear that the cart driver would get up and walk away. Similarly, at the conclusion of *A Hash House Fraud,* the pursuing Keystone Kops fire a frenzied spray of bullets at the escaping automobile, yet no one is hit. Sennett's stated comic philosophy was that in his films "things must go wrong, but not too wrong. . . . Just enough to make you laugh."

The Sennett Style

By 1915 Sennett had established himself as an astute, attentive film producer at Keystone. At the studio many of the directing assignments after 1913 had been turned over to Henry Lehrman, Mabel Normand, Robert Thornby, and the inspired and inspiring Charles Chaplin who first came into Sennett's employ as an actor late in 1913.

Occasionally Sennett consented to direct one-reelers and even longer films including the two-reel comedy *Zuzu the Band Leader* (1913) and a feature-length picture *Tillie's Punctured Romance* (1914). But increasingly his creative input came through his supervisory powers as head of production.

In this catalytic role he was able to sustain the Keystone brand of comedy until the early 1920s. At this time Sennett's popularity slowly began to decline. The popularity slide, plus the advent of sound pictures and the stock market crash at the end of the decade, resulted in a declaration of bankruptcy in 1933.

Sennett's incomparable career as the "king of comedy" sprang from an intuitive sense of the peculiar nature of silent motion pictures. Working without the advantage of comic dialogue, Sennett concentrated his attention on the impact of absurd images and intense movement. He took his inspiration from three sources of theatrical humor: slapstick, chase comedy, and burlesque. To these Sennett added the special cadences available through film editing.

In utilization of the camera, Sennett favored his troupe of clowns rather than fancy angles or an abundance of shot variations. Recognizing that clowns generate humor most effectively with their full bodies, the Keystone films made good use of long shots and for the most part left close-ups to dramatic filmmakers.

The majority of ideas for the Keystone comedies were either born out of Sennett's imagination or refined by it. He knew how to fit ideas to the stars he inspired and cultivated while never suppressing the intuitive instincts of his actors. To a large degree Sennett's success and pioneering standards for slapstick screen comedy were a result of close coordination between a well-executed style of physical comedy and a group of very "physical" comedians.

Sennett's screen innovations are not as easily charted as those of other early film pioneers because of the complex nature of comedy and the ill-defined mechanisms which generate laughter. Suffice it to say that Sennett's comedy worked, time and again, for millions of filmgoers who laughed without ever thinking why.

CHARLES CHAPLIN: THE EARLY YEARS

The place of Charles Chaplin (1889–1977) among the film pioneers who shaped the aesthetic development of cinema was secured through dual roles. He emerged first under the tutelage of Mack Sennett as a screen comedian of incomparable talent. With the development of his acting career Chaplin soon assumed responsibility for the direction of the films in which he appeared. As actor-director he brought to the screen comedies that were perfectly orchestrated and, often, sharply social, even tragic, in tone. The refinement of his little tramp figure into a familiar screen character represented an important achievement for a medium looking to win the empathetic involvement of audiences. Many critics have described the little tramp as the screen's first fully realized, psychologically affective character. Chaplin's ability to attract audiences, as well as generate unparalleled critical praise for his films during the silent era, in itself had inestimable importance for a still emerging industry.

An Unhappy Childhood

Charles Chaplin was English born and spent his early childhood in near poverty with his mother and half-brother, Sydney, in South London. When Chaplin was 5 years old, Hanna Chaplin, a small-time music hall singer, was forced to place her two sons in an orphanage where floggings were a common occurrence.

In 1898, at age 9, Chaplin left the orphanage for work with a music hall group, The Eight Lancashire Lads. He and Sydney formed their own team in 1901, performing together throughout England until 1907 when Charles became associated with Fred Karno's repertory company of vaudeville performers.

Enter the Movies

Karno's company traveled widely, often making trips abroad to France, Canada, and the United States. On Chaplin's second trip to the United States in 1912 Mack Sennett and the Keystone Company, always on the alert for fresh talent for their own developing repertory group of comedy players, saw Chaplin and offered him a contract. At first Chaplin refused the offer which came to him by telegram from Sennett. Then in 1913, on a second offer of $150 a week, Chaplin accepted.

Chaplin's first film at Keystone, released to the public on February 2, 1914, was titled *Making a Living*. Although in style a typical Sennett slapstick action comedy, Chaplin's screen debut caught the attention of the critic for *The Moving Picture World* who wrote:

> The clever player who takes the role of [the] nervy and very nifty sharper in this picture is a comedian of the first water, who acts like one of Nature's own naturals. He is so full of action that it is indescribable, but so much of it is fresh and unexpected fun that a laugh will be going all the time almost. [February 7, 1914.]

The Little Tramp Emerges Chaplin remained at Keystone for a year, appearing in thirty-five films there and continuing to impress the public and critics with his special comic talents. Following his twelfth film, Sennett agreed to allow Chaplin, who was not particularly happy with the *tour de force* slapstick approach at Keystone, to write and direct his own pictures. Chaplin's preferences were for pantomime and distinctive comic characterizations. He had already begun to experiment with an individualized character in his second film at Keystone, *Kid Auto Races at Venice* (1914).

In this film Chaplin had donned part of the costume which would eventually evolve into the little tramp figure: derby hat, oversized shoes, baggy pants, and tight coat. The "messy elegance" of the ill-fitting clothing was innately funny, but also gave hint of an individual attempting to affect an air of worth and self-esteem. Chaplin's dandified tramp carried implications that would with refinement imbue his characterization with an aura of comic pathos.

Chaplin's instincts for sympathetic comic characterization (inspired by France's great screen comic Max Linder) were never fully realized at Keystone. He did, however, appear in the studio's first feature-length comic film, *Tillie's Punctured Romance* (1914), a picture which also starred the theater actress Marie Dressler. Dressler's position as the foremost comic actress of the legitimate stage brought even more attention to Chaplin's young film career. The comic interplay in the earlier parts of the film, which was directed by Sennett, showed Chaplin's abilities to be equal to Dressler's, a fact noted by the many critics who lavished praise on the picture.

Refinement at Essanay In 1915 Essanay Pictures was willing to give Chaplin a contract that paid him a weekly salary of $1,250. This was nearly ten times the amount being earned at Keystone.

He directed fourteen films at Essanay where he began a long association with the cinematographer Roland Totheroh and his favorite leading lady Edna Purviance. Also the year's period at Essanay allowed Chaplin to develop further the little tramp character and to refine his more subtle comic interests. One critic reviewing an Essanay film in 1915 noted that "Chaplin comprehends pantomimic expression (most of his clown confreres do not) which gives a certain value to whatever he does."

The emerging pathos that would eventually dominate Chaplin's comic style is particularly evident in the Essanay-made films *The Tramp* (1914) and *The Bank* (1915). Chaplin is the struggling common man, forever the victim of circumstance, love-struck but always a loser at love *(The Bank)*, disappointedly shuffling down the road at the picture's conclusion *(The Tramp)*.

Chaplin's individual cinematic style also evolved more noticeably in the early collaboration with Totheroh at Essanay. Bright, flat lighting, a predominance of medium and long shots; and a reserved use of editing techniques began to emerge as the selected methods for emphasizing pantomimic action.

The Mutual Films

From Essanay Chaplin moved to Mutual in 1916 where his salary and artistic progress took an even greater leap. The weekly salary was $10,000 and for a year's work he was to receive a bonus of $150,000. The willingness of studio executives to pay a film actor-director such an enormous sum of money held more significance than its recognition of Chaplin's formidable talents. It signaled a general move toward escalating salaries for all stars who had earned favorable box office reputations. Quickly, talent personnel had become a critical factor in the American

Chaplin and Edna Purviance in *The Rink* (1916).

film industry, and out of this business trend would emerge the Star System as a means of sustaining the major studios.

Charlie Chaplin's work at Mutual was remarkable for its comic ingenuity, social commentary, and psychological effect. The movement away from comic caricature to a fully developed, fully human character was finally realized in the dozen films made at Mutual in 1916 and 1917. In *The Rink* (1916), *The Floorwalker* (1916), and *The Cure* (1917) the display of visual gags, the expert realization of comic gesture, and an agile use of physique worked together to produce near-perfect comedies. In *Easy Street* (1917), *The Immigrant* (1917), and *The Adventurer* (1917) Chaplin's social criticism, born from his own years of poverty and a consequent sense of injustice, emerged with tragicomic effect.

The Rink and *Easy Street* contain those elements which made the Mutual films so memorable.

The Rink Chaplin's skill for purely visual humor reached new heights in *The Rink*. This picture, released on December 4, 1916, was his eighth Mutual film and has Chaplin portraying a waiter who is also "posing" as Sir Cecil Seltzer, C.O.D. The comic routines develop in the restaurant where Chaplin works and in a roller-skating rink where he skates during his lunch break. At both places Chaplin is the irrepressible little tramp, mocking convention and pomposity.

The restaurant scenes contain an unrelenting barrage of sight gags as Chaplin deflates every individual in the establishment. Chaplin orders one customer a melon after examining the size of the man's head. To another he serves a cake of soap and a scrub brush between pieces of bread. For another he brings a covered dish which contains under its lid a frightened cat. When the portly Mrs. Stout (Henry Bergman) enters, Chaplin pulls the armchair from beneath her as she goes to sit, then when she gets up off the floor he rips the arms from the chair to call attention to the woman's commanding size.

Comic gestures also abound. Chaplin, with perfect pantomimic finesse, splits an imaginary hair down the middle to test the sharpness of a carving knife. After concocting a drink mixture he takes up the cocktail shaker and his entire body begins to gyrate while the container remains perfectly still in his hands.

These sight gags sprang from a *commedia dell'arte* approach to comedy which permitted improvisation and irrelevancies in the development of comic details. Any type of comic antic which might possibly develop within the context of the plot or location was perfectly acceptable. As Chaplin gained greater control over the artistic style of his films at Mutual, the *commedia*-inspired gags flourished.

Chaplin's physical agility in *The Rink,* as he dons a pair of roller skates, can best be described as strikingly balletic. At the rink, on learning that the rotund Mr. Stout (Eric Campbell) is in pursuit of Edna Purviance against her wishes, Chaplin engages Stout in a roller-skating *pas de deux.* Chaplin, his bamboo cane pressed into Stout's stomach, drives the man around the skating rink with deflating acrobatic flair. Later at Purviance's skating party Chaplin's display of physical agility and acrobatic skills are even more sharply evident as he takes on Mrs. Stout.

The Rink concludes with a typical comic climax—the chase, this time staged on roller skates. The men at the party (and the law) take off after Chaplin through the streets. With the curved end of his cane Chaplin latches onto the bumper of a passing automobile, temporarily victorious as he gets a free ride into the sunset. He laughs at his victory and at his pursuers who have stumbled and fallen on one another. As Chaplin tips his hat, he too trips and falls, thus bringing *The Rink* to a humorous and abrupt climax.

This show of Chaplin's own fallability adds a human touch that was of vital importance to the psychological nature of the little tramp characterization. For Chaplin, victory and order are possible in the chaotic world that he so bravely and resiliently endures, even if the victory is only temporary.

Charlie oversees a newly converted "Easy Street."

Easy Street *The Rink* derived its humor principally from a spontaneous response to locations (the restaurant and the skating arena). *Easy Street,* by contrast, approaches its comic situations within a purposefully poignant social context. Location is important in the latter film as the title *Easy Street* implies; but the title functions as an ironic statement for the social environment depicted in the film.

Life is far from easy on the city block where Chaplin, a reformed thief-turned-cop, aids the poor, oppressed people who live in his precinct. Overpopulation, hunger, brutality, thievery, and drug addiction abound on Easy Street.

Hardly obvious as comic material, these social conditions, nevertheless, provide Chaplin with sufficient opportunities for humor. Efforts to reform the wayward Eric Campbell lead to comic repetitions and chases with pointed moments of slapstick. When Chaplin must rescue Edna Purviance, a social worker, from a drug addict's den, he accidently sits on the addict's needle.

Although a cop rather than a tramp in *Easy Street*, the effect of the character is precisely the same. Chaplin walks the streets with the familiar tramp shuffle, toes pointed outward, twirling a billy rather than a cane. Like a mechanical toy he mounts steps one foot at a time; he is forever falling and tripping after each moment of triumph.

At the conclusion of *Easy Street* the place has been converted into a utopian environment, with the "New Mission" now having moved into the thieves' former headquarters at the head of the street. In the final scene various ethnic types, including the converted Eric Campbell, trek optimistically with Bibles and spouses toward the Mission. Chaplin and Purviance, arm in arm, follow.

At this point the title takes on still another ironic meaning. The transformation has indeed created an "easy street," but it is a utopia devised as a mockery of those optimists who would believe that social ills are as readily curable. Chaplin's own view of the world would never have permitted so easy a solution to the injustices he had observed and experienced. But he enjoyed such absurd fantasies, and later repeated the idea of a slum utopia in *The Kid* (1921).

The ironies and social dimensions of *Easy Street* reveal the breadth of Chaplin's comic resourcefulness. The film conveys a deep understanding of the misfortunate human condition, yet cleverly transposed to laughter. These abilities induced George Bernard Shaw to pronounce Charles Chaplin the motion picture's one true genius.

Silent Features and Independence

Audience response was equal to critical acclaim. In a matter of a few years Charlie's little tramp became the most familiar screen character in the world and Chaplin the most famous actor. With greater fame came more money and more independence. In 1918 Chaplin signed with the distribution-exhibition company First National Pictures for a yearly salary of $1 million. With this financial backing from First National, Chaplin was able to open his own production studio in 1918.

The next year Chaplin, Mary Pickford, Douglas Fairbanks, and D. W. Griffith organized United Artists for the purpose of distributing their own films. Although his contract with First National did not allow Chaplin to distribute any films through United Artists until 1923, all pictures made in Hollywood after 1918 were produced within the freedom of his own studios.

Chaplin's direction from this point on was meticulous and his interest in social commentary grew as evidenced in *A Dog's Life* (1918), *Shoulder Arms* (1918), and *Sunnyside* (1919).

The Kid Chaplin's first full-length picture, *The Kid,* was completed in 1921. In this sentimental comedy, Jackie Coogan portrays an abandoned child who is taken in and reared by Chaplin, an itinerant window repairman. The child becomes a miniature version of the little tramp,

The little tramp and his young charge (Jackie Coogan) in *The Kid* (1921).

joining in partnership with his foster father in both the breaking and mending of windows.

The plot of *The Kid* was cleverly contrived for the enjoyment of audiences who knew the little tramp well and could appreciate seeing Chaplin's beloved character, briefly, rearing a child much like himself. In addition to its cleverness *The Kid* possessed integrity and sincerity which together made it the biggest commercial success of Chaplin's career.

The Gold Rush Of Chaplin's silent films, *The Gold Rush* (1925) stands as the most highly praised; Chaplin himself singled out the picture as the one accomplishment of his career for which he hoped to be remembered.

The ability to combine the comic and the tragic comes to fruition in the plot of *The Gold Rush*. The little tramp, like many another, has traveled to Alaska during the height of the gold rush to seek his fortune. Instead of finding instant wealth, Charlie finds a place of cold, hunger, greed, and loneliness.

In this stark world, comic situations are born from near tragic events. As Charlie makes his way along the frozen trails of the Klondike, he is stalked by a grizzly bear without knowing that the dangerous beast is close behind him. When Charlie is caught in a snowstorm, he and another prospector (Mack Swain) find refuge in the cabin of a murderer, Black Larsen (Tim Murray). Charlie must stave off his insufferable hunger by cooking and eating the leather sole of a shoe; he carves and relishes the leather as if it is a fine steak. Shoestrings are twirled onto a fork as though taken from a side dish of spaghetti and the nails from his shoes are savored as if succulent fishbones.

Big Jim McKay, the other prospector in the cabin who is also mad with hunger, imagines Chaplin to be a plump rooster. The hallucinations lead to wild chases as Chaplin struggles for his life. It is comedy derived from primitive survival instincts that include cannibalism. Such is the tragicomic nature of the film.

The Gold Rush also presents Chaplin's skill for deriving poignant irony from comic pantomime. This talent is illustrated in a scene that involves the one joy of the little tramp's existence in the Klondike, a girl named Georgia who is a dance hall hostess in one of the local saloons. Georgia and two of her girlfriends have become intrigued by the funny, sad Charlie and lead him on. He graciously invites the women to come for dinner on New Year's Eve. Without realizing the cruelty of their action, they teasingly accept.

With money he has earned by shoveling snow in the town, Charlie prepares an elegant dinner, complete with a sumptuous roast and neatly wrapped gifts for the invited guests. He waits for Georgia and her friends in his room a few blocks from the saloon.

As the evening wears on and it becomes clear that the women are not coming, a dejected Charlie sits at the table that he has lovingly prepared and falls asleep. In his sleep, he dreams that Georgia arrives with her friends and together they enjoy his meal.

For entertainment, Charlie announces that he will perform the "Oceanna Roll." He sticks table forks into two of the hard, oval-shaped dinner rolls on the table and performs a soft-shoe dance number for his guests. Charlie's head appears to be magically attached to the little dancing rolls which resemble oversized shoes, creating the illusion of a small figure dancing on the table top. The girls burst into spontaneous applause as Georgia shouts: "Isn't he wonderful!"

The dream fades away and the scene shows Charlie asleep at the table. He stirs and wakens when he hears singing coming from the saloon. It is midnight and the saloon revelers, hands joined in a circle, have begun to sing "Auld Lang Syne." Charlie crosses to the door of his cabin, opens it slightly, and listens. It is a moment of great poignancy in which Charlie's own loneliness is matched through intercutting to the lonely faces in the saloon.

The sadness stands in sharp contrast to the vivid emotions of joy and happiness experienced in the fantasized "Oceanna Roll" scene. The juxtaposition of fictive dream with harsh reality conveys an ironic expression of how human action and thoughtlessness lead to unhappiness.

Charlie makes a gourmet meal from an old leather shoe in *The Gold Rush* (1925).

Performing the "Oceanna Roll."

Chaplin's humanity was never greater than at this moment in *The Gold Rush*. The sequence also reveals the major theme of the film: human goals are far greater than those linked with material possession. Love, companionship, and comfort are universal needs to be sought and valued more highly than a greedy rush for gold. The frozen wilderness of the Klondike, populated by materialistic dreamers, provides the perfect setting for making this pointed statement.

Much of Chaplin's own psychological self appears in *The Gold Rush*. Its ending, which brings Charlie wealth, happiness, and love, usually elusive goals for the little tramp, can be interpreted as yet another instance of a contrived utopia. Knowing full well that he has twisted reality into a happy dream for his common-man character, Chaplin is appropriately scolded by a photographer in the final shot of the film for having "spoiled the picture." The photographer's comment is made in reference to Charlie's sudden movement to kiss Georgia as the camera shutter is released; yet the double entendre is obvious.

Although the happy ending epilogue of *The Gold Rush* has been criticized as incompatible with the remainder of the film, it reveals with telling significance an artistic vision that seems rooted in Chaplin's somber childhood. Amidst the realities of tragicomic situations, dreams of the ideal, at least, are possible in the fictional world of motion pictures. The genius of *The Gold Rush* surely comes in part from expressions of personal catharsis as Chaplin looked toward self-redemption.

This compulsion would continue to manifest itself in Chaplin's important work after the introduction of sound in 1926. A discussion of these sound-era films appropriately appears in Chapter 11 alongside the efforts of other great *auteurs* of the thirties and forties.

BUSTER KEATON

Standing beside Charles Chaplin as the consummate comedian-director of the motion-picture's silent era was Buster Keaton, a former vaudeville performer who made his first film, *The Butcher Boy*, for Fatty Arbuckle in 1917. During the decade that followed, Keaton, working first in two-reelers, then in features, developed a screen persona whose stoic deadpan qualities led to the label, "the great stone face."

Critic Walter Kerr in his important book *Tragedy and Comedy* has succinctly noted the essential differences in Keaton's and Chaplin's approach to silent-screen comedy:

> Buster Keaton produced one kind of comedy, Chaplin quite another. And Keaton's was the purer use of the form. That is to say, there was no admixture of sentiment, no bid for pathos, no confusing of the comic and tragic modes. Keaton was cool, detached and very strictly funny, never suggesting for a moment that we need worry ourselves about what might

happen to him. [Kerr, Walter. *Tragedy and Comedy*. New York: Simon & Schuster, 1967, p. 210.]

Keaton's comedy was derived primarily by placing his immovable figure into competition with the world around him, its man-made objects and its physical laws. Keaton always emerged the victor, no matter how disastrous the event in which he found himself or how complicated the machine he might be pitted against.

In one of his outstanding film shorts, *The Boat* (1921), Keaton's object of contention is a self-made vessel which he attempts to launch while his wife and small sons (carbon copies of their stoic father) observe. In getting the boat out of the house where it's been built, Keaton pulls down the family dwelling. Undaunted, he sets sail with wife and sons, only to encounter a storm at sea. The family finally must float in a small bathtub to land where surely Keaton will find a way of starting anew. *The Boat*, like Keaton's screen persona, avoids sentimentality altogether—showing instead Keaton and his family mutely accepting their fate.

Keaton's unique comic artistry appeared brilliantly in three classic feature pictures which he directed and starred in during the waning years of silent cinema: *Sherlock Jr.* (1924), *The Navigator* (1924), and *The General* (1926). In these works Keaton displayed those qualities which lifted his comedy to a level equal in importance to Chaplin's: the expert comic timing, the visual gags derived from doing battle with mechanical objects, the brilliant acrobatics, and the tight construction of comic routines.

In *Sherlock Jr.* Keaton portrays a motion-picture projectionist who, asleep, dreams that he enters the film screen and becomes the world's greatest detective, struggling to save a beautiful young girl from her captors. Visual stunts and acrobatic tricks abound as Keaton finds his talent for mechanically inspired visual gags enhanced by the magical possibilities of the motion-picture medium.

In *The Navigator* and *The General* Keaton uses a similar idea for comic plot: the hero having to command, alone, an overpowering vehicle. A huge ocean liner forms the background for *The Navigator* with Keaton deriving inventive humor from the disproportionate contrast of the ship's size with his own small self and that of a sole female passenger also on board. Keaton tries boiling six coffee beans in gallons of salt water and two eggs in a pot intended for mass cooking.

Keaton reached the height of his career with *The General* in 1926. The competitive machine in this Civil War farce is a locomotive, and Keaton is Johnnie Gray, the engineer who attempts to command it. Expressionless but indomitable Gray wins his battle with the locomotive and Union forces and, finally, the love of Annabelle Lee. In addition to its comic inventiveness *The General* is notable for its period authenticity and its photographic beauty.

Buster Keaton, forever the victim of objects and machines, in *The General* (1926).

Keaton's *The General* and Chaplin's *The Gold Rush* have often been called silent comedy's finest moments—each an enduring tribute to the genius of their makers.

James Agee has summarized the deeper qualities of Buster Keaton's work:

> Beneath his lack of emotion he was also uninsistently sardonic; deep below that, giving a disturbing tension and grandeur to the foolishness, for those who sensed it, there was in his comedy a freezing whisper not of pathos but of melancholia. With the humor, the craftsmanship and the action there was often, besides, a fine, still and sometimes dreamlike beauty. [*Life,* September 5, 1949.]

Although the historical development of the motion picture can be traced artistically by sampling the efforts of early, innovative directors such as Griffith, Ince, De Mille, Sennett, Chaplin, and Keaton, the process by no means completes the picture.

The growth of the new medium and its establishment as a permanent art form are intricately tied to a group of entrepreneurs who, simultaneously with the formative artist-directors, pressed the motion picture forward from its novelty stage to full maturity.

Collectively, their names (Louis B. Mayer, Samuel Goldwyn, William Fox, Carl Laemmle, Sam, Harry, Jack and Albert Warner, Jesse Lasky, and Adolph Zukor) came to mean the American film industry itself. With almost innocent faith at first, then with real drive and shrewd organization, they began to take hold of the new medium and to exert an influence on the film industry that was not only economic but aesthetic as well. The important role played by these businessmen in the development of film art is the story which follows.

SUGGESTED READINGS

Chaplin, Charles. *My Autobiography*. New York: Simon & Schuster, 1964.
Higham, Charles. *Cecil B. De Mille*. New York: Scribner, 1973.
Huff, Theodore. *Charles Chaplin: A Biography*. New York: Pyramid, 1964.
Kerr, Walter. *The Silent Clowns*. New York: Knopf, 1975.
Lahue, Kalton C. *World of Laughter: The Motion Picture Comedy Short, 1910–1930*. Norman: University of Oklahoma Press, 1966.
Mast, Gerald. *The Comic Mind*. Chicago: The University of Chicago Press, 1979.
Sennett, Mack, *King of Comedy*. Garden City, N.Y.: Doubleday, 1954.

AMERICAN STUDIO FOUNDERS:
THE SILENT YEARS

For more than thirty years I avoided carrying a watch. I never wanted to know what time it was. My day ended when my day's work was completed. Again and again, I didn't go to bed at all during the twenty-four hours. . . .

I was acquainted with every story that was selected by my companies. I read every story they ever produced. I made suggestions in the majority of the stories produced by our companies. In the early years I wrote most of the scenarios. No picture ever produced by the Fox Film Corporation was permitted to be viewed by the general public, until every title it contained had been approved and passed by me.

William Fox, studio founder, quoted in *Upton Sinclair
Presents William Fox,* p. 5, 1933.

William Fox at work under an umbrella.

$\mathbf{T}$he group of men who would eventually sit at the head of the major American studio "families" were individuals who entered the medium in the early phases of the film business. They began as small-time businessmen with an intuitive awareness of the mass marketability of motion pictures that had eluded Thomas Edison. They took their intuitions into store theaters and makeshift studios and, urged on by a favorable public response to their offerings, parlayed the financial returns into big business conglomerates.

As the powerful heads of their own studios, the Hollywood titans lorded over the business and dramatic interests of film production. With now legendary control they infused their showmanship sensibilities into the developing American film. Increasingly, front-office management, as much as the talents of early directors, began to shape the styles and types of films that would dominate Hollywood production.

Each of the original founders of the major American studios possesses a unique and colorful story of pioneering effort.

PARAMOUNT PICTURES: GIANT OF THE SILENT ERA

Considering the fact that many early motion-picture producers retained a close relationship with legitimate theater, it is not surprising that the most successful and important of the silent era film production companies, Paramount Pictures, evolved from a theatrical organization, Famous Players.

Adolph Zukor (1873–1976)—born in Ricse, Hungary, orphaned in childhood, and an immigrant to the United States in his teens—created Famous Players in 1912 after having successfully distributed in the United States the Film d'Art's screen adaptation of *Queen Elizabeth* with Sarah Bernhardt. Prior to this venture he had been a partner with Loew's Consolidated, operators of a chain of vaudeville and motion-picture theaters.

Famous Players: American Film d'Art

The amazing financial returns on his $18,000 investment for the exclusive American rights to *Queen Elizabeth* gave Zukor the idea (and funds) for making his own Film d'Art-styled series with famous actors. Zukor's intention was to present on celluloid popular Broadway actors in their stage successes. The initial title of the organization, consequently, became Famous Players in Famous Plays, a title not quite as pretentious as the French Film d'Art Company but one chosen to convey the same sense of elevated purpose.

Among the early directors hired to handle film adaptations for Famous Players was Edwin S. Porter. Porter oversaw productions of *The Count of Monte Cristo* and *The Prisoner of Zenda* (co-directed with Daniel

The founders of the Famous Players-Lasky Production Corporation in 1916, from left to right Jesse Lasky, Adolph Zukor, Samuel Goldfish (Goldwyn), Cecil B. De Mille, and Albert Kaufmann (Zukor's brother-in-law).

Frohman). Both were released in 1913 to launch Zukor's new organization.

Famous Players' emphasis on acting skills and quality dramatic material paid off handsomely. For the first time important American theater actors were induced to appear in motion pictures. The role of Edmond Dantes in *The Count of Monte Cristo* was portrayed by James O'Neill (the father of Eugene); Zukor was successful in recruiting other stage celebrities of the era for *The Prisoner of Zenda* (James K. Hackett and Beatrice Beckley, two prominent Shakespearean actors, starred). Shortly after the release of these films, actors as prominent as John Barrymore and Fannie Ward consented to act in films for Famous Players.

Merger with Paramount Pictures Corporation

In 1914 Zukor's Famous Players entered into a production-distribution agreement with Paramount Pictures Corporation, an organization founded early that year by W. W. Hodkinson for the purpose of engaging producers in a national distribution exchange. Hodkinson had sought out producers of "quality" films and promised to supply theaters with two films a week—a reasonably manageable promise.

Within a year nearly a dozen producing organizations had contracted with the Paramount Corporation, each agreeing to pay Paramount 35 percent of the box office intake for any feature film handled by the exchange.

The Paramount exchange provided a boost to film expansion through its movement toward unification of production, distribution, and exhibition channels. Famous Players' profits soared, as did those of the other producing companies, and Zukor was stimulated to acquire a more prominent voice in Paramount's activities. In 1916 he successfully won over control of the distribution company by convincing the consortium of film producers that a more efficient organization and greater profits would be had for all if the production forces were united.

With this move Zukor now controlled his own distribution as well as production corporation. To strengthen the producing end of his business enterprise Zukor's Famous Players merged with Jesse L. Lasky's Feature Play Company and several other smaller producing units to become Famous Players-Lasky. In effect, the Paramount Corporation became a distribution subsidiary of the Famous Players-Lasky Production Corporation with Adolph Zukor as its president and Jesse L. Lasky as its vice-president in charge of production. Cecil B. De Mille and Samuel Goldfish, associates in the Lasky company, were declared, respectively, director-general and chairman.

Mary Pickford: A Paramount Star

Zukor's acquisition of prominent actors for Famous Players continued but with a shift in emphasis. The early interest in legitimate stage performers gave way to a preference for celebrities who had earned their reputations as film actors. Sought after in particular were celebrities who had acquired a large public following.

One of Zukor's prize acquisitions was the incomparable Mary Pickford (1893–1979). For her first starring film appearance in Biograph's *The Violin-Maker of Cremona* in 1909 Pickford had earned $25. Her gentle screen presence and sincerity soon prompted Biograph and her favorite director, D. W. Griffith, to raise the salary to $100 a week.

From this point on, increased fame and fortune came to Pickford with each passing year. Although screen credits were still rare in 1910, Louis Reeves Harrison, a critic for *The Moving Picture World* (June 4, 1910) lavished praise on Pickford's performance in Griffith's *Ramona* without knowing the actress' name. The leading character, Harrison said, "is portrayed with an intelligent grasp of fine detail which gives exquisite finish and charm to the play." Pickford was only 17 at the time.

This ability to project charm and earn anonymous praise caught

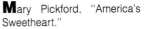
Mary Pickford, "America's Sweetheart."

Zukor's attention in 1913 after the young star had skipped from studio to studio for higher salaries. For the leading role in Famous Players' production of *Hearts Adrift* (1914) Zukor offered Pickford $1,000 a week and marquee and screen credits. Later in the year Pickford's salary rose to $2,000 a week for her work in *Tess of the Storm Country*. To promote this film Zukor labeled his star, "America's Sweetheart," a sobriquet which would identify the actress throughout her career.

In 1916 the Mutual Film Corporation proffered $1 million a year for Mary Pickford's talents and box office appeal; Zukor, whose own fortunes were now firmly enmeshed with the stars he had under contract, went to Pickford with a counterproposal that offered her $1 million annually as well as her own independently run production unit, to be called the Mary Pickford Picture Corporation. Pickford would be allowed to choose her own scripts and directors and would receive a share of the profits from her films.

Douglas Fairbanks

Using a similar contractual arrangement Zukor guided the appealing Douglas Fairbanks (1883–1939) from Triangle Films in late 1916 to the helm of the Douglas Fairbanks Picture Corporation.

Fairbanks ·had come to motion pictures in 1915 after having

established a stage reputation for light comedy. The dozen films made for Zukor in 1917 and 1918 were for the most part social satires written by the gifted scenarist Anita Loos (whose subtitles added to their success) and directed by John Emerson. In each, Fairbanks was invariably the extroverted, all-American boy who breezes through life in a mockery of social convention, e.g., *In Again, Out Again* (1917), *Wild and Woolly* (1918), *Down to Earth* (1918).

Fairbanks gained a large public following with an energetic, dashing style of acting that in the 1920s propelled him into a popular series of costume-action films made for United Artists: *The Mark of Zorro* (1920), *The Three Musketeers* (1920), *Robin Hood* (1922), *The Black Pirate* (1926).

The list of Famous Players-Lasky screen stars grew into an impressive array of talent: Pickford, Fairbanks, Pauline Frederick, Blanche Sweet, Gloria Swanson, Mae Murray, William S. Hart, "Fatty" Arbuckle, alongside such prominent directors and producers as D. W. Griffith and Mack Sennett.

Block-Booking and Changing Quality

As a result of spiraling production costs and the expense of supporting the Star System he had helped create, Zukor increased exhibition fees and in 1916 introduced block-booking which required theaters in the Paramount distribution exchange to take all or none of his yearly output of films.

The guarantees provided by a block-booking system, rather than being a stimulus to imaginative filmmaking, lowered initiative and ultimately the quality of many of the films offered to exhibitors.

Settling on the Exotic

With the acquisition of more theaters (over 500 by 1921) and with the block-booking mandate in effect, Zukor began to admonish producers to trim costs and to streamline the filmmaking process. This new conservatism led to a Paramount-Zukor penchant for studio melodramas built around such exotic stars as: Rudolph Valentino who left Metro for Paramount to make *The Sheik* (1921), an effusive film inspired by *The Four Horsemen of the Apocalypse;* Gloria Swanson who was always exquisitely and provocatively costumed in films such as *The Impossible Mrs. Bellow* (1921) and *Bluebeard's Eighth Wife* (1923), and who soon surpassed (with the help of Paramount's publicity department) Mary Pickford as Hollywood's reigning queen; Pola Negri, a Polish actress who was imported from Germany by Zukor to become a Paramount star.

The presence of Valentino, Swanson, and Negri at Paramount and the types of films in which they appeared in the early 1920s soon pointed up Zukor's emphasis on the exotic, on romance, adventure, lavish costumes, and star mystique. The output was hardly elevated fare, but it was what the filmgoer seemed to yearn for at the time.

Zukor's philosophy of film production was stated clearly in the title of his autobiography, *The Public Is Never Wrong,* and he devoted much of his front-office energies to the task of gauging audience taste. What the public seemed to want Zukor attempted to give them: longer films, popular actors, and pleasing, adventurous stories.

FOX PICTURES (TWENTIETH CENTURY-FOX): MANAGEMENT POWER

From the very beginning of his film career William Fox (1879–1952) was known for his bravura. Fox was among the dozen or so independent film producers whose persistent challenge to the Motion Picture Patents Company helped break the trust's stranglehold on the developing film industry. He began in the business as an exhibitor and boldly entered production in 1912 rather than pay the licensing fees imposed on exhibitors by the Patents monopoly. Together with Carl Laemmle, the pugnacious Fox brought suit against the trust and through this legal action and continued competition forced a dissolution of the Patents Company in 1915.

Fox's record of film enterprise reads remarkably like that of the other important businessmen who helped shape the industry: an immigrant to the United States (from Tulchva, Hungary); a New York merchant (garment maker); nickelodeon operator in 1904; head of a growing film chain; producer; and studio founder.

This classic pattern of business progress resulted in the creation of the Fox Film Corporation in 1915. In his studio, which he moved to California in 1916, William Fox ruled with a power that was considered uncommon even in an industry known for its powerful, uncompromising management. Under his guidance Fox films developed into a strong producing organization, supplying products to the companion Fox exhibition chain which by the late 1920s was composed of 1,000 movie houses in the United States and nearly 300 theaters in Europe.

The Power of the Publicity Agent

Among Fox's astute moves in his developing production organization was the creation of a self-developed stock company of screen actors by the studio's shrewd publicity agents.

Theda Bara An exotic-looking young woman from Cincinnati, Ohio, named Theodosia Goodman achieved stardom at Fox in 1914 under the studio-created name of Theda Bara (an anagram of the words "Arab Death"). Publicity agents claimed that Bara was the child of a French artist and an Egyptian woman. Her first appearance as a screen *femme fatale* came in *A Fool There Was* (1914), a film which also first introduced the word "vamp" to the language. Bara portrayed a woman whose

Theda Bara in *A Fool There Was* (1914).

uninhibited conquest of men—married or otherwise—knew no moral boundaries. Fox's creation of the screen vamp was so successful that Bara made nearly forty films in which she appeared as a mysterious sorceress. Her salary rocketed to $4,000 a week and her public appeal prompted other studios to create their own sultry *femme fatales*.

Fox publicists worked to develop other stars through calculated image-building campaigns. Virginia Pearson, Tom Mix, Buck Jones, John Gilbert, and Dustin Farnum were among the screen actors whose careers were launched at the fledgling studio.

Tom Mix After Theda Bara, the most important of the Fox publicity-created stars was Tom Mix. Mix began making one- and two-reel western films for the Selig Company in 1911, but it was at Fox that he became a major star. After signing a contract with the studio in 1918, Mix rapidly emerged as the "King of the Cowboys."

The screen persona which evolved in the Mix films represented a radical change in the nature of the western hero. The hard-living, hard-hitting loner hero created by Thomas Ince and William S. Hart was replaced by a more romanticized figure with the arrival of Mix. Authenticity, which had been responsible for much of the appeal of Hart's work, gave way to stylization and conventional western stories. Mix projected a gentle, girl-shy image of a cowboy whose horsemanship

William S. Hart and Tom Mix—a study in cowboy contrasts.

skills and acrobatics often got him out of the troubles he usually brought on himself by trying to help others. His horse Tony, full of tricks like Mix himself, became a significant part of the new western format.

With Mix the physical characteristics of the cowboy began to change also. William S. Hart had conveyed a realistic facade of the "good-bad" man living in a frontier environment: craggy faced, grim expression, unkempt look, grimy clothes. Mix projected a polished, rodeo-styled appearance with beaming face, fancy clothes, and symbolic white hat. In a scene from *Western Blood*, made at Fox in 1918, Mix shyly courted his leading lady (Victoria Forde) while the two sat in a side-saddle position on the back of the cowboy's obedient horse.

Tom Mix and horse Tony soon eclipsed William S. Hart in popularity and Fox was proud to publicize the fact that the studio in 1919 was paying the actor a weekly salary of $10,000. Mix stayed at Fox to make more than sixty feature films between 1918 and 1928.

Commercial and Artistic Success

By 1921, Fox Film Corporation was the second most prolific studio in Hollywood (behind Paramount), turning out that year sixty-four feature-length pictures. (Paramount's releases totalled 101 films.) Play-

John Ford's *The Iron Horse*, made at Fox in 1924, revealed the director's ability to utilize the environment as an important element in his action stories. This ability would become a distinctive characteristic of all Ford's films.

ers other than the western stars Tom Mix, Buck Jones, and Dustin Farnum were also making an impression at Fox. John Gilbert achieved leading-man status in 1922 in *Monte Cristo.*

Important directors also spent part of their formative years in the studios at Fox. The most significant was John Ford, who directed two Buck Jones westerns in 1920–1921, then left for a brief period of work at Universal before returning to Fox to direct his most important silent film, *The Iron Horse* (1924).

The Iron Horse along with James Cruze's *The Covered Wagon,* made at Paramount the year before, introduced to the screen a rash of epic films about pioneers on the American frontier. *The Covered Wagon* was filmed on location in Nevada and brought back the authentic western landscape to motion pictures. For *The Iron Horse* Ford also traveled to Nevada with his actors and crew. In the desert he recreated an epic story of pioneers struggling to lay the first railroad across the United States. The film was impressive for its exciting action sequences and its evocative use of the environment as a part of the story's dramatic conflict. These directorial qualities, found in Ford's obvious talent for spirited story-telling and environmental detail, would later distinguish his sound films made during the thirties, forties, and fifties.

Not to be outdone by other studios, William Fox also sought prestigious directors from abroad and felt compelled to produce, along with the studio's many pictures aimed at popular tastes, an occasional work of higher purpose.

F. W. Murnau, the great German director (*The Last Laugh,* 1924), left his country in 1926 for a contract at Fox which promised him, in addition to regular studio assignments, an opportunity to make one film of any type without front-office interference.

Sunrise (1927), the film which Murnau chose for his unbridled American debut, became a silent-screen masterpiece. In a story of passionate love, adapted from Hermann Sudermann's *A Trip to Tilsit,* the silent screen found a new visual expressiveness. Through lighting, settings, and cinematography Murnau was able to present a broad range of moods while treating the story of a simple peasant who attempts to murder his wife for the love of a city woman.

The emotions of ecstasy, passion, and turbulence experienced by the principal characters (Janet Gaynor and George O'Brien) were effectively translated to the screen. Murnau's roving, subjective camera, an expressive element in his heavily psychological films in Germany, was also evident in *Sunrise.* A critic for *The New Republic* (October 26, 1927) wrote: "Not since the earliest, simplest motion pictures, when locomo-

George O'Brien and Janet Gaynor in Murnau's *Sunrise* (1927). O'Brien makes an effort to drown his wife during a boat ride.

tives, fire engines and crowds in streets were transposed to the screen artlessly and endearingly . . . has there been such joy in motion as in Murnau's direction."

The praise lavished on *Sunrise* sprang in part from the film's striking contrast with the other more commonplace pictures being made at Fox in the late 1920s. Holder of a massive studio chain of 1,300 houses by 1927, Fox had geared his operation principally for the production of films intended for corporate use. Fox's driving energy led him to demand personal approval of nearly every script chosen for production at the studio. He also claimed that every picture Fox Studios made in the 1920s was "passed" by him before release to the public.

UNIVERSAL: HOME OF THE LOW-BUDGET PICTURE

The birth of Universal Pictures occurred the same year, 1912, as Fox Pictures and was founded for similar reasons. Carl Laemmle (1867–1939), like William Fox, was one of the principal opponents of the Motion Picture Patents Trust. Even in the face of threats from the trust, Laemmle continued to operate his International Motion Pictures (IMP) studio which he had formed in 1909. IMP supplied films to exhibitors through Laemmle's impressive group of distribution exchanges located in Chicago and other major midwestern and western cities. More than 100 films were produced at IMP in 1910.

Laemmle's business acumen as a beginning producer was remarkably like that of William Fox. Both men understood the value of stars within their production units and both also recognized the role that clever publicity agents could play in generating public interest in screen actors. Even before Fox "invented" Theda Bara, Carl Laemmle enticed Florence Lawrence, "The Biograph Girl," away from that studio and began to promote her as the new star of IMP. Publicity agents issued false reports of the actress' death, which were later discounted by the studio and its star. The gimmick made Lawrence the first widely known screen performer.

In 1912 IMP and five other independent producing organizations formed Universal to strengthen their stand against the Patents trust. Universal continued to turn out low-budget, one- and two-reel films for distribution through its network of exchanges.

In 1914 construction was begun on Universal City, a self-contained studio complex located in the San Fernando Valley outside Los Angeles. Here at Universal City Laemmle's studio established itself as one of the prominent companies of the silent era.

Serials and Sensation

Universal's reputation as the home of the low-budget picture developed early, although this characterization of the studio is not an absolute one.

Carl Laemmle on the Universal City set of *Uncle Tom's Cabin* (1927). Eva is 9-year-old Virginia Grey.

Occasional quality pictures came out of Universal City along with its predominant outpouring of standardized escapist fare.

Serials held a prominent position among the routine types of films produced by Laemmle, including the very popular serial *The Trey of Hearts* made in 1914 with Cleo Madison and George Larkin. Its success helped stimulate an epidemic of serialized stories.

Carl Laemmle's attitude of providing filmgoers with good, clean entertainment resulted in a series of films starring J. Warren Kerrigan and Lois Wilson. The couple always portrayed fun-loving, wholesome American youth.

An occasional venture into more sensational material occurred at Universal. In 1916 the studio produced a sincere, candid film about abortion, *Where Are My Children?* This picture was directed by Lois Weber, who became one of the few prominent women directors of the silent era. Among her other important efforts at Universal was *The Dumb Girl of Portici* (1916), a film which introduced the renowned dancer Anna Pavlova to the screen.

Erich von Stroheim as the lascivious officer in *Blind Husbands* (1919).

Erich von Stroheim and Irving Thalberg

The most exciting period of silent-era production at Universal occurred with the arrival of Erich von Stroheim (1885–1957) in 1918 and Irving Thalberg in 1919 (1899–1936). Thalberg came to Hollywood from the studio's New York offices to serve as Laemmle's secretary and a year later was named general manager of Universal City. Von Stroheim, previously working as a screen actor and assistant director between 1914 and 1917, was hired by Universal as a director after showing Laemmle his script for *Blind Husbands*. This was the first of a series of films made by von Stroheim about triangular love affairs.

Blind Husbands, released in 1919, had von Stroheim as its director, writer, and one of its principal actors. Its story recounted the amorous desires of a woman (Francelia Billington) for an Austrian military officer (von Stroheim) after her husband (Sam DeGrasse) has ignored her sexual needs.

Von Stroheim's directorial debut was impressive for its honest treatment of a sensational subject. Pointed close-ups and detail within the *mise-en-scène* conveyed the bored woman's unfaithfulness with ironic frankness. In his own performance as the Austrian officer, von Stroheim was brazenly seductive and self-confident.

The provocative nature of *Blind Husbands* was responsible for its good reception by critics and filmgoers. Von Stroheim followed its success with two variations on a theme: *The Devil's Passkey* (1920) and *Foolish Wives* (1921).

In *The Devil's Passkey,* an American dramatist living in France bases a play on a rumor of an illicit love affair and later discovers that the woman involved is his wife. *Foolish Wives,* like *Blind Husbands,* was a story of continental eroticism and was written, directed, and acted by von Stroheim. His character was again that of a salacious adventurer.

Each of these motion pictures made profits for Universal but not without causing Carl Laemmle and Irving Thalberg considerable frustration. In each case, von Stroheim exceeded his budget—spending large sums of money on settings and costume details. A set of Monte Carlo used in *Foolish Wives* was erected at a cost of $200,000. An obsessive concern for authenticity in the picture prompted the spending of thousands of dollars on medals and embroidery for use on uniforms worn by military officers. Shooting schedules were also exceeded. Von Stroheim took nearly a year to film and edit *The Devil's Passkey; Foolish Wives* in its original form was the length of two feature films (twenty-one reels) and Laemmle had to order the film trimmed to acceptable length.

When von Stroheim's spending habits once more became apparent during the filming of *The Merry-Go-Round* (1922), Thalberg discharged the director and the picture was completed by Rupert Julian who took considerable liberties with the existing footage. Thalberg soon departed for work at Mayer Pictures and von Stroheim moved to the Metro-Goldwyn Studios where he produced and directed his most important film, *Greed* (1924). This picture brought a new realism to the American screen in its sordid story of the lust for money.

After Thalberg and von Stroheim left Universal, Carl Laemmle was able to turn his attention once more to the steady production of less flamboyant motion pictures. During the 1920s Universal purchased several dozen theaters but did not seek to compete with Paramount or Fox in the acquisition of an extensive chain of movie houses. Laemmle was content serving as a secondary producer for the major film organizations. In this role as one of the minor studios, Universal's releases continued to be low budget and standardized in quality.

In 1925 the studio produced Lon Chaney's *The Phantom of the Opera,* a picture which became the most successful horror film of the decade. This film's public reception, due in no small part to Chaney's incredible makeup and bizarre facial contortions, stimulated a lengthy series of horror films at Universal. In the crucial transitional period to sound pictures and during the uncertain times of the Depression, the horror genre would help sustain the studio.

METRO-GOLDWYN-MAYER: HOME OF THE STARS

The formation of Metro-Goldwyn-Mayer came about through consolidation of the production companies, Metro Pictures Corporation and Goldwyn Pictures, along with the distribution company of Loew's, Incorporated. This merger took place on April 17, 1924, and was a consolidation resulting from the enterprising efforts of three film executives: Samuel Goldwyn, Marcus Loew, and Louis B. Mayer. All were astute businessmen who had emigrated to the United States from abroad and first entered the industry as novice theater owners and producers on the East Coast.

Samuel Goldwyn

Samuel Goldwyn (1882–1974), born Samuel B. Goldfish, became attracted to a show business career after he married Blanche Lasky, a vaudeville entertainer and sister to the theatrical producer Jesse L. Lasky. Goldwyn had built a successful business in glove manufacturing and merchandising in New York after moving to the United States from Warsaw, Poland via England in 1889. He left the glove business in 1913 to serve as a partner in Lasky Feature Plays with the responsibility of promoting early Lasky films (e.g., De Mille's *The Squaw Man*) prior to their release.

In 1916, shortly after the Lasky Company merged with Adolph Zukor's Famous Players, Goldwyn (still Goldfish) left the organization because of administration disputes and founded his own production studios in partnership with Edgar and Archibald Selwyn. The Selwyns were successful Broadway producers.

Goldwyn Picture Corporation, the company's name, was derived by combining the first part of *Gold*fish with the last part of Sel*wyn*. Two years later Goldfish officially adopted Goldwyn as his own last name.

The Goldwyn organization sought to continue the Lasky policy of producing films of the highest possible quality. In an innovative move Goldwyn took out full-page advertisements in national magazines to promote his "quality" films. He was also willing to pay actors and writers premium salaries for their services. Geraldine Farrar, an actress with Lasky and also a former Metropolitan Opera singer, agreed to move to Goldwyn Pictures for a salary of $10,000 a week.

In 1918 Goldwyn Pictures began to shift production from a rented studio in Fort Lee, New Jersey, to the abandoned Triangle studios in Culver City, California. Near the end of the first year in Culver City, the organization decided to purchase the Triangle Studio property outright although motion pictures being produced there had failed for the most part to win the public. By 1920 the organization was so shaky that Goldwyn had to elicit additional financial assistance from studio investors, including the wealthy du Pont family of Delaware. Pressured by this

outside influence and further aggravated by strong internal disputes with members of the board of directors, Goldwyn in 1922 left the studios he had founded to become an independent producer. The company continued to use its original title, although Goldwyn retained only a small share of stock after his departure.

Marcus Loew

Early in 1924 Marcus Loew (1870–1927), a highly successful film exhibitor, offered to purchase Goldwyn Pictures and the valuable studio property that went along with the organization. Loew sought the Goldwyn organization as additional production facilities.

An immigrant from Austria, Loew had parlayed nickelodeon interests into store theaters and store theaters into a chain of movie houses which by 1919 totaled more than 100 theaters. In 1920, to broaden his film enterprise, Loew bought the Metro Pictures Corporation, also a floundering studio, and began making and distributing his own pictures. By a stroke of luck, the first film produced at Metro, *The Four Horsemen of the Apocalypse* (1921), was an enormous box office success whose profits secured Loew's position as a film producer.

With the acquisition of the Goldwyn Company in 1924, Loew was well equipped to expand film production on a grand scale; yet he did not feel that either Metro or Goldwyn possessed a suitable supervisor to head production. An associate of Loew's suggested Louis B. Mayer of

Mayer Pictures as a forceful, creative administrator whose operation always ran smoothly and efficiently. So negotiations were conducted simultaneously with Goldwyn Pictures and Louis B. Mayer. Loew offered Mayer the management of the combined companies. Thus, Metro-Goldwyn-Mayer was born, although Mayer's name would not be officially added to the corporation until later.

While Samuel Goldwyn was only peripherally involved in the legal transactions, the new organization contained his name as well as the motto and symbol of the Goldwyn Picture Corporation. All M-G-M pictures would be prefaced by a logo bearing the words "Ars Gratia Artis" ("Art for Art's Sake") and a "live action" shot of a lion. During the silent years the lion appropriately lay silent but after the advent of sound it rose up and roared the introduction of M-G-M pictures. These logo trademarks had been adopted years before by Goldwyn as promotional gimmicks for his early films.

Louis B. Mayer

Louis B. Mayer's (1885–1957) powerful position at M-G-M had been earned through years of experience in motion-picture exhibition, distribution, and production. Mayer, like Loew and Goldwyn, was an emigrant to the United States. In the 1880s he had come to New Brunswick, Canada, with his parents from Minsk, Russia, and, just after the turn of the century, moved from Canada to the Boston area.

In 1907 he bought his first store theater, the Orpheum, in Haverhill, Massacusetts, where vaudeville acts and short films were presented until the young exhibitor had saved enough money to purchase a second theater in Haverhill. Within a few years he was building his own theaters in neighboring towns. He also founded a film exchange to supply products for his movie houses as well as for competitors in the area.

In 1915 Mayer joined with three other businessmen in New York City to create the Metro Pictures Corporation with the intention of expanding his film business into the production arena.

At first Mayer's involvement at Metro was minimal. Then in a shrewd business move he bought the New England distribution rights for *The Birth of a Nation* in 1915. Profits from road showings of Griffith's film totaled more than ten times the $25,000 investment, and with this impressive sum of money Mayer was able to venture wholeheartedly into film production.

Again shrewd and instinctive in gauging public taste, Mayer, like Zukor at Paramount, concluded that the popularity of films increasingly correlated with the popularity of the stars who appeared in them. This astute assumption would remain a part of Mayer's basic production philosophy as long as he made films.

In 1917, when the competition for stars was intensifying, Mayer was successful in enticing an actress at Vitagraph, Anita Stewart, away from her lucrative contract and into the fledgling Metro camp. The winning bribe was an ego-building promise that Stewart would have her own separate production unit, Anita Stewart Productions. This tactic was inspired by Zukor's success in hiring Mary Pickford away from Biograph and Mutual.

Anita Stewart and Louis B. Mayer were a successful team at Metro. Mayer found excellent scripts for the actress, quality directors, and strong supporting players. Stewart's elegance and beauty which had made her a rising star at Vitagraph were displayed to great advantage at Metro in *Virtuous Wives* (1918) and in *Her Kingdom of Dreams* (1918), both popular successes.

In 1919 production was moved from the East Coast to California where Mayer formed his own small film organization, the Louis B. Mayer production company. Between 1919 and the merger with Metro and Goldwyn in 1924, the Mayer organization profited from strong management and a small, but talented, group of artists. Mayer also surrounded himself with production associates who understood his overriding philosophy that filmmaking was first and foremost a business operation.

One of these associates was Irving Thalberg who came to work for Mayer from Universal in 1923. Thalberg, still in his 20s, rode Mayer's coattails into the Metro-Goldwyn company as second vice-president in charge of production. In this capacity at M-G-M the young Thalberg went on to earn the reputation of Hollywood's "boy wonder" and film producer *extraordinaire*.

An M-G-M Style Emerges

Together Mayer and Thalberg, from the first days of M-G-M's existence, began to forge the economic and artistic future of the studio. Mayer's philosophy demanded an efficient, well-run business enterprise, high technical quality, and the finest possible collection of movie stars. M-G-M's aspiration, articulated in its first year, became "More Stars Than There Are in Heaven."

The emphasis on stars at M-G-M, enhanced by strong production values, resulted in several generations of celebrated screen personalities. Many of M-G-M's early great stars became legends: John Gilbert, Greta Garbo, Joan Crawford, Clark Gable, John and Lionel Barrymore, and Jean Harlow.

Irving Thalberg held the production reins during M-G-M's formative years with an unfaltering sense of self-confidence about public taste. He oversaw budget expenditures, holding production costs on standard films to proposed limits, while willing at the same time to spend extravagant sums of money on pictures that appeared to have unusual box office potential. In 1925 he astutely increased the budget for *The Big Parade;* this war film, directed by King Vidor, was a huge critical and

Louis B. Mayer discusses a star's contract, circa 1928.

popular success at a time when war stories were considered taboo. Its New York run alone lasted for ninety-six weeks.

With this impressive start Thalberg's involvement at M-G-M became all pervasive. He worked in close collaboration with writers, directors, and editors during the preproduction, production, and postproduction stages of filmmaking. It was not at all unusual to command that scenes be reshot or that a picture be reedited after previews. Remarkably, Thalberg's judgment served him well, and much of the early commercial success of M-G-M films can be attributed to his personal style of studio management. This influence would help secure M-G-M's position during the 1930s as the world's dominant motion-picture studio.

WARNER BROTHERS: FAMILY ENTERPRISE

Few Hollywood success stories can match that of the Warner Brothers—Harry, Albert, Sam, and Jack. The business acumen of these men, beginning at the turn of the century and continuing well into the 1960s, produced one of the great, enduring studio complexes. Their enterprising, gambling nature—evident from the time the Warner family bought its first motion-picture projector in 1904—would prove to be a stimulus to the film industry time and again.

The four Warner brothers were the sons of Benjamin and Pearl Warner, immigrants who moved to Baltimore, Maryland, in 1883 from Kraznashlitz, Poland, a small village near the German border. Benjamin, a cobbler and peddler, opened a shoemaker's shop in Baltimore and thus began life in the United States with his wife and 2-year-old son, Harry. The next year Albert was born, followed by Sam in 1888 and Jack in 1892. Four other children, Sadye, Rose, Anna, and Dave, made up the large Warner family.

In 1895 the elder Warner decided to move his family to Youngstown, Ohio, and open a bicycle shop in partnership with his sons. Such businesses were fashionable at the time, although the Warners' shop failed and the men had to take on a variety of odd jobs to support themselves.

Novice Film Exhibitors

It was Sam Warner who discovered the emerging film medium. A machinist friend showed the young Warner how to operate an Edison projector he kept in his shop, and with this knowledge Sam was able to find employment as a projectionist in an Ohio amusement park.

Inspired by the enormous interest shown by customers in moving pictures, Sam Warner talked his family into pooling their resources and

The Warner brothers, film exhibitors, pose in front of a nickelodeon.

purchasing their own projector. They found a used one in 1904, bought it along with a print of *The Great Train Robbery* and began presenting shows.

The decision to purchase *The Great Train Robbery* was an astute one. Although Porter's film had been in circulation for more than a year, the sensational picture continued to generate audiences and excitement wherever it was shown. During 1904 and 1905 the Warners toured Ohio and Pennsylvania with their film presentations. They rented any type of space they could find; if a piano was available, Rose Warner provided musical accompaniment.

With profits earned on their traveling shows the Warner brothers opened a ninety-seat theater in 1905 in New Castle, Pennsylvania. They operated the theater for three years while also expanding their film business to include a distribution service that supplied motion pictures to exhibitors in Pennsylvania, Maryland, Virginia, and Georgia. Financial resources grew from the rental fees and box office percentages collected through the distribution agreements.

In 1910 in a temporary setback, the Warners were forced to sell their distribution exchange to the Motion Picture Patents Company and its subsidiary, General Film Company, which together still controlled film production and the supply of films to exhibitors. Sam in 1911 went back to traveling shows, touring New Jersey and Connecticut with a print of the five-reel Italian spectacle *Dante's Inferno* (1911).

Beginning Producers

Jack and Sam Warner ventured into film production in 1912 with *Perils of the Plains,* a two-reel picture written by Jack and produced in an empty factory building in St. Louis. Encouraged more by the creative stimulation of making films than by the commercial success of their first effort, the two brothers continued producing pictures. In 1915, to elude the Patents Trust, they moved their small, independent production unit to Los Angeles.

Films turned out by the Warners met with little success during the first years in California. Big-name stars were the main drawing power of pictures made at the time and Sam and Jack Warner did not possess the capital to acquire a Mary Pickford, Anita Stewart, Doug Fairbanks, or Geraldine Farrar. Nor did the Warners have the East Coast financial associations maintained by most of the young production companies in Hollywood.

In 1917 the Warners scraped together enough money to produce their first full-length film and realized their first significant commercial success. The film was based on James Gerard's factual story, *My Four Years in Germany,* an account of his tense relationship with Kaiser Wilhelm II while Gerard was the U.S. ambassador to Germany. The Warners' treatment of the wartime story contained enough sensationalism (several intensely violent scenes including a rape) to score well with thrill-seeking filmgoers. Box office receipts totaled more than $1 million.

With new impetus and more funds, a studio was leased in Culver City for the production of low-budget pictures and serials. Popular with filmgoers since their introduction in 1913 with *What Happened to Mary,* serials were inexpensive to produce and easy to peddle as filler material for film programs. In 1919 Warners produced two serials, *The Lost City* and *Miracles of the Jungle,* both adventure stories involving wild animals.

Increased Productivity and Efficiency

In 1923 Warner Brothers Pictures Incorporated was officially established and a studio was built at Sunset and Bronson to house the new organization. An ambitious production schedule was undertaken and the studio turned out five feature-length films in 1923 while also devoting considerable energy to the building of an able staff of directors, writers, and actors.

Slowly the Warner Brothers enterprise began to make an impression in the rapidly accelerating world of studio competition. Hal Wallis, who would later become one of Warners' quality producers, accepted a job as publicity chief at the studios in 1923 and began generating information to boost Warners' image.

In 1924 Darryl Zanuck joined Warners as a script writer for the studio's one major star, the German shepherd, Rin-Tin-Tin. The enormous popularity of the Rin-Tin-Tin pictures sustained the studio as it began to bargain seriously for important actors.

John Barrymore consented to appear with the young Mary Astor in the Warners' production of *Beau Brummel* (1924). Barrymore's stage reputation had made him a great box office attraction in *Dr. Jekyll and Mr. Hyde* (1920). His appearance in *Beau Brummel* and *The Sea Beast* (1926) for Warners marked a triumph for the studio. Profits in 1924 rose above $1 million for the first time.

This did not represent a staggering sum of money, but it was enough to allow the Warners to expand their holdings. Two foreign distribution exchanges were purchased in 1924 as well as the floundering Vitagraph Corporation. Vitagraph, an early important production-distribution company (in the film business for two decades by 1924), was the last existing studio from among the ten organizations which had originally comprised the Motion Picture Patents Company trust. The ironic fact that Vitagraph was absorbed into one of the still young independent units that had fled to California to escape the trust suggests the degree to which the old guard had been replaced by the new.

Along with two production studios, one in the East and one in California, Warner Brothers on closing the deal also acquired Vitagraph's national distribution exchange. Further expansion continued throughout 1925 as the Warner Corporation began to rent and buy motion-picture houses. The acquisition of these houses and the Vitagraph exchange helped combat the problem of distribution which had plagued the organization since entering production.

Production in the Warners studios continued to improve in quality; motion-picture critics took note of the fact, praising Warner Brothers for its screen adaptation of the Sinclair Lewis novel *Main Street* (1924). Ernst Lubitsch, a prominent German director, signed a contract with Warners and created his second American film, *The Marriage Circle* (1924), a comedy with Adolphe Menjou which was praised for its "vitality."

Sam Warner, whose intuition to purchase a motion-picture projector in 1904 had planted the seed for the now prospering family enterprise, again proved himself a visionary. On June 25, 1925, after seeing a demonstration by Western Electric of a sound film, he astutely signed an agreement with Western Electric, a subsidiary of AT&T, for a cooperative venture into sound motion pictures. Western Electric had been engaged in sound recording and sound system improvement for nearly fifteen years but had been unsuccessful in convincing Hollywood studio executives that the introduction of synchronous sound was wise or feasible. Earlier, unsatisfactory experiments with sound, going back to Edison's Kinetoscope, had been a deterring factor; also the fact that the motion-picture industry appeared to be in an irreversible period of growth prompted further resistance to the costly technological innovation that would be required in adapting to sound.

But the Warners, still not a fully secure organization, went ahead with their sound experiments. On October 26, 1927, after two years of experimentation, the studio released *The Jazz Singer,* a sentimental part-talking, part-singing motion picture which helped change the course of film history. The Al Jolson vehicle in effect sounded the death-knell for screen pantomime and the American studios hurried to convert their shooting stages for talking pictures. New types of stories and new stars soon emerged.

United Artists (1919), Columbia Pictures (1920), and Radio-Keith-Orpheum (RKO, 1928) were among the significant, later developing production companies within the rapidly emerging American studio system. By 1920 these three organizations, along with Paramount, M-G-M, Fox, Warner Brothers, and Universal, were responsible for 60 percent of the Hollywood feature-length pictures, although at the time more than forty companies were producing films in California. The dominance of these eight companies would set the standards for American motion pictures as the industry moved into the exciting era of talking motion pictures.

SUGGESTED READINGS

Balio, Tino, ed. *The American Film Industry.* Madison: The University of Wisconsin Press, 1976.

Brownlow, Kevin. *Hollywood: The Pioneers.* New York: Knopf, 1979.

———.*The Parade's Gone By.* New York: Knopf, 1968.

Crowther, Bosley. *Hollywood Rajah: The Life and Times of Louis B. Mayer.* New York: Holt, 1960.

Finler, Joel. *Stroheim.* Berkeley: University of California Press, 1968.

French, Philip. *The Movie Moguls: An Informal History of the Hollywood Tycoons.* Chicago: Regnery, 1971.

Higham, Charles. *Warner Brothers.* New York: Scribner, 1975.

Marx, Arthur, *Goldwyn.* New York: Ballantine, 1976.

Pickford, Mary. *Sunshine and Shadow.* Garden City, N.Y.: Doubleday, 1955.

Rosten, Leo. *Hollywood: The Movie Colony, The Movie Makers.* New York: Harcourt, 1941.

Sinclair, Upton. *Upton Sinclair Presents William Fox.* Los Angeles: Upton Sinclair Publishing Co., 1933.

PART 3

**SILENT CINEMA
ABROAD**

SWEDEN, DENMARK, AND GERMANY (1912–1928)

The Cabinet of Dr. Caligari is a revelation and a challenge. It is a revelation of what the motion picture is capable of as a form of artistic expression. It challenges the public to appreciate it and challenges the producer to learn from it. The revelation is there for all to see. If the appreciation fails, the motion picture itself, and all that it has promised, is in danger of failing.

In *The Cabinet of Dr. Caligari* the motion picture for the first time stands forth in its integrity as a work of art. It is one of the paradoxes of art that it is at the same time an abstraction and something tangible in terms of our bodily senses. It is form and idea.

From a review in *Exceptional Photoplays*, March 1921.

The Cabinet of Dr. Caligari (1919).

At the same time that the American film industry was evolving an efficient studio system geared to the mass marketing of entertainment commodities, national cinema abroad was developing in a varied display of filmic styles and interests. A serious commitment to the expressive possibilities of film art in Sweden, Denmark, and Germany resulted in a large collection of motion-picture classics, many of which stand among the most enduring efforts of the medium's silent era. Inspired by national as well as individual goals, these works were diversified in theme and technique and together they suggested new visions and new roles for the motion picture.

VICTOR SJÖSTRÖM AND MAURITZ STILLER: SWEDISH GIANTS

Victor Sjöström (Seastrom) (1879–1960) and Mauritz Stiller (1883–1928) were the two significant artistic figures in the evolution of Swedish cinema. Both began directing motion pictures in 1912, although each developed unique styles of film expression and varying story interests.

Sjöström

Sjöström, both a film actor and director, came to a motion-picture career from the stage after accepting a role in *The Black Masks* (1912). Between 1912 and 1916 he directed nearly two dozen films while continuing to act in others.

In this early period a strong humanistic sensibility emerged in his work as well as a skillful, efficient directorial style. His continuing experience as a performer provided him with a special talent for directing actors and for clarifying screen characterizations. Settings were economically stylized, yet always a significant part of a film's dramatic mood.

Sjöström also experimented with new structural approaches to plot development. In *Ingeborg Holm* (1913) insanity was treated in an impressive, albeit somber manner. The psychological story was developed through episodic segments in order to present the subject in analytical form.

Later Sjöström further experimented with new methods of story development, including the extensive use of flashbacks which were first notable in *The Kiss of Death* (1916). This film had particular aesthetic significance because of its mosaic approach to dramatic material. The event around which the story evolves is recreated in various versions through a series of flashbacks. This method, original at the time, would later appear as the principal structural device in screen classics such as Orson Welles' *Citizen Kane* (1941), Akira Kurosawa's *Rashomon* (1950), and Ingmar Bergman's *Wild Strawberries* (1957). Bergman, a later

Hilda Borgstrom as *Ingeborg Holm* (1913), a widow whose confinement in a workhouse leads to the loss of her children and eventually mental illness.

Swedish director, clearly found inspiration in Sjöström's methods and themes which at their best were marked by serious, analytical studies of human moods and emotions.

In the 1920s Sjöström came to Hollywood along with many of the great European directors. From 1923 to 1930 he directed nine motion pictures at Metro-Goldwyn-Mayer using the name Seastrom. All except two of these films were unmemorable exercises.

The two notable pictures made in the United States were both literary adaptations of American novels, *The Scarlet Letter* (1926) and *The Wind* (1928). Both starred Lillian Gish.

Sjöström's film career in Sweden had been dominated by adaptations of Nordic sagas and Scandanavian literary works, many by the Swedish writer Selma Lagerlöf. This expertise showed in the atmospheric qualities of *The Wind* and in the successful treatment of the moral issues in Nathaniel Hawthorne's *The Scarlet Letter*.

Sjöström's feeling for landscape and his ability to work effectively with actors were qualities he was able to transport from Sweden to these two films directed for Louis B. Mayer. Lillian Gish, only a few years removed from completing her Griffith tutelage, achieved some of her finest emotional moments in a long, distinguished career as a film performer. The love scenes between Gish and Lars Hanson were particularly memorable, offering superb acting along with strong poetic imagery. Gish praised Sjöström for aiding her education as a screen actress.

The Scarlet Letter and *The Wind* were the last two important films of Victor Sjöström's directorial career. He returned to Sweden in 1930 to direct *Markurells and Wadköping* and in 1937 went to England to direct *Under the Red Robe*. Aside from these two final directorial efforts, the remainder of Sjöström's professional career in motion pictures was spent as an actor.

Stiller

The career of Mauritz Stiller, who emigrated to Sweden from Finland in 1910, paralleled Sjöström's in several ways. Both were originally stage actors, both established reputations as skillful directors of literary adaptations, and both had brief interludes as Hollywood directors in the 1920s.

Stiller came to the Svenska Biograf studios in 1912 after working as an actor and director at Stockholm's Lilla Teatern. The early film work at Biograf consisted principally of directorial assignments on short melodramas and comedies that were adapted from popular fiction and stage plays.

In a series of films made in Sweden between 1918 and 1924, Stiller brought to the screen a number of epic stories in which he displayed a gift for visually imaginative, atmospheric filmmaking. *Alexander the Great* (1918), *Song of the Scarlet Flower* (1919), *Sir Arne's Treasure* (1919), *Gunnar Hede's Saga* (1922), and *Gösta Berling's Saga* (1924) collectively contained those filmic elements which established Stiller's directorial prominence: expressive use of landscapes, vivid action sequences, and a keen sense for authentic historical recreations.

Sir Arne's Treasure, based on a novel by Selma Lagerlöf, has been praised as Stiller's most successful epic film. This period story was set in the sixteenth century in Sweden's stark northern country where snow and ice dominate the terrain. Stiller captures the starkness of the place, a physical and spiritual starkness, with striking visual compositions and a series of somber dramatic sequences.

The film's plot tragically recounts the love of a young woman, Elsalill (Mary Johnson), for a Scotsman who has murdered the woman's younger foster sister. Also willing to sacrifice herself for the Scotsman, Elsalill is accidently killed and her body kept in the hold of a ship that is trapped in the frozen lake. The Scot keeps watch over the dead girl's body until village women come and take the corpse in stark procession across the ice.

A somber procession of black-robed women follows Elsalill's coffin across the frozen lake in Stiller's *Sir Arne's Treasure* (1919).

In *Sir Arne's Treasure* Stiller creates a haunting association between the environment and the characters' lives. As Sjöström's flashback devices surely spurred Bergman's *Wild Strawberries*, similarly Bergman took inspiration from Stiller's dark, environment-based legends. *The Seventh Seal* (1956), *The Virgin Spring* (1960), and *Hour of the Wolf* (1968), among others, reveal Bergman's own skillful and inextricable fusion of landscape with character moods. Bergman's stories of death *(The Seventh Seal)*, violence *(The Virgin Spring)*, and insanity *(Hour of the Wolf)* portray the darker side of the human soul, as did Stiller's work, in symbolic linkage with stark and foreboding locations. Myth, saga, and legend—deeply significant to Scandinavia's cultural traditions—have provided fitting inspiration for Swedish directors from Stiller and Sjöström to Ingmar Bergman.

In addition to his achievements in the area of epic-period film-making, Mauritz Stiller also gained a reputation for creating sex comedies in which he handled innuendo with skillful sophistication. These films, of which *Erotikon* (1920) is the most noteworthy example, have often been compared to Cecil B. De Mille's domestic comedies of the same era. Both share the qualities of risqué subject matter and evocative settings and costumes.

Mauritz Stiller's stay in America proved much shorter and even less rewarding than Sjöström's. Stiller arrived in the United States in mid-1925 with Greta Garbo, the star of his last Swedish film, *Gösta Berling's Saga* (1924). This final effort at home was appropriately an adaptation of a Selma Lagerlöf love story. Its prominent introduction of Garbo to motion-picture audiences was followed by the new star's important appearance in G. W. Pabst's *The Joyless Street* (1925), produced in Germany.

Louis B. Mayer, having successfully enticed Sjöström away from Sweden two years earlier, had the idea to launch Stiller and his protégée, Garbo, simultaneously on American careers at M-G-M. However, Stiller sat idle for a full year waiting for work. In mid-1926 he was named to direct Garbo in *The Temptress*, then was removed from the assignment. Discouraged, Stiller moved to Paramount Pictures where he directed *Hotel Imperial* (1926), *Woman on Trial* (1927), and a portion of *Barbed Wire* (1927) before being replaced by Rowland Lee. Of Stiller's two completed American films, *Hotel Imperial* with Pola Negri and Max Davidson enjoyed the greater success. Stiller's direction was described by critics as "elegant" and "forceful." Unable to cope with the American system of making motion pictures and suffering from poor health, Stiller returned to Stockholm where he died on November 8, 1928.

By this time the rich formative period of Swedish cinema had come to an end. The migration of the country's two principal directors to Hollywood and an arrangement in the 1920s with Germany for joint-production of pictures had drained Swedish film of its spirited originality.

The year 1928 also marked the end of the silent film era and the full-fledged introduction of talking pictures. Swedish-language films further declined in marketability. International cinema, in general, experienced a setback with the advent of sound.

CARL DREYER: VISUAL IMPRESSIONIST

In Denmark in 1920 Carl Theodor Dreyer (1889–1968) directed his first feature-length motion picture, *The President*. With this film Dreyer entered into a long career as a motion-picture director whose eventual stylized and abstract approaches to film content would establish him as an important, original filmmaker.

Dreyer, following the pattern of many other early film directors, started out as a writer: first as a theater critic-journalist, then as a film title writer, editor, and scenarist for the Nordisk Film Company in Copenhagen. Between 1912 and 1919 he wrote more than two dozen

Leaves from Satan's Book (1921), Dreyer's four-part film which imitated Intolerance (1916).

film scripts, many of which were adapted from popular novels and directed for Nordisk by its two principal directors, August Blom and Holger-Madsen.

In *The President* Dreyer's cinematic approach suggested influences of D. W. Griffith, especially in his use of flashback sequences to reconstruct the thriller plot. Following this initial effort there began to emerge in Dreyer's work interests that centered on spiritual and moralistic themes. In *Leaves from Satan's Book* (1921), a multiple-story film that was also apparently inspired by *Intolerance,* Dreyer combined naturalistic settings and large close-up shots to project the theme of satanic evil. His fourth film, *Love One Another* (1922), was made in Germany and offered a pointed statement against anti-Semitism.

The Passion of Joan of Arc

In *The Passion of Joan of Arc,* a film produced in France in 1928, Dreyer created his most important motion picture. This version of the legend of Joan of Arc generated great controversy. British censors banned the film because of its unfavorable depiction of English soldiers, while the film's style stimulated intense debate.

In telling the story of the last six hours of the life of Joan of Arc, Dreyer reconstructed the critical events of the drama (the inquisition, the trial, the death by fire at the stake) almost entirely with close-ups.

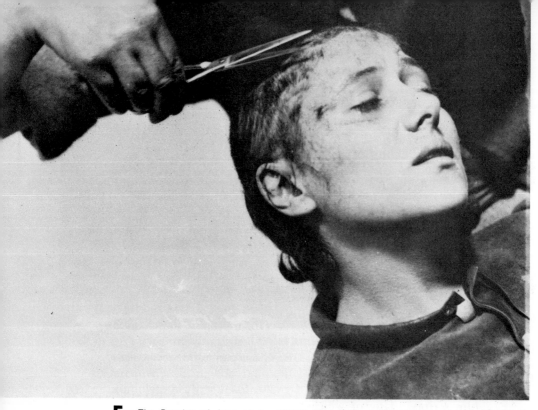

For *The Passion of Joan of Arc* (1928) Maria Falconetti as Joan submitted to harsh indignities in order to give Dreyer the intensity he desired.

Only three full-length shots of Joan (Maria Falconetti) appear throughout the course of the film. The obligatory cover shot of the set, expected in any film dramatization, never materializes. Rather one sees only bits and pieces of locations which appear to have been taken in front of a largely white background.

In Rudolph Maté's camera work actors are photographed without makeup, their emotions often fragmented into huge close-ups of eyes and mouths. Camera angles supply their own meaning within the close-up shots. The inquisitors are photographed from a low angle, looking down at Joan to suggest a continuously domineering position; Joan is filmed from above, always looking up, angles which depict her passion from a subjective point of view.

Frequently in *The Passion of Joan of Arc* Dreyer zooms, tilts, and pans the camera to shift emphasis to another element of dramatic import. These camera movements take the viewer from one detailed close-up abruptly to another.

The concentration of dramatic emphasis into close-up shots, almost exclusively, resulted in a film experience that variously was described as "masterful," "uncinematic," "deeply moving," "impersonal." The accumulative effect of Dreyer's methods was a motion picture unlike any other seen before. For many, he had created a wrenching, painful experience with his unrelenting and probing close-ups; for others, the fragmentation and isolated arrangement of shots were merely disorienting affectations.

Admittedly controversial, the intensity of *The Passion of Joan of Arc*, however, cannot be denied. The actors were driven by Dreyer to "experience" what they were playing through grueling rehearsal procedures that generated feelings of torture and suffering among the cast. Maria Falconetti's hair is shorn, painfully, in the presence of Maté's camera. Together Falconetti's performance and Dreyer's individualistic style produced a motion picture of integrity and compassion. Many critics have claimed that this film, among its other achievements, was the last great silent motion picture.

Following *The Passion of Joan of Arc* Dreyer directed only four feature-length dramatic films: *Vampyr* (1931), *Day of Wrath* (1943), *Ordet* (1955), and *Gertrud* (1964). In each he continued his preoccupation with spiritual themes.

Carl Dreyer's importance in film history was earned through his unique style of expression in treating subject matter of uncommon seriousness. His aesthetic approach represented a radical departure from traditional methods and showed the power of the motion-picture camera for probing beneath superficial realities. Experimental filmmakers, interested in the psychological possibilities of the medium, found inspiration in his abstract scrutiny of screen characters. Ingmar Bergman, Robert Bresson, and other dramatic directors who later sought to reveal psychological values in the development of character also pay homage to Dreyer's pioneering efforts.

GERMANY: STUDIO MASTERPIECES

Germany's "golden age" of filmmaking began shortly after the conclusion of World War I when the defeated nation moved to counter through its motion pictures an unfavorable image being projected in films from abroad. D. W. Griffith's *Hearts of the World* (1918), for example, had offered a negative, one-dimensional depiction of German soldiers. Other war films, often starring Erich von Stroheim as the stereotyped German villain, had looked, in their patriotic fervor, unfavorably on the character of the German people.

The Founding of Ufa

To counteract these negative views and to boost the pride of the nation, the German government acted to reorganize the country's film industry.

A government loan was secured in 1917 from the Deutsche Bank to underwrite a national film production center at the Universum-film-Aktiengesellschaft (Ufa) studios, located outside Berlin at Neubabelsberg. Prominent filmmakers throughout Germany, along with artists and theater producers, were invited to join the government-sponsored organization in collective enterprise.

From its inception Ufa viewed its mission with seriousness. The political rationale on which the studio was founded, plus an attitude among German filmmakers that the motion picture held possibilities beyond its entertainment potential, acted to create an organization of elevated purpose.

With boldness and imagination, Ufa began to turn out films that treated subject matter which was often somber and deeply psychological. The seriousness of theme found expression in innovative approaches to camera usage and visual style, particularly in the more psychological films.

The original quality of German films between 1918 and 1925 grew in large part from Ufa's centralized studio structure. Under the production supervision of Erich Pommer, the assembled German artists, working within a single studio unit, were encouraged to pool their various skills for maximum coordination of each motion-picture project.

Government subsidy of the studio complex made it one of the best-equipped production facilities in the world, and as a result early Ufa filmmakers rarely filmed outside the studio. Consequently, atmospheric studio design with a strong architectural emphasis became a distinguishing characteristic of Ufa-produced motion pictures. Expressive lighting and a fluid, subjective camera were other studio-inspired elements.

Three principal types of motion pictures emerged during Ufa's ascent to international prominence. Historical drama constituted a significant part of Ufa's early output, enjoying great popularity with filmgoers in Germany and abroad and introducing Ernst Lubitsch as a prominent, stylish German director. The stylized fantasy film, of which *The Cabinet of Dr. Caligari* best represented the genre, was a second type of German film which emerged to focus attention on the bold artistry at Ufa. A third type, the psychological or subjective drama, employed a more realistic style of filmmaking as German directors examined the emotions of characters confronting their own destinies. Each of these three types of silent German films was distinctively different in style and subject matter and all were benefactors of Ufa's unified studio approach.

The Historical Drama and the Ernst Lubitsch Comedy

Ernst Lubitsch (1892–1947) was responsible for the first notable Ufa success, *The Eyes of the Mummy Ma*, released in 1918. The picture starred

Pola Negri and Emil Jannings who, like Lubitsch, achieved international reputations as a result of the film's popularity.

Lubitsch, whose theatrical career had begun in 1911 as an actor with Max Reinhardt's Deutsches Theater, came to motion pictures when Reinhardt agreed in 1912 to make screen versions of his stage plays, *The Miracle* and *Venitian Nights*. After acting in these films, Lubitsch worked in a series of comic one-reelers and in 1914 also began writing and directing motion pictures for Germany's Projection-A.G. Studios.

When Projection-A.G. was merged into Ufa in November 1917, Lubitsch went along as one of the directors. As the war moved toward its conclusion he began work on *The Eyes of the Mummy Ma*—a new venture for the comedy-trained director. The film told the story of an obsessed Egyptian (Jannings) who stalks a traveling dancer (Negri) after she has rejected him for an artist. This film of jealousy and revenge succeeded because of Lubitsch's flair for exotic detail.

The enormous popularity of *The Eyes of the Mummy Ma* led to a series of exotic costume spectacles whereby Lubitsch enhanced his reputation as the European master of screen pageantry: *Carmen* (1918), *Madame Dubarry* (1919), *Sumurun* (1920), *Anna Boleyn* (1920), and *The Wife of the Pharaoh* (1922). Most of these films were well received in Europe and in the United States despite fears by Ufa that German-produced films would continue to be boycotted.

Carmen and *Madame Dubarry* starred the tantalizing Pola Negri and caused a sensation when they reached the United States in 1920 and 1921. Lubitsch was praised for his lavish settings and for the bold treatment of often degenerate, earthy characters. The films also possessed an overtone of sexual intrigue, a quality of which Cecil B. De Mille appropriately took note.

Simultaneously with the direction of costume spectacles, Lubitsch engaged himself in a series of sophisticated comedies: *The Oyster Princess* (1919), *The Doll* (1919), and *Kölhiesel's Daughter* (1920).

These films satirized the manners of wealthy Americans, European aristocrats, monks, and Bavarian peasants. Lubitsch's direction was characterized by a light, sophisticated handling of character interaction and nuance, and an amusingly cynical and sexually provocative treatment of the screen persona. His Ufa comedies enjoyed enormous popularity in Germany but never received the wide circulation given his historical films.

After the popular reception of *Carmen, Madame Dubarry,* and *The Wife of the Pharaoh* in the United States during 1920 and 1921, Lubitsch signed a contract to direct Mary Pickford in Hollywood, becoming one of the first of numerous important artists to leave Germany for work in America.

Following unpleasant working conflicts with Pickford during the filming of *Rosita* (1923), he moved to Warner Brothers and thereafter shifted his attention back to the direction of clever, sophisticated comedies of manners. By the 1930s the legendary "Lubitsch touch," employed in the handling of the sexual innuendo, had secured for the director a place in American film history equal in prominence to that of his ten-year German career.

The Stylized Fantasy: *Caligari* Leads the Way

The most startling film produced at Ufa in the studio's first three years of operation was Robert Wiene's *The Cabinet of Dr. Caligari* (1919). This macabre fantasy with its classic illustration of expressionistic devices revealed an audacious departure from screen naturalism. Its story form, developed through the imagination of an inmate in an insane asylum, was boldly original in structure and in psychological implication. The intelligentsia, artists, Freudian adherents, and filmgoers interested in antirealist styles found in Wiene's work a film of unparalleled stimulation.

While Ernst Lubitsch's exacting costume spectacles and satirical comedies had called attention to Ufa, *The Cabinet of Dr. Caligari* provided a true aesthetic advancement in film art. Upon its release Pommer and the studio artists he supervised had suddenly achieved a degree of the international acclaim they had sought.

The Plot *The Cabinet of Dr. Caligari's* plot unfolds through the fantasies of a mental patient. The patient recounts for another inmate a strange tale of a somnambulist who commits a series of murders while under the spell of a mad doctor.

Wiene's opening shot reveals the narrator, Francis (Friedrich Feher), sitting with an older man on a bench in the yard of the mental institution. The older patient apparently has just completed his own bizarre tale, suggested through a title in which the man tells Francis "Spirits surround us on every side." Francis counters with the statement that his own story is "more remarkable than what you have told me." He then begins: "In Holstenwall where I was born . . ."

Through an iris-out, the village of Holstenwall is revealed and the fantasy begins. A strange bespectacled man (Werner Krauss) appears in the village and seeks a permit to operate a concession at a fair which has come to town. The sideshow concession displays a freakish somnambulist, Cesare (Conrad Veidt), who has slept in a wooden box for twenty-five years but wakens to tell the fortunes of those who pay to see him.

Francis and his friend Alan enter the concession. On asking how long he will live, Alan (Hans von Twardowski) is told by Cesare: "You die at dawn." One mysterious murder (that of the town clerk) has already occurred and Alan's reaction is a mixture of amusement and fright.

When Alan is in fact murdered during the night, Francis recalls Cesare's prophecy and seeks to convince village officials that the

Cesare (Conrad Veidt), the somnabulist, wakens in the presence of his master (Werner Krauss) and Jane (Lil Dagover).

concession operator and his charge are responsible for the crimes. Eventually Francis is proven correct after he discovers that Caligari has chosen to emulate a mystical sixteenth-century doctor who trained sleepwalkers to murder at night on his command. The Dr. Caligari who has come to Holstenwall has assumed this identity, Francis learns, while also doubling as the head of a mental asylum.

Francis' story reaches a climax when Cesare's body is brought to the asylum and Dr. Caligari on viewing it goes mad. The doctor's raving reaction confirms Francis' accusations and Caligari is placed in a straitjacket.

At this point the fantasy ends and the film returns to the two storytellers. Francis concludes his tale with the statement that "Today [Caligari] is a raving madman chained to his cell." A longer shot of the asylum courtyard then reveals that many of the principals in Francis' imagined story are fellow mental patients. Similarly, the hospital director enters the yard and he is the same figure as the fantasized Dr. Caligari.

Francis shouts to the other patients that the director is plotting their doom. When the other patients ignore his accusations, Francis becomes irate and must be quieted by a straitjacket. *The Cabinet of Dr. Caligari* ends with a close-up of the asylum director and a title of the director saying: "He believes me to be the mythical Caligari. I think I know how to cure him." This statement is made as the doctor pensively removes his glasses. The comment introduces one final suggestion of ambiguity as the film concludes with an iris fade to black.

Visual Style and Structure The unusual nature of this story by scenarists Carl Mayer and Hans Janowitz was reinforced by a startling visual style. Scene designers Walter Reimann, Hermann Warm, and Walther Röhrig drew inspiration from the expressionist-cubist movement which by 1919 was well-established in German theater, art, and writing. All other dramatic elements in *The Cabinet of Dr. Caligari* also eschew naturalism: lighting, acting, and makeup.

The expressionistic approach to the physical environment serves as a visual metaphor for the principal character's neurotic, distorted view of the world. Settings, space, and movement are all actively linked to the film's psychological story.

In building the sets for *The Cabinet of Dr. Caligari,* the designers worked entirely with cloth drapes and canvas flats, painted to suggest a somber, bizarre mood. A bold contrast exists in the use of black patterns drawn onto white flats. The shapes of the flats and the patterns painted on them rarely fall into perpendicular lines. Representations of pathways, trees, and windows are rendered in twisted and wedge-shaped patterns.

To intensify the unnatural quality of the story, actors often move in concentric or jagged directions to arrive at a location; white makeup gives a starkly stylized appearance to actors' faces; low-key lighting reinforces the dark tenor of the film; foreboding shadows are everywhere.

The camera usage itself is for the most part uninvolving; Wiene simply places the camera into a static, straight-on position and photographs the scenes largely from long and medium views. For emphasis and character reactions, cinematographer Willi Hameister employs the iris-in effect and an abundance of circular masks.

The structure of Caligari's story, on the other hand, brings the viewer into interaction with the principal character's mind, especially at the film's conclusion when Francis' immediate world at the mental institution is exposed as the material source of the fantasy which has unfolded. Particularly intriguing for the viewer is the demeanor of the institute director in Wiene's concluding shot. The ambiguous nature of the doctor's final comment about knowing how to "cure" Francis and his facial expression as he removes his glasses seem to suggest that possibly Francis' paranoia is justified.

The expressionistic nature of story treatment in *The Cabinet of Dr. Caligari* helped open the world of the mind to cinematic visualization. As an evocation of paranoia and derangement, Wiene moved film expression beyond the photographic and into the psychic. The bookended story-within-a-story approach was intellectually stimulating for the manner in which it suggested not reality but a possible reality.

Without its innovative narrative structure and without its expressive decor *The Cabinet of Dr. Caligari* would have been little more than a fascinating horror tale.

Implications Wiene's peculiar story with its ambiguous ending raises numerous unanswered questions. Is Francis really mad? If so, is his madness a fear of authority such as that represented by the institute director? Or is the film's conclusion saying that authority is benevolent? That the director intends to employ Freudian psychiatry to cure the patient?

These ambiguities were partially responsible for Siegfried Kracauer's provocative theory that *The Cabinet of Dr. Caligari* and other German monster films made in the period after World War I possessed more than superficial dramatic values. In his book *From Caligari to Hitler,* Kracauer maintains that the postwar German films such as *Caligari* helped sow the seeds of Nazism by showing the powers that be as both kind and necessary to the welfare of the people—in the case of *Caligari,* frightened and deluded people.

However accurate or inaccurate Kracauer's assumptions may be, certain images within the scenic design do appear symbolically related to views of authority. Authoritarian figures (the city officials, for example, to whom Caligari goes for a concession permit) sit in chairs that rise disdainfully above the villagers who seek assistance. The icon appears to represent a cynical ridicule of authority, rather than a positive attitude. (Initially the scenarists intended that the film be an attack on authority throughout, with Caligari revealed at the end as mad. Pommer, however, changed the story so that its revelation as coming from Francis' imagination would not make it clear who is mad, Caligari or the inmate.) Rather than detracting from the importance of Wiene's work, these plot uncertainties have acted to broaden and enrich critical responses to a strikingly original motion picture.

Other Expressionistic Fantasies

The beginnings of expressionistic fantasy in German cinema can be found nearly a full decade before the release of *The Cabinet of Dr. Caligari. The Student of Prague* (1913), produced by Paul Wegener, represented at least one earlier prototype for the mystical horror film. Its plot, based on ideas from stories by Edgar Allan Poe and E. T. A. Hoffman, recounts the tale of a student who successfully bargains with the evil Scapinelli for unlimited material wealth. In return the student agrees to exchange mirror images with Scapinelli, an agreement which eventually leads the student to self-damnation. In the end he is driven to destroy himself by shooting at his reflected image.

This diabolical story is typical of the many Gothic tales that have fascinated Germans for centuries. As in *The Cabinet of Dr. Caligari,* Wegener's film projects the idea that the world is surrounded by evil spirits which prey on the innocent and the weak. The opening scene of *The Cabinet of Dr. Caligari* notes the German penchant for such tales by having Francis' story of evil spirits immediately follow an apparently similar story by his inmate companion.

After the success of *The Cabinet of Dr. Caligari,* German filmmakers produced a number of other significant motion pictures which emphasized the macabre and the fantastic, including: *The Golem* (1920), directed by Paul Wegener and Carl Boese; *Destiny* (1921), *Dr. Mabuse, the Gambler* (1922), and *Metropolis* (1926), directed by Fritz Lang; *Nosferatu* (1922), directed by F. W. Murnau; and *Waxworks* (1924), a film by Paul Leni. All these films are somber in visual tone, utilize nonrealistic representation within their scenic design, are studio made (except for *Nosferatu*), and tell stories of evil figures who control the innocent and the helpless.

The evil force in *The Golem* is a clay robot, in *Nosferatu* a vampire, and in *Waxworks* a trio of figures who personify evil: Ivan the Terrible, Jack the Ripper, and a tyrannical Easterner.

In Lang's *Destiny, Dr. Mabuse, the Gambler,* and *Metropolis* the forces are more abstract and metaphorical. Lang advocates justice and equality for humankind through film plots in which individuals must strive to overcome spiritually devastating and chaotic forces: "Fate" itself is the antagonist of *Destiny;* scientific nihilism (in the form of a destructive doctor) is the challenge in *Dr. Mabuse, the Gambler;* and a futuristic master race provides the source of social disorder and chaos in *Metropolis.*

Lang's films, with their persistent theme of social upheaval, represented the most political of the silent German fantasies.

The Psychological Subjective-Camera Film

The most realistic of the three major types of post-World War I German films fell into a genre loosely characterized by an interest in the psychological lives of common, contemporary individuals. Because street locations were used prominently by directors as areas of action for many of these common-character films, this category has also been frequently referred to as the German "street" film.

Yet it would be incorrect to regard environmental detail in this group of films as having the same degree of importance as in the romantic spectacles or the stylized fantasies. Often more significant than decor and visual impact is the active, fluid camera which is employed to penetrate the inner lives of the characters being dissected on the screen. The skill with which German cinematographers of the era freed the camera from its stationary tripod and introduced moving shots and subjective points of view as integral story elements remains the genre's most remarkable stylistic quality.

F. W. Murnau's *The Last Laugh* (1924), E. A. Dupont's *Variety* (1925), and G. W. Pabst's *The Joyless Street* (1925) constitute a trio of works which together illustrate the thematic and stylistic interests of the German subjective filmmakers. In these films character emotions and relationships, and the psychology which undergirds the emotions, become the principal dramatic emphases within the narrative. Events, abstract ideas, and universal themes are secondary to penetrating and human views of simple characters.

The Last Laugh Murnau's *The Last Laugh* is based on what would appear to be a most banal and dramatically limiting turn of events. An aging hotel doorman is removed from his job and given another as the attendant in the hotel's basement lavatory. There the man dispenses hand towels to guests.

The film's dramatic exploration centers on the loss of respect and pride experienced by the doorman (Emil Jannings) because of what he regards as a demotion. When the hotel manager demands that the doorman's uniform be turned over to the establishment and in its place gives Jannings a simple white jacket to wear in the lavatory, the old man's imposing figure crumbles. Without his ornate doorman's uniform the old man has lost the one symbol by which he and his neighbors have measured his worth. No longer can he strut proudly through the streets to his home, wearing the elegant tasseled uniform which seems to pull him up as erect as a youthful army officer. Broken and dejected, the once proud man sneaks home in the shadows of the evening.

An improbable happy ending saves the doorman's deteriorating soul when a wealthy American dies in the lavatory, leaving the attendant his fortune. This epilogue, not unlike Chaplin's unexpected, happy ending for *The Gold Rush,* was Murnau's tongue-in-cheek manner of noting that such improbable reversals of fortune are possible at least in the fictive world of motion pictures, if rarely in life. It has also been suggested that the conclusion was intended as an ironic juxtaposition against the realities of the cruel and dehumanizing world depicted in the main body of the film. Again, comparisons with *The Gold Rush* are inevitable.

The theme of *The Last Laugh* was provocative in its implications for contemporary humankind. The old doorman is depicted as a helpless victim of social and economic forces which have increasingly eroded personal security and a sense of well-being. These social concepts are symbolized in the porter's inextricable identification with his uniform.

The old doorman (Emil Jannings) before and after the loss of his uniform in *The Last Laugh* (1924).

Function and self-esteem are shown as interchangeable and, according to historian Lotte Eisner, had particular meaning in Germany where the uniform was considered to be ". . . king, not to say God."

The dramatic treatment of these ideas by Murnau shows the individual's dependence on a uniform to be psychologically damning. Society, likewise, is depicted as having fallen into step with the same assumption, rejecting the doorman with open humiliation rather than offering support for his loss. The hotel manager, neighbors, and even his family refuse to pity the man.

This inhumane rejection can be viewed as double-edged since earlier, before his fall from glory, the doorman had arrogantly flaunted his position of "status" while in the presence of his own lower class of people. At either end of the success ladder, basic human values are shown to have been replaced by foolish pride, alienation, and indifference.

There seems to be little doubt about the social relevance of Carl Mayer's script. The old doorman, like each of the other characters in *The Last Laugh*, is without a name, suggesting that the film's story can be viewed as a microcosm for the modern world at large.

While it is possible to see the doorman as a modern-day prototype, the cinematic style used to delineate the character's emotions keeps the film intensely personal. Murnau's goal was to translate the doorman's internal state entirely into visual images, so that character psychology and sensations would be rendered without the assistance of supporting titles. Except for a title to explain the unexpected happy ending, the film is successful in avoiding verbal crutches.

THE SUBJECTIVE CAMERA With the aid of cinematographer Karl Freund, Murnau employs a variety of imaginative camera techniques to render visible the inner life of the old doorman. At times the camera lens acts as the eyes of the old man: the world outside the Atlantic Hotel, where he proudly performs his duties as doorman, appears magically larger than life—a veritable beehive of activity and an environment that seems hazily alive with sensory pleasures; appropriately angled shots denote the doorman's point of view as he opens a car door for an arriving guest or reaches to lift a heavy trunk from the top of a van; when the doorman disbelievingly receives notice from the hotel manager of his demotion, a close-up view of the letter begins to blur out of focus; the doorman's drunkenness at his daughter's wedding is conveyed by a floundering camera and distorted images that together suggest the physical movements of the character and his sensory perceptions of the milieu.

By panning, dollying, zooming, and tracking the camera, Murnau and Freund are able to transmit impressions of spatial relationships as well as subjective points of view. In the opening scene the camera captures the rhythm of life in the hotel with a dramatic dolly shot through the lobby. The sound of a trumpet blast traveling through space to reach the doorman's ear is suggested by a rapid camera movement out from the trumpet followed by a shot of Jannings reacting to the music.

Often the moving camera serves to focus attention on and emphasize the symbolic importance of objects. Following the sweep of the camera through the lobby during the opening scene, the dolly shot comes to rest with a lingering close-up of the hotel's revolving door, a possible metaphor for the vicious cycle that is *The Last Laugh's* principal theme. A rapid dolly in to the doorman's uniform after it is removed and hung in a hotel wardrobe defines the uniform's importance to the film's theme.

The achievements of *The Last Laugh* reside in Murnau's success in dramatizing through imaginative camera techniques a trivial event and yielding it up as human tragedy. By bringing the camera dynamically into interplay with the old doorman's world and his view of himself, the subject matter transcends its ostensibly banal nature and reveals both personal and universal truths.

Just as *The Cabinet of Dr. Caligari* had proved the motion picture's ability to convey psychological fantasy, *The Last Laugh* served as a model for the film that effectively renders subjective states. Murnau's revolutionary work significantly enhanced the progress of film art while also suggesting a whole new range of subject areas for the motion picture.

Variety E. A. Dupont's *Variety* (1925) was similarly impressive for its use of the camera to dramatize character emotions. The story, although more sensational than that examined by Murnau, again focuses on the psychological spine of a man whose pride has destroyed him.

THE PLOT As a final requirement for pardon, a prisoner (Emil Jannings) confesses to a warden why he committed a murder ten years before. The prisoner's motivations are shown in an extended flashback and form the principal segment of the film.

The flashback confession recounts a story of love and jealousy. Jannings portrays a trapeze artist, Stephan Huller, who performs with a winsome partner (Lya de Putti) in a small circus. Huller is totally devoted to the woman and is willing to act as her servant in return for her somewhat reluctant affection.

After the two performers are invited to work with a famous trapeze artist, Artinelli (Warwick Ward), a love affair evolves between the woman and the debonair new partner. On learning of the affair, Huller's jealousy intensifies to a point where he murders Artinelli. The woman accidentally falls to her death down a flight of stairs as she runs after the enraged Huller. On completing the confession to the warden, the prisoner is given his freedom.

STYLE *Variety* possesses a distinctly expressionistic visual style in the use of settings and lighting during the opening and concluding prison

A sensual celebration party follows the successful debut of the trio of trapeze performers in Dupont's *Variety* (1925).

scenes. The flashback narrative, however, has its inspiration in the subjective realism of *The Last Laugh*.

With Karl Freund again serving as cinematographer, Dupont liberally incorporates moving shots as a principal means of visualizing Huller's emotions. At times the camera not only translates the senses, it actually seems to become sensually provocative in its analysis of the ill-fated story of triangular love.

The opening shots of the carnival activities which are used to introduce the flashback confession also set the mood for Dupont's provocative treatment of locations and events. The camera appears to be no mere observer of the activities, but rather an active participant in the festive arena. Freund positions his camera on the seat of a Ferris wheel to capture the sensation of its revolutions above the carnival grounds. A bold close-up isolates a barker (in the foreground of the shot) blinking his eyes to the rhythm of a weight lifter's flexing muscle, only partially visible in the background. Sharp high- and low-angle shots convey the interaction between the spectators and the performing trapeze artists.

Variety, even more so than *The Last Laugh,* employs carefully selected detail to suggest sensory perceptions as well as to supply the film with an overtone of eroticism. During the celebration party given by Artinelli after his first performance with the Hullers, Freund photographs part of the scene through a small electric fan, its whirring blades making a futile attempt to cool the large table where the celebrants are partying and dancing. The fan symbolically hints at the rapidly accelerating passions that will drive the three principal characters to their destruction.

At times, frame composition is used to convey dramatic innuendo as in the famous shot of the three trapeze artists returning to their hotel rooms after the celebration party. Freund frames the camera so that it looks down the long, empty hotel corridor. As the three performers, walking hand in hand, come into close range of the camera lens, they weave drunkenly in and out of the shot. At one point Berthe-Marie and Artinelli are isolated together in view of the camera; the woman then backs out of view and her husband, Huller, stumbles into the frame. The use of frame space and character interaction within this uninterrupted shot presages the developing alliance between Artinelli and the woman as well as Huller's eventual "stand" against Artinelli.

After discovering that he has been cuckolded, Huller's interior rage is visualized through a variety of subjective shots. The camera spins in a series of 360° revolutions just before Huller destroys a marble table on which he has found drawings depicting his wife and Artinelli as lovers. As he observes Artinelli and Berthe-Marie interacting before their final performance, the two lovers become blurred figures in Huller's vision.

The tension in the final trapeze performance is abetted by Freund's dynamic camera work which again appears to place the viewer in the midst of the action. Movie audience expectations, however, go unmet and Huller's revenge comes not during the trapeze performance but afterward in the darkness of Artinelli's hotel room.

The skill with which Dupont, Freund, and Jannings expose the raw emotions at work in *Variety's* story brought the film great popular and critical success. Evelyn Gerstein, a critic for *The New Republic,* saw in Dupont's work "a tormented, vital beauty having nothing at all to do with the feebled, chastened myths that make the 'movies.'"

The Joyless Street   The last of Ufa's great silent subjective "street" films, *The Joyless Street* (1925), was the work of G. W. Pabst, a director who first came to prominence in Germany at a time when other prominent motion-picture artists were abandoning the country for careers in the United States and Great Britain.

The Bohemia-born Pabst directed his first German film, *The Treasure,* in 1923 and in this effort displayed a stylistic emphasis that was largely expressionistic. However, with *The Joyless Street* two years later Pabst produced a work that many regard as the most socially aware, least romantic of all the German "street" films.

On *The Joyless Street* in postwar Vienna the poor gather outside the unsympathetic butcher's shop, hoping for a small piece of meat.

THE PLOT *The Joyless Street* is set in postwar Vienna where a single dark street serves to expose the somber effects of war. The street's assortment of inhabitants collectively reveal the mental anguish, the physical devastation, and the social disparities of a large cosmopolitan city living in an inflated, indifferent postwar environment.

A butcher (Werner Krauss) acts as both provider to and partaker of the misfortunate inhabitants of the "joyless street." By day he alternately serves or denies meat to the starving; after hours he unblinkingly seeks the pleasure of women who have chosen prostitution rather than starvation.

Asta Nielsen gives a vivid performance as one of these prostitutes and Greta Garbo is the young daughter of a poverty-stricken professor struggling to resist the fate that has befallen Nielsen.

STYLE Through telling camera work and editing *The Joyless Street* creates an unforgettable experience. The film's acting is strikingly naturalistic and subdued with Pabst employing selected close-ups through matched cutting to project character gestures that will convey subtle meanings. Pabst's choice of angles and moving shots aids the film's psychological expressiveness: the impoverished professor is seen in long, wide-angled views, living in bleak alienation in his nearly barren quarters; by contrast, the camera lens is placed in a close, intense relationship with the corrupted dancers in Valeska Gert's nightclub/brothel; and the butcher's haughty dominance over the street's inhabitants is reinforced by a low-angled, up-looking camera position. When appropriate, Pabst tracks and dollies his camera through space to dramatize locations and character relationships. A stark contrast between lights and darks within the film's lighting scheme provides a sense of somberness and environmental chaos.

The Joyless Street succeeded in its social-psychological analysis of a contorted milieu. Pabst's ability to depict class differences and the personal-psychological impact of social disparity overcame the film's melodramatic murder and improbable happy ending in which Garbo is saved from corruption by a handsome American.

The Love of Jeanne Ney: Naturalistic Tendencies

The rich silent period of German cinema was capped by Pabst's *The Love of Jeanne Ney* (1927). In a story adapted for the screen from a novel by Ilya Ehrenburg, Pabst recounts a melodramatic tale of lust and international intrigue. Principals include a communist attaché, the daughter of a French consul, and a beautiful blind girl. The consul's daughter, Jeanne Ney, becomes emotionally caught up in an era of chaos that leads to rape, thievery, and murder. As in *The Joyless Street,* Pabst was again challenged by a story of personal torment and social upheaval.

Objects within settings often define both mood and characters in *The Love of Jeanne Ney.* In the film's opening sequence Pabst's camera sweeps about the sordid, cluttered room occupied by the villainous Khalibiev. The camera's surveillance, with its brief glimpses of erotic art, at once characterizes the nature of the man who resides there. Throughout the film numerous explorative panning and tracking shots discover the material expressiveness of key locations.

Pabst, who had proved in *The Joyless Street* his skill with matched cutting for dramatic emphasis, employs the technique even more liberally in *The Love of Jeanne Ney.* Editing for a change of angle or to present a longer or closer view of a scene is performed only on a character's movement. By cutting on the movement, the spectator's eyes are observing the action and are not distracted by the change of shot. Pabst is able to place emphasis precisely where it is desired without disrupting the viewer's concentration and, thus, enhances the film's naturalistic quality. One scene of little more than two minutes in length contains nearly forty cuts, yet, because of matched cutting, retains a naturalistic flow. Carefully arranged point-of-view shots, achieved by reverse-angle set-ups, also keep the spectator in a logical, nondisruptive relationship with the film's characters.

Pabst's style suggested a shift toward the naturalism that would characterize many of Germany's early important sound pictures.

The Love of Jeanne Ney (1927), a film rich in naturalistic detail.

By the time that Ufa had to face the challenge of sound most of its inspired artists had left Germany for work abroad. Ernst Lubitsch had departed years before for the United States as had the actress Pola Negri. Other directors and stars joined the parade to America in the twilight years of silent cinema: F. W. Murnau, E. A. Dupont, Paul Leni, Emil Jannings, Lya de Putti, Conrad Veidt. By 1930 cinematographer Karl Freund was beginning work on his first Hollywood picture. Erich Pommer had also been lured to the United States in 1926 but remained there less than two years (first at Paramount, then M-G-M) before returning to Ufa and the challenges of sound.

SUGGESTED READINGS

Bowser, Eileen. *The Films of Carl Dreyer*. New York: Museum of Modern Art, 1964.

Cowie, Peter. *Sweden I and II*. 2 vols. New York: Barnes, 1970.

Eisner, Lotte. *The Haunted Screen: Expressionism in the German Cinema and the Influence of Max Reinhardt*. Berkeley: University of California Press, 1969.

———. *Murnau*. Berkeley: University of California Press, 1973.

Hardy, Forsyth. *Scandinavian Film*. New York: Arno, 1972.

Idestam-Almquist, Bengt. *Classics of the Swedish Cinema: The Stiller and Sjöström Period*. Stockholm: Swedish Institute, 1952.

Kracauer, Sigfried. *From Caligari to Hitler: A Psychological History of the German Film*. Princeton: Princeton University Press, 1947.

Milne, Tom. *The Cinema of Carl Dreyer*. New York: Barnes, 1971.

Monaco, Paul. *Cinema and Society: France and Germany during the Twenties*. New York: Elsevier-North Holland, 1976.

FRANCE:
ECLECTICISM (1917–1930)

In the decade following World War I, French cinema, as in Germany, experienced an intense period of stylistic exploration. During this time France gave rise to: impressionism; the first serious experimental film movement; the epic, wide-screen style of Abel Gance; the dreamlike fantasies of Jean Cocteau; and the emerging poetic realism of Jean Renoir. The eclecticism and personal qualities of French film during the 1920s occurred after commercial cinema within the country had steadily declined in quality and appeal.

The popular French chase comedies, which enjoyed considerable success abroad as well as in France during the first two decades of

Napoléon (1927).

motion-picture production, generated little interest after World War I. In 1914 Max Linder, the great comedian-director who inspired Charles Chaplin's comic genius, left France for work in Hollywood, and although the silent star later returned to his native country, his departure signaled the demise of the lively Gallic chase comedy. Ferdinand Zecca, another renowned and prolific director of French chase farces, also moved to the United States in 1914, further diminishing France's comedy output.

The Film D'Art production company, with its theatrical adaptations, was considered by many French cinema enthusiasts to be less than inspiring in the quality of its output. Influential journalist and film critic Louis Delluc launched a campaign in 1917 in which he opposed the static, noncinematic Film D'Art adaptations while proselytizing for unique French films which would exploit the peculiar properties of the medium. Delluc also founded cinema clubs and the journal *Cinéa* with the hope of generating critical interest in film art.

FRENCH IMPRESSIONISM AFTER WORLD WAR I

Delluc, like most other French filmgoers, expressed great satisfaction in works imported from abroad. Most popular were the Swedish films of Stiller and Sjöström, the American westerns produced by Thomas Ince, Charles Chaplin's comedies, and D. W. Griffith's grand-scale spectacles. Delluc in his comparison of French theatrical film styles with those from abroad maintained: "The masters of the screen are those who speak to the masses."

Delluc's expression of affection for a livelier French cinema with French themes inspired a film movement that has been generally categorized as French impressionism. Filmmakers instrumental in the founding of this movement included Delluc, Marcel L'Herbier, Germaine Dulac, Jean Epstein, and Abel Gance. Gance, because of his later experimentation with epic themes and wide-screen formats, deserves his own special category, but his earlier work clearly distinguished him as an impressionist.

In *Fièvre* (*Fever*, 1921) Delluc developed the story of a murder in a Marseilles bar, using an actual flow of time. Spatial unity was interrupted only by occasional close-ups of principals in the bar. Through this restrained, unified approach to time and space, Delluc sought to suggest the ambient mood of the environment and, hence, the tenor of character relationships within it. In his direction of *La Femme de Nulle Part* (*The Woman from Nowhere*, 1922), Delluc also emphasized environmental mood while dealing with character emotions in a restrained manner.

The environmental mood of a Marseilles bar in Delluc's *Fièvre* (1921) helped to convey character relationships—a distinctive quality of French impressionism.

Marcel L'Herbier

The reserved, unsentimental style of Delluc's work gave his films an aura of intellectuality, a quality also characteristic of the early work of Marcel L'Herbier (1890–   ). In *Eldorado* (1921) L'Herbier, a former symbolist poet, utilized a variety of aesthetic techniques, including image distortion and soft-focus photography, to convey character thoughts and emotions within a story that included rape and suicide. Bold camera angles and superimpositions were also employed to suggest impressions of location and of thought. In several scenic shots L'Herbier attempted to capture with filters the impressionistic painting styles of Goya and Velazquez. Many of these same devices also appeared in L'Herbier's *Feu Mathias Pascal (The Late Matthew Pascal,* 1925).

Although L'Herbier often came under attack for the studied artificiality and intellectual approach in his films, his work probably best typified the French impressionist movement. Like Delluc, L'Herbier avoided direct treatment of low-life character actions that were often harsh and somber. Rather, emphasis was placed not on sordid details but on evocative locations and the moods within them. Both filmmakers eschewed melodrama for a studied pictorial style.

Germaine Dulac

Germaine Dulac (1882–1942), who before becoming a filmmaker in 1916 worked as a writer and agitator for women's causes, also created films that were principally visual in their interpretation. In *Les Soeurs Ennemies (The Enemy Sisters,* 1916), *Ames de Fous (Souls of the Untrue,* 1917), and *La Fête Espagnol (The Spanish Feast,* 1919) Dulac earned a reputation as a screen artist with special talents for translating emotions into visual imagery.

Dulac's impressionistic and later surrealistic style appeared most notably in two celebrated films: *La Souriante Madame Beudet (The Smiling Madame Beudet,* 1922) and *La Coquille et la Clergyman (The Seashell and the Clergyman,* 1927).

In *The Smiling Madame Beudet* Dulac visualizes the fantasies of a middle-aged woman who has been ignored by her husband. Both the woman's anger and her romantic fantasies are articulated as she plays a Debussy piece on the piano. Handsome men jump from magazine advertisements and cart away the indifferent husband. The woman's idealized fantasies are conveyed in slow motion; the husband's pompous, demanding ways are displayed in satirical vignettes that employ fast-motion photography.

The Seashell and the Clergyman was created from a scenario by Antonin Artaud and was a more abstract and serious psychological study than that undertaken in Dulac's earlier work. Artaud's scenario involved the terrified flight of a clergyman after the man encounters a woman's ghost. The flight is filled with chaotic situations and grotesque imagery that seem to reveal a subconscious, deeply disturbed emotional state.

The Seashell and the Clergyman contained surrealistic as well as impressionistic elements. Later work by Dulac in the 1920s was capriciously centered on the translation of musical pieces into visual symphonies, e.g., *Disque 927* and *Arabesque,* both made in 1929.

Jean Epstein

The silent films of Jean Epstein (1897–1953), a Polish-born transplant to France, were often praised for their subtle, economic style, quiet rhythm, and vivid impressionistic use of camera and environment. Following *Pasteur* (1922), a documentary tribute to the famous scientist, Epstein directed a screen version of Balzac's *L'Auberge Rouge (The Red Inn,* 1923) and *Le Coeur Fidèle (The True Heart,* 1923), a film similar in style to Delluc's *Fever.* Epstein had served as an assistant on films made by both Delluc and Abel Gance in the early 1920s.

The bored wife in Dulac's *The Smiling Madame Beudet* (1922).

The similarity between *The True Heart* and *Fever* resulted from their evocative use of backgrounds against which the melodramatic stories are set. In *The True Heart* two men battle for the same woman; in a scene at a wine festival Epstein characterizes the accelerating rivalry with a carousel which increases in speed behind the two men. Other background elements aid in exposing small-town village life.

In *La Belle Nivernaise (The Beauty from Nivernaise*, 1923), *Six et Demi-Onze (Six and a Half by Eleven*, 1927), and *La Chute de la Maisón Usher (The Fall of the House of Usher*, 1928) Epstein continued to exploit impressionistic devices and to attempt to create scenic atmospheres that would properly frame his stories. He was particularly successful in achieving a mystical aura for *The Fall of the House of Usher*. Also prominent in this film was one of Epstein's favored impressionistic techniques: slow motion, a device used to intensify character action and mood.

When Epstein returned to documentary filmmaking with *Finis Terrae (World's End)* in 1929, he retained his impressionistic style. The film was photographed on the island of Bannec off the coast of Brittany and focused on the interaction of four fishermen. Although the documentary study contains little narrative content, an injury to the hand of one of the fishermen provides a central incident that gives rise to emotional tensions.

World's End captures the psychology of the island fishermen through a model use of camera, pace, and special effects. Slow motion is effective in communicating the internal meditation of one of the fishermen as he sits by the water's edge eating a piece of bread. As the man chews his food, the slow motion appears to penetrate his thoughts and to project a deeply felt sense of melancholy.

Abel Gance.

Abel Gance

Abel Gance (1889–1981) stands prominently among France's great silent film directors. Often described as the equal of D. W. Griffith because of his pioneering efforts in screen spectacle, Gance enjoyed a long distinguished career as a director whose range of film styles cannot be neatly categorized. In the various periods of his career, he created a number of epic pictures, often using experimental techniques, while also making films which fell clearly into the school of French impressionism.

Gance's diversity in cinematic expression was nurtured by a deep interest in literature and theater as well as a passionate regard for the artistic potential of moving pictures. Gance was born into a bourgeois family (the son of a Paris physician) in 1889, and as a child immersed himself in the study of poetry, literature, and drama.

This cultural activity led to a brief career as an actor, beginning in 1907 when he joined the Theatre du Parc in Brussels, Belgium. The same year he wrote his first screenplay, *Mireille,* and with this project began to shift his dramatic interests to the motion picture. Between 1909 and 1911 Gance acted in and wrote scripts for numerous short films that were produced in Paris.

Impressionism Gance's directing career began with *La Digue ou pour Sauver la Hollande (The Dike or to Save Holland,* 1911), a period film for which he also wrote the script. Several other unmemorable projects followed; then in 1914 under assignment to the Film d'Art company Gance created an uproar with *La Folie du Docteur Tube (The Folly of Dr. Tube)*. This was a comedy exercise with serious overtones (a character is under the effects of hallucinatory drugs). Gance employed unusual image juxtapositions and experimental camera devices, including lens and mirror distortions, to enhance the film's satirical and subjective qualities. These unusual visual effects predated the later impressionistic styles of Delluc, Dulac, and Epstein. The staid Film d'Art company reacted with dismay at the visual experimentation and briefly refused to release the film.

Gance's later work in *La Roue (The Wheel,* 1922) also evinced an impressionistic style as well as an innovative use of accelerated montage which would eventually be associated with films from Russia and with the experimental work of France's rhythmically inspired cinema purists.

In *The Wheel* a character's fatal fall contains a rapid juxtaposition of shots as short as one, three, and six frames in length. Six frames in silent cinema constituted a shot length of one-third of a second. The intention was to give an impression, psychologically and visually, of the character's perceptions of the moment before his death.

Gance's interest in the impressionistic opportunities of camera optics and his elevation of pure visual images to subjective expressiveness were those qualities which led to his association with Delluc's cinematic vision and with French impressionism.

Epics The first of Gance's important epics was *J'accuse! (I Accuse!,* 1919, later remade in 1937), a film born from the director's experiences as a military cinematographer during World War I. This grand-scale, anti-war film employed a variety of trick effects including fast motion, superimpositions, and oblique camera angles; the film also made use of metaphorical image juxtapositions and documentary footage taken by Gance during a battle at St. Mihiel.

It was *I Accuse!* which resulted in Gance's being labeled the "Griffith of Europe," and when in 1921 the film had its American premiere at the Ritz-Carlton in New York, both Gance and D. W. Griffith attended the presentation. Griffith expressed great admiration for the epic film.

Napoléon Gance's experimentation with new visual effects continued in his most celebrated film, *Napoléon,* first released in 1927, rereleased in a sound version in 1934, revived for international distribution in 1971, and again in 1981 by Francis Ford Coppola (with a new score by Carmine Coppola).

Napoléon required five years to complete because of its epic scope (seventeen reels, four hours and thirty-five minutes) and its technical complexity. Originally intended as a six-part study of Napoleon's life, the story was shortened to a treatment of Bonaparte's youth, his activities during the revolution, and the Italian campaign.

A unified triptych projection in Gance's *Napoléon* (1927).

Napoléon's story attracted less attention than Gance's technical virtuosity. Incorporated into the film are four sequences which were projected on to three separate screens that curved around the spectators. This triptych effect was labeled Polyvision and consisted of a center screen bordered by two side screens. The process, requiring three cameras with synchronized motors, had been developed for Gance by André Debrie and allowed the director to film and later display massive crowd scenes for a peripheral impact similar to that introduced in the Cinerama devices of 1952. At other times Gance projected multiimages for metaphorical or contrasting effect.

A variety of other visual and aural effects added to *Napoléon's* remarkable creativity. The imaginative use of a participatory camera often exceeds that of the German subjectivists. At one point the camera appears to have been fired from a cannon; at another the camera tracks the movement of a snowball through the air; a rocking camera movement metaphorically depicts the emotional tenor of a heated debate. To further visualize the volatile nature of the meeting, a superimposed shot of a raging storm appears over the debate scene.

At the conclusion of *Napoléon,* the left screen turned red, the right blue, while the large central screen remained white. Over this tricolor effect, spreading 100 feet across all three screens, Gance projected a huge eagle. This patriotic gesture created a sensation for those who attended the film's premiere at the Paris Opéra on April 7, 1927 (among them Charles de Gaulle).

Metro-Goldwyn-Mayer purchased the American distribution rights to *Napoléon* but reduced the film to what was considered a more tolerable eight-reel version. Also, rather than imposing expensive technical demands on exhibitors, the triptych sequences were rephotographed so that the three images appeared in a single standard frame. Much of the effect of Gance's original work was lost in these alterations.

In 1934 Gance reassembled members of *Napoléon's* cast for voice dubbing and additional dialogue filming. Two years later after extensive reediting, the film was rereleased, becoming the first motion picture to be accompanied by a stereophonic sound track. Gone, however, were the three-screen sequences and the film's original pace. By converting to sound, the older scenes had to be projected at twenty-four frames per second rather than at their photographed speed of sixteen frames per second. The result was a distracting, speeded flow of the action.

In 1971 after Gance's own supervision of the project, this film spectacle was released in still another version and retitled *Bonaparte and the Revolution*. A revival of interest in Gance's pioneering screen work resulted in Coppola's decision in 1981 to reconstruct *Napoléon* for showings of the epic as it was originally conceived.

THE AVANT-GARDE

At the same time that the French impressionists were devising new visual styles and techniques, another film movement surfaced in France. This second development, commonly called the film avant-garde, occurred simultaneously with impressionism, although by 1925 the latter movement was in a decline and the work of the avant-garde filmmakers was on the upswing.

In many ways the theoretical interests and practices of the impressionists and avant-garde experimentalists overlap. Both sought to emphasize with greater purity the visual expressiveness of the motion picture. The impressionists, however, for the most part treated dramatic subject matter while the avant-garde group openly vowed to suppress narrative in their visual experiments.

Much of the nonnarrative experimentation fell into one of two broad categories: either that of surrealism or *cinéma pur,* although it must be noted that the various subcategories of the movement do not permit precise classification. The people who made up the avant-garde group were intellectuals and artists from diverse backgrounds who saw a number of exploratory possibilities in the film medium. Some recognized in film an opportunity to attack social and artistic convention, while others wanted simply to celebrate the medium's possibilities for rhythmic expression. Frequently the avant-garde parodied the film medium itself, while the surrealists often were dead serious in their attempts to use film resources for examining the human psyche.

Surrealism

The most psychological of the French avant-garde filmmakers were the surrealists. As stated by surrealism's principal spokesman, André Breton, the surrealist movement embraced a "belief in the higher reality of certain hitherto neglected forms of association, in the omnipotence of the dream, in the disinterested play of thought."

Much of the inspiration for surrealism came from the Dadaist movement, which originated in Zurich about 1916. Surrealism, like Dada, appeared as a reaction against artistic convention and bourgeois expectations. A manifesto from the Paris-based surrealists in 1925 stated: "Surrealism . . . is a means of total liberation of the mind and of everything resembling it. We are determined to create a revolution."

Because of their reactionary stance against convention, many surrealist filmmakers openly mocked traditional art, sexual morality, politics, and religion.

To achieve their radical goals, the chance arrangement of visual imagery became the principal process of expression. In their poetry, painting, and films, the surrealists pounced on a variety of material phenomena ("object matter") and collected these phenomena together in disparate, nonsensical ways in order to effect subjective and dreamlike meanings.

Man Ray The poet-filmmaker Man Ray (1890–1977), who became one of the leading practitioners of surrealism and Dadaism in the 1920s, employed the illogical materialism common to surrealistic expression in the opening verse of his poem *La Liberté ou L'Amour*

It's in a clean cafe with unpolished mirrors
That we treated humanity like a puppet theater
Past people, future people, canceled visions
And aspects of the word in holy trinity.

The concrete images in this verse have been freed of any clear associations. Their organization prevents objective interpretation, and if at all communicative, the collage of imagery has a dreamlike feel in its absurd flow.

Surrealist filmmakers, like the surrealist poets, also arranged material images in a random and ambiguous manner so that content would carry no preordered meaning. Man Ray's films *Retour à la Raison* (1923), *Emak Bakia* (1927), and *L'Etoile de Mer* (1928), and Luis Buñuel-Salvador Dali's *Un Chien Andalou* (1928) provided classic illustration of the Dadaist and surrealist impulses within the motion picture.

Retour à la Raison (Return to Reason) was conceived as a joke on the audience for whom it was intended. It was made in a single evening for presentation at a Dadaist gathering in Paris. The five-minute film, an exercise in total absurdity, was essentially an out-of-camera creation ("noncamera" film). Ray simply placed objects and fragments of objects found in his living quarters on raw film stock and exposed them to the light for random visual effects.

This process imitated that used earlier by Ray to produce his Dadaist-inspired "Rayographs." In 1921 he had begun his experimentation with noncamera photography by placing objects on photosensitive paper and then exposing the assortment of paraphernalia directly to the

Collected paraphernalia appear in Man Ray's surrealistic *L'Etoile de Mer* (1928), most prominently a starfish.

light. When processed in the darkroom, the shapes of the various objects appeared on the photographic paper as patterns of light against a dark background.

Retour à la Raison was essentially a series of Rayograph snippets on motion-picture stock, fortuitously strung together. The joke on the audience came through the film's contradictory title which in its literal interpretation suggested a movement back to reason and order in artistic expression. Ray's film had no reference to rationality whatsoever.

In *Emak Bakia* and *L'Etoile de Mer (Starfish)* Ray employed photographed imagery that bridged both Dadaism and surrealism. Randomly arranged shots of object matter (flowers, light beams, a car radiator, a huge eye) introduced *Emak Bakia* (1927). The flow of abstract imagery, with its numerous references to an automobile, hinted at a surreal, dreamlike journey. Numerous trick effects, including shot repetitions and superimpositions, reinforced *Emak Bakia's* dreamlike qualities.

L'Etoile de Mer (1928) brought Ray more fully into the then-fashionable area of surrealism for psychological exploration. This exercise was inspired by a Robert Desnos love poem, and while the film's images are randomly abstract, their flow suggests sexual and emotional undercurrents. Two lovers are seen through distorting lenses, filters,

An assortment of disparate imagery prevails throughout *Un Chien Andalou* (1928).

and prisms; a repeated shot of a nude woman on a bed is intercut among various objects (a starfish, most prominently).

Un Chien Andalou The film which remains the most famous work of the French surrealist movement is *Un Chien Andalou* (1928). Luis Buñuel (1900–   ) and Salvador Dali (1904–   ), who were Spaniards living and working in Paris, conceived the film as a satirical commentary on avant-garde cinema—in particular as an attack on surrealist films pretentiously imbedded in Freudian psychology. The film's violent, sometimes repulsive, imagery was designed to shock and horrify those filmmakers who had symbolically and cautiously treated the subconscious.

In their own satirical treatment of psychic subject matter within *Un Chien Andalou*, Buñuel and Dali held nothing back. They sought to be as outrageous as possible within a surrealistic mode, intentionally striving to both repel and attract.

Un Chien Andalou succeeded in its efforts as a satire but also contained symbolic associations that linked its string of images to psychic conflict between personal and conventional morality. Consequently, Buñuel and Dali's work was declared a psychologically provocative masterpiece by the people whom the startling film intended to insult.

The tensions which exist between a man (a cyclist) and a bourgeois woman who appear throughout *Un Chien Andalou* are suggestively sexual in origin. The man bleeds at the mouth with passion after fondling the woman; ants crawl from a hole in the man's palm, a symbolic image of Christian and sexual penalty; a shot of a cocktail shaker in motion precedes the startled close-up of the man as he lies on a bed.

Because of *Un Chien Andalou's* continuity, sexual provocation in one instance appears to have been triggered by a violent act. The couple have watched from their window with combined horror and delight as a woman in the street below pokes with a stick at an amputated hand. When the woman is struck by a passing automobile (a spoof of Pudovkin-inspired editing?), the cyclist becomes excited and begins to pursue his female companion around the room.

The irrational assortment of dreamlike images in *Un Chien Andalou* also conveys impressions of psychic guilt. References to religion, childhood, and death appear subconsciously related to the film's ambiguous sexual tensions. After the cyclist's sexual attack on his female companion, the man pulls two grand pianos into the center of the room. Each piano holds a dead donkey that oozes blood; attached by rope to the pianos are two priests.

Free use of time and space in *Un Chien Andalou* allows a return to a point in the man's life "sixteen years before." In slow motion, the man is seen standing in a submissive position as though being punished by another man (a "stranger") who is in the room with him. A close-up of a child's school desk appears; the stranger takes books from the desk, and thrusts them at the cowering man. The books become revolvers as the stranger turns to walk away, and, in the manner of a western film, the man fires the two guns. In extreme slow motion the wounded stranger falls forward and out of the frame; a matched cut shows the fall continuing in an open meadow where the dying man grasps at the back of a nude woman sitting alone in the open field. A group of pallbearers arrive to lead the dead man's funeral procession.

The meaning of these scenes and events are inexplicit, but their ordering supplies *Un Chien Andalou* with a strong sense of continuity which enhances the opportunities for psychological interpretation. Despite Buñuel's claim that "Nothing in this film symbolizes anything," reactions to the work have suggested that for decades viewers have found their own logic in the film. And even though the film may have lost some of its shock value and satirical bite, the eye-slitting scene at the beginning never fails to jolt. *Un Chien Andalou* remains a startling experience.

L'Age d'Or Capping the surrealist movement in France was Buñuel's *L'Age d'Or,* a film made in 1930 with limited assistance from Salvador Dali in the preparation of the scenario. The work, slightly more than an hour in length, is important for several reasons: its surrealistic structure, its continuation and further development of thematic ideas only hinted at in *Un Chien Andalou,* and its critical place in the early formative years of Buñuel's long, distinguished film career.

L'_Age d'Or_ (1930). The Man in a fit of fury takes up a wooden plough from the corner of a bedroom—one of the many surrealistic juxtapositions within Buñuel's film.

L'Age d'Or, through its assortment of surrealistic vignettes, projects a theme that has been consistently associated with Buñuel, that of human desire attempting to manifest itself in the face of personal, political, and religious repression. Like much of Buñuel's later work, the film boldly attacks organized religion, political institutions, the bourgeoisie, and conventional morality.

The film's position was strongly anarchistic, and its release in Paris resulted in riots and an eventual banning of what its opponents described as a "subversive" work. André Breton, by contrast, called it "the only authentically Surrealist film ever made."

The dramatic vignettes in _L'Age d'Or_ focus on two lovers who struggle against numerous obstacles while attempting to satisfy their sexual passions. Shots of deadly scorpions, Majorcan thieves, and a violently angry crowd, are part of the film's grotesque images. Scenes depict the founding of "Imperial Rome," a bourgeois party that is ridiculously and bitterly ritualistic, and a 120-day orgy in a medieval castle. These bizarre juxtapositions convey an angered view of forces which Buñuel felt curtailed honest self-expression.

L'Age d'Or represented an important event in Buñuel's growth as a film director, and a culminating point for surrealism.

Cinèma Pur

Surrealism by no means dominated the film avant-garde in France during the 1920s. Within the movement there was a group of filmmakers who were advocates of "pure cinema," artists who stated that they were impelled by a desire to return the film medium to its elemental origins. André Maurois defined the pure cinema approach as one where the film "would be composed of pictures arranged according to rhythm, without any intrigue."

Serving as an inspiration to the French cinema purists was the German filmmaker Hans Richter whose *Rhythmus 21* (1921) animated, through stop-action photography, geometric paper squares of various shapes and tones. In Paris René Clair and Fernand Léger began to evince in their work a similar interest in the cadence of objects and images within a film.

Clair The early important works of René Clair (1898–1981) were characterized by a comic zaniness. *Paris Qui Dort (The Crazy Ray,* 1923) and *Entr'acte (Intermission,* 1924) were absurd visual exercises which utilized extensively the trick possibilities of the motion picture. In *The Crazy Ray* a scientist has frozen all activity in Paris except that among a group of people atop the Eiffel Tower. Eventually activities are allowed to resume, but at varied speeds. The trick devices of speeded motion, slow motion, and freeze-frame images are used with delightful visual and rhythmic effect. At the same time they provide moments of social commentary in their fleeting views of Parisian life.

Entr'acte was made by Clair for use during the intermission of a ballet performance; hence its title. This film most closely resembles a Mack Sennett car chase with the car in this instance being a runaway hearse. Events, however, provide no particular narrative unity: two men on a rooftop are engaged in a game of chess; a ballerina (bearded) bounces up and down in the frame; a camel pulls the hearse; the corpse is a magician who causes everyone in the film to disappear.

Entr'acte offered a deliberate mockery of reality, presented in free form. Its form and devices shifted the medium back toward its elemental beginnings, utilizing trick effects associated with Méliès and absurd action common to Keystone comedy and France's own early chase master, Ferdinand Zecca. This film has retained a special significance among avant-garde works because of the prominent artists who appeared in the caper: Man Ray, Marcel Duchamp, and the composer Erik Satie, among others. *Entr'acte's* scenario was written by the Dadaist, Francis Picabia.

Léger Fernand Léger's *Ballet Mécanique* (1924) represents, perhaps as well as any other avant-garde motion picture of the time, the purest

The bearded ballerina in René Clair's *Entr'acte* (1924).

example of abstract expression. Léger, a cubist painter, engaged the American cinematographer Dudley Murphy to assist him in producing a "mechanical ballet" on celluloid. The two chose an assortment of objects (among them many household items) and characters, and utilizing expressive lighting, placed the people and objects in nonassociative rhythms on the screen. Léger's photographed images constituted "art in motion" with the principal values of the film residing in its shapes and its rhythmic flow rather than in any intended communication.

The pure cinema movement drew a whole corps of French film-makers who created works with rhythmic emphases: Henri Chomette's *Cinq Minutes de Cinéma Pur (Five Minutes of Pure Cinema*, 1925); Germaine Dulac's *Disque 927, Thème et Variations (Theme and Variations)*, and *Arabèsque* (1927–1930); Eugene Deslaw's *La Marche des Machines (The March of Machines*, 1928); and Alberto Cavalcanti's *Rien que les Heures (Nothing but the Hours*, 1926).

JEAN COCTEAU AND JEAN RENOIR

The later, important sound work of Jean Renoir (1894–1979) and Jean Cocteau (1889–1963) will be discussed in separate analyses later in this historical chronicle. Their early films, however, influenced the emerging styles of French film in the 1920s and justify notation at this point. Both filmmakers were peripherally associated with the avant-garde movement, while each also developed individualistic approaches to the film narrative which set them apart from other French directors of the silent era.

Cocteau

Jean Cocteau's career in cinema extended over a thirty-year period during which time this highly visible French intellectual-artist also actively expressed himself as a librettist, painter, poet, actor, playwright, and novelist. His films, personal and literary, were shaped by a style that delightfully incorporated myth and fantasy into their narratives. He wrote the scenarios for all of his motion pictures and never hesitated in filling the scripts with his own views of the world. Cocteau admitted to enjoying the opportunity of using the cinema for its "confessional" possibilities.

After studying at the Lycée Condorcet, Cocteau joined with Erik Satie in 1917 as a writer for Satie's ballet *Parade*. During the 1920s, the fascination with music continued while he also began to write for the stage. In this phase of his career, Cocteau produced libretti for Arthur Honegger's opera *Antigone* and Igor Stravinsky's *Oedipus Rex;* his early stage pieces included *Antigone* (1922) and *Orphée* (1924).

Cocteau's early involvement with musical and theatrical projects, most of which had been adapted from the classics and myth, left a lasting influence on his original work as a film writer and director.

Le Sang d'un Poète (The Blood of a Poet, 1930), Cocteau's first film, employed numerous cinematic devices and surrealistic elements common to the methods of the French avant-garde. By utilizing a succession of visual transformations, Cocteau creates a combined surrealistic and impressionistic experience that is intended to reveal the mind of a poet.

The mysterious manner in which the poet's mind alters reality in the creative process served as the rationale for the film's experimental qualities. Statues spring to life, drawings animate themselves, humans are transformed into objects. The camera serves as the mind's-eye with the mind itself allegorically represented by the Hôtel des Folies. Within the hotel, a series of dramatic vignettes, hinting at life's mysteries and traumas, confront the poet.

The allegory contained within this complex film owed much to the Orpheus myth but more to Cocteau's own aesthetic and philosophical views of the personal role and function of the "poet" (artist). The poet's odyssey, rendered in free-flowing, dreamlike images and trick effects, evokes a sense of the contradictions faced by the individual who is committed to a life of artistic enterprise. This concern with the nature of the poetic imagination remained an obsession with Cocteau throughout his film career.

Cocteau's "poet" within the Hotel des Folies, *The Blood of a Poet* (1930).

Renoir

Poetic realism has been the most common label applied to Jean Renoir's directorial style, and properly so. This great French director spent much of his long career as a filmmaker attempting to fuse authentic images with the traditions of French realism. Renoir admitted that the authenticity for which he strove had been inspired by the silent films of Erich von Stroheim (*Foolish Wives* in particular).

While poetic realism is a suitable term for describing Renoir's films made during the 1930s, the director's earlier period exhibits more varied approaches to film direction. In *Nana* (1926) Renoir brought Emile Zola's novel about an embittered prostitute to the screen with a strong dose of subjective French impressionism. The treatment contained many abstract elements in its most cinematic parts while at other times appearing intentionally theatrical in conception. Renoir reduced the number of characters to three and concentrated heavily on the performance of Catherine Hessling in the title role.

For his adaptation of Hans Christian Andersen's *Le Petite Marchande d'Allumettes (The Little Match Girl,* 1928), Renoir filmed the story of a young match seller's death entirely within a theater (in an attic loft of the Vieux Colombier). For the most part, the film evolves as an exercise in fantasy, a visualization of the girl's imaginings as she lies dying in the snow on a city street. Realism and fantasy are combined in such a way that the two elements ambiguously overlap. The young girl (Catherine Hessling) at times resembles a child, at others a woman. These liberties taken in the treatment of the girl's progression toward death were responsible for the film's inevitable comparison with the interests and techniques of the avant-garde.

In *The Little Match Girl* and in the next two films that followed, *Tire-au-Flanc (The Sad Sack,* 1928) and *Le Tournoi dans la Cité (The Tournament in the City,* 1929), Renoir was hampered by limited funds. This fact showed in the imperfect technical effects and poor production values that characterized the three efforts.

For Renoir, these early films, despite their technical limitations and stylistic uncertainties, provided opportunities for cinematic exploration essential to the director's maturity. By necessity, Renoir concentrated his attention on the actor, and on the use of the camera lens and film stock to enhance atmosphere within scenes. Strong acting and simple, expressive images would become trademarks of his many great sound motion pictures.

The period of intellectual and artistic upheaval in France that produced impressionism, surrealism, *cinéma pur,* and fantasy ended almost simultaneously with the arrival of sound and the Depression that had come to France by 1930. Many of the avant-garde filmmakers, who had been inspired by free expression in the silent film, felt uncomfortable with the technology of sound and returned to less complicated, less expensive expression within the traditional arts. René Clair, Luis Buñuel, Abel Gance, Jean Renoir, and Jean Cocteau adapted their styles to feature-length filmmaking and assumed important roles in France's commercial cinema.

The demise of the avant-garde, however, did not destroy the impact of cinematic concepts born during this period of experimentation. Every generation of experimental filmmakers since has found inspiration in the essentially visual expression of the first avant-garde. The American underground, Norman McLaren and the Canadian Film Board's experimentalists, expanded-cinema advocates, and literally thousands of student filmmakers have perpetuated the imagistic, rhythmic traditions that began in France during the 1920s.

SUGGESTED READINGS

Armes, Roy. *French Film.* New York: Dutton, 1970.

Braudy, Leo. *Jean Renoir: The World of His Films.* Garden City, N.Y.: Doubleday, 1972.

Curtis, David. *Experimental Cinema.* New York: Universe Books, 1971.

Gilson, Réné. *Jean Cocteau.* New York: Crown, 1964.

Kyrou, Ado. *Luis Buñuel.* New York: Simon & Schuster, 1963.

Matthews, J. H. *Surrealism and Film.* Ann Arbor: The University of Michigan Press, 1971.

Monaco, Paul. *Cinema and Society: France and Germany during the Twenties.* New York: Elsevier-North Holland, 1976.

Sadoul, Georges. *French Film.* New York: Arno, 1972.

Welsh, James M., and Steven P. Kramer. *Abel Gance.* Boston: Twayne, 1978.

RUSSIA:
NATIONAL CAUSES AND MONTAGE
(1917–1930)

. . . Of all the arts the most important for Russia is, to my mind, that of the cinema.

Lenin, 1919

So, montage is conflict.

S. M. Eisenstein (Jay Leyda, translator).

A strong case can be built for the argument that innovation in cinematic style has most noticeably occurred during periods of social, political, and intellectual upheaval. An antidotal reaction to the hangover of World War I and the impending rise of Nazi power in Germany together stimulated new creativity at the centralized Ufa studios, resulting in film styles that were unforgettably somber in theme and psychological in their visual expressiveness. France, a cultural-intellectual center where international artists congre-

October.

gated during the 1920s, nurtured personal expression and cynicism in the motion picture to an extent uncommon to any period before or after.

In Russia following the 1917 revolution a fledgling motion-picture industry was nationalized by Lenin as a means of supporting the struggling new state. The task of the filmmaker under Lenin's commission (enacted in 1919) centered on efforts to communicate to the country's masses following a time of immense conflict; new methods were explored for recapturing the past out of which the conflict had been born and for forcefully suggesting the course of the future. Didacticism, achieved through a reexamination of history, became the principal challenge of the major Russian filmmakers of the 1920s and 1930s: Sergei Eisenstein, Vsevolod Pudovkin, and Alexander Dovzhenko.

The dedication of these untested filmmakers in serving the state's needs resulted in energetic and innovative approaches to editing and image composition. Led by two important theorists, Dziga Vertov and Lev Kuleshov, the Eisenstein-Pudovkin-Dovzhenko trio gave additional meaning to the concept of montage, while impressing the world with new social possibilities for the motion-picture medium.

THEATRICAL REVOLT

The years immediately following the revolution brought about a reevaluation of the methods and functions of artistic expression in Russia. Efforts to place the arts under state control resulted in many new ideas on how artistic endeavor might best serve and reinterpret the new order. One response by artists and theorists was an effort to disassociate the arts altogether from the methods and values of the past. Bold experimentation began in all the media.

A revolt occurred almost immediately in Russia's theatrical circles that signaled an abrupt change in dramatic expression which would eventually carry over to the motion picture. For two decades prior to the revolution Constantin Stanislavski's Moscow Art Theater had generated new excitement in the dramatic arts with successful methods of achieving realism in the stage setting and in acting. Generously supported by the bourgeoisie, the Moscow Art Theater (MAT) became a model for theatrical naturalism, particularly in interpreting the plays of Anton Chekhov. "Fidelity to life" was among Stanislavski's principal goals as he sought to create stage experiences which would engage the audience and the actor in as empathetic and "truthful" a relationship as possible.

Revolutionary theater producers after 1917 sprang up in reaction to both the bourgeois influence at the MAT and its traditional values. New, abrupt, and less narcotizing forms of dramatic expression were deemed necessary to serve the social needs of the masses. Among the men in the revolt against Russian naturalism were Eugene V. Vakhtangov and Vsevolod Meyerhold.

Eugene Vakhtangov

Eugene Vakhtangov (1883–1922) began as a pupil and protégé of Stanislavski. At the Moscow Art Theater he headed his own company from 1914 until 1920 when he founded the Third Studio, a theater devoted to more varied and progressive approaches than those which dominated the MAT. Vakhtangov did not move entirely away from naturalism, but in the new theater, which later bore his name, there developed a strong interest in merging the humanist's concern for realism with the formalist's regard for art-for-art's-sake. Actors were encouraged to find the "truth" of their characters but at the same time to maintain a detached view of their roles. Out of these ideas came new theater forms that often carried the grotesque to an extreme.

Vsevolod Meyerhold

Following the revolution, Vsevolod Meyerhold (1874–1942) became the first theater producer to join the new government as an artist in service to the state. In 1920 he was appointed head of the Theater Section and set about the task of reshaping Russian theater to fit bolshevist theories.

Meyerhold's work in the theater gave rise to new considerations of the actor's contribution to dramatic expression and to new theories on the relationship of the audience to the production. Within Meyerhold's "biomechanical" system of acting, the stage performer was viewed as an element equal to but no greater than any other element in the production. The refined ensemble playing that had been a major achievement at the MAT was denied.

Meyerhold desired that the audience be conscious at all times of the theatrical performance. To further this goal constructivist sets, depictive of the machine age, often formed the background for productions. Backstage walls frequently remained exposed to the audience, lights were left on in the theater auditorium, and for occasional performances actors wore the worker's overalls rather than illusory costumes.

THE CINEMA IS NATIONALIZED

Meyerhold's mechanical, proletarian attitude toward theater would have its greatest influence, interestingly, on the motion picture. However socially useful theater might be for the needs of the bolshevist regime, the stage could never hope to be as widely accessible as the more transportable motion picture. Government officials recognized this fact when they nationalized the almost nonexistent film industry in 1919;

Lenin in an effort to spur on young filmmakers offered moral support at the time by declaring that "of all the arts the most important for Russia is, to my mind, that of the cinema."

Growth of film production, however, was slow—hampered by a shortage of trained filmmakers and of decent production equipment. The departure of the three major French production companies (Pathé, Lumière, and Gaumont), which had dominated filmmaking in Russia's prerevolutionary years, depleted the country of nearly all its motion-picture resources. Furthermore, production quality prior to the revolution had done little to draw enterprising young artists into the industry. Lavish literary adaptations, rendered in a "canned theater," Film d'Art style, had typified early production.

Significantly, these factors resulted in a five-year incubation period during which theory led practice. The development of efficient methods of film expression, suitable for mass impact, evolved gradually from the ruminations of Dziga Vertov and Lev Kuleshov, leading to the technical expertise of Eisenstein, Pudovkin, and Dovzhenko.

In 1925 Eisenstein, a product of Meyerhold's biomechanical theater school, almost singlehandedly drew the world's attention to Russia and a new era of development in cinematic technique. The movement toward this historic moment offers a fascinating account of film exploration.

DZIGA VERTOV: CINEMA-TRUTH

Dziga Vertov (1896–1954) stimulated the first interest in an invigorating new approach to cinema in Russia. In 1920 Vertov produced *The Anniversary of the Revolution,* a feature-length compilation film composed of newsreel footage taken of the Red and White armies on the country's battlefronts. The film was assembled as a documentary statement in support of the recent revolution.

The young Vertov, who was only 24 years old at the time, became excited by the possibilities of utilizing factual film for instructive purposes. Following *The Anniversary of the Revolution,* he assumed for himself the task of presenting to Soviet film audiences detailed, accurate reports on life within the new state.

To achieve this goal, the documentarist conceived the concept of *Kino-Pravda* ("cinema-truth") for use in the preparation of newsreels. Newsreels produced by the official Soviet news-gathering agency, Kino-nedelia, would employ a candid camera approach in filming with the intention, according to Vertov's own words, of "making the invisible visible, the obscure clear, the hidden obvious, the disguised exposed."

For the production of the monthly *Kino-Pravda* newsreels, begun in 1922, Vertov's cinematographers often used hidden cameras to capture life in intimate detail and filmed events from moving vehicles and other unusual perspectives. Eventually special effects such as double-exposure shots and speeded action were added to filming techniques as additional means of exposing reality.

Arrangement of the recorded images in Vertov's work drew heavily on dialectical editing approaches as various pieces of documentary film were juxtaposed to produce socially useful meanings. These juxtapositions often contrasted the reality of the past with present conditions, the reprehensible with the ideal, old politics against new. Vintage films were utilized along with newly recorded footage to produce statements of an inspirational nature.

Vertov's documentary experiments resulted in a variety of film discourses that included the *Kino-Pravda* newsreels (1922–1925), *Stride, Soviet!* (1926), and the widely seen and studied *The Man with a Movie Camera* (1929).

Stride, Soviet!, as its title suggests, offered a rousing piece of Soviet propaganda through a collection of contrasting images and a liberal use of title inserts.

The Man with a Movie Camera

The Man with a Movie Camera represents a culminating exercise in applied Vertovian theories. The film is a dynamic study of urban life in a large postrevolution Russian city, designed to allow the viewer to see and experience events within the city which otherwise might go unnoticed. Thematically the film advocates an industrial spirit which at the time was considered vital to the success of the new Russian state.

A staccato editing pace dominates the film with the longest shots no more than five seconds in length. Like the rhythmic drive of poetry, however, the dynamic flow of imagery is constantly changing; as the pace of life in the city quickens, Vertov employs speeded motion, accelerated montage, rapid intercutting, split-screen effects, double- and multiple-exposure shots, and unusual camera angles to visualize the energy within the environment. This dynamic treatment offers in animated form a positive vision of a place and its people.

Didactic juxtapositions through montage abound. Shots of a wedding, a funeral, and a woman giving birth are intercut with the scene of a man and a woman engaged in a business transaction. As a medical team loads an accident victim into an ambulance, shots are intercut of a fire engine speeding through the city streets. With the true spirit of the proletarian filmmaker, Vertov arranges shots of a film editor among shots of a barber, a typist, and a clothesmaker to suggest functional equality among all the city's laborers; the linkage argues that artists and factory workers share the same importance within the Soviet state.

The ever-present cameraman, shown throughout the film as he moves from one location to another, acts to deny viewers an illusory motion-picture experience. As in Meyerhold's biomechanical theater, Vertov seeks to keep the audience aware of the artist's role in the

Vertov's *The Man with a Movie Camera* (1929) shows an audience arriving at an empty theater to watch a motion picture, followed by a visually dynamic treatment of life in an industrialized Russian city.

communication process. To further this goal the poetic visualization of the city is introduced by shots of an audience arriving at a movie theater to see the film. These unusual alienating effects, along with the film's dynamic flow, provide a remarkable illustration of Soviet-inspired techniques and ideas.

LEV KULESHOV: EDITING THEORIST

Lev Kuleshov's (1899–1970) importance in film's developmental stages in Russia between 1919 and 1925 grew principally from editing experiments which emphasized the linkage of shots to suggest emotional, ideological, and physical realities. The editorial concepts of montage of attraction, creative geography, and associative editing all came under Kuleshov's close scrutiny, and his findings acted as a stimulus to other emerging filmmakers in Russia, most notably Vsevolod Pudovkin.

Kuleshov's career in motion pictures began before the revolution when he served as a scene designer for Evgeni Bauer, one of the most important Russian directors prior to the overthrow of the Tsarist regime. He directed his first complete film, *Engineer Prite's Project,* in 1918, and with *On the Red Front* (1920), a two-reel film using documentary footage and staged scenes, he began to apply editing theories that he had been formulating since his first involvement with the medium.

In 1920 Kuleshov also founded a workshop where he and his pupils could study the range of possibilities available to the film editor. Because of a shortage of film stock, experiments were often carried out by the reediting of extant films (including some by D. W. Griffith) or by staging theater plays in a cinematic manner.

Creative Geography

Using snippets from different films, the workshop illustrated how screen direction patterns and inserts create a sense of geographic unity. In one experiment a shot of a character, moving toward screen right, was followed by a shot of another person walking toward screen left. An insert of a large white building was then included. Together the three shots, according to viewers who were asked to explain the meaning of the short film, implied that the two people were on their way to meet one another at the white building. In actuality the two people had no relationship whatsoever to each other, and the building, according to workshop students, was a shot of the White House in Washington, D.C., lifted from a newsreel.

This exercise in creative geography was only one of many in which Kuleshov and his pupils experimented with arranged shots to produce a fictive reality. In a most unusual exercise the workshop edited together a series of shots of the parts of a woman's body. Each part was actually taken of a different person.

The Actor's Function

Much attention was given in the Kuleshov workshop to the theoretical possibilities of the actor's function in shot arrangements. It was maintained that the actor gains from contextual placement and need not necessarily express emotion in order to communicate emotion. In the nonfilmed stage exercises Kuleshov instructed his actors not to act at all, but merely to pose.

When raw stock became available, a short film was produced to test Kuleshov's acting theories. The famous Russian actor Ivan Mozhukin posed without expression before the motion-picture camera for several seconds. According to accounts given by Pudovkin, who was by 1922 a student at the workshop, Kuleshov afterward filmed shots of a bowl of soup, a woman in a coffin, and a child playing with a toy. These three elements were intercut with the shot of Mozhukin's emotionless face, causing audiences who saw the experiment to claim that they had seen subtle expressions of satisfaction, sadness, and happiness as the actor "responded" to each of the different cutaway vignettes.

Less obvious experiments in montage of attraction focused on methods of using film construction to suggest the emotional and psychological tenor of dramatic scenes. By careful analysis of environmental elements, intercut with the actors in the scene, Kuleshov showed that it was possible to communicate geographic mood as well as character emotion. It was these experiments which had a great impact on Pudovkin's work.

By 1924 the Kuleshov workshop had begun to produce comic and dramatic films. The most successful was a comedy titled *The Extraordinary Adventures of Mr. West in the Land of the Bolsheviks* (1924). An American-styled cowboy actually performed "western" antics in the streets of Moscow. The workshop was disbanded in 1925, leaving Kuleshov and Pudovkin free to pursue independent careers as film directors. Kuleshov continued to direct motion pictures until 1943, and to teach and lecture throughout Russia on film art until his death in 1970.

VSEVOLOD I. PUDOVKIN: EDITING AS LINKAGE

According to film historian Jay Leyda, Vsevolod Pudovkin's (1893–1953) interest in cinema developed after seeing D. W. Griffith's *Intolerance* in 1920. At that time the 27-year-old Pudovkin was a chemist living and working in Moscow. An avid interest in the arts led to an association with Lev Kuleshov who took the young chemist to see Griffith's innovative film.

Pudovkin was inspired to give up his science career and enroll in the newly formed First State School of Cinematography. There he performed in short films and assisted with production chores until 1922 when he left to join the Kuleshov workshop.

At the workshop Pudovkin enjoyed a principal position as an assistant and collaborator on many of Kuleshov's most important projects. For the successful comedy, *The Extraordinary Adventures of Mr. West in the Land of the Bolsheviks,* he served as a scenarist, actor, editor, and assistant director. The close association with Kuleshov over a three-year period profoundly affected Pudovkin's work as an independent director.

Following his departure from the workshop, Pudovkin directed an instructional film, *The Mechanics of the Brain* (1925–1926), and *Chess Fever* (1925), a comic short centered on a chess tournament in Moscow. To convey character tensions in *Chess Fever,* liberal use was made of Kuleshov shot linkages which associated, satirically, a chess player's intense absorption in his game with the frustrations of an alienated wife who had to sit by and wait.

The release of Pudovkin's classic study of human character, *Mother* (1926), signaled the realization of a unique cinematic style. This style, which combined careful analysis of the social environment, symbolic montage, and intense performances, would continue to mature in his other two silent masterpieces, *The End of St. Petersburg* (1927) and *Storm over Asia* (1928).

Mother

Mother was developed for the screen from a Maxim Gorky story with additional plot elements taken from historical events which occurred during and shortly after an abortive uprising in Tver in 1905. Pudovkin's treatment concentrated on the developing political consciousness of a peasant-mother (Vera Baranovskaya) whose son's involvement in the revolutionary movement leads to her own impassioned commitment. By treating common characters in emotional terms, the story offered inspiration to the Russian masses at large.

Character Analysis As the plot of *Mother* develops, Pudovkin reveals through selected detail the tensions and emotions experienced by members of the peasant family. The family's impoverishment is dissected as the husband attempts to remove a clothes iron and clock from the cottage for pawning at the local tavern. A close-up of the clock establishes its presence just before the husband, depressed and dragging, enters the room. His wife observes his actions, and, when she realizes her husband's intentions, attempts to stop him from taking the clock off the cottage wall. A tussle follows and the clock crashes to the floor, shattering into several pieces. To point up the tragic climax of the scene Pudovkin includes a close-up shot of one of the clock's wheels spinning in a circle on the cottage floor, thus drawing out the agony of the loss.

In the scene that follows, the husband is shown in a tavern asking

The mother visits her imprisoned son in *Mother* (1926).

the tavern-keeper to accept the clothes iron for a drink. When the tavern-keeper refuses, a "comrade" offers to buy the dejected man a drink, an action which provides Pudovkin with an opportunity to convey through montage analysis still another range of emotions. A sequence of rapidly accelerating shots follows to depict the merriment of common men united in a moment of comradeship. The combination of these two scenes, with their contrasting emotions, suggests the spirit (at once defeated yet determined) which would undergird the impending revolution.

Scene Analysis The social setting in each scene of *Mother* is analyzed with equal skill; selected details from the immediate environment are used to convey in an impressionistic manner the dramatic mood of an event.

This impressionistic quality is particularly evident in the scene in which the mother visits her son, Pavel Vlasov, in a Siberian prison. Vlasov has been jailed for his role in a workers' strike and for having hidden guns in the family cottage. By naively believing that confessing her son's involvement will spare him, the mother has been responsible for his imprisonment. The recognition of this fact has radicalized the mother and she goes to the prison with a note telling her son of plans for his escape during a demonstration.

A sharply angled, silhouetted long shot of a guard standing watch over the prison walls introduces the mother's visit, followed by a close-up of a key unlocking a cell door. After a moment, the son appears out of the darkness that shrouds the prison corridor.

Pudovkin cuts to the mother sitting expressionless in the waiting room. A half-sleeping guard is nearby, although the two characters are never visible in the same shot. Intercutting among shots of the woman, the drowsy guard, and the note in the mother's clenched hand gives indication of the contrast of character perceptions as the two await the prisoner's arrival.

The interaction between mother and son occurs while they hold hands through prison bars. An economic selection of shots suffuses the scene with ironic significance. As the mother slips the note to her son and as he reacts to its meaning, shots are intercut of the attendant guard nearby discovering a cockroach in a meal tray and pressing it with his thumb into the food. The guard's smile as he performs this cruel action is preceded by the slow forming smiles of the mother and son, who are enjoying together the knowledge of the impending escape. The juxtaposition of devious smiles reveals Pudovkin's gift for ironic scene construction.

To conclude the mother's visit and to provide the scene with a surge of emotion, Pudovkin turns to metaphorical imagery and associative editing. While the son is being returned to his cell, shots of a spring thaw freeing the waters of small streams, then rapidly moving rivers, are interspersed to symbolize Vlasov's imminent release from prison. The scene concludes with shots of a child laughing heartily while Vlasov is shown exploding with excitement in his cell and smashing his canteen cup to the floor in anticipation of his freedom. Pudovkin likens freedom to the happiness of an innocent child and to freeflowing streams—easily understood metaphors in a film designed to convey the heroic actions of early anti-Tsarist revolutionaries.

The End of St. Petersburg

The End of St. Petersburg (1927) also offered a heroic character study and the recreation of historical events for their propagandistic value. In the film's plot a young peasant boy (Ivan Chuvelov) progresses from a politically naive factory worker who refuses to participate in strikes to a committed and impassioned revolutionary.

This story is combined with the treatment of historical events between 1914–1917 which include: Russia's entry into World War I; the horrors and waste of the war itself; the removal of Tsar Nicholas; the

The End of St. Petersburg (1927).

rise of Kerensky to power; and finally the revolt and march on St. Petersburg in October 1917 that culminated with Lenin's takeover of the city. The film concludes with the victorious revolutionaries assembled at the surrendered Winter Palace (including the peasant lad who is now a bolshevik soldier), anticipating a new state and a new order.

Because *The End of St. Petersburg* was commissioned as a tribute to the tenth anniversary of the revolution, Pudovkin sought to offer an inspiring interpretation of history from a Marxist point of view. His editing arrangements juxtapose the lives of common people against the opulence of the city, the plight of the masses against the wheelings and dealings of capitalists. To make his attack on capitalism forcefully clear, shots of stockbrokers waiting idly for exchange reports and then bargaining greedily for stocks are intercut with soldiers dying in the trenches of World War I.

The city of St. Petersburg is dissected with a flow of dynamic, kinetic imagery. Shots of grand buildings, the city's impressive steel bridges, clouds of factory smoke, patriotic banners waving in the wind, haughty policemen, the wealthy, the powerful, the greedy pour forth to suggest in an almost sensuous manner the city that would become the target of the common people's wrath.

Anatoli Golovnya's camera compositions are at times strikingly formal, at others sharply angled with strong diagonals cutting across the frame. The contrast of angles suggests the mixed ideologies and strife within the Soviets' march to triumph.

Storm over Asia

Golovnya was once more the cinematographer for *Storm over Asia* (1928), an epic dramatization of historical events set in Mongolia in 1918. The plot, which again projects Pudovkin's recurring theme of developing social consciousness, recounts the story of a young Mongol hunter, Bair, who rebels when he discovers that capitalist invaders in Mongolia are depriving him of the fair value of his fox skins. It is the time of the Mongolian Civil War with the invading White army (British) fighting against the Red army.

Following his rebellious act, the young hunter is captured and shot

Bair (Valeri Inkizhinov) as a puppet monarch in *Storm over Asia* (1928).

by the outsiders. It is immediately learned that Bair is a descendant and heir of Genghis Khan. With this knowledge the invaders rush to the badly wounded boy with the intention of establishing him as a puppet ruler of the Mongols. When the young Mongol recovers sufficiently to realize what has happened, he revolts against his captors and leads his people in a charge that forces the invaders from Mongolia. To dramatize metaphorically the driving of the capitalists from the country, Pudovkin intercuts shots of a strong windstorm sweeping across the stark land-scapes of outer Russia.

Because Pudovkin and Golovnya filmed this story on location in Mongolia, the result was a film with strong atmospheric and naturalistic qualities. Landscape shots, dominated by huge expanses of open sky, enhance the more traditional approach to editing and narrative flow.

In the scene in which the young hunter Bair is shot, Pudovkin utilizes precise matched cutting and an ordered editing pace rather than the dynamic treatment of violence notable in *Mother* and *The End of St. Petersburg*. Pudovkin's awareness of differences in the environment and the people of Mongolia creates a more evocative experience for the viewer, while still reaffirming the importance of individual efforts in Soviet causes.

Published Theories

Throughout the course of making his three great silent films, Pudovkin began to write and publish theories on the roles of editing and acting in motion-picture expression. These treatises, published in *Film Technique and Film Acting* (translated into English by Ivor Montagu), focused on the communicative value of relational editing. Pudovkin viewed scene construction (shot selection and arrangement) as the principal method by which the filmmaker seizes the attention of and guides the spectator's "thoughts and associations."

The filmmaker, Pudovkin said, must consider the nature of an event, or the "conceptual line" of a scene (peaceful or excited), and then through shot selection and ordering lead the spectator to an under-standing of the event or dramatic concept. By so doing, Pudovkin maintained that the scene's construction then would "either excite or soothe the spectator." Together the various scenes and sequences must lead to a "final tension" for the viewer in order to bring the film's theme to a proper emotional conclusion.

In a similar manner Pudovkin's theories of film acting emphasized the fundamental importance of relational editing. Whatever detail is most important to a character's presence in a scene must be pointed out for the viewer by shot selection. If an object, action, or another person catches an attentive character's eye, the editor, Pudovkin argued, must show what has seized the character's attention. If a part of the character's body is the important dramatic element (a hand holding a revolver or an escape note) then that detail must be emphasized in close-up. The spectator, if the editing construction is successful, must see the event "as the attentive observer (character) saw it." The actor's function within a scene derives from a contextual relationship with other pieces of film. These ideas reflect the influence of Lev Kuleshov and they are well illustrated in Pudovkin's classic silent films.

SERGEI M. EISENSTEIN: THE COLLISION OF SHOTS

Sergei Eisenstein (1898–1948) and Vsevolod Pudovkin were in many ways unallied partners in Russia's explosive entry onto the international film scene. As contemporaries whose screen expression confirmed the power of montage and whose films were rallying calls for the Soviet masses, they helped redefine the artistic and social potential of cinema.

And yet while alike in endeavor, the methods of these great film masters were marked by significant differences. In their most fruitful periods Eisenstein and Pudovkin amicably, but heatedly, engaged themselves in a dialectical outpouring of opposing theories, particularly with regard to the aesthetics of montage.

Like Pudovkin, Eisenstein came to cinema with a background in the sciences. Born in Riga, Latvia, in 1898, he first studied engineering, then architecture, and during the Civil War worked as an engineer for the Russian army. During his two years with the army, he became interested in a career in the performing arts.

Experimental Theater

Eisenstein's first artistic venture was with Forreger's theater in Moscow as a stage designer. This experience led to an association with Meyerhold's biomechanical theater, followed by work at the Proletkult Theater where he was able to direct several plays with experimental emphases. For his production of Ostrovsky's *Enough Simplicity in Every Wise Man* in 1922, Eisenstein included a short film insert whose content held no particular relationship to the play before the audience. For his most renowned theatrical production, *Gas Masks* (1923), a factory served as the site of the performance.

During his period in the theater Eisenstein began to formulate innovative concepts for achieving socially useful dramatic expression. His beliefs were imbedded in scientific and technological principles which he increasingly sought to apply to his art. The "engineering" of art would not be an incorrect assessment of Eisenstein's socialist intentions.

Strike

When it became clear that the theater severely limited the realization of his goals, Eisenstein transferred his energies to mechanically generated

Intense, chaotic scenes dominate the repression of strikers in Eisenstein's emotionally charged *Strike* (1924).

motion pictures. In 1924 he produced his first film, *Strike,* a boisterous account of a factory rebellion during the time of the earliest uprisings against the Tsarist regime. The crushing defeat of the rebellion by Tsarist forces provided Eisenstein's first film with the same emotional power that Pudovkin's *Mother* had gained by concentrating on a similar period and subject.

Eisenstein's approach, however, was less individualized, more mass-oriented than Pudovkin's. The mother, a model of individual spirit in Pudovkin's work, is replaced in *Strike* by unified throngs whose deaths in the street by Tsarist guns are metaphorically intercut with shots of cattle being slaughtered at a meat factory. This powerful association, achieved by montage of attraction, made Eisenstein's point through symbolic methods, whereas Pudovkin's *Mother* achieved its impact through melodrama and strong characterization.

The Battleship Potemkin

The full range of Eisenstein's aesthetic principles of montage found expression in *The Battleship Potemkin* (1925), one of the most potent motion pictures ever produced. The hero, as in *Strike*, is a collective rather than an individual, and the editing and choice of imagery are once more highly symbolic.

Eisenstein's principal symbol is the battleship itself and his major editing method is the clash and contrast of shots through "montage of collision." As in *Mother* and *Strike*, historical reexamination of an abortive uprising in 1905 serves as plot inspiration.

The Plot Eisenstein's imaginative reinterpretation of history focuses on the mutiny of sailors aboard the ship Potemkin. The horrendous conditions and inhumane treatment of the seamen by Tsarist officers are revealed in the first act of the film through potent images which, in one instance, suggest that in the eyes of the ship's officials the sailors are no better than the maggots which gnaw at their food. Response to these conditions precipitates the mutiny and the seizure of the ship by the disgruntled sailors.

In a classic five-act structure Eisenstein develops: I. The events leading up to the mutiny ("Men and Maggots"); II. The mutiny itself ("Drama on the Quarterdeck"); III. Paying homage to the dead in the Odessa port ("An Appeal from the Dead"); IV. The celebration, then massacre of the people of Odessa ("The Odessa Steps"); V. The sailors

"Drama on the Quarterdeck," the second act of *The Battleship Potemkin* (1925).

back on board the Potemkin encountering another friendly ship at sea ("Meeting the Squadron").

Together these five segments are intended to represent a microcosmic view of the shocking conditions which impelled the revolution, seen through a single event. Consequently, each act consists of a collection of images which are arranged by Eisenstein to develop the narrative and to bring the viewer into an emotional relationship with Russia's recent history. These dual intentions account for the more impressionistic and less traditional continuity of *The Battleship Potemkin*.

Symbolic Imagery Symbols abound throughout Eisenstein's film: the first shots are of huge waves breaking on the shore, included to suggest the imminent uprising; the image of maggots on the sailors' food offers an unforgettable symbol of Tsarist contempt; a plate, on which is written "Give Us This Day Our Daily Bread," further symbolizes the hypocrisy of the Tsarist regime; a pair of dangling spectacles, knocked from the face of the ship's captain, indicate the first blow against the monarchy; pixilated marble lions metaphorically rise up and roar in protest of the Odessa massacre; the smoothly running mechanical parts of the ship's engine in the final act are likened to the values of a unified, efficient collective; the bow of the ship appears to open and consume the entire screen in the film's final shot, as if to take onto the Potemkin all the peoples of Soviet Russia.

Montage of Collision Eisenstein's montage of collision approach in the editing of *Potemkin* is designed for dialectical impact; in his theories he maintained that the task of art for social purposes was to create contradictions, "to forge accurate intellectual concepts from the dynamic clash of opposing passions" (*Film Form*, Jay Leyda, ed.).

Dialectical conflict in *The Battleship Potemkin* takes a variety of different forms: rhythmic, temporal-spatial, and compositional. Individual shots, scenes, parts of scenes, sequences, and the various acts themselves all serve to provide units of conflict and contradiction in both immediate and accumulative effect.

Rhythmic variation in Eisenstein's structuring of the film's major parts follows a consistent pattern of dramatic build from relative calm to accelerating action in each of the five sections. Both internal movement within a shot as well as length of shot accelerate the action until each act reaches a dynamic conclusion. A contrasting caesura, or rhythmic break to slow the action, follows each act. Within individual scenes a static shot is frequently followed and contrasted by one containing a dynamic internal movement.

Temporal-spatial conflict in *Potemkin* is achieved by the expansion and contraction of time through editing. Eisenstein uses this technique to juxtapose new, dynamic views of reality against "traditional" concepts of reality. Single moments and full events in *Potemkin* are subjected to an altered treatment of the time-space continuum.

The people of Odessa gather at portside to pay homage to the men aboard the Potemkin.

Compositional conflict is realized in Edouard Tissé's cinematography through contrasting use of light and shadow, volume (or mass), counterpoint of movement within the frame planes, and contrast of graphic line within the frame. In the case of composition the dialectical montage, according to Eisenstein, is achieved within the shot itself rather than through shot juxtaposition, thus making possible the occurrence of interrelational and internal contradictions simultaneously.

The Odessa Steps The Odessa steps sequence of *Potemkin* (Act IV) provides in close analysis classic illustration of Eisenstein's montage of collision methods at work. Rhythmic contrast occurs by progressing from the even-flowing, lyrical movement of small boats bringing the Potemkin supplies to an ever-increasing tempo of excitement as the mass of celebrants gather on the Odessa steps. The tempo peaks with a title reading "Suddenly," followed by a close-up of marching soldiers' feet and a rapid series of noncontinuous shots (jumpcuts) of a woman flinging her head forward in terror. This disjointed, abrupt evocation of terror introduces the massacre.

The massacre itself contains both rhythmic conflict and spatial-temporal manipulation as Eisenstein disrupts the normal flow of the space-time continuum to depict the event in shocking, analytical detail.

The rhythmic, ordered cadence of the Cossacks' feet, shown in close-up descending the steps, is intercut with long shots of the fleeing crowd. This intercutting provides the sequence with a general framework into which Eisenstein inserts isolated details.

The terrorized crowd's movement down the five levels of stairs, at the pace indicated by the long shots, would have ended the scene in a minute or so. However, by combining documentary views with isolated views of the massacre, Eisenstein denies normal time for dialectical and emotional effect. For example, a long shot of the scene is interrupted by a shot of a wounded man falling on the Odessa steps. Eisenstein expands this moment by breaking the fall into a series of shots taken from different camera angles just after the man is wounded; one of the shots gives a subjective point of view of the fall, thus personalizing the reality of the massacre. The documentary view of the scene (long shot, fleeing masses) is interrupted by dynamic, personal views of the event (extended time/an isolated individual/subjective point of view).

Eisenstein continues to explore visual and rhythmic counterpoint throughout the scene. By the use of medium shots the plight of several individuals is set against that of the anonymous crowd. A small boy is shot by the Tsarist soldiers, and the face of the child's mother is seen in horrified close-up just before Eisenstein returns to a long view of the scene.

To add other opposing elements, the mother lifts her wounded child and starts up the steps to plead for mercy. Her movement up the steps counters, graphically, the downward movement of the soldiers. Dead bodies lie in stillness on the steps around the pathetic mother's ascending figure, suggesting that the massacre has ended. However, a sudden return to a close shot of the soldiers' feet, continuing their unbroken cadence, is followed by yet another long shot of the crowd, fleeing past the bodies of the mother and her child who now in the moment's interval have both been gunned down. The sudden revelation of the mother's fate provides still another contradiction of documentary reality. Graphic, rhythmic, temporal, and volume contrasts are all evident in this brief action involving the mother and son.

Shot Analysis The Odessa steps sequence concludes with the depiction of a final shocking event, also rendered through montage of collision. A second mother, attempting to flee the soldiers, is shot as she prepares to start down the steps with her child who is tucked beneath blankets in a baby carriage. A shot breakdown of this sequence points out the various methods of contrast and collision used within a rapid succession of images: contrast of shot scope, shot length, actual time and extended time, abbreviated time, frame composition, and internal movement. The sequence concludes in the following manner:

1   Medium shot: line of soldiers firing guns, then moving in unison down the steps (faces unseen)

Graphic conflict in *The Battleship Potemkin*. The mother's movement back up the steps —her dead child in her arms —stands in contrast with the methodic downward movement of the soldiers.

2   Long shot: mother, frantically trying to protect baby in carriage
3   Medium shot: soldiers' marching feet, *descending* the steps
4   Medium close-up: mother looking *up* the steps toward soldiers
5   Close-up: baby in carriage
6   Medium shot: mother (looking *up* the steps) trying to protect baby
7   Medium long shot: soldiers *descending* steps
8   Medium shot: mother
9   Close-up: soldiers' marching feet
10 Medium long shot: soldiers in static position, firing at mother (jump cut)
11 Close-up: mother's face as she is hit by gunfire

12 Extreme close-up: carriage wheels teetering at edge of step
13 Close-up: mother's pained face
14 Extreme close-up: mother's blood-soaked hands grasping her metal belt buckle
15 Long shot: fleeing crowd, surrounded by Tsarist soldiers on horseback
16 Extreme close-up: mother's hands on belt buckle
17 Medium close-up: mother's agonized face
18 Close-up: mother's face in closer view (slight jump in time)
19 Medium shot: mother's slow fall to the steps (another slight jump in time)
20 Extreme close-up: carriage wheels teetering at step's edge
21 Medium close-up: soldiers' feet descending steps
22 Medium shot: soldiers' descent
23 Medium shot: mother facing soldiers, falling against carriage
24 Extreme close-up: carriage wheels at step's edge
25 Long shot: wide view of the continuing massacre
26 Medium long shot: view of steps and massacre from different perspective
27 Medium shot: massacre, closer view
28 Medium close-up: mother continuing fall against carriage
29 Close-up: baby carriage
30 Extreme close-up: carriage wheels
31 Close-up: a bespectacled woman, who is apparently observing the mother's fall against the carriage, reacts with horror as she looks back up the steps
32 Medium close-up: carriage starting descent down the steps
33 Medium long shot: carriage speeding down the steps
34 Medium shot: carriage's descent
35 Long shot: extreme wide-angled view of the frenzied massacre (carriage is not visible in this shot)
36 Medium shot: mother's dead body on steps
37 Medium shot: carriage's continuing descent
38 Close-up: same woman observer as before, face frozen in disbelief as she looks back up the steps
39 Close-up: young man looking back up the steps, also apparently observing the carriage and scene
40 Medium shot: massacre
41 Medium shot: moving carriage
42 Close-up: young man's face
43 Medium shot: descending carriage
44 Close-up: baby in carriage
45 Extreme close-up: carriage wheels speeding down steps
46 Close-up: young man reacting in horror (six frames in length)
47 Close-up: soldiers firing guns into crowd at close range (eight frames in length)

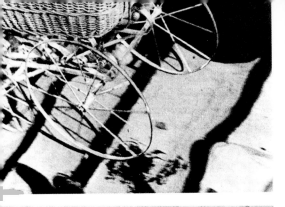

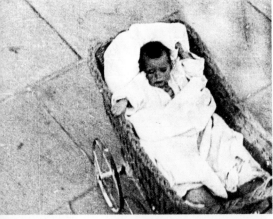

Selected frames from the final moments of the Odessa steps massacre, depicting Eisenstein's powerful use of montage to convey the horrors of the event.

48 Extreme close-up: speeding carriage wheels
49 Long shot: descending carriage
50 Close-up: young man, expectant reaction
51 Medium close-up: carriage
52 Close-up: soldier raising sabre to stab the baby
53 Close-up: soldier's intense face as he brings sabre violently down (slight jump cut)
54 Close-up: woman observer's startled face; a soldier's bullet has just shattered the lens of her eyeglasses

The two final shots of this sequence, each depicting a shocking detail of the massacre in unexpected juxtaposition (sabre stabbing, wounded observer), complete Eisenstein's imaginatively arranged treatment of human torture, and his identification with the causes of the revolution becomes fully clear.

Themes Interspersed between the Odessa steps massacre and the final act are symbolic shots of marble lions in various stages of repose, appearing to rise up and roar in anger as the Potemkin fires its guns at the city's ornate buildings. The future revolution has been justified.

A second theme at work in *The Battleship Potemkin,* incorporated along with the justification of revolution, is that of brotherhood. In Act V, with the ship back at sea, Eisenstein once more draws on the symbolic value of the Potemkin as a unit representative of the whole. By concentrating his attention on the sailors' efficiency and the smooth operation of the battleship's parts (treated in the rhythmic manner of an abstract film), Eisenstein creates a vivid metaphor for the effects of Soviet brotherhood.

In its various parts *The Battleship Potemkin,* commissioned by the Lenin government, reaffirms the 1917 revolution while also making a plea for continued unity within the Soviet state.

October

In *October* (1927), also called *Ten Days That Shook the World,* Eisenstein's methods in treating history are less abrupt than those employed in *The Battleship Potemkin.* Montage again is the principal element of *October's* design, but with less emphasis on the clash and contrast of imagery and a greater use of montage of attraction.

The subject of *October* is the 1917 revolution itself. Made to commemorate the tenth anniversary of the historic victory of the bolsheviks, the film recreates with a mixture of realism and symbolism the same events treated by Pudovkin in *The End of St. Petersburg:* Kerensky's demise and the attack on and seizure of the Winter Palace.

Montage of Attraction The masses, *October's* collective hero, are visual-

In the final shot of *The Battleship Potemkin* the bow of the ship moves slowly toward the camera lens as if to consume the screen and symbolically to take the audience on board with the celebrating sailors.

ized in spectacular action shots as the workers sweep through the streets of St. Petersburg. Interspersed with these bolshevik activities is Eisenstein's metaphorical, highly satirical depiction of the Kerensky government.

Through montage of attraction arrangements, the debates of Menshevik politicians are likened to the music of balalaikas and harps. Kerensky's political ambitions are mocked by showing him ascending, interminably, the grand circular steps inside the Winter Palace. Numerous objects (statues, masks, domestic paraphernalia, architectural details, musical instruments, religious icons, a toy peacock, church spires) are intercut with the film's narrative to make satirical allusions to the arrogant, but faltering, Kerensky government.

In *October's* most vivid images Eisenstein and cinematographer Edouard Tissé include the rise of a drawbridge to depict the suppression of a workers' demonstration in February 1917. As the drawbridge separates to prevent the workers from fleeing the city and returning to their homes, one side of the bridge lifts a dead girl's body, her long hair hanging over the bridge's edge. A dead horse and a cart are raised on the other side. The two images of the girl and the horse are intercut with shots of the frenetic rebellion. The sequence is extended in time until finally the bodies slip from the edges and fall into the river below. A shot of bolshevik pamphlets floating in the river follows to symbolize the failure of the workers' demonstration.

Conclusion The theme of collective spirit emerges in the climactic, epic sequences of *October* as the bolsheviks, led by Lenin, are shown victorious in their seizure of the Winter Palace. These impressive documentarylike scenes give indication of the more realistic qualities of Eisenstein's later work. As a unified film, however, *October* lacks the brilliant cohesiveness of *The Battleship Potemkin*. Eisenstein's broad use of inanimate symbolism produces a work whose self-conscious methods often overwhelm and detract from the treatment of history.

For *Old and New* (1929), his last silent film, Eisenstein approached the subject of collective farming and peasant life in a more direct and lyrical manner than that used for his three earlier films. He referred to the editing of *Old and New* as "harmonic montage."

In 1929 Eisenstein left Russia with Grigori Alexandrov, his collaborator *(Potemkin, October, Old and New)*, and Edouard Tissé, his cinematographer, to learn the technique of producing sound motion pictures. The trio traveled first to Europe, then to the United States, where Eisenstein worked briefly for Paramount, but without completing any of the projects assigned him.

With the financial support of Upton Sinclair, Eisenstein next filmed the ill-fated *Que Viva Mexico!* (1931–1932), an impressive pictorial study of the 1910 Mexican revolution. After numerous disagreements, Sinclair took the unedited footage from Eisenstein and this project was also left unfinished.

Que Viva Mexico! was eventually arranged by Sol Lesser and released in the United States as *Thunder over Mexico* (1933). By this time a disheartened Eisenstein had returned to Russia to teach at the State Film School.

The impact of his experiences abroad, a series of illnesses, and difficulties with cinema officials in Moscow acted to stultify Eisenstein's creativity during the 1930s. It was not until 1938 that he was able to complete his first feature-length sound film, the epic *Alexander Nevsky*. This film would, simultaneously, reestablish Sergei Eisenstein's international stature and stand as a superb illustration of the creative possibilities of sound-image arrangements.

ALEXANDER DOVZHENKO: EPIC POET

Less well-known than Pudovkin or Eisenstein, but no less important in Soviet film history, Alexander Dovzhenko (1894–1956) is a filmmaker whose poetic style and simple themes established him as an important and innovative artist.

Dovzhenko, who was born in the Ukraine on September 11, 1894, the son of peasant workers, committed himself in his various careers as a cartoonist, painter, teacher, writer, and film director to the task of paying homage to the spirit of his homeland. The Ukraine and the common people who lived there were the source of inspiration for all of his artistic expression.

After working as an illustrator and teacher, Dovzhenko sought employment at an Odessa film studio in 1926 at the age of 32. Following three years of apprenticeship, he established his prominence as a film director with the release of *Zvenigora* (1927); this work, which was highly praised by Eisenstein and Pudovkin, gave an account of two Ukrainian brothers who respond differently when the revolution comes to their homeland. One leaves the country, seeking romance and wealth; the other remains at home to fight for the Ukraine.

Dovzhenko utilized numerous impressionistic devices in conveying the fantasies of the brothers' grandfather, who in the film serves as a symbol of the past. By the end, in a plotting detail similar to one used frequently by Pudovkin, the old man converts and joins his patriotic grandson, Tymish, in fighting for the revolution and a new order.

Arsenal

Dovzhenko's first masterpiece, *Arsenal* (1929), is a continuation of the story begun in *Zvenigora*. The film treats the revolution in the Ukraine, showing life at home and on the battlefields. Tymish (Semyon Svashenko) again serves as the central hero, fighting for the bolsheviks and the working class.

In *Arsenal* Dovzhenko's poetic and lyrical style emerges fully, revealing the spirit of the Ukrainian revolution with imagination and feeling. The camera acrobatics are particularly impressive for the manner in which they capture the rhythmic nature of important actions and events.

In one of *Arsenal's* most memorable scenes, a small group of Ukrainian soldiers are taking a dead comrade's body to a burial site where the man's grief-stricken widow waits. The sense of patriotic urgency in this deed is captured through impressionistic images of the speeding horse-drawn cart that carries the body. Oblique "Dutch angle" (canted) shots of the cart and of the passing Ukrainian landscape are intercut with extreme low-angled views of the horses and subjective shots taken from the driver's point of view. This editing arrangement imbues the scene with an experimental and musical quality; more significantly a heroic aura surrounds the simple action of carrying a compatriot to his final resting place.

It was this ability to humanize events that differentiated Dovzhenko's films from Eisenstein's and Pudovkin's. The startling propagandistic ideas that had been the result of Pudovkin's constructive montage and Eisenstein's montage of collision were replaced in Dovzhenko's naturalistic work by mood and feeling.

The battlescenes in *Arsenal* possess a personal quality similar to that achieved by D. W. Griffith in *The Birth of a Nation*. Griffith's influence appears in both the staging of the battles and in the tonal quality of picture composition. The use of bold low-angled shots and diagonally arranged compositions are particularly reminiscent of the Griffith style.

Dovzhenko's desire to symbolize the spirit of his people through poetic expression is illustrated during a scene in which Tymish is fighting on behalf of striking workers at a Kiev munitions factory. The arsenal is about to be reclaimed by National forces and Tymish remains as one of the last bolshevik defenders. When his gun jams, enemy

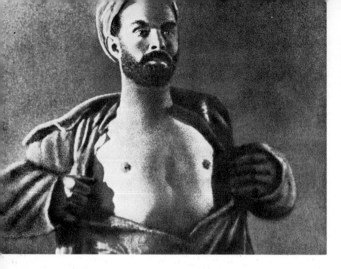

In Dovzhenko's *Arsenal* (1929) Tymish (Semyon Svashenko) rips his shirt open to reveal that he is immune to bullets fired by Nationalist forces.

soldiers charge forward and fire at him. Tymish does not fall, but instead rips open his shirt to reveal that no bullets have entered his body. Symbolizing the spirit of the Ukraine, he is indestructible.

Earth

Earth (1930), the last silent film produced by Dovzhenko, is a cinematic poem about the simple lives of collective farmers in the Ukraine. Technique, like the story itself, is simple and direct. Bountiful images of nature and human life, photographed in black and white with great beauty, are responsible for the film's affective impact. As the collective farmers struggle to achieve unity, life's cycles of love, hate, death, birth, growth, and harvest are rendered lyrically, adding to the film's social theme a larger theme of life's resiliency.

Dovzhenko's naturalism continued in many of his sound films, although never quite matching the visual power of *Arsenal* and *Earth*. Political struggles during the Stalin regime drained him of much of his creativity. He died in 1956 at age 62.

The rich early period of Russian cinema was one born from the excitement of history and shaped in method by political change. Commitment to the new order and to the forces which had created it provided the stimulus for the impassioned work of Vertov, Pudovkin, Eisenstein, Dovzhenko, and other innovative filmmakers who also played a significant role in creating a socially designed film aesthetic in Russia, e.g., Sergei Yutkevich, Abram Room, Victor Turin, and Friedrich Ermler. Often dramatically different in stylistic approach, all spoke, however, with inspired feeling for the unity of the state.

The images in Dovzhenko's *Earth* (1930) create a poetic hymn to the Ukraine—its land, its people, and its collective spirit.

Government policies and increasing conservatism among industry bureaucrats in the 1930s curtailed experimentation significantly, driving filmmakers in Russia back toward more traditional content and to less abrupt methods of expression. Many of the early directors carried on with their careers, but rarely with the same fervor that had characterized filmmaking during the 1920s.

Yet the lessons taught by Russia's morally committed filmmakers of that decade are still intensely studied and applied in contemporary motion pictures. One needs only to examine the methods of the Academy Award winning documentary study of American involvement in Vietnam, *Hearts and Minds* (1974), to realize the lasting power of a montage aesthetic that had its origin in Russia's revolutionary 1920s.

SUGGESTED READINGS

Barna, Yon. *Eisenstein.* Bloomington: Indiana University Press, 1973.

Carynnk, Marco, ed. *The Poet as Filmmaker: Selected Writings by Alexander Dovzhenko.* Cambridge, Mass.: M.I.T., 1974.

Dart, Peter. *Pudovkin's Films and Film Theory.* New York: Arno, 1974.

Eisenstein, Sergei M. *Film Form: Essays in Film Theory.* Edited and translated by Jay Leyda. New York: Harcourt, 1949.

———. *The Film Sense.* Edited and translated by Jay Leyda. New York: Harcourt, 1942.

Leyda, Jay. *Kino: A History of the Russian and Soviet Film.* New York: Macmillan, 1960.

Schnitzer, Luda, Jean Schnitzer, and Marcel Martin. *Cinema in Revolution.* New York: Hill and Wang, 1973.

PART 4

**THE THIRTIES
AND FORTIES**

NEW TECHNOLOGY AND FILMTYPES:

HOLLYWOOD (1927–1939)

[*Hell's Heroes*, 1929] was all sound, the first all-talking outdoor picture Universal made. We were in the Mojave Desert and in Panamint Valley, just off Death Valley. . . . The cameraman was in a glass booth. It was about 120 degrees. In the glass booth it was about 140. Sometimes after a shot we would find that the cameraman had passed out. We had a crew pushing this thing, with a microphone hidden in a cactus here and in the sand over there.

William Wyler, *American Film*, April 1976.

In 1930 a New York newspaper published a short statement by Sergei Eisenstein in which the noted Russian director spoke about the impact that sound technology was beginning to have on the art of motion pictures:

The old dreams of the talking films are becoming realities. Americans have opened the road to the technique of the talking film and have arrived at the

M-G-M's lion roars.

first stages of the realization. Germany is working hard along the same lines. The world is saying that the great mute has found his voice! [*The New York Sun*, June 5, 1930.]

For Eisenstein and other established filmmakers around the world, who were accustomed to the expressive powers of image and montage, the successful integration of sound posed numerous challenges. The desire to retain the visual concepts that had emerged during the medium's "silent" decades was of particular concern. Many feared that the exploitation of sound, especially dialogue and sound effects, would supersede the visual and montage explorations that had made international cinema during the 1920s so diverse and satisfying. Eisenstein spoke of the need to integrate the element of sound into film expression so that it would be "naturally coupled with the visual form."

Briefly the image in motion-picture art did experience a setback as directors struggled to accommodate the presence of microphones and actors simultaneously on the set. But only briefly. Sound technology advanced quickly and soon performers no longer had to stand close by microphones hidden in flower pots and cacti, but were free to move at will beneath follow-booms of remarkable mobility. Technicians mastered the art of sound recording, perspective, and editing and learned to utilize aural elements in both literal and creative ways.

By 1932 film directors in America had come to realize that sound was more than a technological intrusion. It was a valuable tool for intensifying the screen image while also offering rich opportunities for expressive sound-image arrangements.

The path to the successful coupling of sound and image had its rudimentary beginnings, as Eisenstein had noted, in the United States where the first sound synchronization systems were introduced in the late 1920s. Warner Brothers led the way with its Vitaphone sound-disc system in 1926, followed by the superior Case-Western sound-on-film method at Fox which was first demonstrated early in 1927.

As these two studios and, shortly thereafter, their competitors adapted to sound, new film genres and styles emerged. The major Hollywood producing organizations continued on their path toward individual personalities through a variety of responses to the "talking" picture.

WARNERS INTRODUCES SOUND

Sam Warner's agreement with Western Electric in 1925 for a joint venture into the production of talking pictures resulted in the formation of a sound subsidiary, the Vitaphone Corporation, so named because the visual material the studio agreed to provide to Western Electric's sound technicians was to be filmed and edited in the old Vitagraph studio in Brooklyn. The studio underwent a complete overhaul so that the facility could be used for sound recording.

The Vitaphone Preludes

By mid-1926 the Warners people and the Western Electric engineers had successfully produced a number of short films using the Vitaphone sound-disc method of synchronization. At the same time Warners was preparing for the public release of the silent motion picture *Don Juan* with John Barrymore. It was decided that this picture, with its prestigious star, would be an ideal one to launch the Vitaphone system. A synchronized score for the film was played by the New York Philharmonic, and engineers recorded an assortment of sound effects to accompany action sequences.

Don Juan and eight shorter films with Vitaphone sound opened at the Warners Theater in New York on August 6, 1926. Audience members paid $10 for admission. The premiere program, billed as "The Vitaphone Preludes," was introduced with a brief address on film from Hollywood's public spokesman Will Hays. Other short films with prominent musicians followed Hays' predictions that the introduction of sound motion pictures would revolutionize the industry; the program concluded with the presentation of *Don Juan*.

Critics as notable as Robert E. Sherwood declared the Vitaphone premiere "a real triumph," although *Don Juan* was nearly overlooked in the flurry of praise for the shorter films. Will Hays' synchronized voice, a solo of "Vesti la giubba" from *I Pagliacci* (sung by Metropolitan Opera star Giovanni Martinelli), and a violin rendition of "Humoresque," played by Mischa Elman, more accurately suggested the range of possibilities for Vitaphone sound than did *Don Juan;* they were described by Sherwood as "extraordinarily impressive." And the reporter for *Film Daily* wrote:

> It seems beyond human conception that the smallest theater in the smallest hamlet of this country can exhibit *Don Juan* with an orchestral accompaniment of 107 men of the New York Philharmonic Orchestra. This is what the Vitaphone has done. Metropolitan Opera stars . . . spreading their artistry to the far-flung corners of the world for untold millions to hear and enjoy. . . . Can there be any doubt that a momentous event has come to pass in the industry? [*Film Daily*, August 8, 1926.]

Warner Brothers in the meantime was in the process of producing additional sound shorts and scored features which would demonstrate the new system. Sound systems were installed in other theaters around the country and by early 1927 more than a hundred movie houses were equipped for Vitaphone. The early Warners' demonstration programs proved enormously popular with the public and business picked up considerably for exhibitors who showed them.

Al Jolson as *The Jazz Singer* (1927).

The Jazz Singer

The Jazz Singer, **released by Warners on October 26, 1927, served as a culminating moment in the movement toward full acceptance of sound motion pictures. In the film Al Jolson portrays Jakie Rabinowitz, a would-be jazz singer who has pursued his love of popular music against his father's wishes. The young man's father says that he has been "shamed" by his son's desire to become a vaudeville entertainer rather than a cantor at a synagogue like himself.**

The Jazz Singer's ample sentiment and dramatic conflict were drawn from the mother's doting acceptance of her son and the father's continued bitterness. The majority of the film's story was silent, containing only two brief sequences of dialogue and several interludes of synchronized music.

One of the film's most startling moments occurs when Jolson, in a music hall scene, sings "Dirty Hands, Dirty Face." This song is followed by the ad-libbed line: "Wait a minute. You ain't heard nothing yet!," after which Jolson begins a second song. At this point the script reverts to its essentially silent format. A highly sentimental injection of music occurs near the end of the film when Jolson, substituting for the older cantor, sings "Kol Nidre" during a High Holiday service at which his father dies. The final musical number of the film is "Mammy," performed by Jakie, now a star, in a packed theater. His mother is in the audience to help celebrate his success.

Public response to *The Jazz Singer* was phenomenal. The appeal of Jolson's vibrant singing carried the sentimental film to an unprecedented box office success, although Sam Warner did not live to see the startling results of his labor. He died of a cerebral hemorrage just before the film's premiere.

The Silent Era Passes

Industry reaction to the Warner Brothers' success was immediate and other producing organizations moved quickly to adapt their studios to sound stages. Exhibitors rushed to convert theaters to a sound capability. At the time of the release of *The Jazz Singer* only 100 movie houses were sound-equipped; at the end of 1928 there were 1,000 converted theaters and by 1929 nearly 10,000.

The effects of sound on the production of motion pictures were far ranging. Silent stars with unpleasing voices soon disappeared from the screen. Production moved almost entirely indoors in order to overcome the recording limitations of early primitive microphones. Because of inexperience in the editing of sound pictures, the first feature-length films were photographed and assembled as a series of long-shot, master-scene takes.

For a very brief period of time the motion picture in the United States reverted back to its "photoplay" tendencies, but the new sensation for audiences of talking pictures carried the industry through the transitional period without a financial setback. Early in 1929 M-G-M introduced the first film musical, *The Broadway Melody,* and later that year RKO released *Rio Rita,* an adaptation of a Broadway musical hit. Suddenly musical theater had come to Hollywood. During 1929 the American motion-picture industry made more than 300 dialogue films, a statistic which gave proof that the silent era had passed.

Warner Brothers profited from its leading role in the introduction of sound films. Its first all-talking pictures, *Lights of New York* and *The Singing Fool,* both released in 1928, were so successful at the box office that the studio was suddenly catapulted into a top position within the highly competitive industry. By now the studio also owned nearly 500 theaters in its expanding exhibition chain.

Tough Gangster Films

With the release of *Lights of New York* Warners discovered the appeal of the gangster story, popular to a degree during the silent era, but a genre which would be nurtured and exploited with unparalleled success after the introduction of sound. *Lights of New York* recounted a big-city tale of prohibition-era gangsterism in which an innocent young man is drawn into the illegal activities of bootleggers.

Despite its static, talky quality, Bryan Foy's film suggested the screen environment that eventually characterized the genre: the backrooms of night clubs and speakeasies where clandestine activities are carried out by con artists. Chorus girls, of which one is invariably allied with and often betrayed by her gangster boyfriend, stand on the periphery of the big-city underworld.

Missing from the fifty-seven minute film, however, was the automobile which later became a familiar element of the genre. The sound of screeching tires was soon introduced to add a new thrill to the motion-picture chase.

With the development of microphone follow-booms, camera silencers, and sound mixers for blending and dubbing aural elements (achieved as early as 1929), the studios were free to add such sensational sound effects as screeching tires and gunshots, and to keep their screen characters on the move. Warner Brothers continued to explore the narrative possibilities of the crime film and achieved renown in the early thirties with several classic illustrations of the genre. Most notable were *Little Caesar* (1930) with Edward G. Robinson, *The Public Enemy* (1931) with James Cagney, and *I Am a Fugitive from a Chain Gang* (1932) with Paul Muni. The tough, active quality of these pictures exhilarated a country in which real-life gangsterism had also captured public attention.

Little Caesar W. R. Burnett's novel about a gangster who progresses from a ruthless murderer to a victim of his own violent world provided the story material for Mervyn LeRoy's *Little Caesar*. Edward G. Robinson, portraying the leading character, Rico, is eventually shot to death in a vacant lot by policemen. Robinson's ability to project toughness and at the same time an almost boyish quality made the actor a major star.

LeRoy's direction was memorable for its taut, straightforward presentation of a story which avoided moralistic overtones. Critic Richard Watts, Jr., praised the film for "pushing into the background the usual romantic conventions of the theme."

The Public Enemy James Cagney appeared in his first Warners' film, *Sinners' Holiday*, in 1930, but it was *The Public Enemy*, his fifth picture, which established the actor as a virile and dynamic star. His portrayal of a lower-class boy who rises from simple surliness to gangster status is grimly drawn on the screen by director William Wellman.

Critics described Cagney's performance as both sinister and honest, and praised Wellman for refusing to romanticize the principal character. Cagney's screen persona is that of a cold-blooded killer who intimidates and inflicts cruelty on all who cross his path. Women, except for his mother, fare no better than men. Just prior to his violent death, Cagney shoves a grapefruit half into the face of his girlfriend, Mae Clarke. A New York critic labeled the film "the most ruthless, unsentimental

Machine gunfire, breaking glass, and fast moving automobiles were among the sounds that helped to give new life to tough gangster films such as *Little Caesar* (1930) with Edward G. Robinson.

appraisal of the meanness of a petty killer that the cinema has yet devised."

The straightforward analysis of criminal activity in *The Public Enemy* can be attributed to Wellman's direction and to the fact that Warners had hired newspapermen, familiar with big-city gangsterism, to help authenticate the studio's crime films. Ben Hecht, a writer for the *Chicago Daily News,* was among those who made the transition from journalist to screenwriter for gangster films. John Bright and Kubec Glasmon also came to Warners from Chicago newspapers. Their knowledge of underworld life brought a new realism to crime pictures that included injecting into scripts expressively gritty dialogue. Such colloquialisms as "On the spot," "So what?," and "Taken for a ride," were first introduced in gangster films and soon became everyday expressions.

I Am a Fugitive from a Chain Gang Warners' realistic crime cycle reached a peak with *I Am a Fugitive from a Chain Gang* in 1932. This film, starring Paul Muni, moved away from the standardized mythology of gangster stories and presented a vivid picture of prison life.

Muni was Jim Allen, a veteran who has been unjustly convicted of a crime and sent to a southern prison. The script by Sheridan Gibney,

Unforgettable gangster cruelty is captured in *The Public Enemy* (1931) when Tom (James Cagney) shoves a grapefruit into the face of his girlfriend (Mae Clarke).

Paul Muni portrays the victim of a savage penal system in *I Am a Fugitive from a Chain Gang* (1932).

Howard J. Green, and Brown Holmes, and based on the true experiences of a former prisoner, exposed brutalities and injustices existent at the time in the American penal system.

Mervyn LeRoy, as director, brought the story to the screen with a starkly candid style that was uncommon in American films. A series of moving vignettes revealed the principal character's futility in escaping the horrors of the dehumanizing institution to which he is confined, and Muni's intense characterization helped provoke a public outrage against the inequities exposed in the film. In Georgia, where the story was set, efforts to reform the penal system were begun.

Social Dramas and "G-Men"

With *I Am a Fugitive from a Chain Gang*, Warner Brothers enhanced its growing reputation as a studio with a social conscience. Other important social dramas followed: *Wild Boys of the Road* (1933), a film about the plight of unemployed youth during the Depression; *Massacre* (1933), a study of the insensitivity of government agents in dealing with American Indians; *Black Fury* (1935), a story of conflict between management and labor in a Pennsylvania coal mining community; *The Black Legion* (1936), a film about mob violence and the organized hatred of foreigners; *They Won't Forget* (1937), a Mervyn LeRoy picture which exposed the evils of mob violence and retaliation.

The prominent role of Warner Brothers in the production of social message films was earned as pressure against such "editorial" films was increasing. In the early 1930s, Hollywood's self-regulatory Production Code Office stepped up its criticism of scripts which questioned the practices of American society, government, or industry. Warners was required, for example, in 1933 to delete scenes from two pictures which showed policemen in a less than favorable light. Efforts were also made to lighten the treatment of coal industry management in the script for *Black Fury*.

The Production Code's criticism was also often aimed at the studio's realistic crime films. Public protest from concerned civic groups about the effects of violence in gangster pictures forced the Code Office to monitor scripts which might continue to popularize societal misfits.

By 1935 Warners had for the most part left behind the antihero gangster story for crime films that presented law-enforcement characters as the protagonists. G-Men replaced "public enemies" as the tough guys at Warners; this reversal of emphasis projected a clear-cut conflict between good and evil and was, therefore, considered more acceptable to the censors.

Backstage Musicals and Screen Biographies

Faced with public pressure and industry censorship, Warner Brothers turned to other types of film entertainment. Two genres, the musical extravaganza and the biographical film, achieved particular success as Warner-styled products.

The Hollywood studios had persistently turned out unimaginative musical revues and operettas between 1929 and 1932. Warners' musical directors, with Busby Berkeley leading the group, injected new life into the genre with a backstage plotting device.

The backstage story line, as it evolved at Warners, centered on a plot about the efforts of a group of entertainers to produce a musical show. Setbacks and character conflicts in the struggle to get the musical on the stage provided dramatic interest. The musical numbers, usually irrelevant to the plot, appeared at various points throughout the film, and reached an extravagant, lavish peak near the film's conclusion.

Berkeley's success as choreographer in *Forty-Second Street* (1933), the "Gold Diggers" series (1933–1937), and *Footlight Parade* (1933) resulted from an impressive visual display of carefully synchronized, highly

Warner Baxter, a stage producer, gives instructions to a struggling starlet (Ruby Keeler) in *Forty-Second Street* (1933). The young chorus girl achieves stardom when the leading lady sprains an ankle and is replaced by the unknown Keeler. Ginger Rogers, appearing in a small part, looks on from the right.

stylized musical numbers. Beginning with *Forty-Second Street* he had begun to separate the story from the musical elements in order to provide more interesting drama and more visually exciting music and dance segments. His ability to utilize editing and a fluid camera also added to the cinematic quality of his unusual film choreography.

Warners' many film biographies included: *Alexander Hamilton* (1931); *Voltaire* (1933); *The Story of Louis Pasteur* (1936); and *The Life of Emile Zola* (1937). These pictures provided suitable vehicles for Warners' male-dominated stock company which was led by Paul Muni, George Arliss, Spencer Tracy, Edward G. Robinson, James Cagney, Humphrey Bogart, and Errol Flynn. In the latter half of the 1930s Flynn's appearance in a series of adventure films, including *Captain Blood* (1935) and *The Adventures of Robin Hood* (1938), gave Warners some of its most successful pictures.

The studio's small group of female stars was headed by Bette Davis and Barbara Stanwyck, both of whom portrayed strong, independently willed screen characters. Davis, in particular, possessed at times a hardened, unscrupulous quality that matched that of Warners' many tough male characters.

The bold, forward-looking social stance of the Warners studios, its hard-hitting action pictures, escapist musicals, adventure stories, and biographical films sustained the studio through the uncertain 1930s.

FOX: MOVIETONE NEWS AND B-PICTURES

William Fox's boldness as a studio chieftain continued as his studios began to make the transition to sound. Warners' Vitaphone sound-on-disc method had proved a big success with *The Jazz Singer,* but Fox had earlier seen a superior system in a sound-on-film method offered by the Theodore W. Case Laboratory. Case had actually lifted the system from Lee de Forest who had earlier made sound amplification possible with the invention of the audion tube. In 1926 Fox signed an agreement with Case similar to the one which Warners had signed with Western Electric. Fox would provide the visual materials for demonstrating the Case sound system. The organization was labeled the Fox-Case Corporation and the sound system was called "Movietone."

After procuring an amplification system from Vitaphone late in 1926, Fox-Case began to promote its sound-on-film method commercially. Movietone "Preludes," similar to those created by Vitaphone for demonstration with *Don Juan,* appeared in several sound-equipped Fox theaters during the early part of 1927. The offerings were standard: shorts of instrumental performances, songs by well-known singers, and comic skits.

Newsreels

By mid-1927, Fox was presenting in its theaters regularly scheduled Movietone presentations, many of which were newsreels. The Fox-Case engineers had discovered that the Movietone system worked almost as well outdoors as in sound-controlled studios, and had applied this capability to filmed news stories which appeared in theater programs under the heading Fox-Movietone News.

On May 25, 1927, in a sensational display of the Fox newsreel, filmgoers in New York City were able to see and hear Charles Lindbergh's departure for his solo flight across the Atlantic. When the cheers of spectators at Roosevelt Field became audible in the background, filmgoers at the Roxy Theater, reporters noted, also stood and cheered.

Follow-up Fox-Movietone Newsreels showed Lindbergh's tumultuous welcome-home receptions, including the one in the nation's capital, where the remarks of both President Calvin Coolidge and Lindbergh were recorded. By the end of 1927 Movietone News programs were being distributed weekly to the Fox theater chain.

Profits at Fox, as at Warners, took a brief dramatic leap with the introduction of sound pictures. The studio completed total conversion to sound early in 1929, setting aside two of its sound stages solely for the production of Movietone Newsreels.

B-Pictures and an "A" Child Star

Pleased with his success, William Fox, early in 1929, sought to gain even more power by purchasing a controlling interest in the Loew's theater chain. Fox also closed deals that year for the purchase of additional theaters in Europe, further increasing the corporation's holdings and its outstanding debts.

As one of the largest film conglomerates in the world, the Fox organization suffered more than others from the devastating consequences of the October 1929 stock market crash. The studio lost more than $3 million in 1930—a loss which resulted from a $12 million drop in company revenues during the twelve-month period. Because of continuing financial woes William Fox was forced to resign control of the corporation in 1932 and Sidney Kent, temporary studio head, made valiant efforts to keep the organization afloat.

Fox, like other plagued Hollywood companies, turned to the newly introduced exhibition practice of double-feature programming. The enticement of two motion pictures for the price of one was a Depression-inspired gimmick that had originated in New England in 1931.

The Fox organization proved particularly successful in turning out B-pictures of good quality. B-pictures were the less expensive films which appeared on double-feature bills. Characteristically lower in budget expenditure, populated by lesser-known stars, and often formulaic in design, B-pictures, nevertheless, became a specialized commodity at Fox with the guidance of Sol Wurtzel, a producer of considerable ability.

In 1934 a precocious child actress named Shirley Temple signed a contract with Fox and throughout the thirties was responsible for one low-budget hit film after another. Her first film at Fox was a musical revue with Warner Baxter, *Stand Up and Cheer* (1934). Temple's popularity soon surpassed that of Greta Garbo and other female luminaries of the decade. Her seven years and twenty-three films at Fox established Shirley Temple as the indisputable child star of motion pictures, a reputation which has yet to be seriously challenged.

Merger

When Fox films merged with Twentieth Century Pictures in 1935 to become Twentieth Century-Fox, Darryl Zanuck (1902–1979) of Twentieth stepped into the amalgamated studio as vice-president in charge of production. Zanuck earned a reputation as an energetic and efficient

Shirley Temple, Fox's major asset during the 1930s.

supervisor of studio operations. Like his counterparts elsewhere in Hollywood, he immersed himself totally in production activities and significantly influenced film quality and style.

Zanuck had acquired his first film experience in the 1920s as a screenwriter for the Rin-Tin-Tin series at Warner Brothers at a time when the studio was struggling for survival. This education at Warners led to Zanuck's hard-nosed attitude toward efficiency and economy in film production.

Zanuck's philosophy of management plus Twentieth Century-Fox's extraordinary success with its B-pictures resulted in studio products which were distinctive for their formulaic variations, glib, fast-moving stories, one-dimensional characters, and easy solutions to dramatic dilemmas.

Scripts at the studio were nearly always written in groups rather than by individuals. Screenwriter-historian Kenneth Macgowan, a contract writer at Twentieth Century-Fox between 1935 and 1943, has recalled that writers were required to work on stories for which they had no particular feeling; Macgowan personally worked on more than fifty scripts which never went into production because the ideas or treatments were vetoed by production management.

To sell its pictures Twentieth Century-Fox depended increasingly on its stock company of popular stars, most of whom were juveniles and ingenues. A young Tyrone Power, who came to the studio in 1936 at age 22, headed the list of male actors; Alice Faye and Loretta Young were among the ingenues.

The first decade of talking pictures showed that the power which had passed from William Fox to Darryl Zanuck had not significantly altered the aggregate nature of films produced by the studio. Fox's prodigious influence which was felt in studio output prior to 1932 merely shifted to Zanuck. The title of a Zanuck biography, *Don't Say Yes until I Finish Talking*, suggests the degree to which management continued to affect studio style at Twentieth Century-Fox. Zanuck remained as head of production until 1952.

METRO-GOLDWYN-MAYER: PRODUCERS, PRESTIGE, AND GLAMOROUS ENTERTAINMENT

As Metro-Goldwyn-Mayer moved into the sound era, the studio's efficient assembly-line system of making films was tightened to keep the corporation running smoothly. Working under Irving Thalberg's supervision were teams of creative producers, contract directors, writers, talented set designers, sound technicians, costumers, and, indispensably, an ever-growing number of glamorous stock players.

Many of the creative producers at M-G-M were individuals of taste and artistic judgment, whose presence was often more strongly felt in films they supervised than that of the contract directors. Albert Lewin headed production of M-G-M's "prestige" films, an innovative sound-era concept introduced by Thalberg that brought to the screen adaptations of popular literary works: *Anna Christie* (1930), *Strange Interlude* (1932), *What Every Woman Knows* (1934), *Mutiny On the Bounty* (1935), *The Good Earth* (1937). As supervisor of this specialized prestige category and as head of M-G-M's story department, Lewin earned a reputation as a cultured, stylish filmmaker.

David O. Selznick, a creative producer at M-G-M until 1936, personified the production supervisor who left a stamp on every film he produced. During the thirties his creative position was topped only by Thalberg's. In *Dinner at Eight* (1933), *Night Flight* (1933), *Dancing Lady* (1933), *Viva Villa!* (1934), *David Copperfield* (1935), *Anna Karenina* (1935), and *A Tale of Two Cities* (1935) Selznick produced one hit picture after another.

Selznick (also at that time Louis B. Mayer's son-in-law) participated fully in all facets of his filmmaking projects—choosing actors, doctoring scripts, and making final decisions on sets and costumes. In a significant move to improve film sound, he permitted musical composers to become involved in the making of films during production rather than after-

The highly romantic musical operetta, here represented by *Rose Marie* (1936), flourished at M-G-M during the 1930s. Jeanette MacDonald and Nelson Eddy were billed as M-G-M's "Singing Sweethearts" and every element of production—lighting, sets, makeup, costumes—was carefully controlled to enhance their romantic fantasies.

ward in the postproduction stage, maintaining that the early involvement of composers resulted in more appropriate and inspired scores.

Among the notable 1930s contract directors at M-G-M were Victor Fleming *(Captains Courageous)*, Clarence Brown *(Idiot's Delight)*, W. S. Van Dyke *(San Francisco)*, Sam Wood *(A Night at the Opera)*, Sydney Franklin *(The Good Earth)*, and Robert Z. Leonard *(The Great Ziegfeld)*. These individuals functioned efficiently within a studio system where coordination was more important than individual directing styles.

Yet, the versatility of the M-G-M directors showed in a diverse collection of sound films made in the thirties for the family trade. These included the large assortment of literary adaptations, musical operettas with Jeanette MacDonald and Nelson Eddy, and numerous series films: *Tarzan, Andy Hardy, Dr. Kildare, Boston Blackie, The Thin Man,* and *Maisie.*

The goal at M-G-M of producing entertaining star-studded films of high technical quality resulted in recognizably distinctive products. Production values (set design, costumes, artistic lighting) assumed great importance in products which displayed the "studio look" to its fullest advantage. Glamorous stars were photographed in high-key lighting in costumes and settings that were designed to transmit luminous images. In close-up shots, Rembrandt back-lighting added additional glamour and romance to screen visages. A similar meticulous attention was paid by costume and set designers to pictorial details.

The accumulative visual effect of an M-G-M picture was that of a perfectly controlled, artificial environment. Stars such as Norma Shearer, Greta Garbo, Jean Harlow, Jeanette MacDonald, and Joan Crawford

glowed in the hands of M-G-M's skillful cinematographers and technicians. And it would be an omission not to add that so too did male stars. Robert Taylor, John Gilbert, Cary Grant, Nelson Eddy, Franchot Tone, Robert Young, among a host of other leading men, were given a similar "prettified" treatment.

To provide stories for its stars and the eager technical staff, M-G-M assembled a prestigious group of writers that included Moss Hart, Frances Marion, Anita Loos, Charles MacArthur, and William Faulkner. By the time, however, that scripts by these high-caliber writers went through an assembly-line translation to the screen they had been shaped to fit the management's preference for escapist entertainment.

The principal challenge for writers at M-G-M came in trying to find new ways of supplying emotional fervor to romance-filled screen stories. The M-G-M style remained even after Thalberg's death in 1936 and Selznick's departure the same year to head his own production company and to make the greatest of all screen romances, *Gone with the Wind* (1939).

UNIVERSAL: MONSTERS, INGENUES, AND WAR

The advent of sound and the economic plunge brought on by the Depression reinforced Universal's symbiotic relationship with the major production-distribution organizations (Warner Brothers, M-G-M, Paramount, Fox). Carl Laemmle sold the sixty-odd theaters owned by Universal in the early 1930s and the studio settled down to its principal position as a supplier of films for the growing double-feature market.

The horror film, following the example of Universal's earlier silent success, Lon Chaney's *Phantom of the Opera* (1925), remained an important studio staple. In 1931 *Frankenstein,* starring Boris Karloff, helped Universal avert bankruptcy while establishing Karloff as a suitable replacement for Chaney who had died in 1930. Karloff was so successful in imitating Chaney's skillful and grotesque use of makeup that Universal followed *Frankenstein* with a number of spin-offs, including *The Bride of Frankenstein* (1935) and *The Son of Frankenstein* (1939).

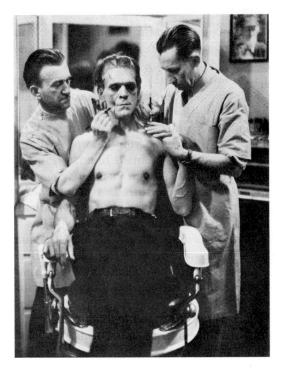

Makeup artists at Universal prepare Boris Karloff for a day's shooting of *Frankenstein* (1931), a film notable for its sympathetic and tragic development of the monster's character.

During the latter part of the 1930s, the studio found a popular star in the teenage actress Deanna Durbin, whose pure soprano singing voice (*100 Men and a Girl*, 1937) and adolescent charm made her Universal's most successful and profitable contract performer.

All Quiet on the Western Front

The most important film produced at Universal during the 1930s, *All Quiet on the Western Front* (1930), managed to give the studio the distinction of having created one of the greatest war pictures of any period and also of having produced one of the first great sound motion pictures. Carl Laemmle, Jr., supervised the screen adaptation of Erich Maria Remarque's pacifist novel shortly after Laemmle's father appointed him head of studio operations at age 21.

All Quiet on the Western Front was a significant achievement for several reasons. It courageously presented German soldiers from a sympathetic point of view, and thereby offered a larger, more tragic understanding of war than that provided by the many anti-German pictures made in the United States after World War I.

Lewis Milestone's sensitive direction of war's personal horrors received great praise. Few individual scenes have exposed the physical and emotional anguish of battle as clearly as the one in which a German soldier (Lew Ayres), in a moment of panic, stabs a French soldier (Raymond Griffith); as the Frenchman lies dying the two youths share

The unforgettable French scene in *All Quiet on the Western Front* (1930). The dying Frenchman (Raymond Griffith) reaches for papers for Paul (Lew Ayres) to send to his family.

their bewilderment over the madness of war. Milestone was lauded for the "immediacy" of scenes such as this one and for his exposé of the "physical suffering and moral prostration" of individuals in military conflict.

Milestone's battle scenes were staged with impressive visual authenticity. Later, in the postproduction stages of completing the film, realistic sound effects of explosions, gunfire, and the battle cries of humans were added to the sound track to intensify the picture's poignant treatment of war.

RKO: TECHNICOLOR, SPECIAL EFFECTS, AND DANCE

The emergence of the Radio-Keith-Orpheum (RKO) studio occurred as a direct result of the advent of sound motion pictures. RKO was incorporated in 1929 as a subsidiary of the Radio Corporation of America (RCA). RCA had profited from its introduction of the Photophone Sound System in 1928 and with the incorporation of RKO expanded its business interests into the areas of film production, distribution, and exhibition.

Because of its late arrival in a well-formed industry, the stylistic identity of the RKO studios was not as apparent in the 1930s as that of the older, more established production companies. In the early years of its existence, RKO was unable to realize a profit despite a surprisingly impressive number of quality films.

Among RKO's early successes was *A Bill of Divorcement* (1932), a film in which Katharine Hepburn first brought her unique physical and vocal qualities before the attention of the filmgoing public. Another soon-to-be star, Leslie Howard, appeared about the same time in RKO's adaptation of Philip Barry's *The Animal Kingdom* (1932). Dolores Del Rio achieved star status in *The Bird of Paradise* (1932), one of RKO's many successful screen versions of well-known stage plays.

Also among RKO's early achievements were *Little Women* (1933) and the first feature-length three-color Technicolor film *Becky Sharp* (1935).

Technicolor

The Technicolor process used in *Becky Sharp*, an adaptation of Thackeray's *Vanity Fair*, culminated a lengthy period of experimentation with methods of supplying color to screen images. The progression led from hand-tinted frames (as early as 1896) to the unwieldy three-color Kinemacolor process (1906) to the improved Technicolor efforts of Herbert Kalmus and Robert Comstock in 1916–1917. Kalmus Technicolor, as the process came to be called, used a double negative lamination system in which red-orange-yellow colors were photographed on one negative and blue-green-purple on the other.

Convincing miniature models and trick photography helped make RKO's *King Kong* (1933) a classic monster film. Here Kong fights off a prehistoric pterodactyl while clutching his beloved Ann (Fay Wray).

This system was first fully introduced in Douglas Fairbanks' costume-action picture *The Black Pirate* (1926). *The Phantom of the Opera*, made the year before, had contained color sequences, but Fairbanks' film was the first to apply Technicolor throughout. Color values in *The Black Pirate*, because of the two-color double-negative system, were not always precisely accurate. By 1932 Kalmus had perfected his process so that a full color range could be photographed on a single celluloid emulsion.

The improved Kalmus process, although expensive, was adopted with great success by Walt Disney in his cartoon *Flowers and Trees* (1932). Disney held the exclusive rights to the process until 1934. When the Disney contract expired and Technicolor became available for general use, RKO, before embarking on *Becky Sharp*, successfully produced a Technicolor short, *La Cucaracha* (1934). Experimentation with the Technicolor process was essential because of the bulky camera and special technicians (provided by Kalmus) required for filming.

Becky Sharp represented a major step toward acceptance of color for other than novelty films. Final acceptance came with *Gone with the Wind* and *The Wizard of Oz* in 1939, although color would continue to be seen by producers primarily as a romantic embellishment until the mid-1950s.

King Kong and the Astaire-Rogers Team

In its first decade RKO achieved additional significance with Willis O'Brien's clever special-effects film *King Kong* (1933), and with a series of dance-films with the talented Fred Astaire and Ginger Rogers.

King Kong employed stop-motion photography to animate the impassioned jungle creature (in actuality only 18 inches tall) who falls for lovely Fay Wray. Masterful miniature settings and trick photography (matte-screen processing) added to the film's illusory qualities. Most notably, however, *King Kong* managed to create dramatic involvement in addition to impressing audiences with its advanced technical achievements.

Beginning with *Flying Down to Rio* (1934), RKO provided filmgoers with a total of nine stylish, delightful dance films starring Astaire and Rogers. By contrast with dance pictures being produced at competing studios, emphasis was placed not on camera choreography and rhythmic editing but on the dancing performances themselves. Astaire and Rogers' dance numbers were photographed for the most part in long shot with minimal cutting. While the approach was clearly more theatrical than Busby Berkeley's dynamic spectacles, the graceful dancing style was extraordinary enough to require no technical embellishments. *Flying Down to Rio, The Gay Divorcee* (1934), *Top Hat* (1935), *Swing Time* (1936), and *Shall We Dance* (1937), all with Astaire and Rogers, ranked among the top box office successes of the thirties. These pictures were vital to RKO's first decade.

With the successful integration of sound into the American motion picture the studio system was at its top form in providing efficiently produced, escapist entertainment. Each studio by the mid-thirties had developed its own business philosophy and creative personality and these in turn were reflected back in the special qualities of its products. Emphasis ranged from the lavish, star-oriented films produced at M-G-M to the unadorned, workaday products from Harry Cohn's Columbia Pictures. Adolph Zukor's good, clean family products at Paramount stood in sharp contrast to the Warner Brothers' more sensationalized, tough character pictures.

Yet the Hollywood system with its varied emphases had one interest in common: each studio sought to avoid failure in a high-cost industry. To avoid failure the studio chieftains often narrowed their vision to their

The graceful Fred Astaire-Ginger Rogers dance team is launched by RKO in *Flying Down to Rio* (1934). Unlike the Busby Berkeley spectaculars at Warners, the Astaire-Rogers dance numbers were carefully integrated into the story and the dances performed without trick effects.

own understanding of the kinds of motion pictures that would best match public tastes. The goal of the American film in the height of the studio years, above all else, was to satisfy the entertainment needs of a large, anonymous public. And that it did!

SUGGESTED READINGS

Bergman, Andrew. *We're in the Money: Depression America and Its Films.* New York: Harper Colophon Books, 1972.

Fielding, Raymond. *The American Newsreel: 1911–1967.* Norman: University of Oklahoma Press, 1972.

Gabree, John. *Gangsters: From Little Caesar to the Godfather.* New York: Gallahad, 1973.

Geduld, Harry. *The Birth of the Talkies: From Edison to Jolson.* Bloomington: Indiana University Press, 1975.

Gifford, Denis. *Movie Monsters.* London: Studio Vista Limited, 1969.

Karpf, Stephen. *The Gangster Film: Emergence, Variation and Decay of a Genre, 1930–1940.* New York: Arno, 1973.

Roffman, Peter, and Jim Purdy. *The Hollywood Social Problem Film.* Bloomington: Indiana University Press, 1981.

Sklar, Robert. *Movie-Made America.* New York: Random House, 1975.

Stanley, Robert H. *The Celluloid Empire.* New York: Hastings House, 1978.

Taylor, John Russell, and Arthur Jackson. *The Hollywood Musical.* New York: McGraw-Hill, 1971.

Thomas, Bob. *Thalberg: Life and Legend.* New York: Bantam, 1970.

Trent, Paul. *Those Fabulous Movie Years: The Thirties.* New York: Crown, 1975.

SOUND IMPRESSIONS ABROAD:
GERMANY, FRANCE, AND RUSSIA

The Blue Angel is notable from the directing angle on account of von Sternberg's clever combination of talking and silent film technique. He uses dialogue sparingly and climatically and employs long sequences of purely cinematic story-telling. In other words, he allows the camera to tell the story whenever possible rather than letting the actor tell it vocally. That, in a nutshell, is the goal of good talking pictures today, now that the ghost of the all-talking picture has been laid.

National Board of Review Magazine, January 1931.

At the same time that the American studios were adapting their popular screen fare to sound, creative filmmakers abroad were proving that they too could make sound an integral part of uniquely styled motion pictures. Directors like G. W. Pabst, Fritz Lang, and Josef von Sternberg in Germany; René Clair, Jean Vigo, and Jean Renoir in France; and Sergei Eisenstein in Russia all

The Blue Angel.

produced important film work in which the element of sound was used in expressive ways. Sound was brilliantly applied to diverse subject matter ranging from René Clair's charming musical fantasies to Eisenstein's historical epics.

While the Depression and political events in Europe during the thirties acted to severely curtail film output, the important contributions made in Germany, France, and Russia to the art of sound motion pictures are worthy of analysis.

GERMANY

Although the talent flow to Hollywood in the late 1920s in effect ended Germany's "golden era" of filmmaking, Ufa's remarkable success with screen naturalism resulted in a surprisingly smooth transition to sound motion pictures. G. W. Pabst directed three outstanding, socially relevant sound films in 1930–1931: *Westfront 1918* (1930), *The Threepenny Opera* (1931), and *Kameradschaft (Comradeship,* 1931). A continuing interest in adult subject matter brought these films international acclaim. Sounds and dialogue were given the same strong naturalistic treatment that characterized Pabst's earlier work.

The Blue Angel

The greatest of the early Ufa-produced sound motion pictures, and a film also distinguished by its forceful naturalistic style, was Josef von Sternberg's *The Blue Angel* (1930). In a reversal of emigration patterns, Pommer brought the Austrian-born Sternberg from Hollywood to Neubabelsberg. Sternberg had earned a reputation in the United States as a director with a special talent for creating screen stories in which the environment played a significant part. He was often described as a director who had been influenced by *Greed* and by the tenets of Max Reinhardt's intimate *Kammerspiele* ("closet play") theater. Sternberg, like Reinhardt, employed intimate details, subdued lighting, and atmospheric settings in his gangster film, *Underworld,* made for Paramount in 1927.

The following year Sternberg directed *The Docks of New York* (1928), another underworld film involving a prostitute (Betty Compson) and a stoker (George Bancroft). Again, the lighting was heavily foreboding and the physical environment precisely identifiable with the violent story.

It was Sternberg's success in applying the methods of European-styled naturalism to these American films that prompted Pommer in 1929 to offer the director the creative supervision of *The Blue Angel*. The project was conceived as a joint Ufa-Paramount production and was filmed simultaneously in English and German language versions.

The Plot *The Blue Angel's* account of the rigidly ordered Professor Rath (Emil Jannings) who falls hopelessly in love with a cabaret singer (Marlene Dietrich) was adapted from Heinrich Mann's novel, *Professor Unrath*. The professor's conversion from an autocratic, severely disciplined school teacher to a cabaret clown is dissected with chilling clarity.

Striking environmental contrasts and a revealing selection of intimate details are Sternberg's principal methods of exposition. Sound, too, works to reveal the differing worlds of Professor Rath and the cabaret singer, Lola-Lola.

The ordered life of Rath is revealed in the opening scene as he has his breakfast and departs for work. The chimes of the town clock coincide precisely with the professor's arrival at school. Before beginning the day's English lesson, Rath neatly orders his books, then with a grand gesture removes his handkerchief from his pocket and blows his nose. This accumulation of details depicts Rath as a mechanical, authoritarian, and aloof creature.

When Rath tracks his students to The Blue Angel cabaret the world he finds there is by contrast one of sensual animation and mystery. A sad-faced clown ominously observes the incongruous presence of the professor; backstage in Lola-Lola's dressing room, an assortment of theatrical characters come and go, letting in the boisterous sounds of the nightclub, then shutting them out as they open and close doors.

The bold Lola-Lola, without inhibition, changes her costume in the presence of the professor, teasingly dropping her underclothing on his balding head. Later, the sensuous woman mischievously opens a make-up case and blows powder into Rath's startled face.

These incidents reveal the staid, ascetic professor being lured into Lola-Lola's simultaneously repulsive and fascinating world. When the cabaret singer takes to the stage to sing one of her distant, smoky-voiced ballads, Sternberg's camera centers not on Lola-Lola but on Rath who watches from a balcony above the club floor. The professor is by this point as trapped in Lola-Lola's amoral world as he was previously trapped by his own sterile existence.

The deterioration that follows—as Rath marries Lola-Lola only to find himself a laughable cuckold—is carried through by Sternberg with an assured use of pointed details. Rath amuses those at his wedding party by happily but uncharacteristically crowing like a rooster; when the new husband lifts his wife's suitcase and it falls open, revealing dozens of publicity photographs of Lola-Lola intended for sale to cabaret patrons, Rath realizes he has married a commodity; later he degradingly peddles the photographs himself.

After several years of traveling the cabaret circuit as a pitiable companion to his unsympathetic wife, Rath finds himself back in his hometown for an engagement at The Blue Angel. In this setting his total degradation is completed. To attract large audiences, it has been decided

that the familiar professor should serve as the assistant to the company manager and conjurer (Kurt Gerron). As Rath is about to go on stage he sees Lola-Lola retire to her quarters with a Strongman who has just completed an engagement at the club. Rath is immobilized, but the magician forces the stricken husband to carry out his performance.

On stage Sternberg creates a scene of unforgettable cruelty and irony through the use of sound, space, and isolated details. The crowd in the cabaret screams with delight when it recognizes the broken professor. The conjurer condescendingly announces the professor as "Auguste, my top student"; then by plunging a knife into Rath's hat, he shows that the "student's" head is empty.

As the magic act proceeds, the crowd shouts its disapproval and Rath attempts to leave the stage. The conjurer demands that his assistant lay eggs for the audience and then that he crow for them. When Rath refuses, two eggs are broken on his head; he glances into the wings where Lola-Lola can be seen in a passionate embrace with her new suitor. Rath begins a pathetic, hollow crowing that echoes with primitive anguish.

Later that evening, Rath creeps through the dark, heavily shadowed streets back to his old classroom where he sits at his desk and dies. The final shots of the film are of an aloof Lola-Lola dispassionately singing "Falling in Love Again," followed by a cut to the town clock with its rotating carousel of gnomelike figures—a symbol of time and tradition moving ahead.

Style and Theme Sternberg's successful combination of atmospheric detail and psychological insights marks the film as stylistically compatible with the Ufa work of Murnau, Dupont, and Pabst. A strongly identifiable German naturalism prevails in the restrained but highly creative use of sound. Sound plays an expressive role in developing a sense of environment and in its naturalistic usage enhances the film's intimate, studio-inspired visual detail.

The thematic implications of *The Blue Angel* hold striking similarities with Murnau's *The Last Laugh*. Rath's foolish sense of pride and lofty view of himself identify him as a character much like that of the haughty doorman. Both believe that their positions have lifted them above all others of their own class, and both strut and flaunt their conceit with a near mocking attitude of disrespect.

The fatal flaw in this attitude resides in the assumption that position is everything. The doorman cannot function without his status-supplying uniform and Rath is vain enough to believe that because he is "Herr" Professor he will be able to dominate Lola-Lola and her world the way he has dominated his students and the classroom.

One sees in *The Blue Angel* and *The Last Laugh* a progressive deflation of two pompous and pathetic characters. It is the loss of uniform that brings down the old doorman, and it is the acquisition of the worldly Lola-Lola that destroys Rath. An unsettling sense of perversity of the human spirit dominates both works. No sympathy whatsoever is shown the doorman following his demotion, and similarly in *The Blue Angel* Rath's former students find delight in his fall.

Sternberg's film is yet another somber view of a middle-class society, devoid of compassion. This theme in one manner or another found its way into many of the great naturalistic, Ufa-produced films of the pre-Nazi 1920s and 30s.

Propaganda

Following the international success of *The Blue Angel*, American motion-picture studios continued to underwrite film production in Germany. This outside influence, combined with Adolf Hitler's stultifying presence, served to hasten the declining importance and distinctiveness of German cinema.

Occasional films, however, continued to carry the high quality of the previous decade of German filmmaking. Pabst's *Kameradschaft* (1931) and Lang's *M* (1931), in particular, received international acclaim and distribution.

As historian Paul Rotha has pointed out, these films made in 1931 "were conceived in a spirit of liberal-minded realism and . . . had liberal

propagandist aims." *Kameradschaft,* in telling a story of a mine disaster, advocated brotherhood and economic justice, and *M,* a study of a psychopathic child killer (Peter Lorre), metaphorically revealed Nazi-like tactics as well as a creeping sickness within the milieu, a sickness that did not appear to be curable.

The compulsive, insidious nature of Peter Lorre's murderous deeds in *M* was conveyed by Lang with brilliant interplay of sound and picture. A Grieg melody, whistled by the unseen killer as he stalks a victim, makes *M's* terror all the more haunting. Lengthy periods of silence and asynchronous sound elements heightened the psychological tenor of Lang's moody study of evil forces.

These liberal films, made in the uncertain period just prior to Hitler's full ascendance, served as a prelude to a total takeover of the film industry for propagandistic purposes. By 1933 Adolf Hitler's Propaganda Ministry, headed by Joseph Goebbels, had seized control of the film industry.

Leni Riefenstahl Under Goebbels' supervision only the documentarist Leni Riefenstahl (1902–   ) attained any real importance. Riefenstahl, a former film actress in many of G. W. Pabst's works, was given unlimited state subsidy to make propaganda films that would glorify the Nazi regime and its activities.

Hitler selected Riefenstahl for this task partly because of her success in 1932 as producer, director, and actor of the mountain film *The Blue Light.* Mountain films at the time were peculiarly popular with German audiences because, critical interpretations claim, they projected in their scenic photography and dramatic action sequences a feeling of spirituality and youthful, heroic enterprise. The adulation of youth, with an emphasis on physical endeavor, had assumed considerable importance in Nazi ideology; mountain films, in retrospect, appeared to reinforce

Himmler, Hitler, and Lutze are architecturally framed by ornamental columns of people as the three men walk toward the memorial monument at Nuremberg. The geometric shapes of the mass of people suggest the means by which *Triumph of the Will* sought to convey Nazi support for Hitler.

and promote the Nazi vision of a physically strong and spiritually pure society.

Riefenstahl had shown in *The Blue Light* remarkable skills as an editor, particularly in her ability to utilize realistic elements for romantic and propagandistic purposes. It was this ability to mold authentic material through editing into propaganda statements that attracted Hitler's attention.

In 1934 Riefenstahl began a lengthy propaganda project that was issued later that year as the controversial *Triumph of the Will*. The film's content offered a study of the first Nazi party meeting held in Nuremberg in September 1934. In design its purpose was to display for the world the support of the Nazi party and the German people for Adolf Hitler.

A massive production crew (135 technicians) photographed the meeting at Nuremberg and the huge rallies and ceremonies that occurred in the streets outside. Like a carefully staged Hollywood spectacle, every effort was made to capture events from the most dramatic, arousing points of view. Lengthy, sweeping travel shots, rare to the documentary film, were carefully executed so that a greater sense of drama would appear within the events. Several scenes involving Hitler were either plotted or staged for maximum effect. Bold camera angles and startling perspectives emphasized Hitler's stature and what would seem to be his intoxicating presence in Nuremberg.

Riefenstahl, working alone, arranged these collected images into a two-hour, Wagnerian glorification of Hitler. The work suggested a near perfect demonstration of the powerful, often undetectable, role of editing in film propaganda. Riefenstahl's mixture of apparent reality and shaped message, underscored by lofty music and cheering crowds, was so superbly executed that some critics declared her editing skills to be equal to those of Eisenstein's.

Siegfried Kracauer, in his observations on German cinema, has described *Triumph of the Will* as an experience in which "palpable life becomes an apparition . . . [achieved through] an inextricable mixture of a show simulating German reality and of a German reality maneuvered into a show." Indeed, on closer examination Riefenstahl's propagandistic film can be seen as a calculated display of theatricality, carefully disguised as documentary reportage.

In 1938 Riefenstahl made the next of her controversial, Nazi-subsidized films, *Olympiad*. This piece of propaganda consisted of a two-part study of the 1936 Olympics which had been held in Berlin. Its focus was concentrated on the physical fitness of Germany's youthful participants—with the intention of reinforcing the Nazi vision of a perfectly conditioned and pure Germanic youth, striving toward Hitler's dreamed-of master race. Once more, Riefenstahl's rhythmic editing attempted to bring these fascist ideas dramatically forward.

Olympiad's ingenious combination of artistry and politics brought additional fame and notoriety to the Third Reich's most visible filmmaker. Riefenstahl prepared different versions of the film for export to a variety of specifically targeted areas; unexpectedly, one of these versions received the Venice Festival prize in 1938. The brilliance of these two treacherous, Nazi-influenced films represented the final gasps of Germany's first innovative period of filmmaking. The unfortunate upheavals of Nazism and World War II quieted cinematic activity in Germany until the mid 1970s when a new group of serious, original filmmakers began to emerge.

FRANCE

French filmmakers who had been primarily interested in the visual and rhythmic possibilities of cinema, not surprisingly, were openly distressed by the arrival of talking motion pictures. As a consequence, many of the important silent directors withdrew from filmmaking rather than struggle with the new technology.

Also, the onset of the Depression drew interest away from artistic experimentation and toward social concerns. Jean Epstein, Alberto Cavalcanti, and other prominent figures in the Paris-based avant-garde found the documentary film more appropriate for the times. The arrival of socially aware films from Russia also had an impact on the demise of the avant-garde and the shift toward more humanitarian interests among French directors.

Commercial cinema in France during the 1930s was characterized by uncertainty and conservatism. As elsewhere, many of the early French sound films were canned-theater exercises lacking in visual imagination. The major studios, like their counterparts in Scandinavia and Germany, had to contend not only with new equipment utilization

The opening panning shot in Clair's *Sous les toits de Paris* (*Under the Roofs of Paris,* 1930). Tenement dwellers in the boulevard below employ song and dance to create an imaginative vision of Parisian life.

but with a language barrier that suddenly threatened the marketability of their products. Consequently, many of the early dialogue films were produced by France's three major studios (Gaumont, Pathé, Paramount) in multilanguage versions, a process which further marked the efforts as largely utilitarian, uninspired commercial ventures.

René Clair

Among the handful of French directors who received acclaim in the early years of sound pictures, clearly the most important was René Clair. Clair's satirical treatment of the bourgeoisie (first explored in his silent film *The Italian Straw Hat,* 1927) reached full maturity in three delightful musical films: *Sous les toits de Paris* (*Under the Roofs of Paris,* 1930); *Le Million (The Million,* 1931); and *A Nous la liberté* (*Liberty Is Ours,* 1932). In these musical films, Clair's familiarity with experimental cinema continued to be evident in his imaginative use of sound to give visual images an expressive life. A scene involving a fight for a lottery ticket in *Le Million,* for example, is accompanied by the asynchronous sounds of a rugby match.

Interplay between rhythmic contrasts such as that in the speeded and slow-motion juxtapositions of *The Crazy Ray* (1924) can also be found in *Sous les toits de Paris*. A group of Parisian tenement dwellers at the film's beginning freeze in position and start to sing a religious song. No movement is perceptible until the eyes of a street singer, who is leading the song, slowly turn toward a prowling pickpocket. Following this static beginning, the pace of the scene quickens as characters burst into life and the action builds to an energetic climax. The nascent rhythm of this action recalled Clair's earlier interests in a cinema of vision and movement.

In 1934 Clair left his native country for work in England and the United States, thus depriving France of its most innovative sound director.

Jean Vigo

The other important figure in France in the early thirties was Jean Vigo (1905–1934). The imaginative young Vigo, whose two films *Zéro de conduite (Zero for Conduct,* 1933) and *L'Atalante* (1934) gave promise of a brilliant new visual expressionist, died of tuberculosis in 1934 at age 29. *Zéro de conduite,* an autobiographical account of Vigo's stark childhood, was particularly impressive for its combination of realistic and symbolic

Rebellious lads in Jean Vigo's *Zéro de conduite* (1933). Their rebellion is a reaction to adult-imposed injustices within a boarding school and is treated by Vigo with autobiographical bitterness.

imagery. Accompanying Vigo's expressive images was a literal, realistic application of sound, an approach which was to have a significant influence on the emerging style of French film during the latter part of the decade.

Others

Without Clair and Vigo, only a handful of directors were left to inject some artistic spirit into the sagging French industry. Most significant were Jacques Feyder, Marcel Carné, Julien Duvivier, and Jean Renoir.

Feyder and Carné both earned reputations as poetic realists whose films were often somber and pessimistic in tone. Feyder's farcical study of Flemish heroics during the seventeenth century, *La Kermesse Héroïque (Carnival in Flanders,* 1935), was an exception. In Carné's *Le Quai des brumes (The Port of Shadows,* 1938), the pessimistic mood of late thirties French films is more clearly evident in a story of political corruption and personal defeat.

Duvivier, also a poetic realist, projected a similar pessimism in *Pépé-le-Moko* (1936), a story of criminal-romantic intrigue in which the antihero (Jean Gabin) is killed by French gendarmes.

The strong feelings of human despair, disillusionment, and uncertainty evidenced in the works of these French directors found their most forceful expression in films being made simultaneously by Jean Renoir: *Toni* (1934), *The Crime of M. Lange* (1935), *The Lower Depths* (1936), *The Grand Illusion* (1937), and *The Rules of the Game* (1939). It was Renoir's most creative period of filmmaking and his work during this time represented the culmination of France's early "golden age" of cinema.

Not until the late 1950s and the arrival of the New Wave movement would French directors again excite the world with sophisticated, intellectual, and philosophical approaches to the film narrative.

RUSSIA AND EISENSTEIN

Due to economic and technical factors, the transition to sound in Russia lagged behind the rest of the world. The first sound picture was not released in the Soviet Union until 1931 and even then sound elements were employed in less than inspiring ways. Many feature-length directors reverted to the prerevolutionary style of treating literary adaptations in a Film d'Art, canned-theater manner.

Dovzhenko created his first dialogue film, *Ivan,* in 1932, as did Pudovkin with *A Simple Case.* Neither film, however, was impressive for its form or its sound, a fact that gave evidence of the stultifying effects of Stalin's first "Five Year Plan" (issued in 1928) which, among other concerns, began to control formalistic expression in the arts. The

The ice battle in Eisenstein's *Alexander Nevsky* (1938), impressive for its close coordination of visual images with Prokofiev's stirring musical score.

art-for-art's-sake approach which had stimulated film creativity in the 1920s was gradually denied as official censors acted to shape cinematic expression toward simpler forms and straightforward, socially useful propaganda.

This concern for socialist realism forced filmmakers to treat in a direct manner contemporary as well as historical heroes who would be an inspiration to the masses. In 1938 Sergei Eisenstein, after recovering from illness and official suppression, was assigned to direct *Alexander Nevsky,* a heroic study of a thirteenth-century Russian prince who defeated Teutonic invaders in an ice battle on Lake Peipus.

Supported by Sergei Prokofiev's magnificent musical score and the splendid acting of Nikolai Cherkassov, *Alexander Nevsky* returned Eisenstein to international prominence. Music and images throughout the film are matched in precise coordination to create a dramatic work of unusual expressive power. The ice battle remains one of the most stirring scenes ever put on film, primarily because of the coordination of Prokofiev's musical score with formal images.

Eisenstein's close matching of sound to image in *Alexander Nevsky* was a departure from his earlier approaches to musical scoring. For his three great silent pictures the prescribed approach required that composer Edmund Miesel's scores work primarily in counterpoint to the screen images. Eisenstein viewed contrapuntal sound during the experimental silent period as an essential part of his montage of collision design.

Eisenstein's last film work, and some of his greatest, appeared in *Ivan the Terrible, Parts I and II* (1944–1946). The two films comprised the

In *Ivan the Terrible*, Part II, the simple-minded Vladimir (Pavel Kadochnikov) is induced by Ivan (Nikolai Cherkassov) to wear the royal robes and crown, thus sending the lad to his death by assassins awaiting Ivan in a cathedral.

first parts of an intended trilogy on the life of Ivan IV, played by Nikolai Cherkassov. Russian officials who commissioned the trilogy saw in Ivan, the country's first Tsar, an inspiring history lesson for the common people. The Tsar, despite his ruthless ways, did much to improve life for workers in Russia during his sixteenth-century reign. Unity of the working class was a major goal of the Stalinist regime in the 1930s and 40s, a goal which Eisenstein's films by implication hopefully would support.

Eisenstein's treatment of *Ivan the Terrible* was spectacular in scope and authentic in detail, a work of such grand scale that the two parts are often described as operatic. Medieval Russia is depicted as a gloomy but opulent place; the passions at work in the film are alternately anguished and hopeful. Prokofiev, once more the composer, produced an impressive musical score to fit the film's pageantry and moods.

Two short experimental color sequences were also incorporated into the second part of *Ivan the Terrible,* primarily for their symbolic value. In one sequence a bluish tint covers the frightened face of Vladimir when the young man, wearing Ivan's robes, realizes that he is about to be killed.

Because Part II (completed 1946, released 1958) characterized Ivan as increasingly maniacal and tyrannical, Stalin refused to allow the film to be shown during his lifetime. Eisenstein went ahead, however, with plans for Part III, but died of a heart attack in 1948 just after he became 50.

Continuing censorship in Russia so suppressed creativity that in 1950 only six feature-length films were released. Not until after Stalin's death in 1953 would Soviet cinema begin to revive.

The 1950s in general would prove to be a time of renaissance for films abroad, reversing the trend of the thirties when America's studio releases soared and European products declined in quantity and quality. Feature films from abroad during the fifties would be on the rebound at a time when Hollywood's studio system was coming apart.

SUGGESTED READINGS

Bazin, André. *French Cinema of the Occupation and Resistance.* New York: Ungar, 1981.
Berg-Pan, Renata. *Leni Riefenstahl.* Boston: Twayne, 1980.
Clair, René. *Reflections on the Cinema.* London: Kimber, 1953.
Furhammar, Leif, and Folke Isaksson. *Politics and Film.* New York: Praeger, 1968.
Hull, David. *Films in the Third Reich.* New York: Simon & Schuster, 1969.

Kracauer, Siegfried. *From Caligari to Hitler: A Psychological History of the German Film.* Princeton, N.J.: Princeton University Press, 1947.

Montagu, Ivor. *With Eisenstein in Hollywood.* New York: International, 1967.

Sarris, Andrew. *The Films of Josef von Sternberg.* New York: Museum of Modern Art, 1966.

Smith, John M. *Jean Vigo.* New York: Praeger, 1972.

DIRECTORIAL STYLES:
HOLLYWOOD (1930–1950)

There are perhaps half a dozen American directors who have such a distinctive way of doing their work that you could recognize it from seeing perhaps half a reel cut from the middle of a picture as you might distinguish the style of Walter Pater from the style of Charles Dickens after reading half a page.

Gilbert Seldes, *Movies Come from America*, 1937.

The history of the motion picture is a dichotomously evolving record of commercial and artistic enterprise. Most films are produced for mass audiences for immediate consumption. Even very successful "releases" (the film industry's pragmatic synonym for feature-length motion pictures) often are appreciated only momentarily as popular entertainment before passing from public view.

As the American film industry, with its sophisticated studio system,

John Ford directing *Stagecoach* (1939).

developed into big business enterprise, executives had to consider each release as a marketable product with a potential return of expenditure. Even abroad, where production costs were generally not as great, most filmmakers soon came to recognize the commercial demands of the medium. This fact is corroborated by the simultaneous production of multilanguage versions of films immediately after the coming of sound technology to the European studios.

The film industry in the 1920s, 30s, and 40s was no different than any other big business operation that offered products to the public. Consistency became the key word in the networking system that included the studios, distribution exchanges, and exhibition houses. If product consumption faltered, each element in the network reacted to compensate: the studios looked for new stories, new stars, and new technical devices, while distributors and exhibitors devised double-feature bills and offered door prizes to woo filmgoers. Industrial response to the ever-changing tastes of a fickle public comprises a fascinating and significant part of motion-picture history.

Tracing the film industry's struggle to survive and to hold its audience is only one way, however, of reexamining the medium's history. Another view is possible through an evaluation of individual artists whose careers have been distinguished by records of great achievement. Directors, in particular, form a significant category of artists whose contributions may be studied as an integral part of film history. It is the director who has stood most prominently at the head of a medium that is critically dependent on collective effort.

The two decades between 1930 and 1950 produced many brilliant films which have survived the test of time. Works by Robert Flaherty, Charles Chaplin, Howard Hawks, John Ford, Frank Capra, and Orson Welles in the United States, and by Jean Renoir, Jean Cocteau, and Vittorio De Sica in Europe are among the great directorial achievements of film history's important middle period. These directors made lasting contributions to cinematic art, and their films of the period continue to be studied and appreciated for their vivid treatment of subject matter as diverse as life itself.

The formative efforts of Chaplin, Ford, Renoir, and Cocteau have been discussed in previous chapters, with a particular emphasis on silent and early sound films which were of critical importance to the development of individual directorial styles. Now the focus shifts to the classic later work of these directors.

Robert Flaherty, a documentarist, also began his film career in the 1920s but continued to produce important films in the 30s and 40s. Orson Welles and Vittorio De Sica first achieved renown in the 1940s and, like the other directors on whom the following chapters focus, are responsible for films of unusual artistic achievement and impact.

The following two chapters do not claim to include all the significant directors of the 1930s and 40s. They seek rather to present a select group of American and European filmmakers whose cinematic styles and themes suggest the artistic genius at work during the motion-picture medium's most commercial period.

DOCUMENTARY TRADITIONS: ROBERT FLAHERTY

Robert Flaherty, (1884–1951) stands apart from other significant directors of his time because his interest in narrative filmmaking was developed through documentary exploration. Often praised as the father of the traditional documentary, Flaherty demonstrated that it was possible to make screen drama from fact, and to make it as exciting as the drama of fiction film. His method of recording and arranging factual material for dramatic and humanistic effect established the guiding principles of the narrative documentary.

Flaherty was born in Iron Mountain, Michigan, attended college in Toronto, Canada, and worked for a while as a mineralogist before beginning to explore on film life in the Canadian Arctic.

Flaherty's first footage, taken during 1917 and 1918 in Baffinland and on the Belcher Islands, was lost in a fire. He returned to the Canadian northland in 1920 and photographed the material that would become *Nanook of the North*(1922).

Nanook of the North

Few documentary films have been as enduring or as charming as Flaherty's simple, humanistic study of an Eskimo family's struggle for survival in the frozen land of Canada's Hudson Bay area. *Nanook of the North* possesses all the fascination of a travelogue, yet it is also a sensitively shaped document of human endeavor, arranged with the skill of a visual poet.

From tens of thousands of feet of filmed material, Flaherty selected those details which would reestablish on the screen the daily and yearly drama he had discovered while living with Nanook and his family for more than a year. This desire to reevoke the conditions that shaped Nanook's life produced the editing aesthetic that would inspire and influence other documentary filmmakers around the world.

Through detail selection Flaherty develops Nanook into a memorable protagonist whose opponent is the environment. Great drama is derived by presenting sequences in which the Eskimo's simple survival skills are revealed and tested in the cruel, ice-covered Ungava landscapes. Shaping tools from animal tusks, hunting, fishing, trapping, training his huskies, building igloos, surviving blizzards, and teaching his own children how to survive—these are the narrative elements that are worked into Flaherty's representation of Eskimo life.

The vicious, seemingly lifeless environment in which Nanook is able to sustain himself serves to create a heroic character of classic proportions. Nanook becomes "Everyman," struggling to conquer nature and to meet the constant challenge of the unknown.

Nanook of the North's remarkable qualities are derived both from the fundamental issues presented by Flaherty and also from the film's many vivid images. In one of the most memorable sequences in the documentary, Flaherty captures Nanook moving slowly into view of camera range as he crawls toward the water's edge to harpoon a gigantic walrus. This scene is presented without editorial trickery so that its drama is contained within a single, rewarding shot.

In another memorable scene Nanook builds an igloo for his family, complete with an ice-block window and reflector to collect the rays of the sun. When he has finished the job and is settled down in the igloo with his wife and children, the little Eskimo smiles directly at Flaherty's camera, acknowledging with gleeful satisfaction his achievement. Charm and drama alternate throughout the film to sustain the appealing nature of Nanook's character.

Documentary Principles

John Grierson, a British documentarist who took inspiration from Flaherty's films and who, in 1926 isolated and published the theoretical principles of the documentary, wrote that *Nanook of the North* was "so intimate in its shots, and so appreciative of the nuances of common feeling, that it was a drama in many ways more telling than anything that had come out of the manufactured sets of Hollywood."

What was impressive to Grierson was Flaherty's method of living with people and events until he had discovered their essence, and then, through shot selection and arrangement of the raw material, recreating that essence as it had been understood. To Grierson this approach created admirable guidelines for the documentarist whose ultimate task involved the "creative interpretation of actuality."

Nanook of the North was not the first documentary film, but it was one of the first to have an international impact and to generate serious interest in the creative possibilities of the factual motion picture. The Lumière and Edison actualities and the more expansive newsreels that followed them had first suggested the potential of the filmed document; Dziga Vertov had taken the factual film a step closer to Flaherty's aesthetic with his *Weekly Reels* (1918–19) in which he spliced together scenes of everyday life in Russia. These films, however, and also the *The Anniversary of the Revolution* (1920), which Vertov produced about the armies on the Russian front, were compilation exercises that catalogued life but did not yet interpret it as Flaherty would do two years later.

In an early sequence of Flaherty's classic study of Eskimo life, Nanook meets his first phonograph at a trading-post.

Moana

After *Nanook of the North,* the Hollywood studios, always keenly observant of motion-picture successes elsewhere, sought to capitalize on the new excitement for the documentary film. Paramount Pictures offered Flaherty a contract and an opportunity to produce a film anywhere he chose. The result was *Moana—A Romance of the Golden Age* (1926).

Like Flaherty's earlier work, this next film focused on everyday life in a distant environment. The setting was the Samoan Islands and the principal character a Polynesian youth named Moana. Flaherty sought to reveal the traditions and rituals which accompanied Moana's progression to manhood.

Without the challenge of environmental hardships that had produced natural drama for his first film, Flaherty was forced to find events in the South Seas which would depict Moana's hardiness. A cult ritual, practiced by earlier generations and involving the painful tattooing of boys entering manhood, was revived and treated in extensive detail. Interspersed with the tattooing sequence were additional ceremonial activities, including a ritualistic dance by a young Polynesian woman. The film's idyllic vignettes resulted in a delightfully romantic documentary which Paramount promoted as "the Love Life of a South Sea Siren" (apparently alluding to the young Polynesian dancer).

While lacking the intense conflict of *Nanook of the North, Moana* utilizes a cinematic style which precisely matches its subject. Large close-ups and extensive camera movement aid in revealing the lovely environment of the South Seas. This treatment, while in direct contrast with the starkness of Nanook's story, contains the simplicity and poetic charm that would typify all of Flaherty's work.

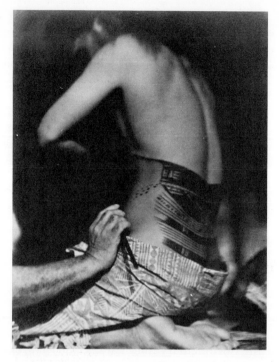

The tatooing of the Polynesian youth in *Moana* (1926).

Visual Experimentation

During the filming of *Moana,* Flaherty became intrigued by the photographic possibilities of camera lenses. This fascination led to a series of films in which he explored new ways of recording factual material: *The Twenty-Four Dollar Island* (1927) was an impressionistic study of New York City's skyscrapers; *White Shadows of the South Seas,* begun in 1927 and completed in 1928 by W. S. Van Dyke, was an attempt to deal through visual contrast and melodrama with changes in the South Seas islands that had been generated by encounters with Western civilization; *Industrial Britain* (1931) profited from extensive camera movement and beautiful photography as Flaherty conveyed the improved working conditions in Britain's modernized factories; *Tabu: A Story of the South Seas* (1931 with F. W. Murnau) continued Flaherty's fascination with Polynesian customs and the lushness of the Pacific Islands.

Man of Aran

With *Man of Aran* (1934) Flaherty once more found a location which suited his thematic interest in filming people in conflict with nature. Photographed on a rugged island off the coast of Ireland, the film's narrative traces the simple daily lives of islanders, principally a father, mother, and son, as they struggle to eke out an existence. The barren land, weather conditions, and the sea are the enemies of people who are observed living in a nearly primitive world. The issues at stake in this combative environment, as in *Nanook of the North,* are fundamental and timeless.

The courageous struggle for survival in *Man of Aran* is revealed through scenes which show the family planting potatoes in rocky soil with seaweed as an enricher, fishing in the turbulent sea, tackling a shark for lamp oil (staged), and fighting to return home from sea during a raging storm. Flaherty's camerawork captures these scenes in vivid, stark images which are often edited together in staccato rhythm.

Peculiarly, an intense appreciation for *Man of Aran's* folk-hero theme in Nazi Germany (where rugged mountain climbing films at the time were conveying similar heroics) acted to make Flaherty's work controversial and to briefly deny its full acceptance by other documentarists.

Films for Conservation

Flaherty's next documentary, *The Land* (1942), was a propandistic study of farm poverty and soil erosion, commissioned by Pare Lorentz,

Man of Aran (1934) brought Flaherty back to a treatment of the theme explored in Nanook of the North: the individual versus nature.

director of the United States Film Service. Flaherty was hired to produce and direct the study at a time when conservation in the United States and abroad had become a major topic for documentary filmmakers.

Lorentz's own reputation as a skillful documentarist had been established with two poetic films which showed the causes of government resettlement and conservation programs: *The Plow That Broke the Plains* (1936), a study of the Dust Bowl tragedy, and *The River* (1937), a visual-aural poem that traced the sources of erosion in the Mississippi River basin and culminated with the creation of the Tennessee Valley Authority.

Abroad in Holland, Joris Ivens' documentary *New Earth* (1934) dealt with the reclamation of land from the Zuyderzee. In Britain during the early 1930s, John Grierson found the documentary film equally useful for inspiring urban working classes.

The use of the documentary format for social analysis and public instruction by these filmmakers led to the formation of the GPO Film Unit in Great Britain (headed by Grierson) and the short-lived United States Film Service with Lorentz at the helm. Lorentz intended that Flaherty's *The Land* be a follow-up study to *The Plow That Broke the Plains* and *The River*.

The final effect of Flaherty's social efforts was an eloquent but depressing picture of the waste which had turned American farm life into a catastrophe during the 1930s. Hopelessness appeared to have drained life and spirit from the faces of the people who were Flaherty's subjects. Because of its painful tone and because the American entry into World War II had precipitated a demand for upbeat, morale-building films, *The Land* on its completion in 1942 was regarded as an ill-timed piece of propaganda. Public distribution of the film was severely curtailed by Lorentz.

Louisiana Story

With *Louisiana Story* (1948) Flaherty completed his film career as he had begun it—returning to a primitive environment to explore life in a precivilized state. The location was Louisiana bayou country and the protagonist a young boy who lives there. It is a film of considerable charm which depicts through documentary and staged elements the boy's primeval world whose serenity is challenged by the arrival of an oil-drilling team.

Life in the Louisiana swamps is shown as the boy sees it: a place of wonderment, where wildlife and humans coexist harmoniously. The boy's domesticated raccoon serves as a major symbol of harmony with nature in the uncomplicated world of the bayou.

With the first explosive sound of the drilling team's dynamite, the focus shifts to another kind of wonderment—that of watching modern

A bayou lad served as the central figure in *Louisiana Story* (1948), Flaherty's poetic study of life in an isolated environment.

technology at work in the search for oil. Flaherty's depiction of this process is as poetic and dreamlike as the boy's earlier vision of his territory. Initial suspicions give way to admiration, and when a huge oil derrick is brought by boat through the swamp waters, the boy observes its movements with the same awe and respect he has held for a crocodile gliding through the bayous.

Ambient sound, along with brief dialogue passages written for the local performers, helps convey the quiet, simple lives of the bayou family. A special musical score by Virgil Thomson unobtrusively incorporates leitmotif themes for each of the principal characters.

Louisiana Story was financed by the Standard Oil Company, but to avoid commercial associations and to retain the film's poetic mood no mention was made of the sponsor.

The distinctive qualities of Flaherty's directorial style grew from his dual role of documentarist-dreammaker. His primary interest was in stories taken from life as it existed in a natural world. Especially thrilling were the harsh challenges of the elements *(Nanook, Man of Aran);* but enchanting, too, were existences in easier environments *(Moana, Louisiana Story).*

Discovering and reconstructing daily behavior of common people became Flaherty's principal method. If restaging an event or detail was necessary to reveal character, he did so without hesitation, but always with respect for the feelings of his subjects. All his films contained strong humanistic qualities which reaffirmed the human spirit.

COMEDY'S GREATS: CAPRA, CHAPLIN, AND OTHER UNIQUE PERFORMERS

The decades of the 1930s and 1940s were rich ones for screen comics and comedy directors. A leading genre of the silent years (to some *the* genre), film comedy not only maintained its public popularity after the advent of talking pictures, but produced some of the most memorable films of a period that encompassed both the Depression years and World War II. These historic events surely contributed to the popularity of motion pictures that offered escape and tension-relieving laughter.

Talent along with diversity and refinement of form were also critical factors in comedy's stronghold. Spirited directors and a host of talented performers developed individual styles that enriched and broadened the genre's range of expression. Frank Capra, Ernst Lubitsch, Charles Chaplin, Mae West, and W. C. Fields were among those directors and performers responsible for unique brands of sound comedy. The ingenious Marx Brothers also generated an original comic style entirely of their own inventiveness.

Keaton and Langdon: Less Fortunate

Missing from the list of prominent sound comedians are Buster Keaton and Harry Langdon, two of silent film's comic stars. Neither was able to achieve success in sound comedies. The stiff, mute quality of Keaton's screen persona was largely responsible for the source of his silent comedy and also for his inability to adapt the character well to talking pictures. Harry Langdon, who also utilized subtle pantomine and who juxtaposed an innocent, clownlike figure against a cruel world, suffered in sound films for the same reasons. Langdon's most successful film, made in 1926, was *The Strong Man,* directed and co-authored by Frank Capra. Work with Langdon on this film and in *Long Pants* (1927) catapulted Capra into directorial prominence while Langdon's career shortly thereafter went into steady decline.

Frank Capra

Frank Capra (1897–   ) was in the forefront of early, successful directors of talking comedies, producing during the 1930s a charming group of domestic comedies and social dramas. The Italian-born director joined Columbia Pictures in 1928 after working as a comedy writer for Hal Roach and Mack Sennett. Following a number of routine

<Harry Langdon, a moon-
faced clown, who projected a
quality of simple innocence
confronting an adult, often
cruel, world.

assignments, Capra established his reputation as a witty, stylish director
with *Lady for a Day* (1933). Robert Riskin adapted the sentimental
Damon Runyon story about Apple Annie for the screen, and with this
film entered into a long, collaborative relationship with Capra that
would prove mutually beneficial.

In 1934 Capra achieved even greater success with the release of *It
Happened One Night.* This screwball comedy with Claudette Colbert and
Clark Gable received the Academy of Motion Picture Arts and Sciences
awards for Best Picture, Director, Writer, Actor and Actress—a feat
which would not be repeated again until *One Flew Over the Cuckoo's Nest*
swept the awards competition for 1975.

The Capra-Riskin style of filmmaking continued to appear in their
subsequent collaborations at Columbia: *Mr. Deeds Goes to Town* (1936),
You Can't Take It with You (1938), and *Meet John Doe* (1941). These pictures
evinced a middle-class view of American life, presented with satirical yet
near idealistic reaffirmation of the country's values. They suited both the
spirit of the times and the personal visions of their creators. The
Depression years and the attacks by Will Hays' office on films given to
national criticism made the unabashed goodwill of Capra's films all the
more appealing. Capra's own view of the country to which he had
immigrated as a 6-year-old child also appeared in his early work.

Gary Cooper as Longfellow Deeds bids farewell to a hometown crowd. He is departing his simple world for life in New York; but, as was typical of Capra's heroes, neither wealth nor big-city corruption would destroy Deeds' abiding honesty.

Mr. Deeds Goes to Town   *Mr. Deeds Goes to Town* was adapted by Riskin from a serialized *Saturday Evening Post* story by Clarence B. Kelland. In the picture, Gary Cooper portrays the naive, honest, and optimistic Longfellow Deeds. Deeds, a country boy who has inherited a huge sum of money, takes his fortune to the cynical, corrupt world of the large city. There, in the midst of an alien environment, he displays himself as a model American—disillusioned by what he has found, but willing to share his wealth with the needy.

The optimism and sentiment of *Mr. Deeds Goes to Town* offered a film fantasy that was enormously appealing to the American public. Its ideas provided more escapism than realism by projecting the "little man" as the ultimate winner in a corrupt and callous world.

You Can't Take It with You   Capra's populist stance continued in *You Can't Take It with You,* emerging through the lunatic activities of an eccentric family who have rejected money and sophistication for a homey, free existence. The father refuses to pay income taxes simply because he does not believe in them; the mother is a painter-writer; a daughter imagines herself a gifted ballerina; a son-in-law makes music on a xylophone; a guest produces fireworks in a basement workroom. This flurry of activity often occurs at once in the family parlor. Riskin adapted the free-spirited screenplay from the stage play by George S. Kaufman and Moss Hart.

Graham Greene, a critic for *The Spectator,* wrote of *You Can't Take It with You:*

> . . . It is useless trying to analyze the idea behind the Capra films: there *is* no idea that you'd notice, only a sense of dissatisfaction, an urge to escape—onto the open road with the daughter of a millionaire, back to small town simplicity on a safe income, away to remote, secure Shangri-La. [*The Spectator,* November 1938.]

Capra's films implied that whether the particular problem for Americans was social, economic, or political, the movement toward a Shangri-La could be achieved through personal redemption, honesty, and goodwill.

Mr. Smith Goes to Washington Working with screenwriter Sidney Buchman rather than Riskin, Capra's *Mr. Smith Goes to Washington* (1939) carries forth similar ideas. James Stewart portrays a Boy Scout leader who is sent to Washington to fill an unexpired Senate term. Awkwardly, yet with idealism and patriotism, Smith leads a twenty-three hour filibuster during an attempt by corrupt senators to remove him from office.

At one point Smith gestures toward the Capitol dome and says "Get up there with that lady that's on top of this Capitol dome—the lady that stands for liberty—and you'll see the whole parade of what man's carved out for himself after centuries of fighting for something better than just jungle law." In the end Jefferson Smith rallies public support and is victorious, the little man once more having won out over the system. In defense of this stance critic Paul Rotha has written of *Mr. Smith Goes to Washington::*

> Its significance, it seems to me, lies not in its truth or falsity, but in its persistence as an idea and its popularity with audiences. . . . It is to be evaluated less as a mirror of life than as a document of human psychology, an index to the temper of the popular spirit. [*The Film till Now,* Middlesex, England: Spring Books, 1967, pp. 452–3.]

Meet John Doe Riskin and Capra teamed again for *Meet John Doe* (1941) in yet another screen story about redemption within a corrupt world.

John Doe (Gary Cooper), after allowing himself to become involved in a fascist-like power scheme, confesses his sins to those whom he has deluded. The normally "goodwilled" public is furious after learning of their idol's involvement with forces of evil. This departure from the typical Riskin-Capra "good guy" hero and the film's less than optimistic

Mr. Smith (James Stewart) holds out against expulsion from the U.S. Senate by way of a lengthy filibuster. Naivete again triumphs over evil in a Frank Capra film.

ending were considered daring by many critics, while Capra personally expressed dissatisfaction over the film's conclusion.

The thematic appeal of Capra's populist films was always matched by a good-humored, energetic style of film direction. Capra displayed a particular gift for developing his folksy characters with combined sincerity and comic touches.

Ernst Lubitsch

Also important in screen comedy's transition to sound motion pictures was Ernst Lubitsch whose comedy interests began in Germany in 1917 and reached new dimensions in Hollywood during the thirties. Lubitsch's capabilities for handling moral discrepancies and sexual innuendo in films such as *Trouble in Paradise* (1932), *Design for Living* (1933), and *Ninotchka* (1939) resulted in some of the most stylish, urbane comedies ever brought to the screen.

Lubitsch's *Trouble in Paradise* was his first straight dialogue comedy, made after directing several musicals for Paramount in the early years of sound pictures. This slick comedy starred Miriam Hopkins, Kay Francis, and Herbert Marshall in a plot involving a thieving couple (Hopkins and Marshall) who weasle their way into the household of a wealthy Parisian widow (Francis). A triangular love affair develops, forcing Marshall ultimately to make a choice between the wealthy widow and his partner in crime.

Lubitsch's treatment of this romantic comedy deftly satirizes life among the wealthy (and those aspiring to such a life) during an era of international Depression. The spirited activities of the pair of crooks and the witty dialogue are further enhanced by a light-hearted musical score that plays continously on the sound track. Art deco settings and glittering costumes also aid in making *Trouble in Paradise* a sophisticated comedy-of-manners whose luxuriously vacuous and scheming world held ironies for the times.

Lubitsch's directorial "touch" is evident throughout the film: in the use of fleeting details to suggest the amoral love play (e.g., shadows on a bed), in the use of quick cutting to emphasize the comic repartee, in the adroit handling of characterization, in the clever skirting of moral codes. An aura of cynicism pervades *Trouble in Paradise* as Lubitsch charmingly exposes the values of the idle upper class.

Director Peter Bogdanovich, a confessed imitator, has defined the Lubitsch "touch" as the "impeccably appropriate placement of the camera, the subtle economy of his plotting, the oblique dialogue which had a way of saying everything through indirection." [*Esquire*, November 1972.]

The Marx Brothers, W. C. Fields, and Mae West

As group comedians, the unique Marx Brothers team, imported to Hollywood from Broadway in 1929, developed a screen style that has been variously described as comedy of insult, surrealistic, absurd, visual and verbal lunacy.

In a series of films beginning with *The Cocoanuts* (1929), the Marx

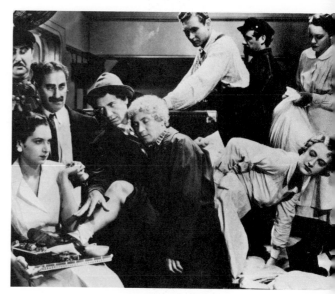

Bodies proliferate within a tiny stateroom in the Marx Brothers' *A Night at the Opera* (1935)—a comedic device which presaged elements employed by theater-of-the-absurd playwrights.

Brothers employed comic elements, including revolutionary object proliferation and verbal mishmash, that would later be associated with the experimental methods of avant-garde theater. These elements are particularly evident in *A Night at the Opera* (1935) where the reading of a contract agreement has the verbal repetitions of Eugène Ionesco's *The Lesson,* and where a stateroom is stuffed with people in a manner reminiscent of Ionesco's material absurdities, e.g., *The Chairs.* More important to general audiences was the Marx Brothers' delightful and hilarious manner of poking fun at pretense and social convention.

W. C. Fields and Mae West brought distinctive styles to screen comedy after earlier careers as vaudeville performers. Both developed comic characters in which physique, vocal delivery, and an irreverent attitude were critical elements and both wrote much of their own material.

Fields, the white-collar worker and perennial cynic, employed an effective throwaway method of line delivery in films where comic situations invariably grew from an unrestrained mistreatment of others, e.g., *The Dentist* (1932), *The Barber Shop* (1933).

West, the master of sexual innuendo, derived comic effect from use of her imposing figure and from glibly cadenced and demolishing retorts. The opening lines of dialogue for *She Done Him Wrong* (1933) go:

Bystander: You're a fine woman.
Mae West: One of the finest women ever walked the streets.

Fields and West combined their unique talents in *My Little Chickadee* (1940).

Charles Chaplin

Of those silent comedians who made a successful transition to sound film, Charles Chaplin, not surprisingly, was the most resistant of all to the new technology. His universally popular little tramp character had dominated loosely structured, episodic films with a brilliant *comedia dell'arte* approach to visual gags and social commentary.

Chaplin's initial reaction to the advent of sound was a belief that silent comedy could coexist amicably with talking pictures. For this reason his first sound-era film, *City Lights* (1931), and the picture that followed, *Modern Times* (1936), rejected synchronous dialogue for the more favored pantomine.

City Lights In a highly sentimental plot the little tramp falls in love with a blind girl (Virginia Cherrill) who sells flowers on a street corner. Chaplin leads the girl to believe that he is a wealthy gentleman who will provide the money for an operation needed to cure the girl's blindness.

Two incomparable comedians, Mae West and W. C. Fields, in *My Little Chicadee* (1940).

Chaplin and the blind flower girl (Virginia Cherrill) in *City Lights* (1931). Although a film without dialogue, a synchronized musical score and comic sound effects helped make the picture one of Chaplin's most successful.

A drunken millionaire, whom Chaplin saves from drowning, eventually supplies the money for the operation. The romantic plot is softened by numerous sight gags, including a boxing match where Chaplin (one of the boxers) displays his balletic abilities with virtuoso effect.

City Lights was photographed by its principal cinematographer, Rollie Totheroh, in much the same manner as earlier films. Long shots dominate and settings remain stylized and unobtrusive. To support the film's story and its visual gags, Chaplin wrote an accompanying musical score and included several synchronized sound effects for selected scenes. In the opening scene where the mayor unveils a statue and reveals the little tramp asleep in its arms, garbled sounds are incorporated to represent the mayor's raspy voice.

City Lights' sentimental love story and well-placed gags allowed Chaplin to win the favor of audiences despite obvious expectations of a talking Charlie.

Modern Times Successful with *City Lights,* Chaplin resisted sound once more in the making of *Modern Times.* In his autobiography he tells, however, of considering, then rejecting, dialogue for the picture:

> Occasionally I mused over the possibility of making a sound film, but the thought sickened me, for I realized I could never achieve the excellence of my silent pictures. [*My Autobiography,* New York: Simon & Schuster, 1964, p. 366.]

In satirizing the impact of increasing technology on the human condition, *Modern Times* draws heavily on visual exaggeration for both comic and social effect. Following the prologue titles which read: "*Modern Times* is the story of industry, of individual enterprise— humanity crusading in the pursuit of happiness," an Eisenstein-inspired montage of attraction brings together a shot of sheep being marched to slaughter with a similarly composed shot of a rush of workers on the way to their jobs.

Chaplin is then seen at work on an assembly line where his job is to tighten two bolts on metal plates that are carried along by a conveyer belt. Gigantic factory machines with an elaborate arrangement of cogs and wheels dwarf the little tramp's figure, suggesting a world where human endeavor has lost its importance.

These thematic ideas are further emphasized with a series of visual gags involving a specialized machine designed to feed workers on the assembly line, thus potentially eliminating the need for a lunch hour. While the feeding machine is being tested on Charlie as he works, a malfunction occurs, and the little tramp shortly thereafter lands in a psychiatric hospital where he is treated for a nervous breakdown. When he is released it is the height of the depression and employment is difficult to find.

Charlie at work on the assembly line in *Modern Times* (1936).

At this point a love odyssey, set in bleak times, begins. Charlie meets a young woman (Paulette Goddard), a gamin, who suffers equally. Existence for the two has been a series of ups and downs and numerous encounters with law officials. He is arrested when he unwittingly marches with a workers' demonstration; she, when she is caught stealing bread for her younger sisters.

Life finally begins to look better for the two when the gamin is hired as a dancer in a cafe and he is taken on as a singing waiter.

Although a failure as a waiter, Charlie is a great success as an entertainer—singing in a pseudo-continental manner that is vaguely suggestive of Maurice Chevalier. His moment of success in the cafe disappears quickly, however, with the arrival of police officers who attempt to arrest the gamin on vagrancy charges. She and Chaplin must once more flee, and in the final shot are seen marching hand in hand down a lonely road toward distant mountains.

Modern Times with its seriocomic story achieves a pathos similar in effect to that of *The Gold Rush*. Both are comedies inspired by rather harrowing tales of efforts at survival (in the cruel Klondike, on the dehumanizing assembly line). In each film Charlie is a loner, a representative victim of society's forces which consume the human spirit and challenge the desire for survival. Both films, in different but poignant ways, also stress the values of friendship and love in bolstering the human spirit when the times, distant or modern, have dragged it down.

For *Modern Times* Chaplin again opted for a sentimental musical

Charlie and the "gamin" (Paulette Goddard), both victims of modern times, offer comfort to one another.

score of his own composing, and the limited use of nonsynchronous speech. In one instance, a radio blurts out a commercial for a product that offers relief from gastritis. During the song routines in the cafe, Chaplin's lyrics remain slapstick gibberish:

> La spinach or la busho, Cigaretto toto bello, Ce rakish spagoletto, Ce le tu la tu la trois! Señora de la tima, voulez-vous la taximeter, La jaunta sur la seata, Je le tu le tu waah!

Although *Modern Times* has been criticized for a lack of narrative unity and for its failure to carry through the promising technological theme to the end, the larger issues of human suffering and disillusionment are threads that tie together this biting comedy.

It is fascinating to contrast the dark ideas of Chaplin's comedy with those in Frank Capra's hopeful, populist comedies made during the same era. Together they provide evidence of the diversity of expression and social comment reaching audiences through Hollywood comedies of the 1930s.

That Chaplin ended *Modern Times* with a vocal number, followed by a nostalgic shot of the motion picture's most familiar character shuffling off into the sunset, held double import. In effect the conclusion signaled the disappearance of the little tramp and, finally, the acceptance of talking pictures. With *The Great Dictator,* released in 1940, Chaplin ventured into new territory—stylistically and dramatically.

The Great Dictator In a bold and prescient gesture, *The Great Dictator* offered a satiric attack on Adolf Hitler (known in the film as Adenoid Hynkel). Chaplin portrays in parallel stories both Hynkel and a Jewish barber serving as a soldier in the Tomanian Army. The barber in typical Chaplinesque slapstick routines bumbles his way through farcical battles, but becomes a hero when he takes control of a plane and saves the life of Commander Schultz. This deed is reciprocated when Schultz, a Party official, later intervenes to save the barber's life as he is about to be strung up by Storm Troopers in the Jewish ghetto where he lives.

In the meantime Hynkel (head of the "Double Cross Party") rises quickly to power, and in one instance exults in his success by dancing a pas de deux to music from *Lohengrin.* His partner is a globe of the world.

Benito Mussolini, in the cartoon presence of a character named Benzino Napaloni (Jack Oakie), also receives satiric treatment as he and Hynkel negotiate plans for the invasion of Osterlich.

The Great Dictator concludes with a case of mistaken identity in which Hynkel is arrested by his own troops who believe him to be the fugitive barber. The barber at the same time is thought to be Hynkel and is taken to a Party rally where he delivers an impassioned speech against totalitarianism. Hannah (Paulette Goddard), a ghetto friend of the barber's, hears the call for freedom over a radio. In a final poetic shot the woman smiles faintly, but hopefully.

The fact that *The Great Dictator's* cartoon approach to politics was followed rapidly by the precipitous and terrible events of World War II has made the film a rich one for critical opinions on Chaplin's groundbreaking work.

Andrew Sarris has noted Chaplin's prescience in "challenging the authority of irrational power at a time when many intellectuals were dazzled by the muscular sex appeal of totalitarianism."

Critic Bosley Crowther wrote that *The Great Dictator* "filled the screen with a job of vivisection that is now recorded history" and "reached heights of metaphorical comment and ironical mockery."

Other critics and historians have noted Chaplin's brilliance in shaping Hynkel's persona by drawing on one side of the tramp's well-established character: the wounded side which in a dozen earlier films had reacted to life's cruelties with similar cruel and destructive responses. It is this side of the tramp that, uncontrolled, became the essence of Chaplin's Hynkel. The other side, that of the essentially good and accepting victim, is separated off into the person of the barber.

SOUND TECHNIQUE In this first talking picture, Chaplin shows a keen comic proficiency with sound technique. Continuing the slapstick approach to verbal expression heard in the song routine at the conclusion

The two opposing natures of the little tramp's personality—the compassionate and the antisocial—are separated to form the characters of the Barber and Hynkel in *The Great Dictator* (1940).

of *Modern Times,* Chaplin again treats words as nonsensical gibberish. Hynkel's dictatorial pronouncements come out "Democratia schtunk, Libertad schtunk, Freisprachen schtunk!" Language, like Chaplin's gestures and mannerisms, serves to mock the dictator's grand conceits. The barber by contrast remains more completely the silent clown whose pathos is derived largely from pantomime.

Direct speech, used in the final monologue's call to freedom, is a contrived appendage in which Chaplin himself is the speaker. He has stepped by necessity out of character to remind filmgoers that the comic events that have gone before hold more insidious implications than their farcical treatment might suggest.

Final Work Two additional feature-length comedies were completed by Chaplin before departing the United States in 1952 for residence in Switzerland: *Monsieur Verdoux* (1947) and *Limelight* (1952). Each film found its ardent admirers.

In *Monsieur Verdoux* Chaplin has totally shed the tramp character for the stylish Henri Verdoux, an out-of-work bank teller who supports his handicapped wife and small son by murdering wealthy women. Verdoux, a cold professional, woos, marries, and then kills one victim after another for her inheritance. Four of these crimes are treated, including a highly comic one that involves the hard-to-do-in Annabella Bonheur (Martha Raye).

The plot for this black comedy was conceived by Orson Welles and developed into screenplay form by Chaplin. Inspiration for the story came from accounts of Henri-Désiré Landru's reign in France as a heartless wife-killer.

Chaplin's apparent interest in such a morbid brand of comedy resided in the plot's satiric possibilities. The elegant businesslike manner by which Henri Verdoux carries out his notorious deeds provided a clever means of likening business activity to murder, and, likewise, murder to business. Verdoux even complains, with domestic casualness, about the taxing demands of his work.

At other times Chaplin's ironic comedy is less oblique. After capture and during his trial, Verdoux advertises himself as merely a small-time businessman, arguing on his own behalf by pointing to greater crimes: "Mass killing. Does not the world encourage it? I am an amateur by comparison." In another instance he proclaims introspectively: "One murder makes a villain—millions sanctify."

During the period just before his execution by guillotine, Verdoux's character is permitted to become philosophical, and it is during these concluding scenes that Chaplin's thematic intentions are realized. Verdoux asks his priest confessor: "Who knows what sin is, born as it is from heaven, from God's fallen angel? Who knows what ultimate destiny is served? After all, what would *you* be doing without sin?"

Such comments promoted public outcries against the brazen *Mon-*

In *Limelight* (1952) Calvero (Chaplin), an aging comic, prepares to turn over the stage to a talented young ballerina (Claire Bloom).

sieur Verdoux, forcing an eventual recall of prints from distributors. Along with *The Great Dictator* it has remained Chaplin's most controversial film. Not surprisingly it failed at the box office, but was revived to considerable acclaim in 1964.

The last American film, *Limelight* (1952), was as sentimental as *Monsieur Verdoux* was morbid. *Limelight* returns to a familiar scene from Chaplin's childhood: a London music hall, circa 1914. The principal character, Calvero (Chaplin), is an aging but dignified comic who has begun to realize that the end of his career is imminent. He has taken to drink and life appears hopeless until one night on the way home he saves a distraught young ballerina (Claire Bloom) from suicide. The woman becomes a source of inspiration to Calvero, and he leads her to success on the ballet stage. In a final moment of glory Calvero appears in a benefit performance with his former partner (Buster Keaton), treating the audience to an uproarious slapstick routine involving a piano and a violin. He is cheered wildly and then, exhausted, dies smiling in the wings just as the young ballerina dances onto the stage.

Limelight's conclusion offered a fitting farewell to Chaplin's comic genius. The clown who entertained audiences for four decades finds himself in a state of crisis, regains his confidence, and departs without regrets. The human spirit has persevered. Furthermore, when the picture ends, it is the young ballerina who holds the limelight, not Chaplin, suggesting that one generation of talent has now passed to another.

Before the premiere of *Limelight,* Chaplin left the United States for travel in Europe and while away was denied a reentry permit. Public reaction to *Monsieur Verdoux,* political innuendo during the House Un-American Activities investigations of Hollywood, and a lively personal life had acted to make Chaplin a public figure of considerable notoriety. He decided to settle with his family in Switzerland and except for the direction of two mediocre comedies, *A King in New York* (1957) and *A Countess from Hong Kong* (1966), he lived quietly there until his death on Christmas Day, 1977.

The critic James Agee summarized the significance of Chaplin's career in this way:

> Of all the comedians he worked most deeply and most shrewdly within a realization of what a human being is, and is up against. The Tramp is as centrally representative of humanity, as many-sided and as mysterious as Hamlet, and it seems unlikely that any dancer or actor can ever have excelled him in eloquence, variety or poignancy of motion. [*Life*, September 5, 1949.]

HOWARD HAWKS AND JOHN FORD: MASTER STORYTELLERS

Of the many excellent studio directors of the thirties and forties, few rose above Howard Hawks (1896–1977) and John Ford (1895–1973) in professional achievement or public regard. Hawks and Ford, often mentioned in the same breath as the master storytellers of Hollywood's golden era, exemplified the studio craftsman who could handle varied directorial assignments with efficiency and style. Both shared a primary interest in the well-made narrative film where plot and characterization are developed through the rapid flow of action.

Hawks

While Hawks' efforts were well-realized in a number of different genres, the qualities of male-oriented toughness in his films and a more typical studio "look" were stylistic differences which separated him from Ford. As script collaborator on nearly every film he directed, Hawks helped shape active stories which, whether comedy or melodrama, invariably drew on plot conventions where the male protagonist's sense of responsibility to his profession or to his gender is dramatically tested. *Bringing Up Baby* (1938) and *His Girl Friday* (1940) were screwball, sex-war comedies in which Cary Grant engaged himself in fast-paced verbal battles with such formidable opponents as Katharine Hepburn and Rosalind Russell.

His Girl Friday was a remake of *The Front Page* which had been a successful stage play and which was first brought to the screen by Lewis Milestone in 1930. Hawks, in rewriting one of the principal roles for a woman (Rosalind Russell), took certain liberties with the original story by Ben Hecht and Charles MacArthur. The fast-talking account of newspaper reporters, however, gained new momentum under Hawks'

Cary Grant and Rosalind Russell at odds with each other in Howard Hawks' *His Girl Friday* (1940).

dynamic direction. Character battles and verbal barbs come at a break-neck pace as the reporters, caught up in an arena of political corruption, interact with one another.

By altering one of the roles to fit a woman, Hawks was able to develop the sex antagonism theme which became a standard of his screwball comedies. Rosalind Russell, star reporter, and Cary Grant, wise-cracking editor, do battle with one another in grand style, engaging themselves in a frenetic game of one-upmanship as they shrewdly mix professional maneuvering with romantic aspirations.

Hawks' love of action is evident in auto-racing films (*The Crowd Roars,* 1932), gangster films (*Scarface,* 1932), and in films about airplane heroics: *The Dawn Patrol* (1930), *Only Angels Have Wings* (1939), and *Air Force* (1943). The latter group of works and Hawks' penchant for action grew from his service in World War I as an airline pilot.

Only Angels Have Wings was a typical Hawks air-action tale about fliers who perform heroically during the most dangerous of situations. Through their brave acts in the air, the mail-transport heroes redeem themselves for inadequacies on the ground. Hawks' male characters, as in all of his action films, are stoic individuals, eschewing sentimentality for the purpose of self-protection. One of the fliers (Cary Grant), a man seemingly invulnerable to emotion, eventually breaks down when his best friend (Thomas Mitchell) is killed in an air crash. Jean Arthur, on discovering Grant's true feelings, is able to enter into a bond of friendship with the flier which had earlier been impossible. The tough quality of Hawks' action story gives way in the end to an honest moment of human interaction. This moment of communication and trust appeared commonly as the climax for Hawks's many action films.

In all his directing exercises, which also included westerns and musicals, Hawks proved himself in skillful command of film technique. He was especially gifted at creating pointed dialogue that was perfectly suited to the constantly moving dramatic action, and at treating his material in a direct clean manner that allowed his tough-minded plots to speak for themselves.

Ford

As a diversified and prolific director who produced an unusually large number of screen masterpieces, John Ford merits detailed analysis as a studio-era stylist. During his long career, he directed more than 125 feature-length motion pictures. Some of his folklore studies of the Old West were so perfectly shaped they set the standards by which all other efforts within the genre were (and often still are) judged. Few westerns have matched *Stagecoach* (1939) in generic achievement. Standard conventions in Ford's hands became poetic tools, supported by a photographic style that was atmospheric and evocative. Conflict and crisis within a frontier environment became Ford's predominant theme.

In addition to finely tuned western sagas, Ford created masterpieces that were set in contemporary times. Invariably they too dramatized the lives of individuals confronting crisis in well-defined environments. *The Informer* (1935), *The Grapes of Wrath* (1940), *How Green Was My Valley* (1941) examined conflicts born, respectively, of the Irish rebellion, the American Depression, and upheaval in Welsh mining territory. The poetic Ford touch and humanistic concerns that established his reputation in westerns carried over well to distinguish these more social-minded studies.

Ford's distinctive style, which first earned critical acclaim in *The Iron Horse* (1924), found easy transition to the sound film in the early 1930s, owing in no small way to a respect for visual story-telling and economy of dialogue. Among the prolific director's important early talking films were *Arrowsmith* (1931), *The Lost Patrol* (1934), and *The Whole Town's Talking* (1935). The international success of these releases also helped to establish the fact that Ford was a director with broad commercial appeal—a factor which in time would distinguish him as a director equally well-loved by the public and by fellow filmmakers.

The Informer With *The Informer* in 1935 Ford tackled an unusual story of some closeness to his heart. Born of Irish parentage as Sean Aloysius O'Feeny (O'Fearna), Ford changed his name but never fully shed his Irish spirit. *The Informer* depicted, in one of Hollywood's first great antihero pictures, an evening during the Irish rebellion of 1922 when the Sinn Fein organization was moving to drive British imperialists from the country.

Dudley Nichols' literate screenplay dealt not with the rebellion in general terms, but with a simple man's desire to be a part of events around him. The man, Gypo Nolan (Victor McLaglen), becomes a victim of his own weaknesses by informing on a friend for a cash reward of 20

Gypo Nolan (Victor McLaglen), mortally wounded, receives forgiveness for his act of betrayal.

pounds. This betrayal leads to increasing guilt as Nolan, pitiably, attempts to forget the act he has committed. Later he is captured, tried by a rebel court, and escapes briefly, only to be gunned down by the rebels. Mortally wounded, Nolan staggers into a church and dies at the altar after receiving forgiveness from his betrayed friend's mother who prays before the votive candles.

Ford's stylized methods of expression, necessitated by a severely limited budget, made *The Informer* one of Hollywood's most experimental film exercises of the 1930s. Joseph August's cinematography and Max Steiner's musical score perform admirably as substitutes for production embellishment. Low-key lighting, nearly expressionistic in tone, covers the sparse settings while simultaneously enhancing the psychological drift of the story. Steiner's music acts to convey Nolan's state of mind (often with melodramatic force), and also to suggest scale and grandeur that do not exist in the intimate treatment. In one instance a close shot of soldiers' marching feet is matched with a large-sounding musical accompaniment to imply a full military unit.

Ford's use of selective details and sound elements to communicate subjectivity create a forceful psychological drama. Ticking clocks, a tapping cane, brief voice-over inserts, and musical coordination imaginatively reveal Nolan's guilt-ridden inner self. The continuous reappearance of a "wanted" poster, carrying the face of the betrayed friend, haunts the doomed informer. Because of its successful application of sounds to screen psychology, *The Informer* suggested a whole new range of possibilities for character interiorization within the motion picture.

Stagecoach Ford's love of action and the western format achieved classic proportions with *Stagecoach* (1939). This grand, entertaining rendering of the western myth that had its screen beginnings in *The Great Train Robbery* generated new appreciation for the genre as well as for Ford's impressive directorial style.

Form and Theme What distinguishes *Stagecoach* from conventional fare is its classic form. The plot centers on the dramatic concept of a "ship of fools"—in the case of Dudley Nichols' screenplay a stagecoach holding nine people who must travel through desolate territory to reach the frontier town of Lordsburg.

In the microcosmic group of characters are a variety of societal types: a prostitute (Claire Trevor) and a drunken doctor (Thomas Mitchell) who have been forced by social pressures to leave the town of Tonto, Arizona for residence elsewhere; a whiskey drummer (Donald Meek) from Kansas City; a pregnant woman (Louise Platt) from the East who is traveling to join her soldier husband; an elegant and mysterious gambler (John Carradine); a banker (Barton Churchill) who is fleeing with embezzled money; an outlaw (John Wayne) who joins the other passengers in mid-journey; the stagecoach driver (Andy Devine) and an accompanying United States Marshal (George Bancroft) who rides shotgun on the trip.

These characters collectively symbolize weaknesses born of western urbanization. The journey away from urban life and into the open wilderness is one of reinitiation and cleansing. As the Overland Stagecoach makes its way through the vast expanses of Monument Valley, the little vehicle once more becomes the lonely western sojourner—cut off from civilization and destined to suffer anew the challenges of the raw frontier.

The journey, an archetypal passage from light to darkness to light, brings the stagecoach occupants into opposition with desert heat, driving dust storms, an Apache attack, and, most significantly, with one another. The banker, gambler, and officer's wife unite against the two social outcasts—the prostitute, Dallas, and the drunken Doc Boone. With their self-righteous and condescending airs the trio of townspeople become more despicable than the outcasts they oppose. Each in a different way has turned a back on basic human values: the banker has absconded with bank funds, the gambler is an uncommitted drifter, and Mrs. Mallory, the pregnant Easterner, chooses to suffer in isolated misery rather than accept solace from a prostitute. The whiskey drummer, too meek to take sides, confesses to having abandoned his desire to become "a man of the cloth" in order to run his wife's inherited liquor business. All those on the stagecoach carry human weaknesses.

It is the environment that ultimately pulls the characters up to more noble stature and draws them closer together. Alone and fully exposed on the open plains, the stagecoach occupants finally unite in an effort to survive the Apache attack. Suddenly the landscape has made them all equally vulnerable to forces far more critical than those nurtured by urban life. Once more a community in spirit, the group fights valiantly against the attackers until rescued by an American cavalry unit.

Included in this classic tale of the purifying journey is Ringo Kid's story of personal revenge. The Kid, as he is fondly called by law officials, is a renegade hero—an essentially good man, but one who has wound up in prison because of differences with the villainous Plummer gang. When the Ringo Kid (John Wayne) joins the stagecoach, he has escaped prison and is on his way to Lordsburg to avenge his brother's murder by the Plummers. A lame horse forces the Ringo Kid to stop the stagecoach, not expecting to find a U.S. Marshal on the driver's seat.

Ringo's characterization follows conventional expectations; a shy but efficient wielder of guns who abides by the code of conduct that governs western conflicts. Nevertheless, he is a gunman of formidable reputation and earned respect. Unlike other characters riding the stagecoach, Ringo holds all women in high esteem and in his simple, kindhearted way both defends Dallas and falls in love with her.

Stagecoach concludes with the vehicle's jubilant arrival in Lordsburg after the cavalry rescue, followed quickly by Ringo's showdown in the darkened streets. The shoot-out with the Plummer boys is sanctioned by the U.S. Marshal in a gesture of respect for Ringo and apparent distaste for the opponents. Successful in his act of revenge, Ringo once more receives favor from the Marshal and is allowed to ride away with Dallas for life together on a distant ranch.

On this happy, upbeat note, crisis and conflict for each of the passengers have been resolved: Lucy Mallory is reunited with her Army husband; Buck, the driver, rejoins his large Mexican family; the now self-confident whiskey drummer prepares to return home to his wife in Kansas City; the banker has been arrested and hauled away to jail; Doc Boone has gained new self-respect after delivering Lucy Mallory's baby and is temporarily sober; the gambler has died a repentant death; and Dallas and Ringo depart to begin life anew. The mythic fantasy is complete.

TECHNIQUE Ford's handling of the environmental and personal elements that combine to form *Stagecoach* has made the film a model for visual and structural analysis. In the story's first few minutes each of the principal characters, except the Ringo Kid, has been introduced to set the personal drama into action. Dialogue is terse but pointed in defining characters as they congregate around the readied stagecoach.

In a swift, economic sweep of events Ford assumes prior knowledge of the western story on the viewer's part. A familiar, stereotyped western-town facade establishes the location of the story without fanfare, and the utterance of the word "Geronimo" (spoken in the film's first minute) portends the ultimate conflict. This rapid exposition indicates that the story is essentially one of action and movement.

Throughout the journey, editing and cinematography work together to produce both grandeur and intimacy. Scenes inside the coach are captured in lingering close-ups as the characters interact. Soft studio lighting heightens romantic moments. Between these intimate scenes are

The superbly photographed landscapes enhanced the poetic and mythic qualities of John Ford's *Stagecoach* (1939).

extreme long shots of the lonely, fragile stagecoach struggling across the barren landscape.

Pictorial composition is often brilliantly conceived. The Ringo Kid's sudden appearance by the side of the road, his saddle over one arm and Winchester rifle in hand, is intensified by a rapid dolly-in from imposing long shot to smiling close-up. A more dramatic or heroic introduction of a screen character cannot be imagined.

Another instance of telling composition occurs when soldiers, accompanying the stagecoach on the first leg of its journey, must depart for another assignment. The departure is staged at a fork in the road where the escorts and passengers pause to say farewell. As the stagecoach and soldiers take up their separate journeys, the two roads become ever-widening, and each foot of movement places the stagecoach further away from protection. In the immediate foreground, at the point where the two divergent roads meet, the skull of a dead horse achieves an ominous presence as the two groups disappear into the distance.

Editing style in Ford's construction of scenes is generally unobtrusive and academic with action and reaction demands dictating cutting points. The stagecoach attack, however, still remains as one of the most exciting and superbly edited chase sequences ever put on film. Again Ford works between close-up shots of the principal characters fighting for their lives and sweeping long shots of the action field. The long shots gain in dramatic value from breathtaking stunt work which involves both men and horses.

Clever parallel editing and dark, expressionistic lighting during the shoot-out scene in Lordsburg allow a climax of sustained suspense. Ford's cutaway methods in this scene as well as the chance arrival of the cavalry in the earlier chase scene were soon widely imitated and became clichés of the western film.

Stagecoach, despite its sometimes stereotyped character delineations and strong moralistic tone, has remained superior to numerous imitators (including a second-rate remake in 1966). Ford's ability to derive drama from the milieu and to handle western conventions in a clear, simple manner are the sources of this film's enduring appeal.

The Grapes of Wrath Following the release of *Stagecoach,* Ford went to work on *Young Mr. Lincoln* (1939), a homey biographical sketch of Abe Lincoln's (Henry Fonda) early years as a lawyer. Considerable pathos was achieved by a largely stylized treatment of Lincoln's character and the forces already working to shape his well-known destiny.

John Steinbeck's epic and controversial novel, *The Grapes of Wrath,* provided Ford with his next directorial challenge. Adaptation rights to the novel were purchased by Twentieth Century-Fox in 1939 and a screenplay was hastily prepared by Nunnally Johnson. Production began despite some public charges that an unfair portrait had been drawn by Steinbeck of Oklahoma landowners and California vegetable growers. In treating the migration of a group of downtrodden sharecroppers from the Oklahoma dustbowl to the labor camps of California, there emerged in Steinbeck's novel a continuous questioning of social justice within America's agrarian classes. Some saw Steinbeck placing blame for the Joad family's plight on the landowners who turn them out and on the wealthy California farmers who offer them no better lot. This was the source of the novel's controversy, one which John Ford's film version, released in 1940, would skirt for a more optimistic conclusion.

With the assistance of screenwriter Johnson and cinematographer Gregg Toland, Ford recreated the essence of Steinbeck's story in simple authentic film images. Johnson's script, out of concession to the time limits and dramatic demands of the motion-picture medium, concentrated its attention on the traumas of the Joad family (led by Henry Fonda) rather than on the larger political issues raised by Steinbeck.

In bringing the script to the screen Ford found much eloquence and pathos in the suffering and disillusioned faces of the principal characters (a style for which Robert Flaherty opted in treating the same subject in his documentary, *The Land,* produced two years later). Conversely, long shots of the Joad's battered pickup truck, moving steadily across the massive, eroded plains, conveyed both the struggle and hope of the uprooted, common people.

To add to the sentimental and stirring nature of the dramatization, familiar American folk songs are used throughout. The songs, such as "Home on the Range," carry their own special ironies and melancholic underscoring.

SOCIAL IMPLICATIONS Coming at the tail end of a period of filmmaking that saw populist statements flourishing (with Capra's films at the forefront), *The Grapes of Wrath* chose to be similarly optimistic in

The faces of Ma Joad (Jane Darwell) and her son Tom (Henry Fonda) are captured with expressive and moving feeling in *The Grapes of Wrath* (1939). Ford's film brought new social realism to the American fiction film.

conclusion. The call for radical change in the American economic system, which many saw as the principal point of the Steinbeck novel, was replaced in the film by a positive view of government. The script in its final part has the Joads arriving at a federally funded camp for migratory workers, where facilities and living conditions have been idealized. In this optimistic setting the family finds new inspiration to carry on against social adversity. Ma Joad (Jane Darwell) offers the final statement of populist sentiment when she speaks colloquially of the indestructibility of common Americans: "We're the people that live. Can't nobody wipe us out. Can't nobody lick us. We'll go on forever."

Viewed in a historical context, the deradicalization of *The Grapes of Wrath* was compatible with the nation's mood—a nation wanting to forget the tragedy of the recent Depression, and one deeply disturbed by threats from abroad. National interests were at stake, and pessimistic views of American life were considered to be demoralizing.

The Grapes of Wrath appears in retrospective analysis a cinematic effort in which both style and theme grew from the overriding social climate. Toland's stark black-and-white cinematography possessed the journalistic appearance of Pare Lorentz' pro-government documentaries, *The Plow that Broke the Plains* (1936) and *The River* (1937). Like Nunnally Johnson's script, each of these films examined dire social adversity but, with positive finality, predicted a better future for Americans through government intervention.

Henry Fonda's Tom Joad characterization also had cinematic relevance to the times. Tough, resilient, and sensitive, Fonda projected a common-man image of mythic proportions that was in many ways remarkably like his heroic but burdened character in *Young Mr. Lincoln* the year before. The Tom Joad and Abe Lincoln characters were only two of many mythic heroes who populated American screens in the 1930s and early 1940s, offering positive doses of reinforcement rather than embittered condemnation. *The Grapes of Wrath* was acceptable for this reason whereas two years later Flaherty's *The Land,* depressing and pessimistic, would be permitted only limited circulation. With *The Grapes of Wrath* John Ford fairly well summarized a critical point in American film history.

The 1940s For Ford the forties was a decade of varied efforts which included: the direction of a second film about socioeconomic conditions for the common worker, *How Green Was My Valley* (1941); documentaries for the U.S. Navy, *The Battle of Midway* (1942), *We Sail at Midnight* (1943); and several artfully constructed westerns, *My Darling Clementine* (1946), *Fort Apache* (1948), *She Wore a Yellow Ribbon* (1949).

How Green Was My Valley *How Green Was My Valley* was adapted for the screen from Richard Llewellyn's novel about the disintegration of a Welsh mining valley. The valley landscape, poetically visualized by Ford through the memory of Huw Morgan (Roddy McDowall), serves as thematic metaphor. Morgan's memory of the once vibrant valley is rendered in flashback as the disillusioned young Welshman prepares to take leave of his hometown and family. Juxtaposed against the romantic remembrances of a lovely place and happy family times are present conditions: economic and spiritual ruin brought on by a failure to properly oversee conditions in the valley's coal mines. The death of Morgan's father (Donald Crisp) in a mine accident provides final motivation to forsake the beloved valley.

Parallels with *The Grapes of Wrath* are inevitable: the family focus, the treatment of social injustices, a sentimental aura surrounding common, decent people whose lives are inextricably tied to the land. The Welsh setting allowed Ford to deal with economic upheaval in a less optimistic manner, but by placing the story entirely in the past Philip Dunne's script offered principally nostalgia within a social context. This approach served up the story and its associations with the American Depression as distant history, while carefully avoiding the bitterness possible in another treatment of Llewellyn's novel.

Ford added to the nostalgic tone of *How Green Was My Valley* by constructing the Welsh village on a California hillside. The romantic, studio look differed significantly from the newsreel quality of *The Grapes of Wrath.*

War Films After the United States entered World War II, Ford, along with a number of other prominent directors whose work had given evidence of social interests, offered his talents to the national cause as head of the Navy's Field Photography Branch. The goal of the Hollywood storytellers-turned-documentarists (Ford, Frank Capra, William

Ford's romantic setting constructed for *How Green Was My Valley* (1941).

Wyler, Walt Disney, John Huston, et al.) was primarily that of informing the American public about war activity and thereby sustaining morale. Capra's *Why We Fight* series (1942–1945), perhaps the best known of all the informational documentaries, explained in seven parts the historical events which had produced the war.

A subcategory of the informational film was the battle document which provided an on-the-spot account of important war campaigns. John Huston's *The Battle of San Pietro* (1944) and Ford's *The Battle of Midway* (1942) were among the memorable efforts in this category.

The Battle of Midway was the first journalistic report to have covered a strictly American war effort, and, like others of its type that followed, visualized the battle for the Pacific island in graphic terms while providing patriotic commentary through voice-over narration. Five hundred prints of Ford's documentary were released for public exhibition during the fall of 1942.

Later Work The postwar years brought Ford back to his favorite arena, the western frontier, and to the chivalrous characters that were the subjects of his most entertaining films. Tombstone, Arizona, and Wyatt Earp provided the dramatic turn of events for *My Darling Clementine* (1946). Earp (Henry Fonda), after driving his cattle from Texas to the Arizona town, finds himself in the midst of killers and rustlers. The murder of a brother in the hostile environment forces an eventual showdown (at the OK Corral) between the surviving Earps and the Clanton gang.

Familiar Ford themes surface in this story: the quest for an honorable revenge, the progression toward civilization in a raw environment, and personal survival in the midst of great adversity. Ford advanced, however, the concept of increasing urbanization to include more than the arrival on the western frontier of gracious eastern ladies and whiskey drummers: a Shakespeare acting company has trekked to Tombstone to perform and suddenly finds itself a part of *My Darling Clementine's* rough action.

The introduction of new values (culture, religion, education) encroaching on western traditions adds to the nostalgic and human appeals of the film. Dramatic camera compositions, precise editing, and simple background folk music were stylistically Fordian in expression.

Subsequent Ford westerns continued to tackle subject matter that emphasized opposing values in a frontier setting. *Fort Apache* (1948) pits not only Indians against a U.S. military outpost, but one military officer (Henry Fonda) within the outpost against another (John Wayne). *The Searchers* (1956) proffers, among other value conflicts, the expressed desire of a kidnapped frontier girl (Natalie Wood) to remain with her Comanche captors. In this film Ford connects western conflict to racial divisiveness, and in *The Man who Shot Liberty Valance* (1962) to political maneuvering and deception.

Ford's work after the mid-1940s was uneven in quality but never impersonal or without the distinctive visual style he had mastered early in his career. Atmospheric command of the milieu and economic but precise use of detail were among Ford's directorial strengths. He was a superb craftsman and lyric stylist who believed in traditional values, sometimes to a point of sentimental extremity. Distractions aside, John Ford at the time of his death in 1973 was one of Hollywood's most honored and revered filmmakers.

ORSON WELLES: AMERICAN EXPRESSIONIST

In 1941 the prodigious Orson Welles (1915–   ) released his first and greatest film, *Citizen Kane*. This classic motion picture, ranked in every poll as one of the ten outstanding films of all time, established Welles' lasting reputation in one brilliant flash of screen creativity. Had he made only this one film, history would still have accorded him a prominent place beside the best of Hollywood's directors.

Welles was a young man of 24 when he left New York City for Hollywood in 1939. He brought with him to California confidence gained from theater work and a brief but sensational career as a radio dramatist, experience which would enter significantly into the realization of *Citizen Kane's* innovative sound track.

Involvement in radio came after apprenticeships at age 16 with the Gate and Abbey Theatres in Dublin, Ireland, followed by acting jobs in theater companies in the United States headed by Katharine Cornell and John Houseman. In 1936 Welles began to take roles on popular radio programs, among them *The Shadow,* and in 1937 he and Houseman created the Mercury Theatre for the purpose of producing stage plays and radio dramas.

It was the Mercury Theatre's radio production of H. G. Well's *The War of the Worlds* in 1938 that turned Welles into a somewhat notorious celebrity. In a docudrama fashion, Welles created a masterpiece of psychological manipulation through the artful arrangement of sounds. By imitating newscaster styles and familiar radio reportage methods, Welles convinced many listeners, already anxious about world events abroad, that what they were hearing was not drama but an actual invasion from Mars. The Halloween eve broadcast, intended merely as a frightening joke, proved through the panic it caused Welles' formidable dramatic skills. He served as both director and narrator of the production.

RKO, impressed by Welles' sensational radio and stage successes in New York, offered the young director a motion-picture contract which promised unusual creative freedom. This freedom allowed Welles to bring with him to Hollywood many of the skilled Mercury Theatre actors and to use them in a film project whose mosaic structure, startling cinematography, and expressive sound track would once more prove his directorial genius. *Citizen Kane*, too, showed Welles in the central role to be an actor of the rarest talent.

Citizen Kane

Not everyone fully understood or appreciated *Citizen Kane* when it was first released on May 1, 1941. The fractured nature of the storyline, plus the investigative and open-ended approach to biographical analysis, left many filmgoers puzzled about Welles' intentions. Accustomed to the well-made narrative, film audiences found *Citizen Kane* a jolting experience.

Story Form *Citizen Kane* is in large part a psychological mystery and the initiating clue (what Alfred Hitchcock referred to as the "MacGuffin") is "Rosebud," the final word spoken by Kane at the moment of his death. In sending a newspaper reporter to interview principals in Kane's life with the hope of discovering Rosebud's meaning and its relevance to Kane's grandiose existence, the mystery is allowed to unfold in a series of flashbacks.

This approach is a modern one, based on the assumption that external analysis of a human being's life is subjective at best and, while every subjective view and biographical detail are pieces in a larger puzzle, the meaning of life is too complex to ever be fully understood. It is the investigative process that makes Welles' film interesting rather than the conclusions. "The point of the picture," Welles said, "is not so much the solution of the problem as its presentation."

Welles' imaginative treatment of a screen biography (inspired by the life of newspaper magnate, William Randolph Hearst) also held ironic implications. The desire to uncover through journalistic investigation the meaning of Rosebud, to find in it perhaps the hidden source of

Kane's drive and egomania and to expose it to the world, can be easily correlated with the journalistic practices by which Hearst built his empire.

This special irony develops after a film editor expresses dissatisfaction with a *March of Time*-styled account of Kane's life and decides to probe more deeply by going after the meaning of Rosebud. The editor selects one of the reporters in the screening room, Thompson (William Alland), and tells him to get in touch with everybody who knew Kane. "Rosebud, dead or alive," the editor says, "it'll probably turn out to be a very simple thing."

Thompson's investigation begins in the Thatcher Library where the first flashback occurs as the reporter reads a manuscript written by Walter Parks Thatcher (George Coulouris), Kane's legal guardian. The flashback traces Thatcher's first associations with Kane as a child, then jumps ahead in time to show disputes between Kane, now a 25-year-old newspaper publisher, and Thatcher over how to run the newspaper.

Additional flashback visualizations take place while Thompson visits: Mr. Bernstein (Everett Sloane), Kane's business manager; Jedediah Leland (Joseph Cotten), one of Kane's top reporters and at one time Kane's friend and confidante; Susan Alexander (Dorothy Comingore), Kane's second wife and a failed opera singer; and Raymond (Paul Stewart), the head butler at Xanadu, Kane's palatial estate.

During the course of the flashbacks, glimpses of Kane's hidden personal life emerge to add to the public knowledge already exposed in the newsreel compilation. Discovered in Thompson's progressive investigation are details of a fragmented childhood, Kane's precocious emergence as a newspaper publisher, increasing material wealth, marriage to a prominent young socialite, political ambitions cut short by a scandalous exposé, the sad investment in Susan Alexander's opera career, the final loneliness in the overly lavish Xanadu. Critical events are seen from different perspectives as the characters recall with open candor affiliations with Kane.

Theme There develops in the course of the flashbacks clues to the value of Kane's life rather than an explicit understanding of Rosebud's relevance. Thompson himself never learns that the word referred to is the name of a sled with which Kane was playing when Thatcher came to take the boy from his mother; only the viewer discovers its meaning when in the final shots of the film the toy is tossed onto a fire as workmen clear Xanadu of its clutter.

While the sled provides the clever structuring device around which the psychological mystery unfolds, it also becomes in the end the principal reference point for Welles' multilayered theme. As Gregg Toland's camera tracks across Kane's massive collection of possessions, one sees a life defined symbolically by an obsession for objects. The

One of Citizen Kane's flash-backs recalls the abrupt ending to the newspaper publisher's brief political career. His opponent brings Kane and his wife to Susan's apartment to announce that he intends to expose the extramarital affair.

camera movement is a materialistic journey back in time, beginning with the gaudy possessions of later life and proceeding to the simple, homey objects of his brief childhood years on his parent's farm. Rosebud is the final object, the end and the beginning of an existence rooted in the search for an elusive happiness through materialism.

In developing this theme Welles and screenwriter Herman Mankiewicz directly correlate Kane's psychological needs with object possession. As Kane's personal life deteriorates, and as he becomes increasingly lonely and unhappy, the objects not only proliferate but grow larger in size.

Welles draws a portrait of an individual desperate for love, but incapable of finding it because he cannot himself love. Charles Kane's value system is one centered on the belief that love can be bought, along with successful opera careers and public adoration. Kane is wrong in every case. Leland verbalizes this aspect of the theme when he says to Thompson: "Love. That's why he did everything. That's why he went into politics. Seems we weren't enough. He wanted all the voters to love him too. Guess, all he wanted out of life was love; that's Charlie's story, how he lost it. Y'see, he just didn't have any to give."

Treatment In treating *Citizen Kane's* story of bourgeois unhappiness, Welles appropriated a variety of cinematic styles, genres, and techniques. It is this evocative, rather than realistic, assimilation of story elements that made the film a revolutionary work of art. Welles mixes newsreels with subjective points of view, expressionism with realism, and satire with tragedy to hint at the essence of a single life.

Citizen Kane's admixture of styles and techniques, its very abruptness, grew from the bold assumption that enigmatic characterizations

One of Gregg Toland's striking deep-focus compositions.

were possible within the motion picture. Every element of cinematic expression is put imaginatively to work to achieve this end: cinematography, settings, sound, lighting, music, editing, performance.

Cinematography Much attention has been focused on the brilliance of Gregg Toland's photography in realizing Welles' goals. Working almost entirely within the studios of RKO, Toland and Welles were able to experiment with new approaches to frame composition. Welles consistently placed his actors in foreground-middleground-background patterns so that compositions carried a sense of visual depth. The triangular, deep-focus arrangements (so greatly admired by André Bazin and later an influence on television directors) allowed character interaction without editorial fragmentation; numerous scenes were played out in single takes, or with minimal change of camera angle.

A model illustration of the uninterrupted scene occurs when Kane's political opponent, Gettys (Ray Collins), announces in Susan Alexander's apartment that he intends to disclose the extramarital affair in order to save his own career. The painful announcement is filmed with long camera runs and in deep-focus composition so that all the principal characters in the drama are emotionally bound to the momentous event: Kane, his wife, the mistress, the political boss.

Toland drew on new lens technology, faster film stocks, and improved lighting instruments to produce sharply defined shots that often revealed a character or object within inches of the camera and other characters positioned far in the background.

For an extreme deep-focus effect, such as that of Gettys observing Kane from high above a speaker's podium, postproduction matte-screen processing and special printing techniques were utilized to increase the distance between the two men. The printer was used to reduce the size of Kane's image, then a separate midground shot along with the close shot of Gettys were matted in over the distant Kane.

Unusually sharp camera angles added their own metaphorical commentary, depicting through low-angled camera positions Kane's early arrogance, and, later, in the long-angled, wide-perspective compositions at Xanadu his complete alienation.

A lengthy, single-take shot keeps all the principals within the frame for the announcement of an intended public disclosure of Kane's "love nest" arrangement with Susan. Dramatic tensions among the four are evident throughout the structurally unified scene.

The dramatic effect of matte-screen processing in *Citizen Kane*.

Lighting and Sound Welles, who admitted to John Ford's influence, is noticeably theatrical in use of lighting and sound. As in Ford's *The Informer*, light and shadow contrasts provide psychological decoration for the story. Patches of light emphasize characters within otherwise dark, exaggerated spaces. An expressionistic aura pervades the film from its first long, misty shots of an obviously hand-painted, cardboard rendering of Xanadu to the final somber scenes in the palace's hollow interiors.

Sound is similarly theatrical and expressionistic. Voices loom larger than life; crashing sound effects serve as dynamic transition devices; Bernard Herrmann's melancholic music ominously underscores every dramatic innuendo. Welles is so thoroughly sound-conscious, a carry-over from radio work, that simply listening to the film conveys Kane's story with surprising clarity. Visual montages of newspaper headlines, for example, are accompanied by verbal readings of the information.

Other radio influence is evident. Character actions are often verbalized as though the script has been written entirely for sound rather than for the motion picture. The scuffle between Kane and Thatcher that takes place when the lad resists leaving his parents' farm is acted out with voice as well as action. When Kane arrives at his newspaper office briefly with his bride-to-be, Emily, waiting in a carriage outside, similar vocal reinforcement of action occurs. Upon discovering Emily's presence outside, a newspaper employee, standing by a window, says with excitement: "Hey, look out here . . . ! " Another employee responds: "Let's go to the window!" Sounds of footsteps follow as the employees rush to get a glimpse of Kane's fiancée.

The extensive use of sound holds significance for the debate that has developed on the relative contributions of Welles and Herman Mankiewicz to *Citizen Kane's* screenplay. Strong evidence of radio styling suggests close collaboration between the sound-wise Welles and Mankiewicz, a seasoned screenwriter of visual orientation who had been working in Hollywood since 1926.

Editing While sound and visuals are vital elements in Welles' daring cinematic style, editing virtuosity also plays an important part. In one of the film's most famous sequences the disintegration of Kane's first marriage is conveyed in a breakfast montage that begins with husband and wife seated at a small, intimate table and concludes with the two in wide separation. Dialogue continues throughout the succession of images as though a single conversation. This glib presentation of an eroding marriage is simultaneously pointed and satiric.

The most striking editing device in Robert Wise's abstract reconstruction of the story is that of sound-image overlap. A line of continuous dialogue connects scenes that are often years apart. Kane's romantic commitment to Susan Alexander, for example, is conveyed in a single dissolve which shows the young woman continuing a song begun for Kane on the evening they first met. The song continues but the dissolve produces a telling change of time and scenery, with the aspiring singer's earlier drab living quarters having been replaced by elegant surroundings.

Acting The remarkable assimilation of cinematic techniques is matched by Welles' undeniably brilliant performance in the central role of Charles Foster Kane. Transition from youth to old age, from ebullience to disillusionment is handled with unfailing physical and psychological credibility. Welles' performance, like *Citizen Kane* as a whole, is a mixture of realism and theatricality—the evocation of a larger-than-life character, but one that never becomes unsympathetic.

Reactions The impending release of *Citizen Kane* was met by efforts within William Randolph Hearst's camp to have the film suppressed. Louella O. Parsons, a Hollywood gossip columnist for the Hearst chain, attended a preview showing at RKO in January 1941, and afterward informed her boss that Welles had created a questionable biography of the newspaper mogul's life. Attempts to keep the picture out of

A dissolve from Susan Alexander's earlier dingy apartment to the new lavishly appointed quarters shown here communicates without words the extent of Kane's attachment to his mistress.

circulation failed, however, and the Hearst people played out their disregard for Welles and RKO by refusing to publish advertisements for the picture.

Initial critical response to *Citizen Kane* after its premiere at New York City's Palace Theater on May 1, 1941 was intense: *The New York Times* critic Bosley Crowther argued that Welles and Toland had "made use of all the best devices of pure cinema." John Mosher at *The New Yorker* said simply, "Something new has come to the movie world at last." Cedric Belfrage, writing for *The Clipper,* wrote of the film's unusual structure, "Here we are really in the cinema medium, in that and nothing else. What other mediums could show so forcefully that truth is not merely objective, but subjective also, and at the same time?"

A precise estimation of *Citizen Kane's* influence on cinematic art is not possible. One can only make note of the fact that Welles' first work continues to generate the same kind of excitement as on its release decades ago. Film critic Dwight MacDonald has maintained that the single most important test of any work of art is that of revisitability—whether old and new pleasures can be found on return visits to reexamine the piece. Accepting MacDonald's criterion as valid, *Citizen Kane* stands as one of cinema's most enduring achievements.

The Magnificent Ambersons

Booth Tarkington's 1918 novel, *The Magnificent Ambersons,* provided the source of Welles' second film (1942). Whereas the explosive *Citizen Kane* had dissected a single character's life, the Ambersons' story examined family disintegration in Indianapolis, Indiana, at the end of the nine-

teenth century. Industrial encroachment rapidly changes the face of the midwestern town and simultaneously ends the grand, romantic lifestyle of one of the area's wealthiest and most prominent families.

Welles' adaptation of the Tarkington book emphasizes the dramatic conflict between the nostalgic past and the rise of a new social order. In so doing the film ambitiously attempts a study of interpersonal relationships dominated by emotional frustration and psychological strain.

The grand Welles style is once more evident in *The Magnificent Ambersons*, but technical virtuosity is downplayed for a more subdued emphasis on social rather than internal realities.

To evoke a sense of bygone grandeur, Welles places his characters in huge houses whose darkly lit interiors seem to be trying to shut out altogether the realities of a changing world. The pace and quality of life in the old order is captured in a lengthy tracking-dolly shot that has the camera move through the doors of the Amberson mansion on the evening of a grand ball and wander about the luxurious settings as though an invited guest.

This sustained deep-focus shot at the ball is only one of numerous instances in which Welles develops scenes in long camera takes. Excessive cutting is avoided for the purpose of maintaining character interrelationships within the expressive settings. A scene in which the brazen young George Minafer (Tim Holt) eats a piece of strawberry shortcake while being scolded by his Aunt Fanny (Agnes Moorehead) is rendered in a single long shot.

As in *Citizen Kane*, Welles' radio sensibilities are critical to *The Magnificent Ambersons'* swift development of narrative. By using a montage sequence of townspeople gossiping impressionistically about the

principal characters, Welles provides an amusing rush of spoken details which, in a matter of seconds, defines the Ambersons and the nature of the impending story.

The montage device and off-screen narrator (Welles' voice) are supported by matched tempo musical scoring (by Bernard Herrmann) that beautifully recreates the spirited mood of late nineteenth-century life. The narrator, uncommon in motion pictures of the time, returns at appropriate places to provide intimate and eloquent commentary that reinforces the story's nostalgic tone.

In other scenes Welles experimented with a naturalistic approach to dialogue, often allowing the characters' speeches to overlap and interrupt. Certain scenes were improvised through lengthy rehearsals to achieve more realistic lines and delivery. Welles sought to make sound an integral part of the environment, to permit it the same range of textures and ambiguities found in his deep-focus images.

At the time of its release in 1942 *The Magnificent Ambersons* was criticized for its intellectual-literary airs and for having failed to properly define the community life which ended the Amberson dynasty. Welles maintained that extensive reediting of the picture by RKO was responsible for critical omissions. Following shooting of the film, RKO officials, already in disagreement with Welles and concerned by *Citizen Kane's* poor box office receipts, took *The Magnificent Ambersons* and trimmed it to what was considered a more marketable length.

In spite of deletions, the film contains an expressive power that is clearly Wellesian. It has continued to gain critical favor over the years as Welles' second most important work, and as a motion picture which together with *Citizen Kane* influenced emerging styles and themes of young European filmmakers in the late fifties and early sixties. Especially meaningful was *The Magnificent Ambersons*' examination of character relationships in a social setting—a prominent concern seen in numerous films from France and Italy two decades later.

Subsequent Work

Later films by Welles never matched the first two works produced while still a novice director. Before his third film, *Journey Into Fear* (1942), was completed, RKO turned the assignment over to Norman Foster for revision. Shortly thereafter Welles' contract with the studio was terminated, his great promise stultified by overriding commercial interests and lack of appreciation for bold innovation.

Subsequent films, *The Stranger* (1946), *The Lady from Shanghai* (1947), *Othello* (1951), *Mr. Arkadin* (1955), *Touch of Evil* (1957), *The Trial* (1962), and *Chimes at Midnight* (1966) were all produced independently and with uneven effect. Still Welles' directorial signature can be found on each: a tragic larger-than-life character serving as principal subject; Welles in a central role; structure and technique abrupt and evocative; visual style dark and brooding. These eclectic elements, unfortunately, never coalesce to provide the heightened drama that ushered *Citizen Kane,* unforgettably, into motion-picture history.

SUGGESTED READINGS

Baxter, John. *The Cinema of John Ford.* Cranbury, N.J.: Barnes, 1971.

Bessy, Maurice. *Orson Welles.* New York: Crown, 1971.

Bogdanovich, Peter. *John Ford.* Berkeley and Los Angeles: University of California Press, 1968.

Calder-Marshall, Arthur. *The Innocent Eye: The Life of Robert J. Flaherty.* New York: Harcourt, 1966.

Capra, Frank. *The Name Above the Title.* New York: Macmillan, 1971.

Chaplin, Charles. *My Autobiography.* New York: Simon & Schuster, 1964.

Giannetti, Louis. *Masters of the American Cinema.* Englewood Cliffs, N.J.: Prentice Hall, 1981.

McBride, Joseph, ed. *Focus on Howard Hawks.* Englewood Cliffs, N.J.: Prentice-Hall, 1972.

Maland, Charles J. *American Visions: The Films of Chaplin, Ford, Capra, and Welles, 1936–1941.* New York: Arno, 1977.

Mast, Gerald. *The Comic Mind.* Chicago: The University of Chicago Press, 1979.

Tyler, Parker. *Chaplin, Last of the Clowns.* New York: Horizon, 1972.

MAJOR EUROPEAN DIRECTORS: (1930–1950)

Now I am beginning to be aware of how I must work. I know that I am French and that I must work in an absolutely national sense. I know also that, by doing this, and only by doing this, I can reach the people of other countries and create works of international standing.

Jean Renoir, 1938 (cited by Georges Sadoul in *Dictionary of Film Makers*).

In Europe as in the United States, there were among the prominent studio directors important filmmakers whose work demanded to be taken seriously. Jean Renoir, Jean Cocteau, and Vittoria De Sica stand within that select circle of film artists. Each was a filmmaker whose vision, themes, and methods of expression made significant contributions to the progress of film art. Renoir as poetic realist, Cocteau as fantasist, and De Sica as neorealist were directors of

Jean Renoir.

both style and substance, and are worthy of inclusion in a sampling of the diverse genius at work in the motion picture during the thirties and forties.

JEAN RENOIR: REALISM AND IRONY

Jean Renoir's achivements as a film director in his native France reached a peak in the late 1930s with a series of brilliantly executed studies of upheaval in the European social order. Austere, ironic, humane, intellectual, metaphorical: all are appropriate adjectives for describing the world created by Renoir in *Toni* (1935), *The Crime of Monsieur Lange* (1935), *La Grande Illusion (Grand Illusion,* 1937), *La Bête Humaine (The Human Beast,* 1938), and *La Règle du Jeu (The Rules of the Game,* 1939).

Renoir cast his personality and individualistic vision of life onto each film, adapting and co-authoring his screenplays, and creating his own repertory of supporting artists, technicians, and actors to sustain his vision. Quantity of work during the 1930s was itself remarkable: fourteen films between 1931 and 1939.

Of this collection two films have been declared model examples of Renoir's thematic and stylistic genius: *Grand Illusion* and *The Rules of the Game.* In theme they entertained the conflict between artifice and reality that characterized conditions within Europe's eroding social order. Stylistically, Renoir's mixture of realism, visual irony, and narrative parallels achieved new dimensions of cinematic observation.

Grand Illusion

Renoir's story, co-authored with the Belgian writer Charles Spaak, is set in a German prison camp during World War I. Two French officers, Captain de Boeldieu (Pierre Fresnay) and Maréchal (Jean Gabin) are captured and brought to the dull camp after their plane is shot down over German territory. French, English, Russian, and Belgian prisoners of war are already housed at the prison, which is supervised by the rigidly aristocratic Commander von Rauffenstein (Erich von Stroheim). The German officer and his French counterpart, Boeldieu, are meticulously disciplined professionals, fully dedicated to both the codes of their military positions and their social class.

From these military and social parallels Renoir extracts a metaphorical study of the illusions and deceits, harbored by the aristocracy, which led to World War I. The plot of *Grand Illusion* also depicts in ironic detail the communal bonds which the German and French officers share. As members of the ruling class, it is suggested by Renoir that the officers transcend national boundaries.

While these officers observe the social and professional rituals to which they are entitled, the proletarian soldiers in the camp react quite differently. They appear nationalistic and determined to escape the camp in order to return to their fighting. These dual ironies which juxtapose upper-class aloofness with lower-class gullibility are profound in their social and philosophical implications. Renoir delineates all his characters as victims of the illusions that generate and sustain wars.

Dramatic Method *Grand Illusion* is as dramatically inventive as it is philosophical. In a series of well-orchestrated vignettes life for all the men in the camp is shown in its various moods. Early in the film a theatrical production (a military camp talent show) is staged by the French and English prisoners as a means of overcoming their boredom. Renoir's camera sweeps back and forth across the stage and toward the audience watching the production to capture this heightened moment.

When Maréchal suddenly rushes onto the stage and interrupts the show to announce that the city of Douaumont has been retaken by the French army, the entire group of captured soldiers rises after several hushed seconds and begins to sing *"The Marseillaise"* to the orchestra's accompaniment. The idea of victory and freedom shatters the excitement of the theatrical presentation; a new excitement, that of patriotic fervor (itself a highly theatrical moment), follows in the singing of the French national anthem. One illusion has been replaced by another. This idea is vividly introduced by a shot of an English prisoner, portraying a woman in the talent show, who removes his wig to lead the singing of the hymn.

Boeldieu, the French officer, is developed by Renoir as a parallel figure to the German officer von Rauffenstein. To depict similarities of background and position, the two men dine together and in one instance von Rauffenstein invites the Frenchman to his room for a conversation. They discuss both the end of the war and the demise of the aristocracy. In the severely spartan quarters the two men address each other with reserved formality, sitting near a window which holds on its ledge a single flower in a pot. Renoir's camera observes this scene in a series of individual close-ups as the two aristocrats strive for an intimacy which neither can properly allow. The flower, a background element in the scene, assumes a symbolic presence as Renoir's reserved treatment of the visit conveys a sense of loneliness and isolation. The flower becomes a clue to other desires denied by "the rules of the game" which the two officers must play.

Boeldieu is the more cynical of the two men. Accepting the impending fate of the caste-bound aristocracy, he offers himself as a sacrificial decoy so that the planned escape by his countrymen can be carried out. Rauffenstein after insisting that Boeldieu stop his charade and return to the camp ground, reluctantly shoots the Frenchman as he runs to divert attention from the fleeing soliders.

The wounded Boeldieu is taken into the castle to die. In the German officer's stark, barren room, Rauffenstein keeps a death vigil by

Boeldieu (Pierre Fresnay) and von Rauffenstein (Erich von Stroheim) meet in the German officer's austere quarters. The flower on the ledge behind the two men, a geranium, becomes one of *Grand Illusion's* expressive symbols.

the bed, the killer standing watch over his victim. The class bonds which unite the two men must be maintained.

When Boeldieu has taken his last breath, Rauffenstein crosses to the window where he snips off the flower (a geranium) seen in the earlier scene when the two had discussed the demise of the aristocracy. Renoir emphasizes this noble act by quickly dollying in to a close-up of the German officer. The gesture, combined with a moving camera shot, takes the viewer to the center of Rauffenstein's deep, but otherwise invisible, compassion for an equal.

Directing Style Such simple, eloquent expression typified Renoir's directorial style which has been accurately described as "photographed realism" by André Bazin. In a manner compatible with French realism which had developed during the 1920s, Renoir employed a stylistic approach in *Grand Illusion* which drew on the accuracy of detail and gesture within a realistic setting.

Renoir insisted on the use of location shooting in order to acquire this realistic effect. The artistic and thematic components of his humane expression were then derived through composition, camera movements, and object and character placement within the decor.

The avoidance of traditional editing approaches to telegraph character nuance or to add rhythmic variety to scenes also enhanced the realistic quality of *Grand Illusion*. Actors function in such a casual manner and with such sustained naturalism that they appear hardly to be acting at all. Von Rauffenstein, wearing a neck brace to hold his battered body erect, carries in his very appearance an unforgettable symbol of military wear and tear. This approach to the treatment of dramatic material is responsible for Renoir's distinguished and austere directorial style. It was a style which demanded more from the viewer, but one which was deeply moving in depicting the tragic ironies of war and human nature.

Grand Illusion concludes with a tense Maréchal and his compatriot, Rosenthal (Marcel Dalio), making their way after escaping through the snow-covered German countryside. The two men are offered shelter in a farmhouse by a German widow, and in a final ironic statement Maréchal and the woman make love. Nationality differences that produce fatal wars are built and sustained by false hatreds that ignore the natural course of human behavior. To reinforce this irony Maréchal says to Rosenthal as they are about to cross from Germany to freedom in neutral Switzerland: "Nature all looks alike. Frontiers are an invention of man."

The Rules of the Game

The themes of artificiality and illusion as a way of life continue in *The Rules of the Game*. Once more the screenplay (written by Renoir, Karl Koch, and Camille Francois) centers on aristocratic society in the throes of transition. Stylistically the film possesses the same economic and naturalistic quality as *Grand Illusion*. Renoir manages to reveal his view of society through narrative parallels that are alternately ironic, poignant, and amusing.

The Plot *The Rules of the Game* follows a weekend hunting party given by the Marquis de la Chesnaye at his country chateau. There the hosts, their guests, and servants act out a complicated social "game" that is played according to strict rules of conduct. The game is a facade backed by social convention, which masks the characters' true desires and needs. As a microcosmic view of a society in ruin, Renoir combines tragedy and farce to create his most complex and stimulating motion picture.

The story line involves a variety of characters: André Jurieu (Roland Toutain), a heroic pilot who falls in love with the Marquis' wife, Christine; Marceau (Julien Carette), a newly arrived servant who engages in his own affair with Christine's married maid, Lisette (Paulette Dubost); Schumacher (Gaston Modot), Lisette's husband and the game-keeper at the chateau who shoots and kills André after he mistakenly assumes that the pilot is his wife's new lover; the Marquis (Marcel Dalio), who graciously and formally forgives Schumacher for the "regrettable" incident that has taken André's life; Octave (Jean Renoir), a pitiable sponger and failed musician who dreams away his life while living off his wealthy friends.

Renoir's picture of social decadence is developed through the two adulterous affairs, one involving the upper class, the other the lower class. Both are carried out according to convention which is insensitive and hypocritical but orderly. In each case adultery is viewed by Renoir's characters merely as an excusable shortcoming—not approved of but ignored in order to protect the social order. The facade is another of life's illusory games, presented in a cynical, yet sympathetic, manner.

The orderliness of aristocratic life with its false pretenses is momentarily shattered when Schumacher kills André during the Marquis' rabbit hunt. The hunt, like life for the aristocrats, is a mechanically elaborate game with its own set of rules and code of conduct. Its construction suggests a ritual whose acceptable cruelties parallel metaphorically the cruel dependence on hypocrisy and idle dreams for sustenance.

When Schumacher kills André, graphic depiction of this act is avoided (unlike the killing of the rabbits) so that the murder remains impersonal. André is merely an unfortunate victim who dies when the rules of the game (not as well understood by the servants) are momentarily violated. The Marquis, after a brief period of confusion, quickly offers his stylish pardon of the gamekeeper, and class solidarity at both levels is restored. The house guests accept the pardon without question or visible remorse and the farce continues.

The hunt in *The Rules of the Game* (1939), another of the highly ritualized *games* played by the aristocracy in Renoir's film. Each hunter, with a gun bearer behind, assumes his assigned position for the killing of game birds.

Cinematic Method Renoir's treatment of *The Rules of the Game* possesses the same pictorial realism that characterized *Grand Illusion* but with further aesthetic experimentation in camera usage. The camera as before is an acute observer of action and detail. In the second half of the film, however, Renoir's camera is put into near constant motion in order to keep a vigilant, roving eye on the action as it progresses from one area of the chateau to the next. This approach provides a structural unity to plot development and keeps dramatic relationships in a continuous temporal and spatial flow.

In following the parallel intrigues at work in *The Rules of the Game*, Renoir's deep-focus, mobile camera serves the function of a curiosity seeker, living among the chateau's inhabitants and observing their actions from a human, lively perspective. Renoir wanted his camera to be inside the film, just as he strove to be "more inside the film" as the director by taking the role of Octave himself.

The realism which Renoir achieved structurally is matched in dramatic effect by sharply revealing character and set details. Mechanical birds and musical instruments, collected by the Marquis and proudly displayed for his guests, symbolize his yearning for orderliness. The overly pampered look of the aristocratic class (both sexes), the ornate hats worn by the women (even during the rabbit hunt), the pretentious Octave's frumpy, worn clothing, and the formality of gestures and manners precisely and correctly delineate the nature of a class rigidly locked in a world of luxurious, removed excesses. Even murder is depicted as an acceptable indulgence.

The Rules of the Game appeared ominously at the edge of World War II, and in time its associations with contemporary history became even more apparent. As French social critic Jacques Joly has aptly noted, Renoir's film offered a continuation of historical commentary that began with an optimistic plea for brotherhood in *Grand Illusion*. In time as the threat of Nazism increased, Renoir's optimism gave way to the pessimistic reflection within *The Rules of the Game*. The affirmation of basic human values in *Grand Illusion* and the film's pacifist stance shifted to cynical, yet poignant criticism of the powerful and indifferent social structures which had helped to destroy those values. The indulgences permitted in *The Rules of the Game,* ironically, became the realities of World War II.

Later Work

Renoir left France in 1941 for the United States where he made six films before returning to his native land.

The first of his films abroad, *Swamp Water* (1941), was a commercially successful melodrama, notable aesthetically for the fact that Renoir broke from Hollywood tradition and filmed the exterior scenes on location.

In *This Land is Mine* (1943) Renoir's social conscience resurfaced with a story focusing on the occupation of France and the difficulties the occupation created for the French people. The stated goal of this picture was to counter American beliefs that the French were Nazi collaborators. These propagandistic intentions and Renoir's distanced knowledge of the occupation made the film one of his most controversial works.

The Southerner (1945) told a simple story of poverty in the South with commendable sensitivity. The direction was reminiscent, in its austerity and quiet observations, of work done in France.

Renoir took his genius back home in 1947 where he would continue his career and receive unparalleled praise for his great films of the 1930s. As a master of French cinema, Renoir stimulated a whole body of new critics (led by Bazin) whose appreciation of film art would culminate for many in directorial careers of their own and the French New Wave.

JEAN COCTEAU: FORMATIVE ARTIST

The formative possibilities of motion-picture art, first embodied in Georges Méliès' prototypical work, have continued throughout the course of film history to stand with uneasy tension beside the medium's realistic leanings. A fascination for creating new worlds rather than merely photographing the old one has attracted ingenious filmmakers from Méliès' time at the turn of the century to the more recent work of Stanley Kubrick and George Lucas.

Fantasy, science fiction, animation, *cinéma pur,* films of dreams, films of conscious and subconscious thought have all been classified as formative expression because their material surfaces are created for the camera lens to reproduce imagined realities. All film creation, however, is formative in varying degrees, whether the appropriated world leans toward documentary or imagined substances. Even *Citizen Kane* with its blend of objectivity and subjectivity, its realism and theatrics, its pure cinema devices (as Bosley Crowther called them) extended our understanding of realities outside the area of facts.

That formative works can hold deeply meaningful realities is also well known. Fables have long been the source of allegorical thought and pointed morals regarding human folly. Stories of the supernatural, as George Lucas' serialized *Star Wars* encounters between *the Force* and Darth Vader revealed, are most frequently adventures in which characters possess unearthly powers for controlling good and evil. The spirits that populate fairy tales usually possess similar powers, plus uncommon wisdom that becomes philosophically and morally instructive.

Jean Cocteau's interests in myth and fantasy as cinematic modes place him clearly in the camp with formative filmmakers. *The Blood of a Poet* (1930) sprang from the Orpheus myth and developed its allegorical theme about the poetic imagination in a free-form flow of images.

Although highly fantastic in form and representation, Cocteau's film was an introspective study of the poet (artist) that suggested objective experiences.

Beauty and the Beast

In approaching motion-picture expression Cocteau delighted in creating themes by drawing on "the frontier incidents between one world and another." His next film after *The Blood of a Poet* was *La Belle et la Bête* (*Beauty and the Beast,* 1946), a fantasy which tenders a lovely story about the mystery of innocent faith. In the introduction to his scenario Cocteau writes:

> Children have implicit faith in what we tell them. They believe that the plucking of a rose can bring disaster to a family, that the hands of a half-human beast begin to smoke after he has killed, and that the beast is put to shame when a young girl comes to live in his house. They believe a host of other simple things.
>
> I ask you to have the same kind of simple faith, and, for the spell to work, let me just say four magic words, the true "Open Sesame" of childhood: "Once upon a time." [Jean Cocteau; Carol Martin-Sperry translator.]

While Cocteau asks for the simple faith of childhood in viewing his interpretation of Mme. Leprince de Beaumont's fairy tale, *Beauty and the Beast* comes across as sophisticated and provocative. The tensions between reality and illusion, between simple fable and objective reflection act to create an imaginative work that is both entertaining and morally perceptive.

The Plot Cocteau places the time of his story in the seventeenth century and centers the tale around the plight of the kind-hearted and lovely Beauty (Josette Day). Beauty's character is Cinderella-like in quality: she is mistreated by her two selfish sisters, Felicie (Mila Parely) and Adelaide (Nane Germon), must bear the responsibility of offering spiritual support to her impoverished father (Marcel André), and must contend with a brother (Michel Auclair) who drinks and gambles.

When Beauty's father, a merchant, becomes lost in a deep forest and is taken hostage by the grotesque-looking Beast (Jean Marais), the young woman decides to offer herself in her father's place. Beauty goes to live in the Beast's magnificent castle where the two maintain separate lives except for the evening meal together. Beast simultaneously admits his ugliness and lack of charm while confessing that he loves Beauty and wishes to marry her. In time the young woman's repulsion softens, but her single desire is to return to her bedridden father. The wish is granted, with the condition that Beauty return to the castle.

At home Beauty is once more torn between the persuasions of her

Beauty (Josette Day) and the Beast (Jean Marais) meet daily for the evening meal. A living hand holds the candlelabra—one of Cocteau's many images that add to the film's sense of mystery.

family to stay with them and her deepening love for the Beast. When finally she goes back to the castle, the Beast is dying of grief. At his death the woman reveals her feelings, a gesture which transforms the dead creature into a handsome prince who says that his imprisonment as a Beast "could only be saved by a look of love." The two are carried aloft into the sky, hand in hand.

Cinematic Methods Cocteau's translation of this familiar story produces its magical spell through sheer inventiveness. Special visual effects in particular add to the film's charm. Returning to tricks reminiscent of Méliès' best work, Cocteau depicts disembodied human arms holding candelabras within the Beast's castle. Marble busts on a mantlepiece come to life, their nostrils emitting smoke and their eyes following visitors' movements. Doors open of their own volition, candles extinguish themselves, a magic mirror allows Beauty to gaze on distant scenes. Marvelous stop-action transformations turn tears into diamonds, peasant clothes into splendid garments, pearls into rags. Cocteau employs reverse-motion imagery, like that in Eisenstein's reconstruction of a statue for *Ten Days That Shook the World,* to magically fill the Beast's hands with jewelry and to bring Beauty through a wall so that it closes behind her.

Much of the film's engrossing effect as a drama comes from Cocteau's superb stylization of the Beast's world. The gentle, animated quality of the castle conveys its occupant not as a creature of ugly bestiality but as a patient individual whose physical appearance cannot hide his inner tenderness. Luminous black-and-white cinematography gives to the translation additional visual appeal and enhances the film's outrageously romantic nature. Dialogue is sparse and camera positions

unobtrusive as Cocteau trusts the settings, costumes, and translucent images to create mood and hold the viewer spellbound. *Beauty and the Beast* possesses a near balletic quality, a stylistic carryover from Cocteau's first theatrical experience as author of Erik Satie's ballet *Parade* in 1917.

The stirring qualities evoked by Cocteau in this innocent fairy tale derive from his ability to render the story so that the viewer sees in the drama a confrontation involving real human values. Questions of the relationship between love and physical appearance, between selfishness and acceptance are clearly provoked. Cocteau utilizes the unreal to explore realities as complex as the forces that mysteriously act to draw two people together. The complexity of love itself is expressed when the handsome prince tells Beauty: "Love can make a beast of a man. It can also make an ugly man handsome."

Aside from the philosophical ruminations offered by *Beauty and the Beast,* Cocteau's work leaves a glowing after-effect that is the result of having realized anew that it is indeed possible to rediscover the innocent faith of childhood and to see that beauty in and of itself can be a remarkable thing.

Because Cocteau's lifetime encompassed work in so many different media (poetry, theater, design, music, ballet, fiction, art) total film output was quite limited. *Beauty and the Beast* was only the second film for which he held the directorial reins and it was also his first feature-length effort. Subsequent films included four features and two 16mm shorts. The major portion of Cocteau's screen effort between 1930 and 1963 was as author of scenarios directed by others.

Later Work

Among the works after *Beauty and the Beast* were two films which reveal Cocteau's continuing interest in mythology: *Orpheus* (1950) and *The Testament of Orpheus* (1959). *Orpheus,* written first as a one-act play by Cocteau in 1925, was in thematic intention similar to *The Blood of a Poet:* an introspective study in mythic form of the poet (artist). A classic conflict between traditional expression and avant-garde interests is explored through two opposing figures, Orpheus (Jean Marais) and Cégeste (Edouard Dermithe). Agonizing self-doubts brought on by the challenge of the avant-garde lead both the celebrated traditionalist and the revolutionary poet into a hellish descent and ultimate rebirth.

In regard to *Orpheus* Cocteau said: "The poet must die several times in order to be reborn." To achieve this philosophical theme, incidents involving the real and the unreal ("the Zone") are brought into interplay, Méliès-like trick shots are incorporated (Orpheus passes from one world to another through mirrors), and stylized expression is used to create an imagistic sense of "other worldness."

The Testament of Orpheus (1959) is likewise a self-questioning exploration of the artist, but loosely structured and intensely personal. Numerous incidents drawn from Cocteau's past are included, some realistically derived, others dreamlike and surrealistic in appearance. Made entirely for his own pleasure, this film provided final indication of Cocteau's expressed delight in utilizing the motion-picture medium for "confessional" purposes.

Jean Cocteau's importance in film history results from his unique position as an artist whose work projected intellectual concerns through boldly stylized expression. Experimental filmmakers, the French New Wave, as well as other contemporary directors have noted Cocteau's influential manner of combining realism and illusion for the sake of personal statement.

VITTORIO DE SICA: NEOREALIST

Jean Cocteau's formative expression was stimulated by the highly personal concerns of an aesthete. Its effect as myth, fairy tale, and artifice lay in cinematic exploration born of the poetic imagination. At the very same time in the late 1940s that Cocteau's allegorical work was influencing the development of cinema styles, a sharply contrasting movement of major importance was afoot: Italian neorealism, as exemplified in the early films of Vittorio De Sica (1902–1974).

Neorealism is Born

Neorealism found its inspiration in the social upheaval resulting from Italian fascism and from the country's involvement in World War II. The bitterness and general hopelessness that followed the expulsion of Mussolini's forces were accompanied by a call for more humanistic consideration within the Italian film industry. As early as 1943 Professor Umberto Barbaro, instructor at the Centro Sperimentale school of cinema studies, had proposed new goals for Italy's filmmakers.

In his four-point program Barbaro asked most significantly that Italian directors avoid the "fantastic and grotesque fabrications which exclude human problems and the human point of view." For inspiration he pointed to "the films of the French neorealism period" in the 1930s. Barbaro alluded to work by Marcel Carné, Julien Duvivier, and Jean Renoir where social consciousness, well-defined characterizations, and individualized directorial styles had been distinguishing qualities. Although these directors are generally referred to as poetic realists, their link with Barbaro's neorealist manifesto is clear. In 1932 Carné had himself wondered when the cinema would "transcend into the streets" and cease "fleeing from life in order to delight in sets and artificiality."

Barbaro looked toward a rebellion against the lavish epics and contrived romances that had long been a part of traditional Italian cinema. Early domestic classics like *Quo Vadis?* (1913) and *Cabiria* (1914) were spectacles whose pageantry and ornate costumes had lasting influence on developing film style at home and abroad.

In later decades film output in Italy began to favor upper-class tastes, and the result was numerous romantic comedies set in a luxurious world far removed from the lives of common people. Because white telephones often appeared in these films as decorative set pieces and as symbols of upper-class luxury, this latter type of unrealistic escapist picture earned the depictive label of White Telephone film.

Barbaro's manifesto was opposed to the "mannered clichés" of the White Telephone film and to the "historical set pieces" borne by the traditions of epic filmmaking. Also requested within the call for a film revolution was a movement away from fascist rhetoric that intimated unfailing national pride. It was believed by Barbaro that the best way to stir the Italian people through cinema was by accurately relating the lives of common people to social realities.

Although well-trained at the Centro Sperimentale school which Mussolini had founded in 1935, and although experienced at the large Cinecittà studio established outside Rome five years later, Italian filmmakers remained for the most part bound throughout World War II to trivial fare and propagandistic demands. As the war and the Fascist regime drew to an end, however, directors began to respond to Barbaro's call for a humanistic cinema.

Ossessione Leading the transition from the White Telephone era to neorealism was Luchino Visconti who, in 1942, directed an unauthorized adaption of James Cain's American novel, *The Postman Always Rings*

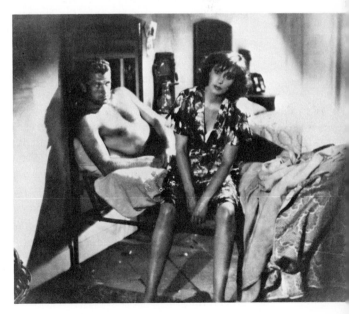

Restless characters, driven by passion, marked Visconti's uncommonly candid *Ossessione* (1942), a precursor to Italian neorealism.

Twice. The film, *Ossessione,* told a searing story of love and infidelity with remarkable honesty. Visconti traced the evolving passions of a wanderer and an innkeeper's wife who eventually murder for love and whose emotions gradually turn from bliss to fatal distrust. The film's sensual, restless qualities, its tragic overtones and realistic, on-location scenes startled Italian audiences accustomed to seeing throwaway, middle-class romances on the screen. Strong attention to character motivation in *Ossessione* showed the influence of Jean Renoir, for whom Visconti had served as assistant during the making of *The Lower Depths* (1936), and *Une Partie de Campagne (A Day in the Country,* 1936, released 1946).

The psychological dimensions and realism in Visconti's treatment resulted in an initial refusal by fascist censors to pass the film. Late in 1942 Vittorio Mussolini, son of the dictator, agreed to release the picture after some revisions. More extensive revision was made just prior to the overthrow of fascism in 1943.

The impact of *Ossessione,* later reconstructed by Visconti from a duplicate print, was first felt in critical circles. Shortly after the film's release Barbaro and other writers for the country's two major film journals, *Cinema* and *Bianco e Nero,* began their reconsideration of Italian cinema and to sense an impending liberation from the constraints which had kept the industry in a state of mediocrity.

The leap taken by Visconti toward social realism and a neorealistic style reinforced interests of Cesare Zavattini, one of Italy's leading scenarists. Zavattini had professed as early as 1941 a desire to present on the screen characters drawn from contemporary Italian life. That year he began a long collaboration with Vittorio De Sica, an actor-turned-director, and together the two progressed toward a new realism of immediacy and concern for human needs.

Open City and Shoeshine

The movement toward neorealism in Italy remained largely hidden from the world until 1946 when Roberto Rossellini's *Open City* (1945) and De Sica's *Shoeshine* (1946) were offered for international distribution. In *Open City* Rossellini presented a poignant account of underground resistance in Rome during the Nazi Occupation that followed Mussolini's fall in 1943. The violence, uncertainty, and disillusionment experienced by resistant Italian workers during the Occupation were captured with near documentary realism. When *Open City* arrived in the United States in March 1946, Bosley Crowther wrote:

> To us who have been accustomed to the slickly manufactured sentiments of Hollywood's studio-made pictures, the hard simplicity and genuine passion of the film lend to its not unfamiliar story the smashing impact of a shocking exposé. And its sharp estimation of realities gives it a rare intellectual quality. [*The New York Times,* March 3, 1946.]

Visual realism, achieved through location shooting, gave authority to De Sica's treatment of social injustice and personal corruption in *Shoeshine* (1946).

When De Sica's *Shoeshine* arrived in New York six months later, critical reaction was similarly favorable. The De Sica-Zavattini study of two shoeshine boys who become innocently, then tragically, caught up in blackmarket activity following Rome's liberation was praised by Crowther for its "pictorial rawness and candor."

To achieve this realistic impact De Sica filmed on location, used nonprofessional actors in the principal roles, allowed the narrative to develop in an episodic, spontaneous manner, and avoided false sentiment and optimism in bringing the story to its poignant conclusion.

Impressive in its spontaneous quality, *Shoeshine* also set a standard for the neorealistic document that sought to examine the plight of common people trapped by social conditions. The two juvenile delinquents are shown being compelled to commit crimes because of rampant poverty and as a consequence land in a crowded jail. Eventually they abandon their regard for each other in an act of betrayal that results in one of the youngsters being killed by the police.

The total corruption of the two boys provided an effective metaphor for conveying the personal impact of social injustice, for revealing the ease with which uncorrected human wrongs at large can tragically destroy individuals, physically and spiritually. The innocent, according to De Sica, become both victims and perpetrators of injustice.

This embittered view of human suffering became the central theme of neorealism. The goal of Italian filmmakers was to report human despair with the hope of learning from it. No solutions to the appalling injustices that followed in the aftermath of fascism and World War II were intended. The original value of the movement was seen as residing in its journalistically styled exposures of contemporary events; Zavattini once remarked that the consummate neorealist film would be a ninety-minute study of a worker in a factory performing routine duties.

In practice, however, Zavattini and De Sica never came close to producing such a Lumière-inspired actualité. Rather, subsequent work after *Shoeshine* revealed a growing tenderness in character development that provided dramatic satisfaction as well as reportage. De Sica became increasingly more skilled in inventing spontaneous-looking actions that revealed emotional realities, and in constructing narratives that, although seemingly following a "flow of life" pattern, were in fact tightly controlled for maximum dramatic effect. Music and camera work, too, began to play greater roles in creating sympathy for the common characters.

The dramatic conditioning enhanced the overall appeal of the neorealist movement rather than detracting from it. Characters became heroic figures whose perseverance against social injustice could be viewed as uplifting if not optimistic. The ugly social statements began to give way to moving human documents of universal value. Nowhere is this more evident than in De Sica's *The Bicycle Thief* (1948), the classic representation of neorealism and a film whose compassionate portrayal of the common worker is enduring.

The Bicycle Thief

The plot of *The Bicycle Thief* (in Europe known as *Bicycle Thieves)* is one based on the most incidental set of circumstances. An unemployed worker, Antonio, is offered a job hanging poster advertisements, a position which requires some means of transportation. Antonio's wife, Maria, pawns her bed linens and uses the money to reclaim the family's already pawned bicycle. On the first day of work the bicycle is stolen as Antonio hangs a glamorous movie poster.

A desperate search begins for the machine which represents Antonio's only immediate hope for a livelihood. The man's son, Bruno, and friends join in the search, trekking through the bleak Roman streets, into churches, brothels, and dingy apartments in their effort to track down the thief and reclaim the bicycle. It is Sunday, so Antonio has a full day to complete his mission. As the day draws to an end and he realizes that his efforts are futile, Antonio attempts in a moment of despair to steal a bicycle that leans against a wall outside a soccer arena. He is caught and humiliated in front of Bruno, but because of the boy's presence is dismissed with only a scolding. Father and son are absorbed into the street crowd as they walk, grief-stricken, toward home.

Directing Methods This simple plot becomes more than ordinary in De

With a feeling of new hope Antonio begins his first day of work as a poster hanger in *The Bicycle Thief*. The poster of a glamorous Rita Hayworth stands in ironic juxtaposition to the realities of postwar Italian life of which Antonio is a part.

Sica's screen translation. Through well-defined character development and well-placed dramatic actions the story is elevated from a sequence of banal incidents to human tragedy. Underscoring the human elements is the film's realistic authority, achieved by photographing the action almost entirely in the streets, by employing nonprofessionals to interpret the roles, and by finding social ironies and objective correlatives for character emotions within the environment's material presence.

Although De Sica's camera images (photographed by Carlo Montuori) are starkly realistic, the imagery is not without visual poetry. When Bruno and Antonio leave together on their bicycle for the father's first day of work, the scene is captured in the soft haziness of early morning. The surge of workers' bicycles into the streets carries a sense of hope ("a new day") that is supported by the swell in Allessandro Cicognini's lyrical music playing beneath the scene.

De Sica also finds considerable poetry in close-up shots of the principal characters. Antonio (Lamberto Maggiorani) transmits in his passive, sculptured face an image of pride, determination, and strength; Bruno, (Enzo Staiola) with his round, cherubic features, becomes a symbol of spirited innocence and hope. Sympathy for these two brave individuals is raised in large part by camera perusal rather than by script development.

Social ironies are also revealed through camera plotting. When Maria takes her bed linens to the pawn shop, a slow tilt up shows bundle

 Antonio captures the bicycle thief—
only to discover that conviction is impossible. The bewildered Antonio then resorts to theft himself.

upon bundle of bridal sheets that have already been offered by others for money. It is a mute statement of the severe economic conditions that prevailed in Italy at the time. Later as Antonio and his team begin their search for the stolen bicycle in a second-hand marketplace, the camera tracks along rows of tables and racks containing in great proliferation used bicycle parts. These objects in abundance provide an unstated commentary on the nature of Antonio's plight and that of Italians at large. The suggestion is that numerous others have also been victimized and their bicycles broken down for resale. Antonio's apparent frustration in the presence of many fragmented bicycles leaps out at the viewer because of this visual reference.

The dramatic thread which gives *The Bicycle Thief* its narrative unity is the relationship that develops between Antonio and his son while they track after the stolen bicycle. De Sica shapes the relationship through a series of dramatic vignettes that are alternately serious and comic, hopeful and desperate, loving and alienating. Dramatic rhythms and emotional contrast are precisely ordered as the father and son are caught in a downpour of rain, locate the thief, lose him, become desperate, recoup their morale in a restaurant, and then take up their journey again only to learn in the end that the thief is an epileptic who has the protection of call girls, neighbors, and the police. Dejected, Antonio in the climactic scene attempts to steal the unguarded bicycle.

De Sica's expertise in developing dramatic vignettes with emotional impact is well illustrated in a scene in which the father's true feelings for his son are made undeniably clear. As the day wears on and tensions grow, Antonio in a moment of frustration slaps Bruno. The boy is deeply wounded by the father's blow and moves away from Antonio physically and spiritually. He walks ahead of the father or behind him and refuses to speak. The man, himself hurt and feeling guilty, tells the boy to wait by a bridge and continues the search alone. After a few minutes, the father hears cries of "help" and realizes that a boy is drowning in the river beneath the bridge where Bruno was told to wait. The father runs to the river bank where the boy's body has been lifted. As he nears the scene, we can see with the father that the arms and legs on the limp body are much too long to belong to the stubby Bruno. The father, relieved, stops and turns rapidly toward the steps leading from the bank up to the bridge. A medium shot reveals Bruno standing on the steps, looking down at his anxious father.

This inventive scene serves as a brilliantly realized objective correlative for emotions and feelings that are not spoken but clearly understood. No amount of private desperation can destroy the love of this father for his child. Such characterizing moments, rendered in actions rather than words, suggest the sensitive, pure nature of De Sica's directorial style.

Bruno, taking his father's hand, acts to offer the love and support that can sustain human beings through the bleakest of times.

Theme *The Bicycle Thief's* theme reiterates ideas found in *Shoeshine*. Once more an innocent individual becomes both victim and contributor to inequities impelled by social hardship. When Antonio steals the bicycle in desperation, his behavior can be viewed as sadly typical rather than atypical. That Antonio is caught and humiliated in the presence of his son acts only to intensify the poignancy of the man's impulsive action. His plight is the plight of all Italy's hopeless—fully exposed in one heartrending moment.

Unlike *Shoeshine*, *The Bicycle Thief* concludes with a positive gesture of unity rather than betrayal. As Bruno and his father, both in tears, move toward the soccer crowd and home, the boy reaches up, takes his father's hand, and in so doing trips slightly, adding a touch of spontaneous humor to the sentimental gesture. Two men, not a boy and a man, are walking home—dejected but wiser and closer. They will survive.

Impact With the enormous critical acclaim bestowed on *The Bicycle Thief* came a clearer understanding of those elements which revealed neorealism at its best: a "flow of life" structure, dramatic action that appears to have been spontaneously taken from the environment, common-people themes shaped by social conditions, realistic imagery which avoids self-conscious camera angles and flashy editing techniques, naturalistic acting, avoidance of false sentiment and easy solutions.

In a terse statement of intention, Roberto Rossellini summarized neorealism as a film movement which sought to say: "This is the way life is." More specifically, advocates attempted to show how unjust social systems can destroy basic values. Pride and courage were offered as the essential elements in struggling against unfair conditions and toward an improved world.

The influence and strains of neorealism outside Italy can be found in numerous works that have concerned themselves in an authentic manner with the problems of common people: in India in Satyajit Ray's *Apu Trilogy* (1955–1959); in Britain's "kitchen sink" films of the late 1950s, early 60s; in France in Truffaut's *The 400 Blows* (1959); and in the United States in *On the Waterfront* (1954), *Sounder* (1972), *Blue Collar* (1978), *Norma Rae* (1979).

Later Work

In Italy neorealism continued briefly into the 1950s with De Sica adhering closely to the movement's stylistic and thematic interests. His *Miracle in Milan* (1950), *Umberto D* (1952), *The Roof* (1956), and *Two Women* (1960) all presented stories of simple people combating degrading sociopolitical conditions.

Even in the whimsical *Miracle in Milan*, where wealth miraculously comes to the poor villagers through oil discovery, De Sica uses the spoof as an ironic statement about the delusions of the working class. This interpretation is reinforced by a final shot of the villagers being carried to heaven on their broomsticks—the only certain solution to the problems of the poor, according to De Sica's pointed satire.

Umberto D, a Zavattini story about a sick, impoverished pensioner, and *Two Women,* which depicts the courageous struggle of a country family during the war, were more grimly neorealistic in treatment.

Late in his career De Sica shifted from the stark black-and-white imagery characteristic of the movement to the more lush world of color photography. *The Garden of the Finzi-Contini* (1971) and *A Brief Vacation* (1973) use color in expressive and romantic ways. In both these works impending death is a central issue and De Sica's lush visual style stands in ironic juxtaposition to death's grim reality.

Neorealism's importance among Italian directors diminished significantly as Italy rebounded from its anguished postwar period. As the dire economic conditions which had helped to sustain the movement improved, the anxious mood of the country shifted to one of hope. Gradually directors began to turn from social realities to studies more attentive to character psychology and to styles that were personal and poetic. These interests suggested a transition to vigorous new themes and styles, not only in Italy but in film industries around the world. The 1950s would be, when all was said and done, a decade of artistic crisis and commercial upheaval that would give rise to the threads of modern cinema.

SUGGESTED READINGS

Armes, Roy. *Patterns of Realism: Italian Neo-Realist Cinema.* Cranbury, N.J.: Barnes, 1971.

Braudy, Leo. *Jean Renoir: The World of His Films.* Garden City, N.Y.: Doubleday, 1972.

Cocteau, Jean. *Cocteau on the Film.* New York: Roy Publishers, 1954.

De Sica, Vittorio. *The Bicycle Thief.* Translated by Simon Hartog. New York: Simon & Schuster, 1968.

Gilliatt, Penelope. *Jean Renoir: Essays, Conversations, Reviews.* New York: McGraw-Hill, 1975.

Leprehon, Pierre. *The Italian Cinema.* New York: Praeger, 1972.

Mast, Gerald. *Filmguide to "The Rules of the Game."* Bloomington: Indiana University Press, 1973.

Nowell-Smith, Geoffrey. *Luchino Visconti.* Garden City, N.Y.: Doubleday, 1968.

Renoir, Jean. *My Life and My Films.* New York: Atheneum, 1974.

PART 5

NEW DEVELOPMENTS IN AMERICA AND EUROPE

THE 1950s AND 60s:
NEW TECHNOLOGY, INFLUENCES, THEMES COME TO HOLLYWOOD

Joe Gillis: You were a big star once.
Norma Desmond: I'm still big. It's the pictures that got small.
Exchange between William Holden (Joe) and Gloria Swanson (Norma) in *Sunset Boulevard* (1950).

For the motion-picture industry in the United States, the period following World War II and leading into the 1950s was one that saw public response to the medium in a state of rapid and critical alteration. *Film Daily Yearbook* estimated in 1947 that motion-picture attendance the year before had broken all records, with an average 90,000,000 tickets sold each week during 1946. By 1952 this weekly figure was only slightly more than 50,000,000—representing a 45 percent drop in ticket sales. Another report, released in 1950, had

Sunset Boulevard.

revealed that only twelve of 146 films made in Hollywood during 1948 had realized profits in their United States distribution.

SOCIETAL FLUX AND TELEVISION

Major changes within American society had begun to affect motion-picture attendance. With the war over, tensions abated and many who had found emotional release in the standardized screen fare of the early 1940s simply stopped going to the movies.

This was also a time of mass exodus to the suburbs, away from conveniently located metropolitan and neighborhood movie houses. With suburbanization came changing lifestyles—more travel and new diversions to compete for entertainment allowances: night baseball, bowling alleys, and racetracks. Increased spending on home products occurred as installment buying became a widely available merchandising practice. The television set, most significantly, was among those home products which many purchased "on time."

At the beginning of 1948 there were an estimated 100,000 television sets in use in the United States; during that year manufacturers placed more than a million additional receivers on the market for eager buyers thrilled with the possibility of "free" entertainment. By 1950, 18 percent of American households owned receivers, indicating that television was no passing fad.

Despite early Hollywood assumptions that the novelty of television would soon pass, the industry was openly wary of its new competition. In the late 1940s studio executives banned their contract players from appearances on television programs, and halted the "airing" of old movies from their stockpiles.

ANTIMONOPOLY ACTION

Television, however, was only partially responsible for Hollywood's increasing woes. A 1948 Supreme Court decree ruled after years of deliberation that the industry's studio-theater chain corporations violated antitrust laws, and that the studios must divest themselves of their theaters. This antitrust action resulted from the conclusion that block-booking, long required of exhibitors by their affiliated studios, constituted a monopolistic practice that prevented fair competition. The studios were given three years to comply with the divestment decree.

When it became clear in 1946 that the antitrust decision was imminent, reaction within the film industry was drastic. The large studios, most anxious of all, effected production cutbacks, layoffs, and wage decreases. In a single year, 1947, M-G-M reduced its payroll by 40 percent. Warner Brothers' roster of contract players dropped from 120 in 1945 to three dozen in 1951. Production of the B-movie, a studio staple and a vital commodity in the block-booking system, began to taper off in the larger studios as the assurance of guaranteed outlets dimmed.

It became clear to all that the American film industry, which had held its own through wars, depressions, and the ever fickle tastes of filmgoers, had entered into a serious crisis that required new consideration of its future. A general philosophy began to develop among Hollywood executives that fewer, more intelligently made films would be a wise response to the uncertain times. Consequently, "Movies are Bigger and Better than ever!" emerged as the rallying cry of the 1950s.

TECHNICAL GIMMICKS

Within the campaign to convince filmgoers that movies were in fact "Bigger and Better" came the wide-screen, technical-gimmick movement. Certain that television competition was a principal cause of its commercial problems, the Hollywood studios turned to new improved screen devices with the hope of drawing video viewers away from the "box." New projection systems and wide-screen formats introduced in 1952 and 1953 included Cinerama, 3-D, CinemaScope, VistaVision, Panavision, Todd-AO, and a host of additional "visionscope" mechanisms. The goal was to provide audiences with a "total" theatrical experience.

Cinerama

Cinerama was the first of the new exhibition processes to be offered commercially. The process, which had been invented in 1935 by Fred Waller, utilized three-image projectors, a curved screen that circled around viewers, and a stereophonic sound system with localized speakers to match sounds to screen-image position. By projecting the separate images simultaneously, peripheral vision permitted a sensory experience. Viewers felt as though they were in the center of the action. The novel effect of airplane and roller coaster rides delighted audiences who attended *This Is Cinerama,* a travelogue-styled demonstration of the process released to selected theaters in September 1952.

Curiosity made *This is Cinerama* a successful venture, but dramatic applications did not fare as well. The necessity of incorporating novelty effects to satisfy audience expectations interrupted character and plot development, e.g., *The Wonderful World of the Brothers Grimm* (1962). Coupled with the considerable expense of equipping theaters for Cinerama (approximately $100,000 per theater) the process found limited use despite its immediate commercial appeal.

An artist's drawing captures the expanse of the Cinerama screen that permitted audiences to experience the effect of a roller coaster ride.

3-D

Three-dimensional films, employing a stereoscopic process, followed Cinerama's unveiling by only two months. *Bwana Devil,* the first full-length 3-D effort (directed by radio's suspense master Arch Oboler) was released in November 1952, and two months later Warner Brothers provided *House of Wax* for audience amusement.

Demonstrations of 3-D processes had taken place as early as 1936. To achieve the stereoscopic effect, two images of a scene were photographed simultaneously from slightly separated points and projected onto the screen in a similar manner. Polarized eye glasses permitted the viewer to combine the images so that a sense of depth and solidity was experienced.

As with Cinerama, producers discovered that the novelty created by 3-D pictures held audiences only temporarily. Many filmgoers found that putting on cardboard glasses made them feel a bit foolish and most others considered the polarized spectacles a nuisance. Interruption of plot occurred frequently as directors attempted to jolt audiences with sensational displays of the process. In *Fort Ti* (1953) arrows and flaming torches were fired toward the viewers; The Three Stooges, in a trailer short that preceded the feature, thrust hypodermic needles at the audience.

After a half dozen such films in 1953, the sensation soon melted into cynicism. One unconvinced critic summarized critical reaction to 3-D's cinematic effectiveness by concluding that the "potency of movies depends upon the quality of their dramatic articulation, not upon the working of hocus-pocus on the eyes."

Wider Screens

Of the new technical devices introduced in the 1950s the wide-screen, anamorphic lens processes proved to be the most durable. Known under various trade names as CinemaScope (Twentieth Century-Fox), Superscope (RKO), and Panavision (Paramount), the anamorphic process allowed increased screen expansion at reasonable cost (as low as $5,000), while offering clear artistic possibilities that went beyond mere gimmickry.

In 1927 Henri Chrétien, a Frenchman, had perfected the first anamorphic lens, an optical device for photographing scenes of considerable width and squeezing them onto a standard-size frame area. By placing a similar anamorphic lens on the projector, the distorted image could be increased to an aspect ratio of 2.35:1 (sometimes 2.55:1), resulting in a projected screen image that was more than two times wider than it was high. Standard aspect ratio prior to the introduction of the anamorphic lens was 1.33:1 (a width-height relationship of 4 to 3).

Twentieth Century-Fox revealed the possibilities of the anamorphic lens in its CinemaScope release of *The Robe* in the fall of 1953. Adapted from Lloyd C. Douglas's best-selling novel, *The Robe* was assured large audiences; with the added attraction of CinemaScope images, the picture (a Biblical spectacle) became one of the most successful commercial ventures of the decade.

A publicity agent's exaggerated promotion of a 3-D version of *Kiss Me Kate*, released in 1953.

An anamorphically squeezed image from *The Robe* (1953) and one from the same film projected to full width to fill the CinemaScope screen.

Aesthetics *The Robe* pointed out the aesthetic demands imposed by new wide-screen formats. Traditional approaches to composition (e.g., the over-the-shoulder shot) was no longer as effective in CinemaScope framing, and new methods of blocking had to be devised to fill the wide screen in a visually interesting manner. Even simple camera angling had to be curtailed because of the panoramic lens. Further, the widened scope prevented free use of standard editing procedures. Compositional considerations forced long runs of the camera and fewer close-ups; dynamic or emphatic editing approaches, to which filmgoers were accustomed, had to give way to greater dependency on the appeal of spectacle. Many critics of the time feared the loss of intimacy and personal drama available to standard formats.

With careful planning, however, Hollywood directors soon learned to choose and adapt their scripts to the new dimensions. Among the aesthetic discoveries made by directors while working in CinemaScope and Panavision was that creative lighting could serve as a vital tool in achieving maximum flexibility and variety. If the narrative required itimacy, the side edges of the scene could be left in darkness, thus reducing the lit image to a more standard size. Intense key lighting, focused on principal characters, and localized sound placement were other ways of directing attention in a panoramic shot.

New Frame Sizes

Efforts to increase actual film size followed these developments, although the requirement of installing still another new projection system was met with some resistance by exhibitors. Producer Mike Todd, willing to install his own equipment in leased theaters, sponsored a 65mm version of the popular musical *Oklahoma!* released in 1955 in a process known as Todd-AO. The following year Mike Todd Associates used the 65mm width for *Around the World in 80 Days*.

By the early 1960s film width had been expanded to 70mm, a format with an approximate 2.5 to 1 aspect ratio and one that has since remained popular for use in screen spectacles. More conventional aspect ratios also showed the lasting impact of the big screen movement, widening from the earlier 1.33:1 ratio to a new standard of 1.85:1.

Stereophonic sound systems were considered a necessary complement for further enhancing the realism and novelty of the wide-screen processes. Eventually Dolby Sound and other such "multiphonic" systems would further intensify screen spectacle.

Enduring Technology

Three major elements of modern cinematic expression, all long available to film producers, achieved lasting importance during the highly technical 1950s: the adoption of wider screen formats, new aesthetic

consideration of sound, and a dramatic shift to color production. In 1951 only 25 percent of Hollywood-made films were in color; three years later the figure had risen to nearly 60 percent.

In the face of television's competition (then entirely black and white), film producers found color to be a distinct advantage that was corroborated by statistics. Of the top ten money-earning films of 1956 only one, *I'll Cry Tomorrow,* used a black-and-white emulsion. Significant, however, is the fact that *I'll Cry Tomorrow,* a study of singer Lillian Roth's recovery from alcoholism, was the most realistic of the big money makers, ranking fifth in the list that included in order: *Guys and Dolls, The King and I, Trapeze, High Society, I'll Cry Tomorrow, Picnic, War and Peace, The Eddy Duchin Story, Moby Dick,* and *The Searchers.*

Producers were still holding onto the assumption that journalistically styled narratives such as *I'll Cry Tomorrow,* with black-and-white images, possessed greater authority than color films. This was a carry-over from a long-standing tradition of utilizing expensive color processes only for romance, spectacle, and historical pageantry. Not surprisingly, when color came to television, motion-picture producers shifted away from black-and-white feature production almost entirely—in large part to assure later sale of films to the video networks.

Economic necessities during the 1950s forced acceptance of valuable technology that had been held in abeyance by the film industry.

While the innovative devices were proving temporarily successful in increasing box office revenues, it became apparent that story content also required a more modern look; aural and visual sensation alone could not save the motion-picture industry. Stronger, more effective scripts were also needed.

FREER EXPRESSION

Gradually, and somewhat reluctantly, Hollywood discovered the selling power of bolder, more candid films. During the 1950s, stories dealing with such themes as drug addiction, sex, and violence increased in number on American screens. To treat this material, external and self-regulatory censorship procedures had to be significantly liberalized.

Statutory Censorship

In 1915 the United States Supreme Court had declared in *Mutual Film Corporation V. Industrial Commission of Ohio* (236 U.S. 230) that "the exhibition of motion pictures is a business, pure and simple, originated and conducted for profit, like other spectacles, not to be regarded, nor intended to be regarded . . . as part of the press of the country, or as organs of public opinion."

This decision had underwritten the numerous municipal and state censorship boards which had sprung into action to oversee the "moral fitness" of films before the medium was a decade old. Chicago had created the first city board in 1907, and Pennsylvania the first state reviewing committee in 1911. By 1922 two-thirds of the American states had enacted or had pending some form of legislation for regulating the motion picture.

Film producers found the varying, uncertain reviewing procedures of the numerous boards frustrating. With such widespread censorship decided by individual interpretations, it became impossible for filmmakers to know what was acceptable in their films and what was not. Postproduction deletions were common around the country while the 1915 *Mutual* decision went unchallenged. Many films were banned altogether in one place or another.

Self-Regulation

As if statutory censorship were not bad enough, the industry acted in 1930 to devise a self-regulatory code of moral standards for use as a production guide. The well-intended Motion Picture Producers and Distributors of America (MPPDA), sponsors of the guide, had concluded that an internal code might lessen outside censorship.

Included in the 4,000 word document was a listing of specific and general taboos, prohibiting the treatment of miscegenation, illegal drug use, pointed profanity, illicit sex, undue suggestiveness, and methods of crime. Producers and screenwriters were cautioned to show due respect for religion, national feelings, and for law and justice.

The MPPDA code (in time the "Hays Code," after Will Hays who headed the organization) was initially an optional guide; but with the potential boycott power of the newly formed Catholic Legion of Decency in 1933, enforcement was considered necessary. Thereafter producers were required to submit their scripts to the MPPDA Code Administration for a "seal of approval."

The stultifying effects of double-pronged censorship practices on motion-picture content are well known. Candor often gave way to moral hypocrisy as producers attempted to work around both the code and the legally sanctioned reviewing boards. For *Uncle Harry* (1945), a film in which a character murders his sister, the code requirement that sinners must be punished was circumvented by revealing at the film's conclusion that the brother's deed had only been a dream.

The Miracle Case

The challenge to legal censorship began in December 1950 when Roberto Rossellini's short film *The Miracle* (1948) opened at New York's Paris Theater. Various Catholic organizations charged that the Italian film was "blasphemous" and "sacrilegious" in its depiction of a simple woman (Anna Magnani) whose confused religious fervor leads her to believe that she has conceived immaculately. Spurned by her neighbors, the woman must deliver her child alone under the overhang of a church.

Critical interpretations assessed *The Miracle* as an allegorical statement about social and institutional insensitivity to basic human needs. Still, Catholic groups, most specifically the Catholic War Veterans, pressed to have the film banned.

These ambivalent interpretations became the significant issues in a two-year court battle that was finally resolved by the Supreme Court. In a unanimous decision regarding *The Miracle*, the Court ruled on May 26, 1952 that the film was not censorable because of a single group's interpretation of sacrilege.

In its reversal of the 1915 *Mutual* decision, the Supreme Court offered social status to the motion picture and the assurance that prior restraint of films was no longer constitutional. *The Miracle* decision did not end statutory censorship, but the case represented the beginning of a lengthy period of liberal thinking on the part of Chief Justice Earl Warren's court toward freedom of expression for the motion picture.

Code Breakdown

The progressive climate that prevailed after *The Miracle* decision and

In *The Miracle* Anna Magnani's rendezvous with a man (Federico Fellini) whom she thinks to be Saint Joseph leads the woman to believe she has conceived immaculately. Through a Supreme Court decision Rossellini's allegorical film won social status for the American motion picture.

throughout most of the 1960s helped to bring about a relaxation of Hollywood's self-regulatory practices.

A first mild relaxation of code standards occurred in 1954 when the MPPDA Administration dropped its ban on the treatment of miscegnation, the drinking of hard liquor in films, and the use of mild profanity. An urgency to further loosen internal restrictions became evident in 1955 when the Code Administration refused a seal of approval for *The Man with the Golden Arm,* a film about drug addiction. Producers distributed the film anyway. In 1956 director Elia Kazan refused to delete scenes from his independently produced film *Baby Doll* in order to meet Legion of Decency and Code standards. Numerous foreign films with candid material were also receiving wide distribution without official Hollywood sanction.

Impelled by these developments to allow American producers greater freedom of content selection, Code restrictions were significantly eased late in 1956. Specified taboos against the treatment of abortion, "illicit sex," prostitution, kidnapping, and drug addiction were abolished at this time.

The Rating System

Ten years later a major move began to replace the self-regulation Code with a classification system for rating films according to their content and suitability for various age groups. Devised by Jack Valenti of the Motion Picture Association of America (MPAA), and announced in 1968, the rating system was comprised of four categories: G, general audiences; M (later changed to PG), mature audiences, "Parental Guidance" advised;

R, restricted, adult accompaniment required for anyone 17 or under; X, no one under 18 admitted.

Problems inherent in an interpretive rating system became apparent even before it went into effect: the difficulty of precise categorization; changing standards within the MPAA Rating Board; public interpretation of the various categories; and a tendency on the part of producers to alter or delete material to satisfy category standards rather than artistic standards. Stanley Kubrick, a strong opponent of motion-picture censorship, was nevertheless willing to delete a satirical sex scene from *A Clockwork Orange* (1971) in order to receive a rating change from (X) to (R). Had this film been made five years later when Rating Board standards were looser, Kubrick's work likely would not have received an (X) rating in the first place.

The sequence of events which led to the disappearance of the Code (the disintegration of the studio system, television competition, a liberal legal climate, independent and foreign film distribution) was accompanied simultaneously by other significant developments that would also affect motion-picture content. Trends in the American theater in particular interacted with Hollywood's liberalization to propel the screen toward an acceptance of new themes and new candor.

OUTSIDE INFLUENCES ON HOLLYWOOD CONTENT

A more serious-minded Hollywood was suggested by several important films made just after the conclusion of World War II: *The Lost Weekend* (1945) portrayed the nightmarish world of an alcoholic; *Crossfire* and *Gentleman's Agreement*, both made in 1947, examined anti-semitism issues; *Pinky* and *Intruder in the Dust*, both filmed in 1949, dealt with the theme of racial prejudice; *All the King's Men* (1949) brought to the screen Robert Penn Warren's incisive study of a corrupt politician.

World War II found its most poignant statement in William Wyler's postwar production *The Best Years of Our Lives* (1946)—a film which presented sympathetic accounts of three servicemen attempting to make transitions back into civilian life. As the twentieth century approached its midpoint the American film industry gave notice of an emerging realism and a new social awareness.

Two motion pictures produced in 1950 can be viewed in retrospect as symbolic points of departure for an industry that was in fact leaving behind one generation of filmmaking and moving ahead to another. That year, with *Sunset Boulevard*, Billy Wilder presented a darkly expressionistic film of metaphorical significance. His story centers on a once great screen actress, Norma Desmond (Gloria Swanson), who survives on glorified memories of a career and a Hollywood that have passed.

Wilder's dissection of the actress' vanity avoided sentimentality altogether, and in so doing exposed the myths that deluded golden era screen personalities and rendered them unable to separate the fantasy of their work from its reality. Norma Desmond's decaying mansion with its somber reminders of a past grandeur stood in 1950 in ironic synchronization with Hollywood's newly collapsed studio structure, its rapidly fading Star System, and its dwindling box office receipts.

Fred Zinnemann's realistic study of paraplegic war victims, *The Men*, was also released in 1950. The pivotal importance of this film was twofold: its emphasis on character psychology, and the appearance of Marlon Brando as the principal character in his first film role. Brando, a celebrated stage actor, projected a vivid new style of acting (known as The Method) in interpreting the mental and emotional realities of his paraplegic character.

Brando's arrival in Hollywood at the very time that *Sunset Boulevard* was looking sardonically at the "star" mythology, signaled a transitional period for the screen actor. The image of the old Hollywood star, cast dramatically onto film by Swanson's Norma Desmond, would be further eradicated by this new breed of actor represented in Brando. Other performers, trained in Method acting, arrived soon after to interpret roles which, like Brando's *The Men*, demanded psychological, introspective attention.

The Actors Studio

The 1950s would bring an intense interaction not only between the motion-picture and prominent theater actors but with directors and playwrights as well. The Actors Studio of New York, which had given rise to Brando, served as a major source of new talent. This training school was an offshoot of The Group Theatre—an organization found-

Marlon Brando: the prototypical "method" actor who emerged during Hollywood's uncertain 1950s.

ed in 1929 and dedicated to Stanislavski acting principles. Lee Strasberg, an organizer of The Group Theatre, founded The Actors Studio in 1947 to continue performance training in The Method style where emphasis was placed on discovering inner realities ("psychological truthfulness") and on presenting a naturalistic, fully concentrated character.

Elia Kazan

Hollywood producers, groping for new material, began bringing to the screen adaptations of plays which had catapulted the Strasberg-trained actors to fame. Late in 1950 Marlon Brando began work on the film version of *A Streetcar Named Desire,* repeating the searing Stanley Kowalski role which he created for Broadway in 1947.

Tennessee Williams' Pulitzer Prize-winning study of frustrated sex and neurosis was brought to the screen under the direction of Elia Kazan, (1909–   ) a co-founder of The Actors Studio, who also directed the stage play and who had directed his first feature-length dramatic motion picture, *A Tree Grows in Brooklyn,* in 1945. With *A Streetcar Named Desire* Kazan began a lengthy theater–motion-picture association with Williams which included directing assignments for *Camino Real* (1953, stage); *Cat on a Hot Tin Roof* (1955, stage); *Baby Doll* (1956, motion picture); *Sweet Bird of Youth* (1959, stage). In each of these Williams scripts Kazan showed an unusual talent for directing actors.

Kazan's interest in serious material and first-rate acting placed his screen efforts of the 1950s among the decade's best American films. *On the Waterfront* (1954), scripted by Budd Schulberg, was a vivid, authentic account of industrial corruption battling the rights of the common worker. Brando appeared as Terry Malloy, an uneducated longshore-man whose love for a young woman (Eva Marie Saint) awakens him to a new awareness of waterfront racketeering. Compelled to stand up against the mobsters who take advantage of simple, unthinking people like himself, Malloy becomes a symbol of simplistic but brash idealism.

To achieve visual authenticity for *On the Waterfront,* Kazan filmed on location in New Jersey where the bleak environment and harsh lighting gave the images a newsreel-like quality. Many scenes were composed from low-angled camera positions and set against stark backgrounds.

Additional realism was provided by the film's remarkable acting. Brando managed to project character sensitivity through a combination of personal charisma, vocal delivery (that appeared to be tied to an inner turmoil), and a naturalistic, improvised approach to dramatic action. In one scene a glove, dropped accidently by Eva Marie Saint, is picked up by Brando and withheld from the woman as the two walk and talk. Her efforts to retrieve the glove and Malloy's refusal to give it back convey his unexpressed, growing attachment to the woman.

The poignancy of Brando's brutish, searching character reached its greatest intensity in a taxicab scene where Malloy recounts for his

In the back seat of a taxicab in *On the Waterfront* (1954) Terry Malloy (Brando) tells his brother (Rod Steiger) that he could have been "somebody."

brother (Rod Steiger) a lost dream of becoming a great boxer and, hence, "somebody." Here, Kazan achieves an affective mood through a naturalistic, impromptu approach that presents the ideals and aims of Method acting at their very best. The impact of this single scene on the changing course of screen acting has been well noted by observant critics and by dozens of film and stage actors who have followed Brando's lead.

Kazan's regard for screen naturalism was evident in other important films of the decade: in *East of Eden* (1955) with James Dean; in *Baby Doll* (1956) with Karl Malden and Caroll Baker; in *A Face in the Crowd* (1957) with Andy Griffith and Patricia Neal; in *Splendor in the Grass* with Natalie Wood and Warren Beatty (1961). Sometimes accused of emotional excesses in the treatment of film material, Kazan nevertheless played an important role in altering film styles and themes. His introspective studies of alienated heroes progressing toward new self-realization set the tone for numerous films with similar protagonists that appeared during the 1950s and 60s.

Other Actors, Other Writers

Other actors who arrived in Hollywood from New York to recreate stage roles included Julie Harris whose sensational theater success, *The Member of the Wedding* (1950), was adapted to film in 1952. Harris, also schooled in the psychological naturalism style, recaptured the intense and delicate qualities of an awkward girl approaching womanhood.

Similar traits were displayed in creating Abra for Kazan's *East of*

Julie Harris and James Dean in *East of Eden* (1955), one of many films made during the 1950s about adolescent anguish.

Eden. In this adaption of Steinbeck's novel of generational differences, Harris and James Dean (Cal) exemplified the internal conflicts and restlessness of youth that emerged as a popular theme in American films of the fifties and sixties. Their physical presence on the screen seemed to embody a combination of inner turmoil and pained gentleness; Dean's interpretation clearly owed much to Marlon Brando and, consequently, was attacked by critics for its imitative qualities.

In 1952 Shirley Booth, an established actress but also an adherent of Stanislavski methods, appeared in the motion-picture version of *Come Back, Little Sheba,* the William Inge play which had brought her Broadway acclaim in 1950. Booth's screen interpretation of Lola, a housewife whose life has been irreparably saddened by an alcoholic husband (Burt Lancaster), won her wide praise and an Academy Award.

Daniel Mann, director of *Come Back, Little Sheba,* had also been an instructor at The Actors Studio, a fact of significance in the successful adaption of Inge's play.

Inge *Come Back, Little Sheba* represented initial Hollywood contact for William Inge (1915–1973), a writer of import to content trends through the decade. Inge offered in his screenplays just the right mixture of sexual innuendo and psychological analysis to appeal to producers and audiences of the time. *Picnic* (1956), *Bus Stop* (1956), *The Dark at the Top of the Stairs* (1960), and *Splendor in the Grass* (1961) all presented Inge's interest in average American characters confronting sexual and emotional insecurities. The Freudian overtones of these films were often heavy and their solutions simplistic, but the combination of poetry and candor placed Inge among the serious writers in the "New Hollywood." Tennessee Williams won favor for the same reasons in *The Rose Tattoo*

(1955), *Baby Doll* (1956), *Cat on a Hot Tin Roof* (1958), *Suddenly, Last Summer* (1959), *The Fugitive Kind* (1960), *Summer and Smoke* (1961), *Sweet Bird of Youth* (1962).

Chayefsky Paddy Chayefsky (1923–1981), another writer of importance to Hollywood's transitional fifties, made his screen reputation with *Marty* (1955). The independently produced *Marty* impressed the film world with its modest budget, neorealistic look, and sensitive story of romance between two very average people (Ernest Borgnine and Betsy Blair). This film offered further proof of Hollywood's progression away from old-style filmmaking.

Chayefsky followed *Marty* with *The Bachelor Party* (1957), another low-budget film about ordinary people. Both screenplays had been first written for live television, a fact which accounted for their intimate qualities and the concern they gave to fundamental human relationships, treated without dramatic bravado.

The Goddess (1958) found Chayefsky taking a sardonic look at the Hollywood actress (Kim Stanley) who is unable to cope with movie stardom. Drugs and alcohol gradually overtake the woman's fragile mental state; her "goddess" status (created in large part by Hollywood publicists) is exposed as a dubious achievement and as an awful burden for so insecure a figure. The elements of truth in this story (directed by John Cromwell) were carried with unusual realism by Chayefsky's dialogue and by Kim Stanley's internal performance.

Chayefsky's gift for brilliant dialogue would continue to appear in

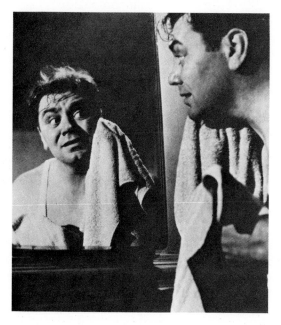

A very different-looking romantic lead reached the screen with Ernest Borgnine's appearance in *Marty* (1955).

Hollywood's period of serious self-examination during the 1950s produced *The Goddess* (1958), Paddy Chayefsky's memorable study of an insecure film star (Kim Stanley).

the probing social satires written during the 60s, 70s, and 80s: *The Americanization of Emily* (1964), *Hospital* (1972), *Network* (1976), *Altered States* (1981).

Independent Producers

As new writers, directors, and actors paraded their forthright characters across American screens, independent production accelerated. Greater freedom in content selection and opportunities for profit sharing provided the incentives for producers to manage their own financial and production arrangements. Studio layoffs also inspired independent production.

Filmmaking outside the studio structure offered opportunities for more individualized attention to projects not always available in studio assembly line processes. Location shooting became common practice, partially due to realism demands, but also to stay within low-budget allocations for less ambitious projects. By 1958, 60 percent of all feature films released in the United States were made by independent producers; by 1970 this figure had risen to 85 percent.

This dramatic shift did not destroy the Hollywood studios, as some voices of doom had predicted, but rather propelled the old corporations into new roles within the film industry. Sound stages were offered as rental space for independent production and for filmed-for-television projects. The established studios acted as prestigious distributors for the majority of independent producing companies, an arrangement which studio executives soon learned worked to their advantage because of distribution fees and contract agreements that guaranteed them a percentage of gross receipts. Smaller investments by the distributing studios often meant profits not realized by the film's producers whose investment was considerably larger.

Television Production

Freed largely from their role as feature-film producers, the studios were able to justify a more prominent involvement with the television industry. As independent production grew and as the temporary relief provided by the big-screen-gimmick movement wore off, in-studio production was reorganized to help satisfy television's voracious appetite. By 1965 television subsidiaries existed within most large Hollywood corporations, turning out prime-time series programs and made-for-television movies with the same fervor (and, usually, quality level) that in earlier decades had gone into making the B-picture.

Hollywood-based production completely dominated television dramatic programming by 1970, and it is estimated that at this time 80 percent of Hollywood's artist and technical guild members earned their livelihood through television-related work.

These rapidly developing changes meant that the now rarer American feature film must sustain itself on a product-by-product basis. Every release, like Broadway productions, was a risk. This uncertainty resulted in the fads-and-fancy approach that began to characterize American film output during the 1960s. Producers were quick to gauge current successes and to offer motion pictures of a similar sort. Film cycles spurred by a fashionable theme, a popular genre effort, or an escapist trend setter formed a sizeable portion of American film history in the years immediately following the hectic 1950s and uncertain 60s.

SUGGESTED READINGS

Carmen, Ira H. *Movies, Censorship and the Law.* Ann Arbor: The University of Michigan Press, 1968.

Ceplair, Larry, and Steven Englund. *The Inquisition in Hollywood.* Garden City, N.Y.: Anchor, 1980.

Ciment, Michel. *Kazan on Kazan.* New York: Viking, 1974.

Dowdy, Andrew. *The Films of the Fifties: The American State of Mind.* New York: Morrow, 1973.

———. *"Movies Are Better Than Ever": Wide-Screen Memories of the Fifties.* New York: Morrow, 1973.

MacCann, Richard Dyer. *Hollywood in Transition.* Boston: Houghton Mifflin, 1962.

Stuart, Frederick. *The Effects of Television on the Motion Picture and Radio Industries.* New York: Arno, 1976.

THE FRENCH NEW WAVE
AND LUIS BUÑUEL

A Bout de Souffle (Breathless, 1959) was the sort of film where anything goes; that was what it was all about. Anything people did could be integrated in the film. As a matter of fact, this was my starting point. I said to myself: we have already had Bresson, we have just had *Hiroshima,* a certain kind of cinema has just drawn to a close, maybe ended, so let's add the finishing touch, let's show that anything goes. What I wanted was to take a conventional story and remake, but differently, everything the cinema had done. I also wanted to give the feeling that the techniques of filmmaking had just been discovered or experienced for the first time.
Jean-Luc Godard, *Cahiers du Cinema,* February 1962 (translated in *Godard on Godard,*
1972).

With the shift away from studio dominance in the filmmaking process, a new type of "star" emerged to replace the screen actor in audience favor: the director. The uncertain 1950s, which included new experimentation in cinematic expression,

Breathless.

also led to a growing awareness of individual directors whose probing themes and innovative techniques excited film enthusiasts appreciative of more serious, personal cinema. Simultaneously, academic examination of motion-picture art on college campuses intensified during the fifties and sixties to spark wide-scale interest in not only new but older directors as well.

Much of the directorial excitement was generated by films made in Europe and Asia where stylistic experimentation was particularly intense. Directors in France, England, and Italy, in Sweden, Japan, and Eastern Europe led a cinematic renaissance characterized by personal commitment and by narrative exploration which sought to integrate more fully form and content.

By isolating the distinctive qualities of such national movements as the French New Wave and of the influential directors who emerged in the 1950s, it is possible to see the extraordinary diversity that revitalized world cinema during one of the medium's most creative periods.

INSPIRATION

Two aesthetic forces sustained French cinema during the transitional years between the country's fertile poetic realism era (ended by World War II) and the New Wave revival in the late 1950s: intense critical activity, largely under the influential André Bazin; and the directorial genius of Robert Bresson.

André Bazin

In 1947 André Bazin (1918–1958) founded the criticism journal *La Revue du Cinéma,* which in 1950 became the vital *Cahiers du Cinéma.* Bazin drew a whole school of young writers who followed the journal's dedication to serious appraisal of the motion picture. François Truffaut, Jean-Luc Godard, Claude Chabrol, Eric Rohmer, Jacques Rivette, Jacques Doniol-Valcroze, and Alexandre Astruc were among the gifted *Cahiers* critics, all of whom developed a deep love of cinema that inspired and conditioned their own later careers as prominent directors.

It was this group which led the French revival and inspired a new generation of energetic film artists. They were people compelled not by a unified vision but by an urge to apply their studied knowledge of film practice and style to personal creations. The catch-all phrase *New Wave (Nouvelle Vague)* appeared after 1959 as a convenient label for the full range of "new director" releases which began to surface at that time.

Robert Bresson

The importance of Robert Bresson (1907–   ) was solidified in the period when critical activity at *Cahiers du Cinéma* was most intense, and in

A stark, dominant landscape envelops the spiritually disturbed curé of Bresson's *Diary of a Country Priest* (1950).

large part because of praise its critics lavished on this rigorously austere director. A devout Catholic, he made his first film, *Les Affaires Publiques (The Public Affairs),* in 1934, worked as a screenwriter during the late 1930s, then after a year and a half in a prisoner-of-war camp in 1940 and 1941, directed his second film, *Les Anges du Péché (The Angels of Sin, 1943).* This work and *Les Dames du Bois de Boulogne (The Women of the Bois de Boulogne),* made two years later in 1945, suggested a developing interest in spiritual themes wrought from a confining milieu. *The Angels of Sin* had as its setting an isolated convent where religious activity centers on the reformation of female vagrants. A confrontation between a novitiate and an inmate ultimately leads to spiritual exaltation for both. Communion through love and acceptance denies a woman's attempted betrayal of her rival in *The Women of the Bois de Boulogne.*

This idea of spiritual transcendence as resolution to personal crisis served Bresson as the principal theme of his most important films: *Le Journal d'un Curé de Campagne (Diary of a Country Priest,* 1950); *Un Condamné à Môrt S'Est Echappé (A Man Escaped, 1956); and Pickpocket (1959).* Bresson's unique, much analyzed approach to film direction also manifests itself in these works.

Diary of a Country Priest The central character in *Diary of a Country Priest* is a young curé who is deeply anguished by shortcomings in dealing with parishioners. The crisis of faith intensifies when the priest discovers that he is terminally ill with cancer. Bresson's study (adapted from Georges Bernanos' novel) is one of rigid attention to the priest's inner turmoil, the camera concentrating so intently on the man's face that the effects of the cancer (physical and spiritual) are painfully conveyed.

Bresson limits dialogue and camera embellishment, preferring instead close scrutiny of the principal character in the environment at hand. A first-person voice-over narration translates the priest's agony. The narrative progresses in a disjunctive manner as Bresson moves from one moment or event to another to capture important psychological and emotional reactions. The accumulation of aural and visual images provides, rather than a well-ordered dramatic plot, the spiritual progression of an isolated individual.

The young priest's suffering, which ends with his transcendence to grace at the moment of death, is supported visually by stark landscapes and by the muted, lonely sounds taken from the environment. Bresson's success in treating emotional complexity is undeniably intense.

A Man Escaped* and *Pickpocket The same austere, intense methods appear in *A Man Escaped* and *Pickpocket*. Each is a story about a criminal whose social and physical confinement promotes personal turmoil that leads to spiritual awareness. Isolation or, expressed another way, condemnation to solitude provides Bresson's troubled characters with physical conditions that force movement of the soul through darkness toward an exalted state.

Because of their interior nature, these two films also use first-person narration and concentrate attention on the protagonists' environments with their expressive sounds and material objects. Essential emphasis, as in all Bresson films, remains on internal characterization through elliptical observation of critical actions and reactions. Nonprofessional actors again portray the screen characters.

A cinematic ascetic, inspired by intellectual and moral commitment, Bresson's vision and directorial style were uniquely his own. His small body of films (eleven) made between 1934 and 1971 ignored commercial trends, disregarded audience expectations, and demanded, even from the most appreciative viewer, patience.

Bresson's stylistic integrity and dedication to personal filmmaking separated his work from the grandiose mannerings that typified much of traditional French cinema. *Cahiers* critics, taking note of the differences, praised Bresson as a serious artist to be admired alongside France's most vigorous, imaginative filmmakers.

NEW WAVES

Several important French films appeared in 1959 to signal to the world that aesthetic reconsideration of the motion picture was taking place there. Three of them attracted international attention: Truffaut's *The 400 Blows,* Alain Resnais' *Hiroshima Mon Amour,* and Jean-Luc Godard's *Breathless.* Entirely different in substance and form, this trio of films showed that the diversity of directorial styles which *Cahiers* critics had advocated in writings throughout the decade was indeed possible in their own country.

François Truffaut

François Truffaut (1932–   ), in particular, had expressed disdain for the French film industry at large, contrasting its lack of creative spirit with Hollywood's where studio-bound directors were often able to evince personal style in a variety of genre offerings. His own career as a director was one impelled by a desire to exercise artistic liberty in film expression.

Following three short dramatic exercises, *Une Visite (A Visit,* 1954), *Les Mistons (The Mischiefmakers,* 1957), *Une Histoire d'Eau (A History of Water,* 1958, with Godard), Truffaut began work on *Les Quatre Cents Coups (The 400 Blows)* when he was barely 26 years of age. A year later it earned him the 1959 Cannes Festival Grand Prize. The critical importance of this first feature effort resided in its sensitive theme and its free-style approach to treatment of idea. Truffaut proved himself to be a director with strong humanistic leanings, a distinctive trait which would characterize much of his work.

The 400 Blows Truffaut's first feature contained autobiographical references in presenting the story of a young lad whose life is a series of

Antoine Doinel (Jean-Pierre Léaud), shunned by his family and unhappy, steals a typewriter—an act which lands the boy in a reform school. *The 400 Blows* (1959) was spontaneously free in its use of Parisian street locations.

Shoot the Piano Player (1960), Truffaut's breezy tribute to the American gangster film. The story alternated between suspenseful melodrama and parody full of cinematic references.

oppressive home and school experiences that lead to petty theft. Officially declared a "juvenile delinquent," the boy is institutionalized for psychiatric help, eventually escapes, and runs frantically along the seashore to demonstrate his freedom. In the final shot a freeze-frame captures the boy's ambiguous expression as he darts within close range of the camera lens, symbolically holding him captive forever by an uncertain future which promises little chance for the freedom he desires.

As a youth Truffaut was himself arrested for petty theft, charged with school truancy, and convicted of military evasion. His one strong interest as a boy had been in cinema study; as a founder of a ciné club, Truffaut came to know André Bazin who helped the young man through his difficulties.

In treating the story of Antoine Doinel (Jean-Pierre Léaud), his screen counterpart in *The 400 Blows*, Truffaut gave indication of a sensitivity in revealing character while providing an entertaining film experience. His subject matter, that of the wayward youth, was easily understood as a universal truth. Such a character, depicted by Truffaut in a developing stage where cynical resignation is not yet evident, offered a gentle, tragicomic reminder of life's corrupting forces.

An eclectic approach to cinematic technique in *The 400 Blows* adds to its insightful effect. Fluid camera movements follow the boy when he romps freely; alternating close-up shots convey the tensions between the youth and his parents; improvised action adds spontaneity to comic scenes; a candid, hidden camera set-up films the lad as he is interviewed by the institution psychiatrist (who remains unseen); lyric music interweaves among the documentarylike passages to constantly pull the film back into an emotionally evocative framework. This stylistic combination of realistic and sentimental elements showed separate influences of Jean Vigo, Jean Renoir, and Roberto Rossellini, all greatly admired directors.

Shoot the Piano Player Truffaut paid tribute to the American film with *Shoot the Piano Player* (1960), his second feature and a work inspired by the Hollywood gangster picture. The plot reports incidents from the life of a piano player (Charles Aznavour) who has sought solitude following his wife's suicide. Flashbacks reveal the man as a once important concert performer whose career ambitions had led to the wife's death and subsequently his detachment. As the story develops, the piano player is once again pulled back into life after he offers to help two brothers evade gangsters; tragedy recurs, including the death of a second woman to whom the piano player has attached himself.

Nowhere is there greater proof of the *Cahiers* years' nurturing influence on New Wave directors than in *Shoot the Piano Player*. It is as thorough an exercise in studied filmmaking as *The 400 Blows* was personal statement of autobiographical inspiration. Truffaut borrows techniques from favorite films and directors (Hitchcock, Guitry, Clouzot, Aldrich). Numerous references are made to cinematic conventions for Truffaut's own enjoyment, including the glib introduction of avant-garde elements uncommon to action thrillers. Mood alternates throughout, from well-styled melodrama to comic parody to psychological analysis.

Jules and Jim With his self-indulgent impulse satisfied, Truffaut returned in *Jules and Jim* (1961) to the lyrical subject matter and sensitive treatment of character that would carry as distinguishing stamps into the 1980s. *Jules and Jim* is a story of the love of two friends for the same woman beginning in Paris just prior to World War I. The film depicts in very personal terms the complexities of relationships where the parties are friends as well as lovers. Central to Truffaut's exploration is Catherine (Jeanne Moreau), a spirited, free-living woman who first attracts Jules (Oskar Werner), then Jim (Henri Serre). Ultimately unconvinced by a woman so whimsical and domineering, Jim rejects Catherine and she kills him and herself by driving her car off a pier.

Time and setting are vital components in Truffaut's theme of romantic idealism. The pre-World War I Paris setting invites memory of an era linked with unconditional freedom for youthful intellectuals. Postwar scenes which reunite the trio unfold in ironic parallel with the impending realities of historical events. The love story begins in 1912 and ends just after the three attend a movie newsreel showing book burnings in Nazi Germany. *Jules and Jim* is also a treatment of a special period's demise as well as a study of the difficulties of unorthodox love.

In adapting *Jules and Jim* from a 1953 novel by Henri-Pierre Roche, Truffaut denied all charges of literariness (so despised by *Cahiers* critics

The unusual triangular relationship that is the theme of *Jules and Jim* (1961) was brilliantly captured by Raoul Coutard's lyrical camera compositions.

in traditional French cinema) by drawing on every imaginable filmic device. Moving camera shots abound, as do special *verité* methods of filming scenes. Composition and framing are studiously varied, music precisely matched to fit the editing rhythms.

The showy display of technique creates an appropriate lyrical style that is compatible with the exuberant characters' lives. By spontaneously integrating form and content for poetic impact, Truffaut produced a masterpiece.

Later Work Work following his first three important feature-length motion pictures alternated between failure and success, between studied exercises and light-hearted themes about youth. *Fahrenheit 451* (1966), a Ray Bradbury adaptation, showed Truffaut treating an intellectual-philosophical scenario with heavy-handed styling. *The Bride Wore Black* (1968) and *Mississippi Mermaid* (1969) were mannered thrillers with too-rigid dedication to Alfred Hitchcock, a director idolized for his understanding of the medium's manipulative possibilities.

Truffaut was at his best in a return to more personal themes and in particular to the Antoine Doinel character of *The 400 Blows* who reappeared (each time with Jean-Pierre Léaud) in *Love at Twenty* (1962), *Stolen Kisses* (1968), and *Bed and Board* (1970). Obvious affection for the characters in these self-confessional films about innocence confronting an adult world made them equally appealing to audiences. Their free, nonmoralizing, and eclectic quality suggested the true personal vision that established Truffaut as an important director in his own right. *The Wild Child* (1969) and *Small Change* (1976) carried forth thematic interest in childhood themes with a clear expression of faith in the tough, resilient nature of innocent youth.

Alain Resnais

Alain Resnais (1922–   ) differed from Truffaut so significantly that only timing linked the two as members of the New Wave. Contrasting Truffaut's breezy, humanistic films were Resnais' highly formal, intellectual, and philosophical studies. While personal referencing gave rise to Truffaut's childhood universe and cinephile preferences inspired his Hitchcock-styled thrillers, Resnais was given to dramatic abstraction which provoked larger questions about society, politics, and the human imagination. The best of Truffaut's work seemed to be merely happening in its narrative progression, whereas Resnais' expression was rigidly ordered in choice of editing arrangement, image composition, and sound track.

Resnais prepared for a film career in Paris at IDHEC, the French cinema school, where he enrolled during 1943–1944. Although he has said that a dislike for the school's theoretical emphasis caused his departure, the instruction there left an undeniable influence. The exacting nature of his work and the temporal-spatial manipulations that convey his themes reveal a near academic interest in film as art; these qualities sharply contrast with those of the *Cahiers*-tutored directors whose films showed a more spontaneous interest in retrieving the best of cinematic practice.

After a brief period as an actor, Resnais began directing short films, most notably a series on art subjects: *Van Gogh* (1948), *Gauguin* (1950), and *Guernica* (1950). The structural approach in these films displayed an editing virtuosity uncommon to the genre as visual and aural elements were evocatively ordered.

Night and Fog Resnais' talent for lyric construction manifests itself prominently in the much acclaimed *Night and Fog* (1955), an emotionally charged reminder of World War II's concentration camp horrors. Resnais sets the short film's components into contrapuntal arrangements: colored picture postcardlike views of the Nazi camps as they look ten years after the war dramatically oppose grainy, black-and-white newsreel shots taken of terrible events as they actually occurred at Auschwitz; lyrical music and a poetic voice-over narration (hauntingly written by Jean Cayrol) overlay the stark, mute documentary images. The awful past charges the apparently serene present for a dialectical statement about war's recurring possibilities and its incredulous extremities that time's distancing perilously blots from memory.

With *Night and Fog* Resnais established two primary characteristics of a personal style that would distinguish him from his contemporaries: controlled montage that thematically shifts between past and present, between memory and reality; strong collaborative scripting as an impetus to intellectually styled cinematic exploration.

Hiroshima Mon Amour *Hiroshima Mon Amour* (1959), a film whose dramatic form evolves through memory, was brought to the screen from an original screenplay by Marguerite Duras. Resnais commissioned Duras, an established literary figure, to write a love story set in the bombed city of Hiroshima with the idea of reevoking the past and its imposition on an amorous relationship.

The Resnais-Duras collaboration resulted in a complex time-space narrative involving a French actress (Emmanuelle Riva) and a Japanese architect (Eiji Okada) who meet in Hiroshima where the woman has come to perform in an antiwar film. They fall in love and at the beginning of the story are shown in a love embrace, their bodies covered with a glittering, radioactivelike dust.

The architect quietly begins to narrate his memories of Hiroshima's devastation while Resnais' camera tracks subjectively through a museum filled with reminders of the atomic bomb's horrible toll. These remembered experiences jolt the actress' own terrible war memories in the French village of Nevers where an affair with a German soldier ended in tragedy and public humiliation.

In Proustian-styled construction, Resnais as editor of *Hiroshima Mon Amour* shifts freely between past and present, leaping from images in Hiroshima to episodes in Nevers as the woman's memory forces an emotional catharsis that she has long suppressed. Her presence in Hiroshima, with its wartime realities, is a stimulus to personal history and tragedy whose scarred evidence cannot be enclosed in museum cases, but which remains all the same. The jigsaw arrangement of past and present condition, of public and private horror, skillfully expands into intellectual, emotional, and philosophical terms the lasting effects of war.

Last Year at Marienbad Resnais' fascination for memory as dramatic substance continued with even greater abstract treatment in *Last Year at Marienbad* (1961). The script by experimental writer Alain Robbe-Grillet (with contributions by Resnais) eschews traditional narrative progression and plot for a cinematic experience imbedded in the implications of time and thought. A narrator (Giorgio Albertazzi) speaks in repetitive phrasings about a time past (the year before?) and an acquaintanceship with a woman (Delphine Seyrig) who has promised to meet him again. The setting, possibly the intended meeting place, is a baroque chateau whose impressive architectural details pass before Resnais' constantly roving camera. In effect, mind (narration) and eye (camera) probe the chateau's spaces, pausing to catch snippets of conversations, and to reflect on the meaning of objects as the man attempts to convince the

Remembrance of a time past leads the actress (Emmanu-elle Riva) in *Hiroshima Mon Amour* (1959) to painful ca-tharsis.

woman (and himself) of their previous encounter and plans for a future (permanent?) engagement.

The outcome of the persuasive efforts are never made explicit and the relationship between the couple remains ambiguously suspended in time. *Last Year at Marienbad* has continued to be of critical interest primarily because of its formalistic, graphic images which are proposed as mental process and as "illusion" (the narrator in conclusion refers to the hotel as "a structure of illusion"). Efforts to convincingly interpret the film's meaning have proved impossible and even Resnais and Robbe-Grillet differed on whether the man and woman had actually met before. Resnais said yes; Robbe-Grillet no.

Later Work Later films reveal a less cold, less oblique Resnais, con-cerned most frequently with characters who are attempting to redeem themselves through memory of events from their past: *Muriel* (1963); *La Guerre Est Finie (The War is Over,* 1966); *Je t'Aime, Je t'Aime (I Love You, I Love You,* 1968). *La Guerre Est Finie,* the most successful of this group, examines a veteran's inextricable ties to the long-past Spanish Civil War and the challenge posed by contemporary politics to the man's life commitment that has been all-consuming.

Stavisky (1974) proved an unusually engrossing dramatic experience in a story of political intrigue written by Jorge Semprun. Based on the life of a famous swindler who manipulates the wealthy and the powerful, Resnais effectively recaptures the mood of France during the 1930s while drawing parallels between politics and personal corruption.

Memory and the past, illusion and appearance—essential elements that gave Resnais' career its consistency—found their way into *Providence*

(1977) through a decaying old novelist (John Gielgud) who fitfully reconstructs family relationships for a final book. Disparity between recall and actual appearances provides the familiar Resnais juxtaposition. In *Mon Oncle D'Amérique* (1980) Resnais presents a seminar-length lecture on human behavior, tracing the lives of three characters from their childhood years of behavior instruction through to the reactive patterns evident in adult rituals of survival and conquest. Dramatic and scientific illustrations of behavior theories commingle throughout the film.

Jean-Luc Godard

Jean-Luc Godard, (1930–   ) a third member of the figurative New Wave triumvirate, stands closest to the center of the movement's derivative interests. His pleasure in imitating favorite filmmakers, in retrieving admired techniques, his fresh, independent and free-wheeling filmmaking style, combined with anarchistic, existential views of life make him the quintessential, totally original representative of the movement.

Godard was 24 when he joined the writing staff of *Cahiers du Cinéma* in 1954, coming to Paris after the war from a television cameraman's job in Switzerland. Like Truffaut, Godard entered film direction with a group of short exercises that includes both documentaries and fictional films. A whimsical comedy, *All the Boys Are Called Patrick* (1957), anticipated the Godard style of informal, rapid filmmaking where improvisation adds to the spirited quality. Cinematic referencing (a poster of James Dean, a reflected view of the camera) showed Godard's respect for film and simultaneously his lack of intimidation by the medium.

During his years as a critic for *Cahiers du Cinéma*, Godard wrote appreciatively of the American B-movie, citing among other favored genres the *film noir*-styled gangster and intrigue films that flowed unpretentiously from Hollywood during the declining studio years. Nicholas Ray, considered among the best of the *noir* directors, was especially admired by Godard for his films about youthful, alienated protagonists who combat societal forces—most commonly in losing battles, e.g., *They Live by Night* (1948), *Knock on Any Door* (1949). Violence and criminal activity ensnare Ray's naive heroes here and in later works: *In a Lonely Place* (1950), *Born to Be Bad* (1950), *On Dangerous Ground* (1951), and *Rebel without a Cause* (1955). These stark character studies with their violent, nihilistic undercurrents helped inspire Godard's first feature, *A Bout de Souffle (Breathless)*—a gangster-tailored film which was offered in tongue-in-cheek homage to Monogram Pictures, a small American studio that turned out, exclusively, low-budget B-movies.

Breathless The plot of *Breathless* projects key elements representative of the early Godard: the difficulties of communication in a repellent

A detached sense of self is conveyed in Jean Seberg's characterization of Patricia. Godard's images in *Breathless* (1959) often support the American girl's feeling of personal confusion.

society, characters aggravated by personal indifference and moral collapse. Godard's principals (in a script idea suggested by Truffaut) are Michel Poiccard (Jean-Paul Belmondo), a young car thief (who sees himself as a Humphrey Bogart hero), and his offbeat American girl-friend, Patricia Franchini (Jean Seberg). Poiccard kills the policeman who pursues him and flees to his girl. He is shot to death after Patricia turns informer.

These familiar plotting ingredients suggest a standard action story when in fact they have been appropriated less for thriller value than for the dialogue that follows between the two lovers. The two are contemporary heroes: self-centered though hardly self-aware. Patricia considers herself "free," but not happy; she is excited by life only through the anticipation of new experiences—one being the betrayal of her hoodlum lover. Michel is equally detached, finding emotional stimulation in his criminal activity and, seemingly, in the end, liberation. He smiles self-mockingly at Patricia as he lies dying in the street—no more concerned about death than life.

Whereas Resnais' drama grew from the weight of the past, Godard's concern in *Breathless* remains always within the present as he delineates characters who are products of fractured times, conducting their lives impulsively on a day-to-day basis. His cinematic method carries its own feeling of abrupt contemporaneity. Handheld shots, taken on location by cinematographer Raoul Coutard, dominate the casual, cluttered-looking settings.

Further Generic Exploration Godard continued during the 1960s to generate films aesthetically linked to popular genres, with personal effect in each case. *Le Petit Soldat (The Little Soldier,* 1960) is a spy intrigue that involves its introspective characters in the Algerian crisis. *Une Femme Est une Femme (A Woman Is a Woman,* 1961) employs the musical comedy, wide-screen format for a personal statement about female needs, specifically those of Anna Karina (the actress portraying Angéla and also Godard's wife). *Les Carabiniers (The Soldiers,* 1963) draws on elements common to war movies and pushes them to absurd extremes for a Brechtian effect that raises more questions about the implications of military engagements than are answered. Godard uses the comic book, science-fiction plot of *Alphaville* (1965) to treat, metaphorically, communication failures and personal delusion, a theme repeated in *Pierrot le Fou (Pierrot the Crazy,* 1965)

These earlier films are the work of a director whose response to the medium was one of intellectual detachment and impatience with traditional approaches to character analysis. The rather conventional plotting outlines that formed Godard's narratives are revealed in a torrent of words, images, and self-conscious effects. Characterization is random (often worked out during filming) rather than well ordered, and reality is an ambiguous, informal flow of events loosely tied to melodramatic maneuvers.

Polemics Increasingly, Godard shifted from the film narrative to political statement and an anarchistic attitude that brought even more revolutionary approaches to film expression.

Intrigued by the political opinions and personal life styles of Parisian youths in the mid-60s, Godard in *Masculin-Féminin* (1966) explored the world of four outspoken characters from "the Marx and Coca-Cola generation." The film's fragmented narrative is presented in improvised interviews with fifteen separate "acts" relaying, among other concerns, the frustrated love of Paul (Jean-Pierre Léaud) for Madeleine (Chantal Goya). He is a recently graduated student, romantically committed to revolutionary causes and in Paris looking for work. The trivial Madeleine is an aspiring pop singer whose uncommitted involvement with Paul leads to his death, likely a suicide, and pregnancy for her.

Masculin-Féminin's content is impressionistic. Critical events in the characters' lives occur between recorded conversations while dramatic situations happen around the principals with unexplained casualness. Five violent deaths (Paul's and four others) are built into the film, with causality revealed in only one instance: a self-immolation in protest of the Vietnam War. In his elliptical probing Godard touches on character alienation in a specific time and place. The informal technique avoids psychological analysis but implies a great deal about Paul's generation.

Preoccupation with the complexities of modern life resulted in the simultaneous direction in 1966 of *Made in U.S.A.* and *Two or Three Things I Know about Her.* Each is intended as a statement about sociological and political mutations in French life—the former a detective intrigue made

Two representatives of the "Marx and Coca-Cola" generation, Jean-Pierre Léaud and Chantal Goya, engaged in conversation but clearly emotionally dislocated from one another.

to dissect American influence, and the latter using an anecdote about housewife prostitution in a high-rise apartment building for a metaphorical essay on materialistic concessions that Godard said were sweeping the country.

These two transitional films began Godard's commitment to the direct treatment of ideas. Subsequent works are political discourses on a variety of topics: anti-Vietnam sentiment in France, *Far from Vietnam* (1967); youth activity that would swell to create the student riots in Paris in 1968, *La Chinoise* (1967); abstract political protest, *One Plus One* (1968); artistic nihilism, *Le Gai Savoir (The Joy of Learning,* 1968); revolution and cinema, *Le Vent d'Est (Wind from the East,* 1969).

Godard's cinematic process in this political phase, like his subject matter, is radical. Sounds and aural imagery increase in significance with lengthy monologues, documentary interviews, and political debates (frequently including Godard) directly incorporated into polemic exercises lacking any recognizable organic structure.

Weekend (1967), the best-known example of Godard's later radical cinema, mixes realism and metaphor with brutal force. A weekend trip to visit relatives progresses from a casual journey to scenes of human carnage on the highway to a warring world where barbarism is rampant. Along the way, truck drivers (in actual interviews) debate colonialism. Such interruptions point out the essential Godardian style and its unconventional role for cinema in contemporary society.

Godard's later political abstractions failed to win the public at large; yet this phase of his work in the late sixties and seventies made vital contributions to film aesthetics as did the more personal earlier period.

Other Directors

The French New Wave brought in its creative rush between 1959 and 1964 hundreds of new films and several dozen important young directors. Claude Chabrol in *Le Beau Serge* (1958) and *Les Bonnes Femmes*

In *Weekend* (1967) Godard employs weekend tourists and the brutal defense of their automobiles for a scathing attack on the extremes of bourgeois materialism.

(The Good Women, 1959) showed a developing interest in bourgeois relations and character interplay leading to emotional destruction for the weak. This theme becomes more complex in later Chabrol works where emotions are used to create sophisticated psychological intrigues: *Les Biches (The Does,* 1968), *La Femme Infidéle (The Unfaithful Wife,* 1968), and *Le Boucher (The Butcher,* 1969).

Le Signe du Lion (The Sign of Leo, 1959) was the debut effort of yet another *Cahiers* critic turned filmmaker, Eric Rohmer, a delightfully genteel director whose work reached full maturity a decade later in a series of comedies of manners: *Ma Nuit Chez Maude (My Night at Maude's,* 1969), *Le Genou de Clair (Clair's Knee,* 1970), *L'Amour l'Aprés-Midi (Chloe in the Afternoon,* 1972).

Louis Malle and Roger Vadim, already established by 1959, contributed to the New Wave excitement with continued interest in sexual themes: *Les Liaisons Dangereuses (The Dangerous Liaisons,* Vadim, 1959); *Le*

Feu Follet (The Fire Within, Malle, 1965). Vadim's *And God Created Woman* (1956) with Brigitte Bardot and Malle's *The Lovers* (1958) with Jeanne Moreau had been liberating factors in the progression to cinema revival in France. Malle's ability to produce stylish studies of sexual passion achieved new heights in *Pretty Baby* (1978).

Impact

The influence of the New Wave movement was lasting. It provoked reconsideration of film art so that the medium would never be quite the same again, while suggesting new possibilities for personal expression. Numerous developing directors, commercial and independent, attached themselves to the movement's free spirit.

In England and the United States alone the evidence of influence mounted. Godard's narrative obliqueness appears in Arthur Penn's *Mickey One* (1965); his political dialecticism and cinematic self-consciousness in Haskell Wexler's *Medium Cool* (1969). Resnais' time maneuvering is seen in Stanley Donen's *Two for the Road* (1967), Joseph Losey's *Accident* (1967), and in Jack Clayton's *The Pumpkin Eater* (1963). Truffaut's humanistic, free-spirited concern for anarchistic youth carries over into Tony Richardson's *The Loneliness of the Long Distance Runner* (1962) and into Richard Lester's *A Hard Day's Night* (1964).

LUIS BUÑUEL

After a lengthy absence from film directing, the Spanish expatriate Luis Buñuel resumed his career in Mexico where he settled in the late 1940s

Los *Olvidados* (1950), a film populated by vicious delinquents who use city slums as a "playground" for their sadistic activities.

before returning to France in 1955. He proved in a series of superb films made during this second burst of creativity that his artistic interests and appeal transcended national boundaries.

Buñuel's last film in the earlier period had been an extraordinary documentary study of poverty in Spain, *Land without Bread* (1932), a work which broke from the surrealist symbolism that made *Un Chien Andalou* and *L'Age d'Or* classics. The realistic strains of *Land without Bread* carry over into the best of the Mexican works, *Los Olvidados (The Young and the Damned,* 1950), a shocking, sometimes surrealistic account of juvenile delinquents living outside Mexico City. Buñuel integrates stark documentary visualization with telling dream sequences so effectively that the delinquents' world is translated with psychological as well as social import. The film earned him the Cannes Festival Best Direction Award and reestablished his importance after eighteen years of relative obscurity.

Following this triumph Buñuel settled into the characteristic style that became unmistakably his own: a preoccupation with themes of sexual obsession and repression, presented in a matter-of-fact manner and with such an air of normalcy that dramatic circumstance is heightened to surrealistic intonation.

This approach and a recurring motif which attacks restricting social conventions and religious-taught morality dominate Buñuel's personal vision in film after film: *El (The Strange Passion,* 1952), *Viridiana* (1961), *The Exterminating Angel* (1962), *Belle de Jour* (1967), *Tristana* (1970), *The Discreet Charm of the Bourgeoisie* (1972), and *That Obscure Object of Desire* (1977). Made in France, Italy, Spain, and Mexico with international financing, the recurrent vision in this body of work reveals the extent to which Buñuel was able to maintain his uncompromising individuality. So sure was he of his established role as the supreme anarchist-surrealist that two different actresses were cast in the leading role for *That Obscure Object of Desire* without explanation or thematic justification.

Buñuel twice proved himself a great, personally commited director and in so doing offered inspiration to French cinema activity during both the vital avant-garde and New Wave movements.

SUGGESTED READINGS

Allen, Don. *Truffaut.* New York: Viking, 1974.
Armes, Roy, *The Cinema of Alain Resnais.* New York: Barnes, 1968.
Cameron, Ian, ed. *The Films of Robert Bresson.* New York: Praeger, 1970.
Durgnat, Raymond. *Luis Buñuel.* Berkeley: University of California Press, 1970.
Graham, Peter. *The New Waves.* Garden City, N.Y.: Doubleday, 1968.
Kyrou, Ado. *Luis Buñuel.* New York: Simon & Schuster, 1963.
Monaco, James. *The New Wave.* New York: Oxford University Press, 1976.

Roud, Richard. *Jean-Luc Godard.* Garden City, N.Y.: Doubleday, 1968.

Sadoul, Georges. *French Film.* New York: Arno, 1972.

Ward, John. *Alain Resnais, or The Theme of Time.* Garden City, N.Y.: Doubleday, 1968.

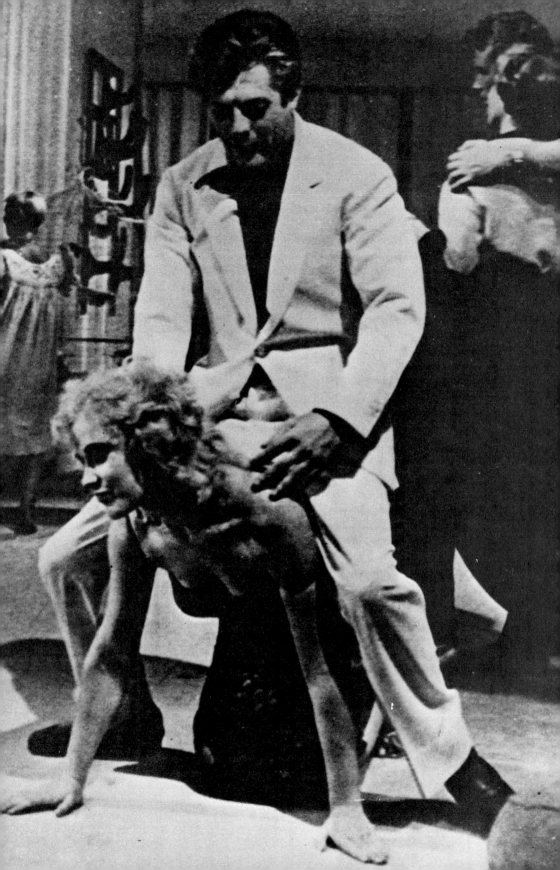

ITALY AFTER NEOREALISM

La Dolce Vita is intended to be both a testimony and a confession. The film attemps to dedramatize (and not merely demystify) certain aspects of the world we live in, and to accustom us to facing up to our monsters, one after the other. . . . In La Dolce Vita everyone can see his own reflection, providing he is sincere enough first to look for it and then recognize it.
Federico Fellini explaining La Dolce Vita at the 1960 Cannes Film Festival (quoted by
Pierre Leprohon in The Italian Cinema).

The 1940s and neorealism brought new vitality to Italian cinema in works spurred by social conditions and the deeply humanistic concerns of a handful of commited artists. As the economy improved during the following decade, established directors turned their sights to more personal themes, introducing bold subject matter and innovative methods of expression that were radically different from the thematic and stylistic interests of neorealism.

La Dolce Vita.

The revolution, led by Roberto Rossellini, Federico Fellini, Luchino Visconti, and Michelangelo Antonioni did not cast out realism by any means; instead it merely shifted toward more expansive views of reality than were possible in the traditional forms of expression.

The year 1960 was to new Italian cinema what 1959 had been to the French New Wave: a year which brought undeniable proof that a change of direction had taken place within the country. Fellini's *La Dolce Vita* and Antonioni's *L'Avventura* both appeared that year to convey intentions and experiences unlike any seen before them.

FEDERICO FELLINI

La Dolce Vita, directed by Federico Fellini (1920–   ), opened in Italy and elsewhere with shocking and controversial impact. Its episodic view of life in Rome at the end of the 1950s evolves as a newspaper journalist (Marcello Mastroianni) makes his rounds through the city; professional and personal experiences interweave. The reporter covers the arrival of a famous movie star (Anita Ekberg), attends the site of a "miracle" which has been faked by two children to produce a media event, is visited by his father who has a heart attack during a rendezvous with a show girl, engages in his own affair with the unquenchable Maddalena (Anouk Aimée), contends with his mistress' attempted suicide, and shares an orgiastic evening with a group of arid bourgeoisie.

Marcello's world is one of rapidly changing events, each oddly fascinating to the reporter. Yet, the picaresque journey seems to further confuse an individual seeking some greater personal satisfaction than is offered by the decadent environment and its "sweet life."

Much of the power of *La Dolce Vita* comes through its startling images. The opening shot reveals a helicopter carrying a statue of Christ (arms outstretched in blessing) over Rome and past the crumbling walls of the San Felice aqueduct. Marcello rides in a follow-up helicopter, taking photographs of the event and calling out playfully to young women who sunbathe on the rooftops below. This opening imagery advances an ironic, satirical statement of the contradictory values pressing Roman life at the time. Concluding shots juxtapose the eye of a dead fish with a young girl's innocent smile to symbolically confront Marcello the morning following the all-night orgy.

Autobiographical Inspiration

La Dolce Vita was one of numerous works of autobiographical conception. Earlier Fellini had traced formative experiences in *I Vitelloni* (1953), concluding the imaginative narrative with the young Moraldo's decision to depart his small provincial town for a new life in Rome. *Il Bidone* (1955) extends treatment of the roustabouts' way of life begun in *I*

The opening images of *La Dolce Vita* (1960) carry a symbolic statement about contemporary Rome.

Vitelloni; and Marcello of *La Dolce Vita* may be considered the man that Moraldo became after arriving in Rome.

Fellini's own life paralleled this progression. He left the seaside town of Rimini as a young man, first at age 12 to join a circus, then to Florence and Rome at 17. There he worked as a journalist and cartoonist before becoming a film scenarist (collaborating with Rossellini on numerous scripts including *Open City* and *Paisan*).

His first film as full director, *The White Sheik* (1952), was a comedy which describes early experiences as a cartoon artist. *Amarcord* (1974) returned to Rimini and childhood impressions of life there during the rise of fascism. Autobiographical references to the creative demands of film directing served as material for *8½* (1963), a self-portrait of the artist that blends reality and imagined thought with masterful skill. A made-for-television film, *The Clowns* (1970) and *Roma* (1972) are impressionistic studies in quasi-documentary form that engage Fellini's memory respectively of the circus and the Eternal City as he first experienced them.

Style and Themes

A fascination with time and place, revealed through the semi-detached eyes of an observer (a character such as Marcello, or Fellini's camera as in *Roma*), is a stylistic characteristic inherent in all the autobiographical

Fellini's *La Strada* (1954), a transitional film for Italian cinema. The larger social concerns of humanity, treated by neorealism, gave way to the treatment of individual needs and the tragic failure of human communication.

films. The city, large and small, provides a suitable environment for investigating human values and emotions within a particular time frame. The experience itself is shaped always by Fellini's poetic imagination which can be alternatively satiric, ironic, and poignant.

These directorial qualities also apply to a series of films designed to display the major talents of Giulietta Masina, Fellini's actress-wife, and to two films set in earlier periods of Italian history.

Masina's international prominence was established with *La Strada* (1954), a work which gave evidence of Fellini's (and Italy's) dramatic break with neorealism. As a feeble-minded waif enslaved to a wandering entertainer (Anthony Quinn), Masina embodies the innocent spirit that is easily crushed by brutish oppression.

In *The Nights of Cabiria* (1957) Masina and Fellini continue exploration of life's cruelties in a story of a downtrodden prostitute whose lot never improves. As in *La Strada* Masina is a disadvantaged, trusting victim of forces beyond her control.

By 1965 Fellini's preoccupation with mixed fantasy and realism placed Masina in *Juliet of the Spirits* (1965) where she is a frustrated wife whose subconscious thoughts are revealed in lavishly colored images. Subjective reality is double-layered as Fellini creates a vision of what he imagines a wife's sensual thoughts and fears to be—a fact which might help to explain the film's surreal, rather lifeless quality.

Fellini Satyricon (1969) and *Fellini Casanova* (1976) turned away from contemporary Italy for explorations of worlds where sexual compulsiveness is all-consumptive. *Satyricon's* pre-Christian paganism and the legendary Casanova's sexual drive are revealed as collectively and individually corrupting: sex without love that renders the partakers impassive beyond a quest for physical pleasure.

The fascination for psychedelic analysis of the contemporary Italian woman reappears in *City of Women* (1980) with Marcello Mastroianni portraying a beleaguered male who must combat a variety of feminine types. Like much of Fellini's later work it is a satiric, dream-laden exercise of intricate personal design, spectacularly decorative, and constructed in a sketchy, episodic manner.

MICHELANGELO ANTONIONI

Fellini and Michelangelo Antonioni (1912–   ) share developmental backgrounds. Both wrote scenarios during neorealism's early period, entering film careers after work as newspaper journalists. By the early 1950s each had begun to turn from social-problem themes to particularized character studies.

Antonioni's greatest achievements focus primarily on alienated, wealthy individuals—most prominently women—for whom life has become boring and meaningless. Characters are restless, agonizing souls who function in cold environments as stagnant as the central figures' lives.

The first feature-length dramatic film, *Cronaca di un Amore (Story of a Love Affair,* 1950), presented an account of failed romance between a rich woman and an impoverished lover who together plot the murder of the woman's husband. When the husband dies instead in an automobile crash, the two lovers find themselves guilt-ridden and drained.

Beginning with this film Antonioni suggested the personal style that would reach full power in later works, most noticeably an ability to relate environment to character psychology while shrouding his narrative in mystery. Male-female relationships between strong, bored women and weak, common males are established as a thematic motif that recurs in *Le Amiche (The Girl Friends,* 1955) and *Il Grido (The Cry,* 1957).

The Malaise Trilogy

With *L'Avventura (The Adventure,* 1960) and two films which followed, *La Notte (The Night,* 1961) and *L'Eclisse (Eclipse,* 1962), Antonioni created a superb trilogy centered on the emotional-malaise theme. As controversial as Fellini's *La Dolce Vita* in its time, *L'Avventura* was met with boos when screened at the 1960 Cannes Festival, but it has survived as Antonioni's masterpiece.

Plot is minimal: Claudia (Monica Vitti) and Anna (Lea Massari) are vacationing with a group of friends in the Aeolian Isles off the coast of Sicily. When Anna mysteriously disappears, her fiancé, Sandro (Gabriele

Claudia (Monica Vitti), deeply concerned, searches the barren island for Anna in Antonioni's unresolved *L'Avventura* (1960).

Ferzetti) and Claudia remain behind to search for the woman. In their wanderings they enter into an affair which produces emotional confusion and guilt feelings. Anna cannot be found, and the two lovers return to the mainland and a Sicilian town where Claudia soon discovers Sandro with another woman. Claudia's inner conflict deepens when she realizes Sandro's lack of commitment; still, her fears draw her back to the man despite the relationship's tenuous nature.

Initial criticism of *L'Avventura* centered on Antonioni's failure to resolve Anna's strange disappearance and on the unconventional treatment of subject matter. Dialogue is tediously glib and emotional relationships ambiguous. The film's intent is social observation rather than melodrama, its issues concerned not merely with romantic intrigue but with the complexities of human behavior among the morally bankrupt.

Antonioni derives ennui and a prevailing mood of alienation through a distinctive camera style and vivid use of the milieu as an emotional correspondent. Long shots and lengthy, uninterrupted sequences provide a rigid attention to character, an approach that is ultimately penetrating. The rocky barrenness of the volcanic island and the lifeless Sicilian town become visual metaphors for character states. Monica Vitti as Claudia evokes Antonioni's intentions perfectly, testimony to the director's assured control of all production elements.

La Notte continues the malaise theme by reporting a series of incidents involving a married couple, Giovanni (Marcello Mastroianni) and Lidia Pontano (Jeanne Moreau). The episodes, occurring in a single day, show the husband and wife visiting a dying friend, going to a nightclub, then a party where both display erotic behavior, and finally ending the night by making love without feeling.

Giovanni and Lidia's marriage is an empty one—he is sexually compulsive and she is bored and disillusioned. Again, Antonioni's compassion remains with the woman, the stronger figure. Milan's bleakness matches the emotional tenor of the relationship.

The sketchiest of narratives forms *Eclipse*. A woman, Vittoria (Monica Vitti), ends her love affair with Riccardo because of his emotional neglect, after which she takes up with a young stockbroker (Alain Delon) whose marriage offer is rejected because Vittoria also sees him as deficient. Antonioni's title suggests the film's intentions: Vittoria places herself in emotional eclipse, refusing to enter into an unsatisfactory relationship like those that anguished Claudia and Lidia in *L'Avventura* and *La Notte*. The decision to bear life alone rather than live in resigned misery moves Antonioni's principal character in a new direction and thus he puts to rest his trilogy on female despair.

Later Themes

With international acclaim secured, subsequent work revealed Antonioni seeking revitalization. For *The Red Desert* (1964), color was added to the obliquely familiar story of a woman, Monica Vitti again, striving for emotional comfort in an industrial setting that is depicted as stultifying. Color motifs delineate theme and psychological response: flights of fantasy are vividly bright, the industrial environment bleached and dull.

Antonioni went abroad to film *Blow-Up* (1966), *Zabriskie Point* (1969), and *The Passenger* (1975)—works rising from particular environments and each continuing experimentation with color abstraction as thematic articulation.

Blow-Up *Blow-Up* is set in London during the Mod 1960s, where the protagonist, Thomas (David Hemmings), is a successful fashion photographer bored by his life and looking for new direction. He is an extension of his work, finding in his photographic sessions a release which is likened to sexual fulfillment.

In an effort to alleviate the boredom of his fashionable world, Thomas has begun preparation of an album depicting social realities. One day while photographing in a London park, he snaps pictures of a man and a woman (Vanessa Redgrave) in amorous play. The woman's efforts to retrieve the exposed film activates the photographer's curiosity, leading him to believe that he has been witness to a crime. Subsequent photographic enlargements of the scene reduce details to grainy abstractions that appear to contain shadowy images of a face, a gun, and a body.

A photographic session in *Blow-Up* (1966) possesses sexual connotations. Human feeling has been superseded by occupation.

Although Thomas returns to the park at night and discovers a corpse, a second trip finds the body gone and the mystery remains unsolved.

Antonioni's direction is essentially visual as he allows dramatic incidents to pull the ambiguous intrigue along. Dialogue is absurdly irrelevant. The provocative ideas raised by the film—basically the contradiction between artistic perception and reality—are borne in large degree by color abstraction. Cool blues and whites define the clinical nature of the photographer's studio. An unnaturally lush green covers the park—posing questions from the outset about its "realness." Buildings are painted in garishly bright colors that depict the surreality of the time and place.

Antonioni's energetic achievement is his cleverness in using photographic communication as both method and theme. As a result *Blow-Up* became his one large commercial success.

Zabriskie Point Antonioni filmed *Zabriskie Point* in the United States for M-G-M, presenting a somewhat incoherent account of student activism among the well-heeled. Environment again plays a major role in a self-consciously styled exercise that mixes realism and fantasy. An understanding of the characters is never convincingly projected, and Antonioni resorts to a showy pyrotechnic display, capping the film with an explosion in extended slow motion.

The Passenger An archetypal journey gives shape to *The Passenger*,

Antonioni's provocative study of switched identity in a North African setting. David Locke (Jack Nicholson) is a documentarist in Africa looking to produce a story on guerilla warfare. When a gun supplier dies in a hotel room next to Locke's, the documentarist seizes the opportunity to assume the dead man's identity as an escape from personal and professional frustration. He takes up the gun supplier's appointment itinerary, picking up a beautiful companion (Maria Schneider) along the way, and finally arriving at his ultimate destination, the Hotel de la Gloria. There Locke dies mysteriously, killed perhaps because he is believed to be the arms agent. Antonioni's roving camera refuses to look on the murder. Locke's journey has been a movement not toward freedom but toward destiny's final appointment, death. The hotel's name is fatefully symbolic.

Antonioni's approach in *The Passenger* is again essentially visual. His story is derived from human boredom and dissatisfaction and the plot is filled with unexplained mystery. In theme the standard issues also arise—illusion in conflict with reality, the difficulty of media in providing truth.

Locke (Jack Nicholson) finds a gun supplier dead and uses the discovery to switch identities in *The Passenger* (1975). In taking up the dead man's itinerary, Locke's own fate is sealed.

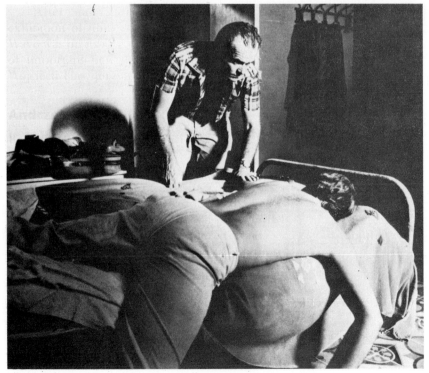

LUCHINO VISCONTI

The earlier importance of Luchino Visconti (1906–1976) in Italian film history was secured through the explosive *Ossessione* (1942), a precursor to neorealism. His most realistic work was a documentarylike study of horrendous working conditions in Sicily, *La Terra Trema* (1948).

But Visconti was a member of Italy's aristocracy, and his brief flirtation with common-people themes soon gave way to interests in other classes of society. His artistic temperament for rich theatrical screen experiences found its fullest expression in a series of atmospheric social dramas that often placed sex and politics in uneasy tension. Opulent uses of color, appearing as early as 1954 in *Senso,* became an important element in the later films. *Senso* was a period study of infidelity set in the nineteenth century and a work that revealed Visconti's developing taste for lavishly rendered stories of upper-class society in a state of flux.

Only *Rocco and His Brothers* (1960), made in part to quell criticism that he had abandoned earlier commitments, reveals neorealistic strains. Rocco (Alain Delon) is a member of an impoverished family that moves from southern Italy to Milan, naively expecting an improved life.

After *Rocco and His Brothers,* Visconti's transition quickens. *The Leopard* (1963) returns to the nineteenth century for a lush adaptation of Lampedusa's novel about upper-class decline. *The Stranger* (1967) translates Camus' novel to the screen, and *The Damned* (1970) exposes with near expressionistic extravagance the corrupting interplay of wealth, politics, and sex in Germany during the rise of Nazism.

Death in Venice (1971) brought both praise and attack for the screen version of Thomas Mann's novella. It was the most atmospheric of all Visconti's films. The story of artistic obsession that symbolically relates physical and spiritual death is vividly rendered through music association (Mahler) and color abstraction. Visconti's second career as a theater and opera director is evident in this work; by combining his mastery of screen composition and visual design with well-applied theatrical skills, *Death in Venice* became Visconti's unique achievement.

A last film, *The Innocent,* released after Visconti's death in 1976, contained the vivid colors, expressive settings, and formal elegance that characterized all his period studies. Set at the turn of the century in the opulent homes of Italian aristocrats, it is a triangular love story of passion and destruction. Tullio (Giancarlo Giannini), an aristocrat, becomes enamored of a free-living woman (Jennifer O'Neill) but holds onto his own wife (Laura Antonelli) as a friend and confidante. The wife enters into her own affair and in so doing rearouses her husband's passion for her. His reborn attention is shattered with the revelation that his wife is pregnant with the other man's child. Tullio's jealousy increases until he acts to destroy the baby.

Visconti's nonsentimental treatment of the two women reveals a

Decay, corruption, and disease surround Gustave von Aschenbach (Dirk Bogarde) in the concluding parts of Visconti's *Death in Venice* (1971).

society at a particular time and place seeking to respond to new needs, but incapable of knowing precisely how to do so. *The Innocent,* with its theme of passion, jealousy, and destruction appropriately book-ended with *Ossessione,* each supporting Visconti's long, distinguished career of bold and original filmmaking.

ROBERTO ROSSELLINI

Roberto Rossellini (1906–1977) continued to make films until his death. After his important neorealist work, he turned to more personal expression, stimulated by Ingrid Bergman's arrival in Italy and appearance in *Stromboli* (1949), *Europa '51* (1952), and *Voyage in Italy* (1953). An affair, then marriage to Bergman, reached scandalous proportions and acted to deny these works full consideration—particularly in the United States where Rossellini's *The Miracle* (1948) had already stirred a major religious controversy.

In each of these four later films women protagonists are presented in dire situations, torn between individual needs and societal conventions: a simple peasant girl (Anna Magnani) is cajoled, mocked, then ignored for her claim of immaculate conception in *The Miracle;* Karin (Bergman), an alienated war bride in *Stromboli,* marries to escape a prisoner-of-war camp only to find herself trapped on a lonely island with her fisherman husband; a mother (Bergman), despondent over the death of her child in *Europa '51,* attempts personal redemption through social work but is scorned by her family and friends; and in *Voyage in Italy,* Ingrid Bergman portrays a bored British wife whose trip with her husband to exotic Naples aggravates an already uncertain relationship. These films received greatest attention among *Cahiers'* critics in France who were especially appreciative of Rossellini's personalized character studies.

Rossellini again found fleeting international acclaim with *Il Generale della Rovere* (1959) and *Era Notte a Roma* (1960), both reappropriating World War II themes of collective courage and employing neorealistic methods along the lines of *Open City.*

After 1960 much of Rossellini's creative energy was spent on theater work and historical documentaries made for European television: *The Iron Age* (1964), *The Rise of Louis XIV* (1966), *The Age of the Medici* (1973), *Leon Battista Alberti* (1973), among others.

ERMANNO OLMI

Ermanno Olmi (1931–   ) had a lengthy career from 1954 to 1961 as a documentarist for Edison Volta, producing and directing more than thirty studies of life in the large industrial factory. When he turned to feature filmmaking with *Time Stood Still* (1959), he carried forward his interest in the relationship of occupation to personal conduct. *Il Posto* (1961), *One Fine Day* (1968), and *The Tree of Wooden Clogs* (1978), the best of Olmi's works, are all strongly humanistic and rich in visual quality.

Il Posto follows a young man's entry into a Milan factory, first as a messenger then as a desk clerk. The shy boy's reaction to the large, impersonal plant and his relationship with a young woman who also works there form the tender story. Appropriately bleak black-and-white cinematography and a nonprofessional cast add neorealistic authority.

The Tree of Wooden Clogs looks at peasant life in Italy in the early 1800s. Olmi's evocative treatment bears comparison with Bertolucci's *1900,* especially in its success at recreating a sense of place and time past.

The young couple in *Il Posto* (1961), Antonietta (Loredana Detto) and Domenico (Sandro Panzeri), offer one another relief from the impersonal world of industry.

The script, written by Olmi, is essentially impressionistic in tracing daily life for five families in a Lombardy farming community. Remarkably, Olmi also served as cinematographer and editor for this simple, beautiful film. He again gains impact with a full company of nonprofessional actors.

NEW GENERATION DIRECTORS: PASOLINI, BERTOLUCCI, AND WERTMÜLLER

Pier Paolo Pasolini (1922–1975), Bernardo Bertolucci (1940–   ) and Lina Wertmüller (1926–   ) emerged as important new Italian directors at the very moment the country's established directors were reclaiming their international reputations. Pasolini created his first film, *Accatone,* in 1961 with Bertolucci as assistant director. The following year Bertolucci directed *La Commare Secca (The Grim Reaper,* 1962) based on a short story by Pasolini. Lina Wertmüller directed her first feature, *The Lizards,* in 1963. Each became leading figures in an emerging new generation of Italian directors.

Pier Paolo Pasolini

Pasolini had come from northern Italy to Rome in 1950 where he worked alternately as a fiction writer and scenarist. As author and director of *Accatone,* his cinematic sensibility as a humanist with external neorealist leanings became apparent. Nonprofessionals appear in Pasolini's story of materialistic corruption that involves a young pimp, Accatone (Franco Citti), whose efforts to earn a decent living go unrealized. Camera style is unadorned and narrative structure is episodic. Accatone's death at the end hints at the violent impulse in Pasolini's vision that would grow with subsequent work.

The Gospel according to St. Matthew* (1964) brought wide acclaim by presenting a simple, direct account of Christ's life within a social-realist context. Pasolini's scenario drew on Biblical scripture to frame an unusually effective reconstruction that gained spontaneity from nonactors and *verité* filming methods. The view of Christ as an intent human figure was considered provocatively engaging by most, including Catholic groups that usually agitated against liberal trends in Italian cinema.

A shift in style becomes apparent with *Teorema* (1968), a controversial film in which symbolism and realism are freely mixed. A mysterious young man visits a bourgeois household, sexually satisfies each of the residents (father, mother, son, daughter, and maid), then departs. Each household member, except the maid, is dramatically altered by the encounter. Pasolini's intentions are not made clear, but his biting humor appears to attack middle-class social structures.

Sexuality interests imbedded in loosely framed tales inspired

The realistic tenor of Pasolini's *The Gospel According to St. Matthew* (1964) and its close attention to faces added to the film's impact.

Pasolini's trilogy *The Decameron* (1971), *The Canterbury Tales* (1971), and *The Arabian Nights* (1974). These works allowed an imaginative portrayal of sex in distant times when values were different from Pasolini's. At his death in 1975, Pasolini was completing *Salo or The 120 Days of Sodom* (released in 1976), centered on material generated by the writings of the Marquis de Sade. It received wide censure.

Bernardo Bertolucci

Bertolucci's career also moved in the direction of controversy. His importance on the international film scene was secured with *Before the Revolution* (1964), a story of political and emotional tension in Italy immediately following World War II. This theme continued to fascinate Bertolucci and reappeared in variations within *The Conformist* (1970), and *The Spider's Stratagem* (1970).

The Conformist, based on a novel by Alberto Moravia, is a complex account of a young man's efforts to find release from guilt through political conformity. Marcello (Jean-Louis Trintigant) is sexually traumatized as a child through a homosexual encounter with the family chauffeur. Using flashbacks, Bertolucci links this experience to Marcello's insecurity that drives him to membership in the Fascist Party and a willingness to kill for political causes.

Time interweaves freely throughout the film, picking up events occurring on an afternoon in 1917 when Marcello was a child, on a date in 1938 when he helps assassinate Professor Quadri (Enzo Taroscio), and on the evening that Mussolini falls from power. In the end Marcello must confront his real self that can no longer be repressed by conformity.

The Spider's Stratagem also entails a progression toward self-awareness and assumption of personal responsibility. A young man returns to his hometown where childhood memories (in flashback form)

Marcello (Jean-Louis Trintignant) is willing to act on behalf of the Fascist state in *The Conformist* (1970), including assisting in the assassination of a former professor. The professor's wife (Dominique Sanda) screams at the passive Marcello after his deed.

interweave with contemporary conditions to reveal personal as well as political truths. The roots of fascism are exposed through the intricate structure. Bertolucci's close friendship with Godard during the 1960s is evident in films made in this period.

Thematic interests shift dramatically with *Last Tango in Paris* (1972), a controversial work which teamed Bertolucci with Marlon Brando and Maria Schneider. Brando and Schneider portray a couple who agree to enter into an anonymous affair after they meet in an empty apartment. Bertolucci involves Paul, Brando's aging American-in-Paris character, in introspective analysis and sadistic gestures that suggest total self-alienation. Paul's interest in Jeanne (Maria Schneider) appears impersonally sexual; her involvement is one of adventure from an aloof fiancé.

It becomes clear that the woman is being used as a receptacle for the American's residue of anger (expressed verbally and sexually) that remains after his wife's unexplained suicide. Ultimately Paul acts to engage Jeanne in a more personal relationship and she leaves. When he goes after her, she kills him.

The power of *Last Tango in Paris* comes from Bertolucci's sheer display of pained emotion. Brando's performance recalls earlier work where inner turmoil rises to the surface through searching, improvisational methods. He is so spontaneous that other sequences without him appear stylistically anomalous.

For *1900* (1976) Bertolucci turned to the epic format and Italian history. Its importance resides mainly in its ambitious effort to chart life for two families (one poor, one wealthy) during social and political upheavals in Italy from early twentieth century forward. Bertolucci's gift for evocative visualization of time and place is vividly on display.

Luna (1979) returned to a theme of emotional crisis with Jill Clayburgh as a widowed American singer in Rome. Conflict is derived from her declining career and a near-incestuous obsession with a young

son. Bertolucci's direction approaches melodrama and except for some outstanding operatic sequences the film is undistinguished.

Lina Wertmüller

Lina Wertmüller's creative explosion during the 1970s brought her international popularity and a critical reconsideration of earlier films. Her first feature, *The Lizards,* was made after work as a puppeteer and an apprenticeship with Fellini (as assistant on *8 ½*).

From the onset of her film career Wertmüller revealed an impressive talent for sociopolitical satire, expressed most commonly through studies of vain male protagonists whose lives become politically entangled. Sex and politics are inextricably bound to one another, and through their response to each Wertmüller usually makes her men look quite foolish.

The Lizards projected a collective view of the male in small-town Italy, living aimlessly but in smug expectation of a better life. Still another impressionistic account of men followed with *Now Let's Talk About Men* (1965), with Wertmüller filming four short stories so that each would satirically reveal a facet of the male personality.

Popular fame came with a trilogy of satires that starred Giancarlo Giannini as a Wertmüller prototype who is naively caught up in both love and politics: *The Seduction of Mimi* (1972), *Love and Anarchy* (1973), and *Swept Away* (1974).

The Seduction of Mimi Giannini is Mimi, a man caught between political factions and within a web he spins by sexual dalliance. The Mafia drive Mimi out of his hometown after he votes a Communist ticket, forcing him to leave behind his wife and seek work in Turin. There he falls in love with another woman who has his child; his wife has her own affair with a city official who leaves her pregnant also.

To save face Mimi decides to seduce and impregnate the official's uncomely wife. When the official is murdered, Mimi is blamed, sent to prison, and when released is greeted by two "wives" and seven children. The Mafia on whom he is now totally dependent for employment have "seduced" him. He pounds his fists on the prison door, seeking reentry.

Love and Anarchy Giannini portrays a man who is out to assassinate Mussolini after Fascist action kills one of his friends. His hideaway is a Roman brothel where he falls in love with Trippolina, one of the women there. Out of fear for his life she acts to prevent the assassination attempt; he goes berserk, shoots several soldiers, is captured and executed. The man's foolish efforts at social usefulness are bared with tragicomic force.

Swept Away Giannini portrays Gennarino, a working-class Communist who is stranded on a Mediterranean island with a beautiful woman, Rafaella, who represents the wealth and politics of the capitalistic bourgeoisie. After a storm sweeps them to the island, away from the woman's luxurious yacht on which Gennarino serves as a crew member,

Mimi (Giancarlo Giannini) in an act of personal revenge prepares to seduce the wife of a city official. At the end of *The Seduction of Mimi* (1972) it is Mimi who is seduced, domestically and politically.

the two are forced to co-exist in the new world. He alters positions by forcing Rafaella to play his servant while he acts the role of lord and master. Gennarino's "re-education" of the woman is brutal, forcing her eventually into sexual submission that leads to emotional dependence as well.

As in *The Seduction of Mimi,* Gennarino is eventually trapped by his forceful acts and left to face a world that offers no romantic illusions, only practical problems to be solved. Political irony is the end result of Wertmüller's gamey interplay between males and females. Both Mimi and Gennarino are moved toward new political positions in an effort to escape their traps. Mimi must accept the Mafia, and Gennarino resorts to capitalistic enticement in an attempt to hold onto Raffaella when they are cast back into the real world.

The raw, intense quality of Wertmüller's trilogy generated controversy but an even greater amount of appreciation from filmgoers and critics who admire spirited satire. Her work clearly owed much to the presence of Giannini—a dark, intense performer who seemed to embody the cunning charm and chauvinistic attitudes of the male type that Wertmüller exploited in setting up her sexual-political dichotomies.

Seven Beauties Giannini is again the principal character, Pasquilino, repulsive on the one hand as he says of himself, yet somehow mysteriously attractive to women for indefinable qualities. Pasquilino lives in Naples with his mother and seven plump sisters—a self-confident figure who espouses honor and dignity as he struts about the city and acts as overlord to his female family. When an older sister seeks to marry Totonno, a brothel owner, Pasquilino murders the man and is sent to jail.

Pasquilino (Giannini) possesses "the seven beauties," unexplainable qualities that are the source of his attractiveness to women in *Seven Beauties* (1976).

The arrival of World War II leads to Pasquilino's release to fight for Italy. At war he is captured and put in a concentration camp where torture and death prevail. To survive, he comes upon the idea of seducing the concentration camp's female commandant—a grotesque mound of flesh.

The seduction, a mixture of comedy and repulsion, serves to set up the film's final irony. On returning home to Naples after the war, Pasquilino discovers that his entire family as well as his young fiancée are all prostitutes—a fact now understandable to him because they, like he, have been able to survive by using similar methods. Once again a Wertmüller film is resolved through ironic conversion, sexually induced.

An effort to work in English resulted in the failed *The End of the World in Our Usual Bed in a Night Full of Rain* (1977). Wertmüller handled the story of marital conflict between a Communist journalist (Giannini) and his feminist wife (Candice Bergen) with an excess of verbiage, forewarned by the film's title. *Blood Feud* (1980) had a Sicilian setting with Giannini as a Mafioso type, once more doomed by sexual-political forces to which he readily exposes himself.

Wertmüller's vision of the world cajoles, provokes, and titillates—qualities shared by the best of Italy's many spirited postneorealistic filmmakers.

SUGGESTED READINGS

Cameron, Ian, and Robin Wood. *Antonioni.* New York: Praeger, 1969.
Fellini, Federico. *Fellini on Fellini.* New York: Delacorte, 1976.
Leprohon, Pierre. *The Italian Cinema.* New York: Praeger, 1972.
Nowell-Smith, Geoffrey. *Luchino Visconti.* Garden City, N.Y.: Doubleday, 1968.
Willemen, Paul, ed. *Pier Paolo Pasolini.* London: British Film Institute, 1977.

GREAT BRITAIN:
STRUGGLE FOR IDENTITY

We should welcome American and Continental directors as long as they justify themselves by helping to make better and more widely acceptable British pictures.

A British writer in *Film Weekly*, February 20, 1932.

Both Great Britain and her commonwealth country, Canada, have long found their film industries existing under Hollywood's lengthy shadow. Throughout the 1930s and 1940s Hollywood releases dominated the marketplace in Great Britain; Canada was virtually an extension of the American market. Ambitious British-made films at the same time relied heavily on U.S. distribution to help recoup costs. The best artists soon found themselves being enticed to California, a tendency continuing into the 1980s.

Alfred Hitchcock.

Efforts at reducing the number of imported products and spurring at-home production occurred in Britain through a quota imposition that was ordered in 1927 and a heavy importation tax (75 percent) levied in 1947. The quota requirement, which demanded that exhibitors show a specified percentage of British-made pictures, had both good and bad results—increasing output and stimulating industrial growth, but soon revealing filmmakers turning out quantity rather than quality to meet percentage demands. The harsh 75 percent importation tax of 1947 was followed a year later by a more acceptable agreement with Hollywood companies that required them to reinvest within Britain 75 percent of profits earned there. As a consequence, American production in British facilities increased significantly, once more challenging a self-sufficient home industry.

In the movement toward this sequence of events feature filmmakers in Britain sustained themselves with products of assured marketability, while the nation at large took pride in the unmatched quality of its state-funded documentaries made during the 1930s and the upheaval brought by World War II. The John Grierson-led model for factual films in a national cause was one that presented socially useful information in a straightforward manner without emotional embellishment, e.g., *Song of Cyelon* (1934), *Night Mail* (1936).

The dramatic film in Britain had its most prolific period following the Quota Act of 1927 with Alfred Hitchcock and Alexander Korda standing prominently among those individuals who helped bring international esteem to the country.

HITCHCOCK: BRITAIN'S MASTER OF SUSPENSE

Alfred Hitchcock (1899–1980), a strong visualist with a cunning sense of humor, had spent a brief period of time during the early 1920s working in the Ufa studios where he observed the imaginative use being made of decor in Germany's psychological films. Ufa's influence can be seen in Hitchcock's own method of cinematic expression during a lengthy, distinguished career.

British Films

His first major film in Britain was *The Lodger* (1927), a suspense story of misplaced suspicion. Hitchcock directed Britain's first synchronous sound picture, *Blackmail,* in 1929, revealing at this early date an intuitive understanding of sound-image relationships in creating screen suspense. In this film's exciting climax, which included a run through the British Museum, Hitchcock established the chase in a familiar setting as a plotting device. Throughout the 1930s he continued to garner critical acclaim and popularity with well-styled suspense thrillers, e.g., *The Man*

The final chase of Hitchcock's *Blackmail* (1929) took place at the British Museum, the first of many familiar settings that would be used to frame final confrontations in the director's suspense thrillers.

Who Knew Too Much (1934), *The Thirty-Nine Steps* (1935), *Sabotage* (1936), *Young and Innocent* (1937), and *The Lady Vanishes* (1938).

In these films Hitchcock's working methods became clear as he proved himself an artist with a theoretical, intellectual, and sophisticated approach to motion-picture entertainment. He avoided the traditional British whodunit, favoring emotionally active thrillers over intellectual exercises. His subjects were average people, rather than professional criminals or detectives (an option which Hitchcock said increased audience identification), e.g., a young couple on a Swiss vacation in *The Man Who Knew Too Much;* a film exhibitor in *Sabotage;* an elderly woman and her young traveling companion in *The Lady Vanishes.*

Through a dramatic turn of events (Hitchcock's MacGuffin device) the principal character becomes caught up in extraordinary events: an assassination plot in *The Man Who Knew Too Much;* a bombing episode in *Sabotage;* a spy intrigue in *The Lady Vanishes.* Situations develop through carefully controlled release of suspense elements with a clever interplay between expectations that go unfulfilled and genuine surprises that come when least anticipated. Hitchcock once observed that the most terrible things in life happen not in the dark but in full daylight. Illusion and understatement are additional elements that add unmistakable style to the thrillers.

American Work

Hitchcock's British films were followed by work in Hollywood where he maintained his reputation "as the master of suspense." Many of his important films in the United States bring character psychology more noticeably into the theme: *Suspicion* (1941), *Spellbound* (1945), *Stage Fright* (1950), *Psycho* (1960).

Hitchcock's wit included fleeting cameo appearances in his films. Here he appears (top) as a train passenger in *Blackmail*, and (below) as a model for a newspaper advertisement in *Lifeboat* (1944)—a film with only nine characters and one confined entirely to a ship's lifeboat.

Psycho, Hitchcock's most celebrated work, begins seemingly as a tense chase film with a bank clerk (Janet Leigh) fleeing town with embezzled money. A brief encounter with an unsuspecting policeman is merely diversionary suspense; the relieved woman complacently continues on her way toward a lonely motel and brutal death. Character and viewer are equally lulled, hence caught off guard by the sudden appearance of the psychopathic killer (Tony Perkins)—a classic Hitchcockian trick studiously copied in the opening sequence of Brian De Palma's *Dressed to Kill* (1980).

An ingenious knack for avoiding the clichéd conventions of the suspense thriller occurs in *North by Northwest* (1959) when Cary Grant is being chased by armed killers. The standard method would be to drive the hero into an enclosed area. a building or a deadend alley, offering no outlets. Hitchcock's way is to put the killer in an airplane overhead and Grant below in a barren field, surrounded by endless open space. The suspense derived from this imaginative staging defies description because, like much of Hitchcock's best work, it has the effect of a horrible nightmare.

Hitchcock achieved his screen impact through meticulous preproduction planning that left nothing to chance, aided by a brilliant gift for directing actors. He was knighted by Queen Elizabeth II just prior to his death, but more significantly he was admired and imitated by numerous filmmakers (Chabrol, Truffaut, Rohmer, de Palma) who considered Hitchcock a director's director because of his understanding of the medium's innate possibilities.

KORDA: LITERARY AND HISTORICAL MASTERPIECES

A popular brand of British-styled motion picture emerged with the release of *The Private Life of Henry VIII* (1933): the well-tailored historical romance. Alexander Korda (1893–1956), a Hungarian emigré, was the producer of this internationally successful effort. Drawing on Britain's unrivaled supply of acting talent and theatrical technicians (many also emigrés from the Continent), Korda continued to produce character studies in period settings: *The Private Life of the Gannets* (1934), *Catherine the Great* (1934), *Rembrandt* (1936), and *Knight without Armour* (1937). Charles Laughton, one of the motion picture's greatest character actors, appeared in the title roles of *Henry VIII* and *Rembrandt,* bringing interpretations to the screen that were richly dimensioned. Korda's brother, Vincent, was responsible for the artistic design of these and other important British films including Carol Reed's *The Third Man* (1949).

At his Denham Studios, founded in 1936, Korda supervised production until 1939 when he left England for work in Hollywood. Later production back in England included *The Fallen Idol* (1948) and *The Third Man,* both directed for Korda by Carol Reed and developed from original screenplays by Graham Greene.

Other fine literary films were produced in England during the 1940s, most notably Laurence Olivier's screen versions of *Henry V* (1944) and *Hamlet* (1948). At the Cineguild Company David Lean further strengthened Britain's reputation for adapting the literary classic with *Blithe Spirit* (1945), *Great Expectations* (1946), and *Oliver Twist* (1948).

Elsewhere in Great Britain the Ealing Studios gained international respect after World War II with an outpouring of low-budget satrical comedies, best represented by *Kind Hearts and Coronets* (1949) and *The Lavender Hill Mob* (1951).

The Private Life of Henry VIII (1933)—an Alexander Korda film of lavish design and superb acting, particularly by Charles Laughton in the title role. It was Britain's first internationally successful film after the arrival of sound.

Laurence Olivier both starred in and directed Henry V (1944). The adaptation remains one of the most cinematically pleasing of numerous Shakespearean translations.

Numerous British actors were catapulted to international fame in the postwar period: James Mason, Terry Thomas, Alec Guinness, Peter Sellers, John Mills, Ralph Richardson, Edith Evans, and Trevor Howard.

NEW REALISM

In 1956 John Osborne's play, *Look Back in Anger,* was unveiled at London's Royal Court Theatre. This and following works by Britain's "angry young men" helped trigger a revolution in British filmmaking.

Osborne's play is focused on a male protagonist, Johnny Porter, whose outbursts against upper-class values and unhappy social circumstances are expressed with verbal eloquence: "I may write a book about us all. . . . And it won't be recollected in tranquility either, picking daffodils with Auntie Wordsworth. It'll be recollected in fire, and blood. My blood."

Jack Clayton

The tone of Osborne's restless words signaled the beginnings of a new social consciousness among British writers that soon extended into the motion picture. In *Room at the Top* (1958) Jack Clayton (1921–   ) served notice that young film directors in the country were moving away from commercial traditions (bound by literary heritage and pageantry) toward "freer" expression that allowed the treatment of contemporary themes. An awareness of Britain's restricting class structure, the central theme of *Room at the Top*, became a spirited issue that continued until the mid-1960s.

The scenario for *Room at the Top* was taken from a novel by John Braine and followed the calculated efforts of Joe Lampton (Laurence Harvey) to win social and economic status. Lampton's tactics involve sexual exploitation of a well-to-do industrialist's daughter. Adding poignancy to the story of cold ambition is Lampton's emotional relationship with Alice (Simone Signoret), a sensual and caring woman who does not, however, fit into the opportunist's ultimate plans.

Clayton's treatment offered a stark, realistic portrayal of the industrial environment while the romantic sequences with Signoret and Harvey are memorable for their bold sensuality. The contrast provides a dramatic account of one's urgency to escape class and earn personal position at all costs.

Alice (Simone Signoret) offers Joe Lampton (Laurence Harvey) a sensual love in *Room at the Top* (1958)—a love which he willingly discards in order to climb out of his slum past and into a higher social and professional position.

Tony Richardson

Tony Richardson (1928–   ) brought *Look Back in Anger* to the screen in 1959 with a first-class cast that included Richard Burton, Claire Bloom, Mary Ure and Edith Evans. Richardson, who had also directed Osborne's play at the Royal Court Theatre, rendered the film version in a cluttered, naturalistic apartment setting—an effect which led to the descriptive label "kitchen sink realism."

Look Back in Anger was Richardson's first full-fledged directorial assignment. Earlier he had co-directed *Mamma Don't Allow* in 1955 with Karel Reisz, an innovative study of a North London jazz club and the working-class youths who frequent the place. The documentary was offered as part of the National Film Theatre's initial Free Cinema program (1956), an exhibition concept devoted to the showing of films from Britain and abroad with personal, social points of view. Altogether six programs were presented between 1956 and 1959 under the Free Cinema heading.

Richardson's film career continued to move in social directions with three notable screen adaptations that described the realities of contemporary British life: *The Entertainer* (1960), *A Taste of Honey* (1961), *The Loneliness of the Long Distance Runner* (1962).

The Entertainer, taken from John Osborne's stage play, presented Laurence Olivier as Archie Rice, an elderly, fading comedian whose life has become a hollow exercise in spiritual and professional maintenance. Olivier's dissection of Rice tenders a brashly pathetic figure, conveyed through Richardson's intense use of close-ups.

In the film version of Shelagh Delaney's play, *A Taste of Honey,* naturalistic scenes, taken from depressed locations by cinematographer

Anger and frustration dominate Tony Richardson's screen adaptation of *Look Back in Anger* (1959).

The "kitchen sink realism" of earlier work gave way to open space and eclectic style in Richardson's *The Loneliness of the Long Distance Runner* (1962), but the angry attitude toward the establishment remained.

Walter Lassally, add visual authority to character studies of an unmarried pregnant girl (Rita Tushingham) and a homosexual friend (Murray Melvin) who offer each other emotional support. The film draws on conventional attitudes toward the personal circumstances of the young couple's lives, attitudes which ultimately destroy the delicate relationship.

With his adaptation of Alan Sillitoe's story, *The Loneliness of the Long Distance Runner,* Richardson opened up his treatment of class-conscious themes to fuller, less stage-bound expression. The film begins in a grim industrial setting where 18-year old Colin (Tom Courtenay) reacts to his dreary existence with a rebellious attitude. After he is sent to a boys' reformatory in Borstal for stealing money, the institution director discovers Colin's superior ability for long-distance running and enters the lad in a competition with a middle-class boarding school. On the way to certain victory Colin holds back rather than win for the director, a statement of continuing rebellion against the establishment. During the running sequences Richardson alternates memory flashbacks and lyrical shots of the passing landscape to suggest the tension between social resentment and personal freedom.

John Schlesinger

John Schlesinger (1926–   ) arrived as a socially conscious director of major talent at a time when other directors were beginning to expand their range of interests. His first dramatic feature, *A Kind of Loving* (1962), examines the problems of modern British life with a realistic approach that reflects earlier work as a documentarist for the BBC. Taken from a novel by Stan Barstow, *A Kind of Loving* looks at the

The tensions that occur as the result of an unusual triangular affair are treated subtly and sympathetically in Schlesinger's *Sunday, Bloody Sunday* (1971).

difficulties experienced by a young couple (Alan Bates and June Ritchie) following their forced marriage (she is pregnant).

Billy Liar (1963), a transitional exercise, moved Schlesinger into personal analysis through a young undertaker (Tom Courtenay) who fantasizes away his dreary existence.

Transition From here, Schlesinger and other prominent directors who had established themselves during Britain's important renaissance would, as Italy's neorealist filmmakers had done in the 1960s, move away from working-class themes and toward more personal, psychological explorations. The well-used northern industrial milieu was replaced with increasing frequency by London settings; stark black-and-white images gave way to an expressive use of color.

Schlesinger's developing interest in characters attempting to conduct their lives in impersonal, big-city environments brought him critical acclaim with *Darling* (1965), then popular success with *Midnight Cowboy* (1969). In *Darling* Julie Christie portrays an ambitious London-based model who uses all available means to attain her career goals. *Midnight Cowboy* deals with loneliness and alienation in New York City, represented by a displaced male hustler (Jon Voight) and a sickly native (Dustin Hoffman) who dreams of a healthier life in Florida. Schlesinger captures the impersonal mood of New York City with garish colors and telephoto recordings of street scenes that reveal the principal characters as one-dimensional, cardboardlike figures.

Schlesinger returned to London for *Sunday, Bloody Sunday* (1971). The screenplay by writer-critic Penelope Gilliat presents a complicated *ménage à trois* involving a homosexual doctor (Peter Finch), an employment counselor (Glenda Jackson), and a young pop artist (Murray Head). Again the subject matter is treated with sympathetic care (including an authentic rendering of a bar mitzvah). Colors are richly expressive.

Widely disparate styles and themes appear in Schlesinger's later work: period spectacle and romance in a translation of Thomas Hardy's *Far from the Madding Crowd* (1967) and in *Yanks* (1979); social analysis and surrealistic satire in a version of Nathaniel West's *The Day of the Locust* (1975); melodramatic suspense in the thriller, *Marathon Man* (1976).

Schlesinger's career fairly well typifies the path of the British director after 1965, hopping back and forth across the Atlantic for assignments that reflect the uncertainties of motion-picture production at the time in both Britain and the United States.

FILMS FOR DIVERSION

Strictly diversionary fare also continued to pour out of England's studios during its realist period: Gothic horror films from the Hammer studios (*The Two Faces of Dr. Jekyll*, 1960); period romances from Anthony Asquith (*The Doctor's Dilemma*, 1958); and beginning in 1962 with *Dr. No*, the comic-book-styled James Bond thrillers.

Peter Sellers appeared in Blake Edwards' *The Pink Panther* in 1964 to introduce the first of a series of slapstick comedies centered on the fumbling Inspector Clouseau.

Richard Lester drew on the Beatles' unrivaled popularity for two successful films which integrated spontaneous comedy with songs from the singing group: *A Hard Day's Night* (1964), *Help!* (1965). "Pure cinema" devices added to the energetic quality of these comedies. In time Lester was also drawn into large-scale production, e.g., *The Three Musketeers* (1974), *Robin and Marian* (1976), and *Superman II* (1981).

LOSEY, RUSSELL, KUBRICK, AND ROEG

As the British film industry moved toward the seventies, American money dominated production ventures that were "internationalized" by mixing home-grown talent with artists and technicians from abroad. Further, with the emergence of television, motion-picture attendance declined dramatically, forcing exhibitors to close their doors. By 1977 Britain's movie houses had dwindled to less than 1,000—down from 3,400 in 1960. A shrinking market, coupled with rapidly inflating

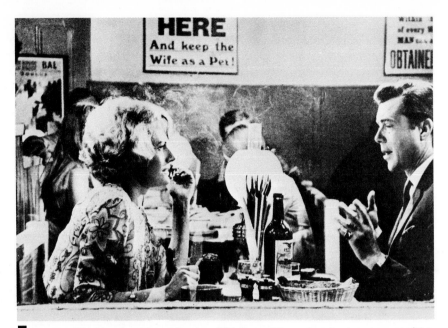

Francesca (Delphine Seyrig) and Stephen (Dirk Bogarde), a university don, are part of the sexual interplay in *Accident* (1967). Stephen, stimulated by the mysterious Anna, consoles himself by having a brief affair with Francesca.

production and promotion costs, continued to force dependence on the American film.

Among the handful of important directors who continued to work extensively in Britain were Joseph Losey, Ken Russell, Stanley Kubrick, and Nicholas Roeg.

Joseph Losey

Joseph Losey (1909–   ) an American director of long-standing reputation (*The Boy with Green Hair,* 1948), moved to Europe after HUAC investigations led to his blacklisting. Following several directorial efforts, Losey teamed with playwright Harold Pinter to create a provocative study of human destruction in *The Servant* (1963). Tony (James Fox), a young, upper-class man, employs a servant (Dirk Bogarde) who is able to completely dominate and corrupt the master. Losey's visually somber film focuses on the inherent dangers of living within a class system that is obsolete.

In *Accident* (1967), another Losey-Pinter collaboration, Oxford serves as the serene location for a seething, beneath-the-surface account of sexual and emotional tensions generated by a beautiful young woman (Jacqueline Sassard).

This preoccupation with cool surfaces, torrid inner tensions within an upper-class milieu, is the recurring motif of Losey's most interesting works, including *The Go-Between* (1971), also with a screenplay by Pinter. In this effort, as in the earlier two collaborations, Pinter uses an outsider (a 13-year-old boy) to expose hidden aspects of life in upper-class society. Losey's treatment is consistently unsentimental; his camera concentrates heavily on material details (often ornate and baroque) in an attempt to expressively relate characters to the setting.

Other Losey works in the 1970s included *Figures in a Landscape* (1970), *The Assassination of Trotsky* (1972), *A Doll's House* (1973), *Galileo* (1974), and *Mr. Klein* (1976). An interest in themes of emotional tension and moral confusion within established social structures remains central to Losey's cinematic vision. Although an expatriate, his class-conscious films made in the sixties and seventies place him among a very small group of outstanding directors whose work after 1965 was distinctly and continuously British in inspiration.

Stanley Kubrick

Another expatriate achieving new renown in England during the late sixties and seventies was Stanley Kubrick, (1928–   ), an American director whose best-known works in the United States were *Paths of Glory* (1957) and *Spartacus* (1960). *Paths of Glory* took an antimilitary stance in dealing with a court-martial incident in France during World War I and was a highly acclaimed, albeit controversial, film.

After the large-scale epic *Spartacus*, Kubrick moved to England where he began work on an adaptation of Vladimir Nabokov's novel of love between a very young girl and an older man, *Lolita* (1962). Nabokov's own screenplay made significant concessions to the film medium, focusing primarily on societal conflicts brought on by the obsessive relationship rather than on the passion and interior despair experienced by the principal character, Humbert (James Mason). The shift of emphasis made the translation merely a curiosity piece.

In his next three films, *Dr. Strangelove, or How I Learned to Stop Worrying and Love the Bomb* (1963), *2001: A Space Odyssey* (1968), and *A Clockwork Orange* (1971), Kubrick projected cynical views of the human condition in futuristic settings. Power figures and advanced technology are the oppressive forces in his pessimistic vision.

Dr. Strangelove satirically exposes events leading toward total nuclear disaster. Adapted by Kubrick from Peter George's novel, *Red Alert,* the film uses sharp camera angles, expressionistic black-and-white imagery, and comic caricatures of military-political figures. Superb ensemble acting aids Kubrick's wry criticism of man-made doom. Popular music is incorporated to satirize dramatic vignettes.

The achievement of *2001: A Space Odyssey* lies both in its own

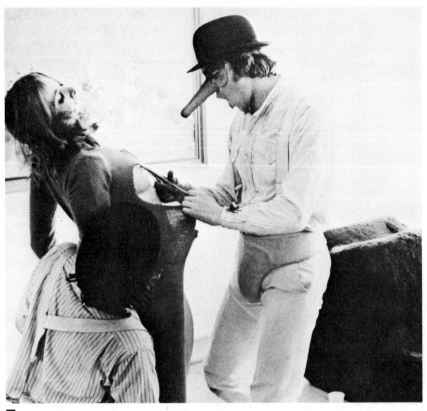

Expressive settings and costumes are part of the perverse world treated by Kubrick in *A Clockwork Orange* (1971).

technical virtuosity and its theme of technological manipulation in the twenty-first century. Kubrick engaged Britain's masterful special-effects artists in creating a coolly metaphysical experience in the guise of a science-fiction adventure. Through improved mobility devices and specially devised in-studio projection systems that permitted exact double-exposures, the illusion of space travel is vividly realized. In concept *2001* reveals humankind as subservient to its technology, destined for an uncertain fate. Kubrick depends almost entirely on the power of his images for his wry understatement about human progress.

A Clockwork Orange translated Anthony Burgess' novel for the screen in a bold, energetic treatment that brought the film controversy and commercial success. Kubrick presents a stylized story of a teenage gangleader, Alex (Malcolm McDowell), whose violent acts are carried out in a bland city of the future. Authorities effect behavior reversal by forcing Alex to watch on film repelling scenes of violence and sex. Relieved of his desire for sadistic action, Alex finds life unbearable and regains his will to live only after he is able to revert to his earlier self. The disarming effect of Kubrick's treatment results from the use of violence to raise provocative questions about social oppressiveness and individual will. Expressionistic settings and costumes define Alex's perverse world and once again Kubrick puts familiar music on the sound track to counterpoint dramatic content. Beethoven's *Ninth Symphony* and "Singin' in the Rain" accompany acts of violence.

For *Barry Lyndon* (1975) Kubrick went back in time to eighteenth-century England and an adaptation of William Thackeray's picaresque novel. In treating the story of an adventuresome young Irishman (Ryan O'Neal) who progresses from rags to riches and back again, Kubrick once more trusts the power of his images to convey the narrative and evoke a sense of time and place. Formally paced editing rhythms, authentic visual details, and vivid color compositions aid Kubrick's effort to reexperience a distant world.

The Shining (1980), filmed in Great Britain, moves into new territory, the suspense melodrama, but with Kubrick continuing to reveal himself as an unerring visual stylist.

Nicholas Roeg

Nicholas Roeg made a reputation as a superb cinematographer before directing his first film, *Performance* (1970), a story of triangular interaction in a household containing a pop singer (Mick Jagger), a gangster (James Fox), and a young woman (Anita Pallenberg). The two men adopt each other's personalities in an ambiguous, sometimes surreal account of shifting realities.

Roeg's second film, *Walkabout* (1971), has two middle-class Australian children being cared for by, and learning to communicate with, an aboriginal; but ultimately the three are unable to reach full acceptance of one another.

Don't Look Now (1973), a large-scale thriller about an architect (Donald Sutherland) with psychic powers, was internationally successful and showed Roeg's matured skills as a visual and structural stylist. A love scene with Julie Christie and Sutherland uses evocative parallel editing. Subdued color toning creates an appropriately somber Venice where much of the intrigue takes place.

David Bowie portrays *The Man Who Fell to Earth* (1976), Roeg's fragmentary view of how earthlings affect a visitor from outer space. It is yet another instance of a preoccupation with juxtaposed realities, imbued with surreal qualities.

Ken Russell

Ken Russell, Britain's most visible director in the 1970s, established his film reputation after working for BBC television in the sixties. There he directed two important series studies, one on contemporary artists and another on musical composers. Through this work Russell developed a growing interest in biography that examined both the public and personal lives of his subjects. Psychology (and later sex) receives significant attention in the dissection of character.

Women in Love (1969) became Russell's most highly praised feature film. D. H. Lawrence's novel is transferred to the screen with candor and visual richness. An ability to convey psychological mood and reveal sexual undercurrents lifts the film above other Lawrence adaptations, and Russell's work is marred only by a weak, drawn-out ending.

Beginning with *The Devils* (1971) subject matter and treatment become intentionally and increasingly more sensational. Sexual horrors are openly displayed in this work taken from Aldous Huxley's *The Devils of Loudun. The Boy Friend* (1972) is an extravagant version of Sandy Wilson's intimate musical. *Mahler* (1974), *Tommy* (1974), *Lisztomania* (1975), and *Valentino* (1977) all make excessive use of costumes, settings, music, and sexual innuendo. Lack of restraint in later work detracted from Russell's overall importance to recent British film history.

Feature film production in England at the end of the 1970s was limited almost entirely to outside projects, commonly American-financed spectacles seeking the assistance of Britain's special-effects technicians, e.g., *Superman* (1978). Industry artists were forced to find work in television, to teach, or to go abroad.

The emerging British influence on the Hollywood film could be seen in Peter Yates' charming rendering of *Breaking Away* (1979), and in Michael Apted's sincere *Coal Miner's Daughter* (1980). The keen surveillance of the American countryside by these British directors matches well Joseph Losey's observations of British life.

Britain's stylish, upbeat *Chariots of Fire*—recipient of the Oscar as best film of 1981—hinted at new activity by home directors with a desire to treat once again indigenous subject matter.

SUGGESTED READINGS

Butler, Ivan. *Cinema in Britain.* Cranbury, N.J.: Barnes, 1973.

De Vries, Daniel. *The Films of Stanley Kubrick.* Grand Rapids, Mich.: William B. Eerdmans, 1973.

Kulik, Karol. *Alexander Korda: The Man Who Could Work Miracles.* London: W. H. Allen, 1975.

LaValley, Albert J., ed. *Focus on Hitchcock.* Englewood Cliffs, N.J.: Prentice-Hall, 1972.

Leahy, James. *The Cinema of Joseph Losey.* Cranbury, N.J.: Barnes, 1967.

Manvell, Roger. *New Cinema in Britain.* New York: Dutton, 1969.

Phillips, Gene D. *Stanley Kubrick: A Film Odyssey.* New York: Popular Library, 1975.

EASTERN EUROPE:
INTERNATIONAL SUCCESS

I find I am using more and more heterogeneous material. It is not true that you cannot mix different materials. . . . This interrelationship of different materials creates a rich spiritual field. Each separate mono-stylistic point is a layering that only film can create. So you have a complete web of interrelated associations that can be political, sociological, psychological.
Dušan Makavejec, Yugoslavian director, *University Film Study Center Newsletter,*
December 1975.

Prior to World War II, films in Poland, Hungary, Czechoslovakia, and Yugoslavia were made primarily for the enjoyment of home audiences. International achievement was rare, and efforts by Hollywood studios in the 1930s to enter into co-production arrangements (e.g., Paramount in Poland) proved unsuccessful. Technical facilities, however, were ample and in the case of Czechoslovakia, where government subsidy supported the industry,

Makavejev's *WR: Mysteries of the Organism* (1971).

highly advanced. Feature-film production was dominated after the arrival of sound by literary and musical adaptations and by frivolous satires. Some of these films were imported by national groups living abroad, but language barriers made wider distribution impractical.

Important work in Eastern Europe during the prewar period was done by Gustav Machatý in Czechoslovakia, Wanda Jakubowska and Aleksander Ford in Poland, and István Székely (Sekely) in Hungary. Their films showed an interest in nationalistic themes with social and personal concerns. Ford and Jakubowska had their early training in documentary filmmaking. Machatý began as an actor; his treatment of sex in *Erotikon* (1929) and *Extase* (1933), inspired by von Stroheim's work, brought him wide notoriety and directing assignments in Hollywood. Ford's best known documentary was *Street of the Young* (1936), a realistic exposé of poverty among the Jewish people of Poland.

Nazi occupation of Eastern Europe had a devastating impact on film production. Feature filmmaking was prohibited altogether in Poland, and in Czechoslovakia less than a dozen films were produced during the war years. Aleksander Ford fled Poland for work in the Soviet Union where he founded the Polish Army Film Unit, a vital force in postwar Polish cinema. Wanda Jakubowska was arrested for Resistance activity in 1942 and incarcerated at Auschwitz and Ravensbruck, an experience which she poignantly recalled in one of Poland's outstanding postwar films, *The Last Stage* (1948).

After the Nazi period, the rapid emergence of Communist governments, and, consequently, Russian influence in Eastern Europe, provided cinema with different incentives. Film industries were nationalized as state organs and, although intended as avenues for propaganda, guaranteed subsidy proved to be a stimulus to artistic innovation. The founding of a national film archive in Czechoslovakia (1943) and a national film school in Poland (in 1948 at Lodz) were other stimulants to artistic growth. By 1948 Czechoslovakia, Poland, Hungary, and Yugoslavia had all begun to make a slow but impressive rise from cinema obscurity to international prominence.

POLAND

Poland took the lead in establishing a prominent corps of filmmakers. Most looked to the immediate past and to the Nazi experience for subjects: Leonard Buczkowski's *Forbidden Songs* (1947) revealed the unfailing Polish spirit in Nazi-occupied Warsaw; Jakubowska exposed the tragic way of life in the concentration camp in *The Last Stage;* and Ford's *Border Street* (1948) studied treatment of Jews in a Warsaw ghetto.

The creative outpouring of these postwar films was one of personal release spurred by national trauma. In the meantime pressure to support state causes through the cinema led to close control of content

by the Central Committee on films. Expression until the mid-fifties was fairly well confined to socialist realism but without the revolutionary spirit which fired directors in Russia during the twenties.

With Ford's *Five Boys from Barska* in 1953, evidence of more personal themes and styling began to appear. The work presented an honest account of youth delinquency in Poland following the war and the efforts made to deal with the problem. Ford's work earned him the 1954 Cannes Film Direction prize.

After Stalin's death in 1953, control of film projects eased and exhibition of films from outside Poland increased; soon a Polish New Wave was on its way, bringing with it between 1954 and 1962 a number of important new talents, including Andrzej Wajda, Andrzej Munk, Wojciech Has, Jerzy Kawalerowicz, and Roman Polanski.

Andrzej Wajda

Between 1954 and 1958 Andrzej Wajda (1926–   ) created a remarkable trilogy dealing with youth heroism and tragedy during Nazi occupation of his homeland. *A Generation* (1954) thrusts romantic Polish youth into military encounters; *Kanal* (1957) takes them into Warsaw's sewers during the 1944 uprising; *Ashes and Diamonds* (1958) places a young political assassin at a pivotal point in Polish history.

Ashes and Diamonds is considered Wajda's early outstanding work. The young hero's efforts to kill a Communist official on the day that peace comes to Poland, ending instead with his own death, represents the ultimate, ironic loss of individual spirit that struggled against the Nazis for a free Poland. The young man's fate is sealed by the unalterable course of history.

A strong mixture of realism and romantic lyricism creates a sense of personal and national tragedy. Wajda's individual style is expressed through bold camera compositions, careful control of editing to create

Awaiting the assassination attempt in *Ashes and Diamonds* (1957)—a suspense thriller and a film with symbolic national meaning for Poland.

dramatic tension, and evocative use of lighting and music. Zbigniew Cybulski's intense performance as Maciek earned great praise.

Andrzej Munk, Wojciech Has, and Jerzy Kawalerowicz

Andrzej Munk, (1921–1961) like Wajda, was a graduate of the Polish film school at Lodz but began his career as a state-committed documentarist. He produced only four feature films before dying in an automobile accident: *Man on the Track* (1956), *Eroica* (1957), *Bad Luck* (1960), and *Passenger* (released in 1963). *Eroica,* a satirical essay on heroics directed at peers such as Wajda, showed Munk at his best: a gifted ironist and austere stylist.

Wojciech Has (1925–   ) and Jerzy Kawalerowicz (1922–   ) were less concerned with war themes than their contemporaries. Has' *The Noose* (1957) freely incorporates subjective points of view into a study of a lonely alcoholic. Kawalerowicz exhibited a strong interest in psychological exploration and traditional narrative: *Night Train* (1959) was a thriller, meticulously constructed in plot and dimensioned in its analysis of character. *Mother Joan of the Angels* (1961), his early masterpiece, is a symbol-laden film in which Kawalerowicz treats the Devils at Loudun incident.

Roman Polanski

The critical success and varied styles of these films indicated the progress being made within Poland toward full artistic liberation. When Roman Polanski (1933–   ) arrived as a feature director in the early

The conflict that develops between the two men in *Knife in the Water* (1962) is handled by Polanski subtly and openly, as here in a knife-throwing contest.

sixties, an even sharper turn was taken away from thematic preoccupations of the previous decade. After creating the brilliant parable *Two Men and a Wardrobe* (1958) as his senior project at the Lodz film school, he continued to make short symbolic films noticeably influenced by an interest in theater-of-absurd methods, especially the use of material objects and repetition as satirical commentary.

Knife in the Water (1962), Polanski's first feature, was declared a masterpiece for its skillful handling of sexual tension. Plot on the surface is uncomplicated. An older man and his wife on their way to a lake give a young hitchhiker a ride; they invite the drifter to join them for a weekend of sailing. On the boat, beneath-the-surface conflicts build between the two men, with the woman mutely aware of the tension. In a scuffle the young man is knocked overboard, disappears, but returns after the husband swims ashore to report the mishap. The drifter makes love to the woman and leaves. Later she confesses to her husband who pretends not to believe her.

Polanski's study is one of emotional violence, presented in an austerely naturalistic style. Unlike earlier work in his film shorts, symbolism is absent except for the drifter's knife. An observing camera carries the incisive study, treating innuendo and behavioristic details with clinical observation.

After this film Polanski moved to England where he made *Repulsion* (1965) and *Cul-de-Sac* (1966), both also films with sexual themes. Later work in the United States included *Rosemary's Baby* (1968) and *Chinatown* (1974), each a stylish thriller that makes effective use of the spare, observing style seen in *Knife in the Water*. For *The Tenant* (1976), a French production, Polanski returned to surrealistic expression that suffered from a lack of restraint. *Tess* (1980), also made in France, brought new respect as well as commercial success.

Visibility of Polish films went into a decline in the late sixties, in part a result of political upheaval and revived controls. New activity in the late seventies brought treatment of contemporary social themes which included divorce, alcoholism, and suicide.

CZECHOSLOVAKIA

At the end of World War II, the Czechoslovakian government acted immediately to nationalize the film industry and to create film study centers. Artistic progress closely parallels that in Poland with a small group of filmmakers achieving prominence in the late forties, a brief hiatus in the fifties, then an explosive burst of new talent to bring notice to the country during the sixties. Most prominent in the immediate postwar period was the puppet animator Jirí Trnka whose social-political allegories are often darkly bitter, e.g., *The Devil on Springs* (1946).

Bringing international regard to Czechoslovakia in the sixties were Milos Forman, Jirí Menzel, Pavel Juracek, Jan Kadar, Jan Nemec, and Véra Chytilová. Forman's *Loves of a Blonde* (1965) and *The Fireman's Ball* (1967) are ironic satires that examine the personal effect of outmoded social convention within Czechoslovakia. The low-budget, spontaneous filming style used by Forman (including nonprofessional actors) gives his biting comedy realistic authority.

The Shop on Main Street (1965), co-directed by Jan Kadar and Elmar Klos, earned the distinction of becoming the first feature film from Czechoslovakia to win an American Academy Award. Its story is located in a small Czechoslovakian village during Nazi occupation where anti-Semitic cruelty that was rampant at the time is personalized through the relationship of an itinerant carpenter with an old Jewish shopkeeper. The film's achievement is in its effective development of characters and its exposure of the individual compromises which allowed anti-Semitism to prevail tragically.

The following year Jirí Menzel's *Closely Watched Trains* (1966) also succeeded in capturing an Academy Award. Mixing comedy and trage-dy, Menzel juxtaposes an assistant stationmaster's initial fumbling at-tempts at sex with the political realities of Nazi-occupied Czechoslovakia. The film ends with the death of the young initiate while he is blowing up a German ammunition train. This black-comedy approach to the well-used theme of resistance heroics was refreshing at home and abroad.

Jan Nemec and Véra Chytilová

Jan Nemec (*The Report on the Party and the Guests,* 1966) and Véra

A formal party incongruously set within a forest serves as the setting for Němec's political allegory *The Report on the Party and the Guests* (1966).

Chytilová (*Daisies,* 1966) revealed formalistic impulses and an anarchistic approach to subject matter, proving themselves to be the most radical of Czechoslovakia's New Wave directors.

The Report on the Party and the Guests begins with a man hosting an elegant feast for a group of guests. The Host's expressed desire is to please. When one of the guests departs unhappily, he is pursued by the remaining members of the party who use hunting dogs in their chase. Nemec's allegorical theme implicitly criticizes totalitarian oppression that squelches individual will, and the film was banned for two years, released, then banned again after the Soviet invasion of 1968. The allegory's visual style studiously copied familiar works of art and the principal characters were portrayed by Nemec's friends; Evald Schorm, another important Czech director of the time (*The Return of the Prodigal Son,* 1966) appeared as the Guest Who Refused to Be Happy. Nemec's political stance led to exile.

Chytilová's career as a director began in 1962 and her work thereafter was characterized by varied interests and methods of expression. Many of her earlier studies were *verité* accounts of young women confronting themselves and their values in contemporary Czechoslovakia, e.g., *Ceiling* and *A Bag of Fleas* both made in 1962. *Daisies* (1966) takes two young women with nothing else to do on a hedonistic romp. Surrealist and avant-garde techniques appear throughout, including a mixture of color and black-and-white images. Chytilová's formalistic sensibilities led to decreased output in the seventies; however, her appearance in New York City in 1979 to discuss her work suggested new activity.

Political uncertainty after the 1968 invasion disrupted progress of Czechoslovakia's brief but fruitful New Wave period. As in Poland the censors were once more forcibly at work, suppressing individual effort, and driving many of the country's best directors abroad.

HUNGARY

In Hungary film art had had a spiritual father in Béla Balázs, one of the medium's first great theorists and teachers. After living and writing in exile for a quarter of a century, Balázs returned to Hungary in 1945 to lead his country's film industry to a revival. He trained young filmmakers and began writing screenplays dealing with postwar life in Hungary. In *Somewhere in Europe* (1947), which Géza Radványi directed, Balázs and his co-writers offered a realistic study of dire circumstances for a group of orphans.

With the establishment of a Communist government in 1948, the film industry was nationalized as an organ of the new regime. Achieving prominence in the period that followed were Lázló Ranódy, Kalman Nadasdy, and Zoltán Fabri. All dealt with Hungarian themes from a social point of view. Fabri's studies of rural life, first as author (*Mattie the Goose Boy,* 1949), then as director, were particularly impressive.

Movement toward a Hungarian New Wave was interrupted by the 1956 uprisings whose devastation affected all aspects of life in the country. Rebound came in the mid-sixties after the founding of the Béla Balázs Studios in 1961. István Szabó and Miklós Jancsó were the most visible of Hungary's new talents.

István Szabó

Concern for the future of Hungarian youth, presented through six representative characters, formed the theme of Szabó's *The Age of Daydreaming* (1964). The film's pessimistic tone indicated new social relevance among emerging directors. Szabó continued to explore the theme of questioning youth in *Father* (1967).

Miklós Jancsó

Jancsó's work was prolific, unique, and internationally acclaimed. His features in the sixties included *Cantata* (1963), *My Way Home* (1964), *The Round-up* (1965), *Silence and Cry* (1968), *The Red and the White* (1968), *The Confrontation* (1969), and *Winter Wind* (1969).

Jancsó's vision characteristically draws on wartime situations as a means of examining human relations. *My Way Home* takes place in a rural setting in 1945 where a Hungarian schoolboy is captured by Soviet forces in the country. A friendship with a young Russian soldier leads to disillusionment and confusion for the Hungarian youth. Jancsó's expressive use of landscape emerges as a distinctive element of future work. Much of *The Round-up,* an account of Hungarian peasant resistance during the Austro-Hungarian empire, is set on a barren plain, a timeless place.

The Red and the White also locates a war story (Russia's Civil War of

Humiliation—physical and psychological—is one of the methods employed by Austro-Hungarian soldiers to break peasant resistance in *The Round-up* (1965).

1918) on vast, somber landscapes that are further emphasized by a wide-screen format. War's absurd methods are exposed in a depersonalized view of characters. A constantly moving camera further distances.

A similar application of space to theme is made in *Agnus Dei* (1970) where Hungary's own Civil War of 1919 is the subject for visualizing "irrational" (the director's word) human behavior. Jancsó's unconventional approach to narrative and imagery made him the most provocative of the Hungarian New Wave directors, and one whose bleak vision reflects his country's agonized history.

YUGOSLAVIA

Except for its important role in modern animation, the film industry in Yugoslavia until the late sixties remained relatively undistinguished. Feature output was sparse and only with the arrival of Dušan Makavejev (*A Man Is Not a Bird*, 1965; *The Switchboard Operator*, 1967), and Vatroslav Mimica (*Monday or Tuesday*, 1966; *Kaja, I'll Kill You*, 1968) did dramatic films begin to receive international distribution.

Makavejev's early works showed him to be a strong ironist with an unusual flair for editorial experimentation that mixes elements freely. His iconoclastic approach is well illustrated in *WR: Mysteries of the Organism* (1971), Makavejev's best-known work outside Yugoslavia. His hilarious attack on contemporary decadence includes narrative mixed

A Klee-like figure serves as the inventive hero of *Ersatz* (1961).

with news footage, interviews, and self-conscious references to communication media.

Mimica's *Kaja, I'll Kill You* renders an impressionistic study of Yugoslav life on the Adriatic coast during Italian occupation there in the early forties. Atmosphere suggests memory and tension along the lines of Fellini's *Amarcord* (1974). Mimica's major importance within Yugoslavia prior to turning to feature filmmaking was as an animator, the area of cinematic expression that brought the country its greatest acclaim.

ANIMATION

In 1950 a cartoon group was founded in Zagreb, Yugoslavia, which has almost singlehandedly pointed the direction for modern screen animation and animation theory. This government-sponsored group, known as the "Zagreb school," devoted itself to highly graphic, nonrealistic animations which are charged with political and social thought.

Ersatz and *The Wall*

The first film to call critical attention to the Zagreb school was a cartoon produced in 1961 called *Ersatz* (*The Substitute*). *Ersatz* became the first foreign film to win an Academy Award in a nonforeign film category. The drawing technique of Dušan Vukotić is reminiscent of the artists Paul Klee and Joan Miró. The humor and theme are urbane.

Vukotić presents a small, Klee-like man who arrives at a beach for a swim. The man takes geometric scraps of colored paper from his automobile and using an airgun, inflates the pieces of paper into necessary beach paraphernalia: a beach ball, a rubber raft, a cooking grille, fishing gear. For companionship, a bikini-clad woman is created, but immediately deflated when she resembles, too closely, a naturalistic female. A second, more graphic figure is produced from another scrap, and the man, pleased with his creation, engages himself in romantic pursuit. When the woman goes for a swim, the man produces a shark so that he might rescue the endangered beauty and prove his worth. A he-man figure appears on water skis and competes for the woman's affection. The first man is distraught and deflates his female creation. The he-man commits suicide by pulling his own air-plug. The first man inflates his automobile, deflates the beach objects, produces a highway with his air gun, and drives away. As the car rounds a curve it strikes a rusty nail on the pavement, instantly destroying all material objects in the scene except the nail.

Ersatz's theme has a double significance. Vukotić treats, satirically, modern kind's fate, the obsession with and easy possession of material objects. The ironic ending suggests the potential self-destruction of man through his genius for invention.

The theme of this short film also can be interpreted as a visual manifesto of the significant differences between the Zagreb school and the animation traditions established by naturalistic animators. Vukotić shows that the animator creates an imaginary world from colors and scraps of paper. The hero's pneumatic gun in *Ersatz* is also the animator's drawing pen. Vukotić does not pretend that his drawings are anything but those of a graphic artist.

An example of the trenchant thought in contemporary Zagreb animation appears in a short cartoon by Ante Zaninović, *The Wall* (1965). A distinguished gentleman in green suit and bowler hat sits idly by a stone wall that blocks his path. A second man, unclothed, appears and attempts to traverse the wall by scaling it, by firing a cannon at the wall, by springing over. He fails, cries against the wall, becomes desperate, finally backs up and runs furiously at the wall, bursting a hole through the barricade, but dying under the pile of crumbling stones. The gentleman, who has been waiting passively, walks through the hole, only to find a second wall identical to the first. Again, he sits and waits.

The Wall offers one of the central thematic concerns of Eastern European animation: the individual caught in a social environment, presented in allegorical form and characterized by cynicism.

Ralph Stephenson, in his important book *The Animated Film,* claims that the Eastern European countries, Yugoslavia along with Poland and Czechoslovakia, have "produced more original, more serious, finer, wittier work, more satiric work even, in the last twenty years than the world of free enterprise in the last fifty."

Themes

Yugoslavian, Czech, and Polish animators often create works with similar themes. One of the most common is that of the individual trapped in an urbanized and mechanical world.

Jan Lenica, Poland's foremost animator, has drawn numerous cartoons around this theme. In *Labyrinth* (1961), he tells the story of a surrealistic, desolate city and the loneliness of the individual who is trapped there. The city (the labyrinth) is a nightmarish, Kafkaesque place.

In other of his films, *Janko the Music Maker* (1961) and *Cages* (1967), Lenica mocks mechanization and society's dependence on and acceptance of authority. Lenica's cartoon characters are depicted as prisoners of the world in which they live. Classically, Lenica projects a modern artist's view of the impact of technology and urbanization on individuality.

In *Monsieur Tête* (1959), Lenica presents another common theme in satirical form, that of conformity. The film is about a man whose head is constantly in revolt, doing eccentric things and being anticonformist. Monsieur Tête is labeled a "bad head" by others and ultimately, out of frustration, hits himself over the head with a large hammer. The head is shown filling with lead, after which Monsieur Tête becomes a model citizen, and wins numerous awards as a head "like everyone else's."

The theme of conformity appears elsewhere in Eastern European cartoons, e.g., *Icarus* (Jerzy Zitman, Poland, 1970); *Crazy Leg* (Branko Ranitovic, Yugoslavia, 1971).

Jan Habarta, a Polish animator, creates an automated and insensitive world in *No. 00173* (1966). A small, red butterfly enters an automated factory where modern men—all exactly alike—work in perfect unison. One of the factory workers becomes concerned for the safety of the butterfly among the machines and attempts to protect it. But the operation of the factory cannot be interrupted. A robotlike figure captures the butterfly, destroys it, and places it in a small display case labelled No. 00173, alongside hundreds of other preserved butterflies in similar cases.

Eastern European animators continue to produce films with dark, cynical ideas and further distinguished by their graphic appeal.

SUGGESTED READINGS

Butler, Ivan. *The Cinema of Roman Polanski*. New York: Barnes, 1970.
Fuksiewicz, Jacek. *Polish Cinema*. Warsaw: Interpress Publishers, 1973.
Holloway, Ronald. *Z Is for Zagreb*. South Brunswick, N.J.: Barnes, 1972.
Liehm, Antonín J. *Closely Watched Films: The Czechoslovak Experience*. White Plains, N.Y.: International Arts and Sciences Press, 1974.

Liehm, Mira, and Antonín J. Liehm. *The Most Important Art: Eastern European Film after 1945*. Berkeley: University of California Press, 1977.

Michatek, Bolestaw. *The Cinema of Andrzej Wajda*. New York: Barnes, 1973.

Stoil, Michael Jon. *Cinema Beyond the Danube*. Metuchen, N.J.: Scarecrow, 1974.

Whyte, Alistair. *New Cinema in Eastern Europe*. New York: Dutton, 1971.

PART 6

RECENT
VISIONARIES

INTERNATIONAL
VISIONARIES

It was fairly obvious that the cinema should be my chosen means of expression. I made myself understood in a language that by-passed words, which I lacked; music, which I have never mastered; and painting, which left me unmoved. Suddenly, I had the possibility of corresponding with the world around me in a language that is literally spoken from soul to soul, in terms that avoid control by the intellect in a manner almost voluptuous.

Ingmar Bergman, accepting the Erasmus Prize, 1965 (translated by Keith Bradfield).

The international explosion of new creativity in film expression during the 1950s established the importance of directors from practically every corner of the world. Although many of these filmmakers had been active for years, the revived interest in international cinema made new "stars" of directors in Sweden, Japan, and India—artists of the caliber of Ingmar Bergman, Yasujiro Ozu,

Winter Light (1962).

Akira Kurosawa, and Satyajit Ray, among the most respected names in all of motion-picture history. Works from the imaginations of these filmmakers and other directors from their countries expanded the ever-growing body of film classics.

SWEDEN: INGMAR BERGMAN

Ingmar Bergman (1918–   ) was born in Uppsala, Sweden, on July 14, the son of a Lutheran minister. Early interests in theater led to work in amateur productions while a university student and later a brief career as a professional stage manager at Stockholm's Royal Opera. By 1946 Bergman had established himself as a skillful director in several of Sweden's prominent municipal theaters.

Involvement in cinema began as a script editor and screenwriter at Svensk Filmindustri. First acclaim came with Alf Sjöberg's *Hets* (*Frenzy/ Torment,* 1944), a film about adolescent trauma with Bergman writing the screenplay and serving as assistant director. Sjöberg's somber interpretation of the story left a lasting impact on Bergman's own approach to cinematic expression.

The following year Bergman directed his first feature, *Kris* (*Crisis,* 1945), taken from a Danish stage play and, like *Torment,* concerned with adolescent anguish. It received only fair notices, but Bergman went on to explore again a youth theme in *It Rains on Our Love* (1946) and achieved commercial as well as critical success.

Stylistic Eclecticism

An individual style was not yet fully evident in these earlier works, but expressionistic methods to achieve introspective analysis were. Also evident was Bergman's interest in the darker side of human existence—a concern carried forward from Swedish theater (especially Strindberg) and the early film work of Victor Sjöstrom and Mauritz Stiller. *Prison* (*The Devil's Wanton,* 1949), a study of prostitution and suicide revealed the extremes of this earlier work about the despair of adolescents.

In the meantime *Port of Call* (1948) had drawn on neorealistic methods for a documentarylike account of love between a confused young woman (Nine-Christine Jonsson) and a seaman (Bengt Eklund).

Bergman's career took yet another stylistic turn with *Secrets of Women* (1952), the first of a series of sophisticated pictures centered on matrimonial foibles. Subsequent works in this vein include *A Lesson in Love* (1954), and the Cannes Festival winner, *Smiles of a Summer Night* (1955). Erotic, farcical, and stylish, *Smiles of a Summer Night* is a love intrigue set at the turn of the century and involving an assortment of men and women whose lives intermingle during a midsummer's eve-

The Knight (Max von Sydow) and Death (Bengt Ekerot) are dark foreground figures engaged in a life-death game of chess. In the background a young family—Bergman's symbol of hope—sits bathed in light.

ning. Bergman's lighthearted screenplay fairly well exposes the nature of human love and all its deficiencies.

The fame and regard which *Smiles of a Summer Night* brought was increased with the appearance of *The Seventh Seal* in 1956. This work and that which followed the next year, *Wild Strawberries* (1957), exploded onto the international film scene as provocative exercises of assured style and deeply serious purpose.

The Seventh Seal

The Seventh Seal presents in the form of an allegory a life-death struggle (spiritual and physical) set in medieval times. Death (Bengt Ekerot) stalks a knight (Max von Sydow) who has recently returned to Europe from the Crusades and who is disheartened by what he sees around him. A plague is sweeping through the country, taking its toll of human life, while sin and religious fanaticism give evidence of a squalid society. As the knight wanders about, seeking some hopeful sign of meaning to life, he is continually confronted by Death. The two play an ongoing game of chess for the Knight's right to live, with Death the certain victor.

Bergman's direction is somber in visualization, his expressionistic images laden with heavy shadows. Bright light is absent except in the scenes with a juggler, his wife, and small child—representatives of virtue who become the Knight's means of release from spiritual despair just before his death. A silhouetted "dance of Death" against a severe landscape provides the film's most powerfully telling image—an abstraction of life's mystery and fate presented in playful terms. Landscape and nature compositions are used extensively to evoke a poetic feeling of medieval futility.

Bergman's control of actors is also apparent. The stoic Max von Sydow as the Knight illustrates Bergman's ability to make transparent inner tensions in reserved performances.

Wild Strawberries

Wild Strawberries also uses impending death as a provocation to personal quest. A renowned medical professor, Isak Borg (Victor Sjöström), is returning by automobile to the scene of his college days to receive an honorary degree. The trip frames a journey back in time, as the professor remembers events from his past, while also dreaming of his death. He observes in a grainy, overexposed fantasy the movement of a caisson that carries his own coffin. Bergman takes the character, unseen, in and out of flashback vignettes which ultimately reveal detachment and selfishness as the causes of Borg's unhappy life. Accepting this conclusion, the professor in the end sees the meaning of love and takes a step in that direction. He is at peace.

The method of presentation in the form of a journey (a metaphor for life's passage) owned inspiration to Strindberg's *The Road to Damascus* and Sjöberg's screen version of *Miss Julie* (1951). It appears as a recurring motif in other of Bergman's character studies. Sjöström's performance, his last, brilliantly sustained a character questing for final clues to the meaning and value of his life. Gunnar Fischer's cinematography showed him to be one of the medium's great chiaroscurists, painting psychological and nostalgic moods with an expressive use of light and shadow.

In the period that followed *The Seventh Seal* and *Wild Strawberries*, Bergman continued to examine the dark side of the human condition, alternating among a realistic study of grief in a contemporary maternity ward, *Brink of Life* (1957); a symbolic parable of artistic humiliation, *The Magician* (1958); and a mythic ballad of medieval horror, *The Virgin Spring* (1960). In each of these works the principal character is driven to self-knowledge.

Religious Questioning

Bergman's strict religious upbringing reveals itself in his preoccupation with a search for God and evidence of value in life. Thematic explora-

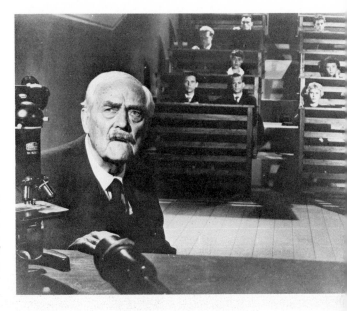

Professor Borg (Victor Sjöström) is returned to a lecture classroom from his medical school days. Memory materializes itself throughout *Wild Strawberries* (1957) to bring the old man to a new recognition of himself.

tion of this theme places doubt and reaffirmation in uneasy tension: the knight in *The Seventh Seal* goes to his death with only a hint of hope after witnessing the innocent love of the juggler's family; the father (Max von Sydow) in *The Virgin Spring* vows to build a church on the site of his daughter's murder after avenging her evil death. A spring bubbles to life as a symbolic sign of reaffirmation.

The recurrent theme of religious questioning was the focus of a trilogy of works (which Bergman referred to as "chamber plays" because of Strindberg's influence and their limited scope and isolated placement of small groups of characters): *Through a Glass Darkly* (1961), *Winter Light* (1962), and *The Silence* (1963).

Through a Glass Darkly is set on a Baltic island where a father, negligent of his family, begins to reach out to his son after his daughter's mental deterioration. To the schizophrenic daughter, God is a large spider hovering over her head. The father's gesture of engaging his son in conversation (consolatory love) is a positive sign of faith in humanity.

Winter Light reveals a Lutheran pastor, Tomas Ericsson (Gunnar Björnstrand), in a progressive state of emotional and spiritual confusion, provoked initially by his wife's death and by his failure to rouse a congregation. The film opens with a formally composed shot of a nearly empty church, emphasizing a place of worship devoid of spirituality. Administering and receiving communion is, simultaneously, an empty gesture. (See illustration on page 438.)

The pastor's doubts grow when he is unable to offer reassurance to a parishioner plagued by fears of atomic holocaust. When the fearful parishioner commits suicide, the pastor suggests self-awareness and

The searching, the anguish, and the innocence that are part of *The Silence* (1963) are all evident in a single shot of Bergman's isolated characters.

effort at communication by offering an evening service though only a lone woman is in the church.

As a study of spiritual crisis in isolation, *Winter Light* begs comparison with Bresson's *Diary of a Country Priest*. Both make use of bleak landscapes and natural sounds as correspondences for dullness of the soul.

The Silence brings Bergman's quest for religious meaning to a negative conclusion, suggesting in the end failure of communication altogether and total isolation. The story is that of two sisters, Anna and Ester, on a journey through a foreign country. Anna's young son is traveling with them. In the city of Timoka they take a hotel room, but are unable to speak the city's language. The streets harbor military activity; odd, sinister people inhabit the seedy hotel rooms and corridors.

In their isolation within the strange city the three sojourners bear their burdens without mutual support: Anna's sexual compulsiveness, Ester's illness and incestuous attachment to her sister, the son's helpless displacement. The two sisters are emotional cripples, motivated by basic instincts that prevent any meaningful relationship. Anna and her son move on, leaving Ester to die alone in the alien hotel room. Ester in a final gesture at communication has translated a few words of the foreign language for Anna's son.

The Silence connects selfish instinct to hellish incarceration, offering no evidence of God's presence or hope for salvation through human contact. The camera work by Sven Nykvist (Bergman's cameraman after 1956) makes extensive use of moving-camera shots, a method of conveying the hotel as a place of turbulent passion and human unrest.

Artistic Questioning

The dual-personality approach in *The Silence* repeated itself as the framework of *Persona* (1966), a masterful piece of cinematic construction in which Bergman explores human psychology while questioning the value of artistic expression. A famous actress (Liv Ullmann) suffering from psychosomatically related muteness, and Alma, a nurse (Bibi Andersson) who cares for her, interchange personalities after becoming dependent on one another. Individual identity is lost, indicated by double-exposure which fuses the two women's faces into one. The relationship is destructive with Alma—seemingly the stronger of the women—becoming more insecure while the actress rebounds. Bergman incorporates shots of a motion-picture projector and other alienation devices (including the sound of the director's voice), apparently to indicate that film, like life, can be deceptive and illusory.

Artistic introspection and personal crisis examined earlier in *Sawdust and Tinsel/The Naked Night* (1953), and *The Magician* (1958), continued throughout the 1960s to stimulate Bergman's creative urges. *Hour of the Wolf* (1968) locates an artist (Max von Sydow) on a desolate island where he has apparently come to recover from emotional and mental disturbances. The artists's fears, agonies, and mental distortions are visualized, including an inability to distinguish between illusion and reality during a puppet-theater presentation. Eventually the man mysteriously disappears, leaving his wife (Liv Ullmann) alone on the island to question his whereabouts.

Shame (1968) and *The Passion of Anna* (1969) also put the artist in a state of isolated introspection, uncertain of his role in a society of political upheaval and human failings. Bergman's view of the artist is one of identity crisis: an individual plagued by inadequacies in reflecting the human condition—hence the self-conscious awareness of the medium in *Persona* and *The Passion of Anna* that aims to alienate the viewer from full illusory experiences.

Later Work

Bergman's best works of the 1970s, *Cries and Whispers* (1972) and *Scenes from a Marriage* (1974), are psychosexual studies employing, respectively, symbolic expression and *verité*-styled recording techniques.

Cries and Whispers (another "chamber" play) places four women in an elegant home where decor is dominated by deep red colors. Characters appear in contrasting gowns of pure white. Physical pain, sexual tension, and memories of the past agitate beneath the splendid surfaces to suggest a world of detached interaction. Bergman's theme is rendered in large part through color values which are alternately passionate, airy, weighty, void, and, in the treatment of the mother figure, a caring servant, earth warm.

Bergman's fondness for light and shadow was replaced by a bright documentary look in *Scenes from a Marriage* (1974), an unusually direct treatment of male-female relationships.

Scenes from a Marriage was filmed for television in six parts over a fifty-five-day period, exploring in minute detail the progress of a troubled marriage (taken partly from Bergman's own experiences). Eventually released as a theatrical feature and as an international television special, this uncharacteristically direct work found acceptance among general audiences—many unfamiliar with other Bergman films. Liv Ullmann as the wife, Marianne, gives an extraordinarily sensitive performance of both transparent and intricate texturing.

In modern cinema few artists can challenge Ingmar Bergman in prominence. The consistency of his vision and the intensity of his personal and philosophical ruminations greatly enhance the best traditions of Swedish culture. His abilities as a film practitioner suggest genius, one capable of drawing great performances from a favored stock company of players, of exposing the face as a mask for human suffering while willing at the same time to reveal the medium in which he works as an illusory device incapable of fully grasping the mysteries of human existence.

Others in Sweden

Other directors achieved prominence in Sweden and abroad during the 1960s and 1970s, most notably Bo Widerberg and Jan Troëll. Widerberg's *Elvira Madigan* (1967) proved internationally successful as a lyric-romantic study of star-crossed love. Likewise, *Adalen '31* (1969) dealt with a political incident in romantic terms.

Troëll's success came within an epic format, showing himself to be a masterful storyteller in *The Emigrants* (1971) and *The New Land* (1975), continuing accounts of Swedish emigration to Minnesota. Troëll's gift for creating period drama and telling incidents is especially noteworthy.

JAPAN

A long tradition of outstanding filmmaking within Japan had gone largely unnoticed outside Asia until Akira Kurosawa's *Rashomon* (1950) captured the Venice Film Festival Grand Prize in 1951. With the entry of this provocative motion picture into the international market, critics and historians began to recognize the unique styles of noted Japanese directors and to afford them the international acclaim they deserved. Yasujiro Ozu and Kenji Mizoguchi stand together with Kurosawa as the giants of Japanese cinema.

Yasujiro Ozu

Yasujiro Ozu's (1903–1963) reputation was earned in Japan during the 1920s and 30s with a series of silent comedies and dramas about family relationships, a theme which he continued to treat throughout his forty-year career. The earlier period in Japanese film history, like the American studio years, was characterized by mass-production output aimed for studio-owned theater chains. Although budgets were usually minimal, established directors of Ozu's rank were able to impose their artistic temperaments on assignments, and often to choose or write their own screenplays. Ozu's style, which has been described as the "most Japanese" of all Japan's cinematic effort, and his thematic interest in the lower-middle-class family, evolved under such conditions in the pre-nationalistic 20s and 30s.

I Was Born, but . . . (1932) is representative of Ozu's familial social comedies made in great but memorable abundance during the first decade of his career (1927–1937). In an open-ended story, Ozu shows an office clerk whose salary advancement has allowed him to move his family into a new neighborhood. The uprooting dismays the man's two young sons who react to the new environment with staged fights and then observe with disbelief their father's foolish efforts to please his boss at a party. This revelation of adult aspiration and social convention, viewed through a child's perspective, conveys universal truths with satirical charm. Ozu avoids moralizing altogether, allowing the title *I Was Born, but* . . . to suggest the young boys' resigned attitude at the film's conclusion.

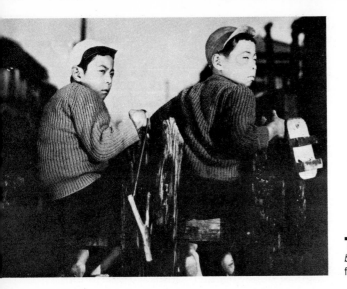

The two lads in Ozu's *I Was Born but . . . .* (1932) turn their backs on their father's new way of life.

Altogether Ozu directed nearly three dozen such satires in the ten-year period, working in a leisurely style that emphasized character relationships within middle-class environments. Ozu's camera takes the position of an observer, with scenes often filmed in long shot from a straight-on, low-angled camera position (the position of a person seated on a tatami mat) and played out fully without editorial emphasis.

Ozu's effectiveness as a filmmaker comes in large part from the respect he shows his subjects, even when the social criticism is biting. The father's foolishness in *I Was Born, but . . .* is counterbalanced by an unfailing honesty. Such regard, matched by a quietly observant visual style, imbues his films with admirable gentility.

When Ozu turned to more serious treatment of Japanese family habits after World War II, the same tenderness prevailed. His delicate study of a father-daughter relationship, *Late Spring* (1949), typifies postwar work where he continues to assay character response to life's transitions. A beautiful daughter, happy and perfectly content at home serving her equally satisfied father, nevertheless gives in to expectations that she will marry and begin her own family. The subtle dissection of resistance to change, then acceptance, emerges as an understated account of human resignation. A fragile mood, captured through character detail and visual distancing, evokes a sense of time's passage and the quiet but important alterations it brings to all families. In the picture's final shot, the father is shown after his daughter's wedding, alone in his favorite armchair, peeling a piece of fruit. Life must go on.

Ozu's directorial greatness and appeal grew from the unforgettable quality of these simply derived revelations which thematically reinforce the Japanese philosophy of *mono no aware:* acceptance of life's fate as a condition of spiritual growth. This philosophical value is encompassed in all of Ozu's later, widely praised films including *Early Summer* (1951); *Early Spring* (1956); *Tokyo Twilight* (1957); *Good Morning* (1959); *Floating Weeds* (1959); and *An Autumn Afternoon,* released in 1962, the year before Ozu's death on his sixtieth birthday.

Kenji Mizoguchi

Kenji Mizoguchi's (1898–1956) prolific film career began in 1922 with *Resurrection of Love,* the first of more than ninety motion pictures directed over a thirty-five-year period. Like Ozu, Mizoguchi chose themes that were distinctly Japanese in inspiration and similarly was able to develop an individually styled body of films while working in a highly commercial-minded industry.

Typical of the Mizoguchi style are two films made nearly twenty years apart: *The Sisters of Gion* (1936) and *Ugetsu* (1953). In both instances the principal focus remains on female-male relationships and conflict generated by personal ambition.

Two women who are geisha in the city of Kyoto serve as prototypes in *The Sisters of Gion,* a classic study of traditional values pressed by individual interests. The traditional "sister" (a familiar name used by geisha of the same house) feels dutybound to her male patron, even when he can no longer support her. A younger "sister," modern and exploitative, uses her profession entirely for selfish interests and regards the traditional geisha as foolishly naive. Mizoguchi presents the opposing positions without offering a solution.

Cinematic style in *The Sisters of Gion* is remarkably reserved. To maintain environmental awareness and character relationships without editorial intervention, long camera takes dominate filming of scenes. Only an occasional tracking shot (for psychological emphasis) interrupts the sustained set-ups. Psychological mood is enhanced by the film's high-contrast black-and-white images. Scenes are often bridged by pictorial cutaway shots to a river or a street to suggest the larger, on-going world in which the two sisters' drama is unfolding, a stylistic trait also evident in Ozu's films and related to the Buddhist belief that one person's story is only a minute, transient detail of existence.

Ugetsu (1953) moved back in time to the sixteenth century and stories of two peasants who leave their wives and families to satisfy personal ambitions: one seeking to achieve great wealth and the other to become an honored samurai warrior. Parallel accounts of the adventure-some men and their abandoned wives' fates express Mizoguchi's interest in women's position in Japanese society. One wife is violently murdered; the other, after being raped, turns to prostitution. Eventually the two men return to their senses and their villages (the wealth-seeker to live with his dead wife's ghost).

Mizoguchi, a painter before becoming a filmmaker, used *Ugetsu's*

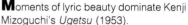
Moments of lyric beauty dominate Kenji Mizoguchi's *Ugetsu* (1953).

jidai-geki ("period film") possibilities to display his skill at atmospheric story-telling. Images are formally composed and theatrically beautiful in lighting, setting, and costume design. At times pictorial imagery is stylized to a point of self-consciouss enhancement—an effect which adds to the spiritual and emotional tenor that transforms *Ugetsu's* feudal story into an imaginative, heightened experience rather than documentary reality. Because of this stylistic quality, which is so vividly compatible with Japan's artistic traditions, *Ugetsu* is often labeled as the nation's supreme cinematic achievement. *Sansho the Bailiff* (1954), one of Mizoguchi's last films, also turned ancient legend into near mystical visualization.

Akira Kurosawa

The arrival of Akira Kurosawa (1910–) as an energetic, style-conscious director occurred during World War II when Japanese censors demanded nationalistic themes; consequently his first film, *Judo Saga* (1943), told the story of a judo expert's rise to fame with an appropriate mixture of physical and spiritual fervor suitable for the times. Occupation forces later noted Kurosawa's apparent "militaristic" stance and destroyed prints of the film.

Kurosawa was well established in Japan when *Rashomon* (1950), his twelfth film, brought unexpected world acclaim through its triumph at Venice in 1951. His achievement gave indication that Japanese cinema had rebounded from wartime constraints and was ready to display its mature, brilliantly styled, and philosophical films for all to appreciate.

Rashomon *Rashomon* was as startlingly complex in concept and structure as it was exotic to Western audiences unfamiliar with Japan's period films. Its narrative, set in medieval times, repeats four accounts of a rape and murder (suicide?). The incident in factual detail involves a merchant (Masayuki Mori) and his beautiful wife (Machiko Kyo) who are attacked by a bandit (Toshiro Mifune) as the couple travels by horseback through a dense forest. Tricked by the bandit, the merchant is tied helplessly to the ground, his wife seduced, followed by a sword fight between the two men in which the merchant is killed. The bandit flees with the couple's horse.

The four "flashback" accounts of this incident develop as three men, curious about the incident, huddle under a crumbling Kyoto gatehouse during a rainstorm. As they sort out rumors, one of the men, a wood cutter who claims to have witnessed the event, introduces the stories. Each is presented by the vagrants as though they are offering court testimony. Subjective, self-serving perspectives unfold as the dead merchant (using a medium), his wife, the bandit, and finally the woodcutter "remember" the rape-murder. Each version is revisualized by Kurosawa's camera with circumstances altered slightly to depict individual interpretations.

The merchant maintains that his wife willingly gave in to the bandit and then sought her husband's death. It is implied through the medium that the husband took his own life.

The wife professes innocence, viewing herself as forever debased and no longer acceptable to her husband. When she awakes from a faint, she claims to have found her own dagger in the dead husband's breast.

In the bandit's account the wife readily acquiesces and he kills the angry merchant during an "honorable" sword fight for the woman's favor.

The woodcutter's version reveals the wife freeing her bound

In the bandit's version of the crime in *Rashomon* (1950) the wife attempts to protect herself with a tiny dagger, but her resistance only excites the man more. The bound husband observes in the background.

husband and pleading that he avenge her rape. Both men fight reluctantly and ungracefully until the bandit finally kills the merchant. This more realistic, straightforward rendering of details (presented without the colorful background music that accompanied the others) seems to give the woodcutter's story greatest credibility. The woodcutter's story becomes suspect, however, with the revelation that he stole the merchant's dagger following his death.

Rashomon's mosaic narrative lends itself to limitless possibilities of interpretation. Issues are raised by the contradictory testimony that place the very nature of perceived reality under philosophical scrutiny. The notion that individual "truth" suffers when strained by guilt also appears relevant in interpreting Kurosawa's fractured story. Significant, too, is the manner by which *Rashomon* unveils the idea that artistic (filmic) versions of reality are, like human accounts, illusory and subjective. Contradictions and ambiguities abound in art as in life.

Equally important are the film's spiritual dimensions and Kurosawa's questioning of the universal goodness (or badness) of humankind. The final scene in which the woodcutter offers protection to an abandoned baby suggests a reaffirmation. Amidst the ruins of the depressed city, a priest commends the woodcutter for his kindness, saying: "I have regained my faith in men."

Other Masterpieces *Rashomon's* popular success was followed by other important films that showed Kurosawa's diversity in a wide range of subjects. Moving between period and contemporary stories (*gendai-geki*), he brought forth the notable *Ikiru* (1952), *The Seven Samurai* (1954), *The Bad Sleep Well* (1960), *Yojimbo* (1961), and *Dodes'ka-den* (1970), among other popular works.

Ikiru/To Live and *The Bad Sleep Well* contained themes developed in modern settings. *Ikiru's* eloquent account of a terminally ill bureaucrat (Takashi Shimura), who acts to achieve social usefulness before his death, is sentimental and humanistic in effect. Presented in two parts, the first section recounts the bureaucrat's efforts at personal redemption by leading the successful campaign for a children's playground; the second part, following the civil servant's death, shows fellow civil-service officials quibbling over the value of the project and debating who should receive credit for it. An ironic view of bureaucratic insensitivity is humorously, but pointedly, developed by this juxtaposition of narrative elements.

In *The Bad Sleep Well* Kurosawa presents a gripping detective story with moral relevance. A young executive, convinced that his father has been murdered for personal gain, is compulsively driven to discover the truth and in his efforts creates tragic consequences for himself and his family.

Kurosawa's fascination with great fiction resulted in the screen adaptations of Gorki's *The Lower Depths*, and in *Throne of Blood* (a rendering of Shakespeare's *Macbeth*). These dark, violent stories also fit a career-long concern for characters in a state of moral and spiritual crisis. Each of these efforts was appropriately stylized for compatibility with their Japanese settings. *Throne of Blood* freely incorporated lyrical elements of the classical Noh form, including extensive use of mime to convey well-known Shakespearean passages.

Samurai Films A great lover of action, Kurosawa achieved some of his widest popularity with period films that examined value systems through the traditions of samurai warriors. *The Seven Samurai* and *Yojimbo* are classic representatives of this category, revealing Kurosawa's gift for screen spectacle and intense action to be equal in power to his trenchant social dramas.

The epic *Seven Samurai* recalls a warring period in sixteenth-century Japan and the efforts by peasant villagers to protect themselves by engaging professional soldiers *(ronin)* in defense against invading bandits. The plot is derived from the absorption of the seven chosen defenders into village life and from the exciting series of battles they must wage before achieving total victory.

Three and one-half hours long in its original version, *The Seven Samurai* sustains interest through its fully dimensioned, fascinating characters and through its brilliant visualization of the action sequences. Well-known character portraits add nobility to the battle scenes, while implying the value of cooperation and personal courage in times of societal upheaval.

Natural elements enhance the epic realism of *The Seven Samurai* (1954).

Pictorial compositions supply additional grandeur. Kurosawa's camera is continually exploring landscape and environmental elements with atmospheric effect. The final battle scene is photographed in a driving rainstorm. To allow greater visual variety in editing of the action sequences, scenes were filmed in multicamera setups. The result was a striking combination of deep-focus shots and shots filmed at extreme close range, shots taken from varied dramatic angles, some at normal sound speed and some filmed in slow motion—all serving to heighten the drama.

Also evident in *The Seven Samurai* is Kurosawa's skill in directing actors. The intense characterizations are each individualistic and humanly realized. Toshiro Mifune's performance as the seventh samurai offers an engrossing combination of humor, compassion, and simple strength. Kurosawa's real achievement, however, came from the remarkable sense of ensemble acting rather than single performances.

Yojimbo (1961), the second of Kurosawa's great samurai films, rivaled *The Seven Samurai* in popularity. Often compared with the American western, particularly personal-courage action films such as *Shane* and *High Noon, Yojimbo (The Bodyguard)* has Toshiro Mifune, a down-and-out samurai swordsman, arriving in a small town divided by feuds and straightening things out with an incredible and hilarious display of personal might. Again, the action is visually varied and exciting in pace.

Kurosawa's influence on American directors and his general importance as a storyteller were confirmed by outside versions of *Rashomon* (*The Outrage,* American, 1964), *The Seven Samurai* (*The Magnificent Seven,* American, 1960), and *Yojimbo* (*A Fistful of Dollars,* 1964, produced in Italy with Clint Eastwood). None of the imitations, however, contain Kurosawa's magic.

Later work in the 1970s, e.g., *Dodes'ka-den* (1970) and *Dersu Uzala* (1975) reveal imaginative screen studies of modern characters in a state of personal turmoil. *Kagemusha* (1980) returns to the sixteenth century and a period-action tale of character deception and growth.

Prominent Contemporaries

Among the other outstanding Japanese directors to receive world-wide attention in the 1950s and 1960s were Kon Ichikawa and Hiroshi Teshigahara. Ichikawa's *The Burmese Harp* (1956) was notable for its pacifist stance in a sentimental story about the travesties of war. A young Japanese soldier-harpist wanders through Burma at the end of World War II, anguished by what he sees. Spiritual conversion causes him to remain and bury his dead countrymen rather than return home with his unit. Ichikawa's images are poetically beautiful and the musical score unabashedly emotional.

Masaki Kobayashi also gained importance as a Japanese director of strong social consciousness. His best-known films, *The Human Condition*

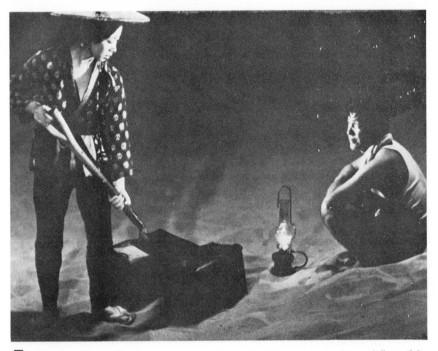

Eiji Okada observes Kyoko Kishoda, the "woman of the dunes" whose daily activity consists primarily of moving sand. Their lives together eventually merge in textured harmony with the environment.

trilogy (1959–1961) and *Hara-kiri* (1962) attack the violent impulses that lead to war and personal vendettas. *Hara-kiri*, a period film of samurai inspiration, exposes damaging codes of conduct which Kobayashi saw as relevant to on-going Japanese culture. An aging samurai swordsman seeks to avenge the deaths of family members by a staged suicide in the presence of samurai peers. His action, told in real time, leads to personal catharsis and repulsion for a system in which he has been a dedicated participant. William Wellman's *The Ox-Bow Incident* (1943) had similar intentions by showing how accepted codes of the old West can unjustly victimize.

Women of the Dunes (1964) created a sensation when shown at the 1965 New York Film Festival and established Hiroshi Teshigahara as a director with great talent for allegorical, philosophical filmmaking. The film treats the story (from Kobo Abe's novel) of a man who, after being trapped in a desert sand pit, is forced to adapt to the lifestyle of the woman who resides there. His efforts to chart the life cycle of a rare desert insect are thwarted, but the man soon sheds his worldly ambitions for the peace and serenity offered by uncomplicated life in the dunes. Teshigahara's reduction of conditions to a primitive state comes through well-ordered pacing, sustained mood, and graphic visual detail. Expressive black-and-white images capture the texture of the environment and reveal its elemental, symbolic power. Teshigahara's film is, on the surface, simple—on reflection, deeply complex.

Shiro Toyoda became a highly regarded translator of Japanese fiction with such films as *The Mistress* (1953, from Ogai Mori's novel, *Gan*), and *A Cat, Two Women,* and *One Man* (1956, based on the novel by Junchiro Tanizaki). The majority of Toyoda's screen work is light-hearted but humanistically revealing. In *The Mistress* a young woman (Hideko Takamine) bears without remorse her role as mistress to an older man and the lost chance for the love of a young medical student.

Nagisa Oshima's films, *The Sun's Burial* (1959), *The Catch* (1961), *Double Suicide* (1967), *Boy* (1969), *The Ceremony* (1971), and *In the Realm of the Senses* (1976) have been characterized by outrageous, sometimes perverse, views of modern Japan. *The Ceremony* presents a variety of recognizable society figures (criminals, political prototypes, the common), with the values they hold being revealed during a succession of family ceremonies. The film's microcosmic intentions are charged by a mixture of psychological and political finger-pointing that made Oshima one of Japan's boldest directors.

Commercial films in Japan after 1960 drew heavily on anamorphic, wide-screen processes, initially to give impact to the dominant action film, but soon well used by directors at large. Color, once resisted by serious directors, also found wide acceptance.

Among the extensive range of Japanese film styles, genres, and themes are common qualities: the important regard for expressive imagery in carrying dramatic ideas; the formal use of camera; stylization of dramatic action; serious philosophical approaches to subject matter; sensitivity to the human condition and traditional values. Together these qualities represent distinguished national achievement of the highest order.

INDIA: SATYAJIT RAY

India's best-known film director, Satyajit Ray (1921–   ), achieved international acclaim with a motion-picture trilogy based on the popular Bengali novel, *Pather Panchali,* written by Bhibuti Bannerjee. The three parts, *Pather Panchali (On the Road,* 1955), *Aparajito (The Unvanquished,* 1956), and *Apur Sansar (The World of Apu,* 1959), were Ray's first efforts at filmmaking after years of observing motion pictures as a devoted cinèaste. Highly impressed by De Sica's *The Bicycle Thief* and inspired by Jean Renoir's encouragement after the French master went to India to film *The River* in 1950, Ray decided to undertake the Bannerjee novel.

After nearly four years of scraping together funds and weekend shooting sessions with a nonprofessional cast, the first part of *Pather Panchali* was released. The film's sensitivity in treating the way of life for

Ray's *The World of Apu* expresses India's sometimes painful progress toward change and modernity in a single image: a closeup of Apu's country wife (Sharmila Tagore) gazing tearfully upon Calcutta from a window in the couple's apartment.

a simple Bengali family, supported by a neorealistic, near-documentary look, attracted admirers wherever Ray's work was shown. Critical success at the 1956 Cannes Film Festival gave Ray the encouragement (and financial assistance) needed to complete the remaining parts.

The film trilogy presents the continuing story of Apu and his family from the time the boy is seven years of age until he reaches young adulthood. The first part is ethnographic in quality as Ray depicts the native customs, family rites, and needs of the five-member Bengali family. In the second part Apu's characterization is further developed for dramatic effect as he struggles with his mother's wishes that he become a scientist and his own instincts to become a creative writer. Part three places Apu in Calcutta where he is idly serving his apprenticeship to life and a writing career. A tragic marriage forces his initiation into the painful realities of human experience.

The Apu trilogy offers a tender account of progress from innocence to knowledge, presented within well-defined and telling social settings. Its character study also holds metaphorical implications for a traditional India moving toward new challenges as a modern, independent nation.

Ray's directorial style is strikingly simple yet masterful. His neorealistic observation of life carries the best qualities of that filmic style: humane, philosophical, quietly revealing film expression. Ray also can, when suitable, employ Eisensteinian editing to suggest abstract or mental concepts. A suicide wish in *The World of Apu* is constructed through montage methods associated with Russian filmmakers of the

1920s. A strong sensibility for effective composition and for use of music to underscore mood and tension are other Ray qualities.

In addition to the Apu trilogy, Ray's important work includes *The Music Room* (1958), *Devi* (1960), *Charulata* (1964), and *The Chess Game* (1977). He has remained the only filmmaker in India whose work has been widely distributed outside the country.

ACTIVITY IN GERMANY AND AUSTRALIA

Carrying the tradition of spirited national cinema into the late 1970s and early eighties was important new work from Germany and Australia.

Germany

The German revival was led by Rainer Fassbinder, Werner Herzog, Alexander Kluge, Volker Schlöndorff, and Wim Wenders—all of whom embarked on directing careers in the 1960s when audience interest in cinema was still largely dormant in West Germany. By 1975 each had established domestic and international reputations; new audience receptivity was also evident by that time as German filmgoers responded favorably to the provocative motion pictures being turned out by both feature and avant-garde directors.

Fassbinder has been the most productive of Germany's new generation directors, often releasing as many as five motion pictures a year. Among his most widely seen works are *Mother Kusters Goes to Heaven* (1975) and *The Marriage of Maria Braun* (1979). A woman involved in a tense, passionate drama serves as the principal character in each case, a

Maria Braun (Hanna Schygulla) is a character who is simultaneously hardened and enticing. Fassbinder draws parallels between the woman's determination and Germany's own economic recovery after World War II.

A tin drum and a lad who refuses to grow up are primary symbols in Schlöndorff's allegorical study of indifference and chaos in Nazi Germany.

creature struggling to survive at all costs after the loss of a husband. Fassbinder's character studies always carry social implications. Maria Braun's wily ways of surviving suggest parallels with the economic drive that catapulted Germany back to prosperity during the late forties and early fifties.

Werner Herzog's best-known films, *Even Dwarfs Started Small* (1970), *Aguirre, Wrath of God* (1973), and *Nosferatu* (1979) display imaginative imagery in tales with extraordinary plots. *Even Dwarfs Started Small* depicts dwarfs, isolated on an island, in rebellion; *Aguirre, Wrath of God* chronicles the increasing madness of a man in search of El Dorado during the sixteenth century; *Nosferatu* recreates the famous German tale of a vampire who preys on the weak. Through these unusual, removed stories Herzog is able to offer telling new perspectives on the human condition.

Volker Schlöndorff first called attention to his directing talents in *Young Törless* (1966), a stark adapatation of Musil's novel about the effects of sadistic activity on a lad in a military boarding-school. As an Academy Award winner, *The Tin Drum* (1978), brought Schlöndorff new acclaim with its provocative rendering of the Günther Grass novel. The long, epic film offered an allegorical story of a 3-year-old boy who, after observing the ways of the adult world, decides to stunt his growth (through an act of will) so he will remain forever a child. Schlöndorff proves himself an evocative craftsman in *The Tin Drum*. Like the best of earlier German cinema, the mood of the film is starkly expressionistic and the camera work often subjective in depicting the bizarre world at hand. Evil appears to be everywhere.

Wenders' works, e.g., *Alice in the Cities* (1974) and *Kings of the Road*

Three Australian soldiers on trial in South Africa during the Boer War are the subjects of Bruce Beresford's thematically rich *Breaker Morant* (1980). The film serves as a statement for Australian nationalism, points up the moral discrepancies of war, and offers a poetic view of the human spirit in times of trial.

(1976), invariably place characters on an extensive journey that reveals social conditions in a naturalistic and satirical manner. Dialogue is kept to a minimum while contemporary popular music is allowed to dominate the sound track.

The activity of these directors turned attention once more to Germany's long-standing appreciation of the diverse and serious possibilities for cinematic expression.

Australia

The creation in 1971 of the Australian Film Development Corporation (later the Australian Film Commission) lifted in a single decade the Australian film industry from obscurity into international prominence. Created to subsidize and promote home production, the Commission spurred an impressive body of films that received worldwide distribution and acclaim, including: *Picnic at Hanging Rock* (1975), *The Last Wave* (1977), *Newsfront* (1978), *The Chant of Jimmy Blacksmith* (1978), *My Brilliant Career* (1979), *Breaker Morant* (1980), and *Caddie* (1980).

Style and theme in these efforts are diverse, ranging from Peter

Weir's mystery fantasy *Picnic at Hanging Rock* (depicting the disappearance of a group of schoolgirls) to the probing social analysis in Fred Schepisi's *The Chant of Jimmie Blacksmith,* an account of racial attitudes in Australia as viewed through reactions to a man who is half white, half aborigine.

My Brilliant Career, directed by Gillian Armstrong, is a beautifully photographed and charming character study of an independent-minded young woman living in Australia at the turn of the century. Bruce Beresford's *Breaker Morant* is a study of a miscarriage of military justice during the Boer War, and *Caddie,* the work of Donald Crombie, presents an appealing story of a barmaid in Sydney during the Depression.

A distinctive national quality and vivid imagery distinguish many of the outstanding Australian films. The directors have found in the country's past both pleasure and displeasure and, consequently, have tended to set their films at the turn of the century when many Australians still lived within the social sphere of British tradition, while struggling to break away. The impact of this move toward individuality, juxtaposed against Australia's sprawling open landscapes, resulted in cinematic works of unusual tension and beauty.

SUGGESTED READINGS

Barnouw, Erik, and S. Krishnaswamy. *Indian Film.* New York: Columbia University Press, 1963.

Baxter, John. *The Australian Cinema.* Sydney: Pacific Books, 1970.

Cowie, Peter. *Sweden I and II.* 2 vols. New York: Barnes, 1970.

Donner, Jorn. *The Personal Vision of Ingmar Bergman.* Bloomington: Indiana University Press, 1964.

Richie, Donald. *The Films of Akira Kurosawa.* Berkeley: University of California Press, 1965.

———. *Japanese Cinema: Film Style and National Character.* Garden City, N.Y.: Doubleday, 1971.

———. *Ozu.* Berkeley: University of California Press, 1973.

Wood, Robin. *The Apu Trilogy.* New York: Praeger, 1977.

———. *Ingmar Bergman.* New York: Praeger, 1969.

THE STRAINS OF
CONTEMPORARY
AMERICAN CINEMA

The real drama of *Apocalypse Now* . . . is not the meeting of Willard and Kurtz—which is neither faithful to Conrad nor the least bit appropriate to the Vietnam War—but the saga of getting the movie made. In the personalized calculus of the new movie culture, with director as superstar and moviemaking as the height of creative aspiration, the sufferings of Coppola and company easily dwarf the agonies of the Vietnam War. Obsessed with his subject, the director, like Napoleon in Russia, finally displaces it and becomes obsessed with his own obsession.

The schizoid quality of *Apocalypse Now*—part genre film, part surreal personal testament—is an especially revealing paradigm of the split within younger filmmakers in the seventies. Like the French New Wave directors from whom they learned so much, they alternate between wanting to make great big versions of the films they grew up on and looking to far more problematic and unusual projects that could never have been made thirty years ago.

Morris Dickstein, American Film, December 1979.

Apocalypse Now.

By the mid-sixties Hollywood was a vastly different place than it had been two decades earlier. Many of the large studios were experiencing serious financial difficulties, most prominently Paramount which was bought by Gulf and Western in 1966 and Metro-Goldwyn-Mayer which had to sell property to stay afloat. Columbia and Universal were concentrating heavily on the production of filmed materials for television. Warner Brothers was devoting itself almost entirely to the support of carefully selected independent projects.

The sorting out of important artists and major trends in American cinema after 1965 reveals a fascinating interplay among societal conditions, industrial struggle, and personal endeavor. The interaction helps define the motion picture's immediate past and hints at the uncertain future of the medium.

AUDIENCE TRANSITION

The 1960s was a troubled decade which saw numerous American theaters closing their doors and hundreds of Hollywood personnel being added to unemployment rolls. Increasingly, tell-tale signs of audience preferences became difficult to ascertain. Trends begun in the fifties carried over only briefly into the new decade: successful Broadway plays remained popular sources of screen material, e.g., *Sunrise at Campobello* and *Inherit the Wind* in 1960, and *A Raisin in the Sun* and *West Side Story* in 1961; experimentation with sexual candor continued in *The Apartment* (1960) and *Splendor in the Grass* (1961); the big novel still provided popular material for cinematic treatment in 1960, e.g., *Exodus*

A revealing sign of an industry in trouble.

and *Elmer Gantry*. All these works offered mass entertainment in conventional form and all were commercially successful on a broad-scale basis.

By the middle sixties, however, discernible signs of audience response to available fare pointed in new directions. *The New York Times* critic Bosley Crowther included only three American-made films on his 1966 list of "Ten Best Pictures of the Year": *The Russians Are Coming, The Russians Are Coming, Who's Afraid of Virginia Woolf?* and *A Man for All Seasons.* The remaining seven choices were provocative works from abroad: *Dear John* (Lars Magnus Lindgren, Sweden), *The Shop on Main Street* (Jan Kadar/Elmar Klos, Czechoslovakia), *The Gospel According to St. Matthew* (Pier Paolo Pasolini, Italy), *Morgan* (Karel Reisz, Britain), *Loves of a Blonde* (Milos Forman, Czechoslovakia), *Georgy Girl* (Silvio Narizzano, Britain), *Blow-Up* (Michelangelo Antonioni, Italian-British made).

These selections were those of a single observer of motion-picture art, but they reflect the inroads that had been made by foreign films into the American market. Discriminating filmgoers, especially college students whose love affair with the motion picture continued to grow throughout the decade, were echoing Crowther's approval with their box office patronage. The support given by the young to these films and the simultaneous failure of many of Hollywood's mass-market efforts, e.g., *Doctor Doolittle* (1967), and *Star* (1967), seemed to suggest that the country's most dependable audience was made up of the committed cinéaste and the young.

Youthful Enterprise

This assumption was reinforced by the remarkable success of a number of youth-oriented films that arrived just as the decade was drawing to a close. In 1967 Mike Nichols' *The Graduate,* a seriocomic study of youth malaise in an affluent American family, scored critically and commercially, establishing itself as one of the most popular Hollywood films ever made. Ben Braddock (Dustin Hoffman) cannot motivate himself to enter the mainstream of American life as envisioned by his middle-class parents. The hero's perceptions of his environment are cleverly conveyed through an impressionistic use of camera while the script's dialogue and treatment of sex possess a strong contemporary flavor. This urbane approach to the theme of youth alienation and uncertainty was the source of the film's wide acceptance by the young.

The incorporation of an LP-length set of songs (by Simon and Garfunkel) into *The Graduate's* sound track was another factor contributing to Nichols' resounding success. Audiences were able to listen to a full record album of popular music while also enjoying a film—an innovation of significance at a time when young Americans were just beginning to prove themselves a generation of entertainment consumers. This trend, which accelerated throughout the seventies, prompted many of

the major American film companies to develop music subsidiaries as part of their expanding conglomerate enterprises.

Rock Documentaries Music continued to play an important role in the film experience, both as a critical element of the sound track and as the inspiration for individual works designed to reach young audiences. The year after *The Graduate's* release, 1968, brought *Monterey Pop,* the first of a series of rock documentaries which depicted on film popular musical performances in vast outdoor settings. D. A. Pennebaker's film offered lengthy musical segments as well as an extensive treatment of the throngs of young people who attended a rock concert in Monterey, California. Verité and direct-cinema filming techniques were combined with crosscutting between performers and audience to create a spirited record of youth culture at the time.

Monterey Pop's success led to other similarly styled displays of musical happenings, most notably Michael Wadleigh's *Woodstock* (1970), Albert and David Maysles/Charlotte Zwerin's *Gimme Shelter* (1970), and Pennebaker's *Keep on Rockin'* (1973). *Woodstock* received critical as well as popular attention and was awarded an Academy Award as Best Feature Documentary Film of 1970. Its huge profits also proved to be a financial boon to the troubled Warner Brothers' studio which distributed the film.

Counterculture Films The cultural reflection within the rock documentary and *The Graduate* hinted at a widening generation gap and a youth mood commensurate with the late sixties. Two other important films that followed extended screen treatment of restless young people questioning established moral and political values: *Easy Rider* (1969) and *Five Easy Pieces* (1970). The protagonists of these works are antiheroes, alienated from society and drifting through life without any commitment beyond the search for self-liberation. The settings through which the characters travel provide a social barometer for assaying contemporary American life.

In *Easy Rider* two long-haired young men, Billy (Dennis Hopper) and Wyatt (Peter Fonda), take to the road on their motorcycles to try to understand the country in which they live. Their journey exposes them to the drug scene, to others who are disillusioned, including an alcoholic lawyer (Jack Nicholson), and ultimately to the violence of antagonistic bigots. In keeping with cinematic trends, a pastiche of popular and rock songs appears on the sound track as lyrical accompaniment to the odyssey. Dennis Hopper received the Cannes Film Festival prize for direction by a newcomer.

Disaffection with American life is expressed in *Five Easy Pieces* through Bobby Dupea (Jack Nicholson)—a classically trained musician who has chosen to deny his auspicious beginnings by wandering about as a hard-hat laborer. Dupea's negative attitude is expressed virulently when he says to a fellow worker: "You keep telling me about the good life! It makes me puke." Called home to visit his father who has suffered a stroke, Dupea admits his shortcomings in a confession that can receive no reply from his paralyzed father. The failure of communication between generations finds a vivid metaphor in this poignant scene, staged with Dupea and his mute father alone on a stark beach of Washington's Puget Sound. Dupea's personal catharsis, however, does not alter his desire to keep moving.

For the film's sound track director Bob Rafelson found country-western singer Tammy Wynette's melancholic lyrics suitable accompaniment for Dupea's picaresque way of life.

Easy Rider and *Five Easy Pieces* offered through their drop-out characters romantically engaging views of youth cynicism that was

Jack Nicholson portrays a drifter in *Five Easy Pieces* (1970), a lyrical study of the counterculture antihero of the 1960s.

assumed to be a result of unalterable American politics. Bitter racial upheaval within the country and involvement in Vietnam had moved students to agitate for social-political change while simultaneously bringing a commitment to lifestyles opposed to the perceived norms of the society. The rebellion, mythically, was expressed through long hair, unconventional clothing, 'free" personal conduct, and a disposition toward love as an immediate means of countering the country's failures. According to the myth, individual freedom—wrenched from a restrictive society—compelled the disaffected young.

It is this idea that is rendered poetically in *Easy Rider* and *Five Easy Pieces*. The characters' cynicism forces them to the road—a familiar cinematic metaphor for uncertain new beginnings, e.g., the Joads of John Ford's *Grapes of Wrath* (1940). In the case of *Easy Rider* and *Five Easy Pieces*, however, the journey is movement away from commitment rather than toward it. Bobby Dupea says: "I move around a lot—not because I'm looking for anything really—but because I'm getting away from things that get bad if I stay."

The screen's antihero drifter, drawn against the passing American landscape with its inconsiderate waitresses *(Five Easy Pieces)* and deadly rednecks *(Easy Rider),* embodied feelings that many filmgoers found to be meaningful reflections of a generation in spiritual crisis.

More Contemporary Issues Disaffection with the establishment did not always center solely on the personal freedom issue. Other variations of the theme sought to analyze specific societal failures and to ponder methods of change. Arthur Penn's *Alice's Restaurant* (1969) dealt with youth rebellion in light-hearted terms, depicting dropouts in an experimental search for companionship which would support their new way of life. A ballad by Arlo Guthrie satirically pointed out the difficulties of the quest.

Haskell Wexler's *Medium Cool* (1969) and Stuart Rosenberg's *WUSA* (1970) both presented media news reporters torn between personal values and the hypocritical methods of the broadcast companies for which they work. In each case the hero's crisis is related to contemporary issues: in *Medium Cool* to the Chicago youth riots of 1968 and in *WUSA* to opportunism in the guise of patriotic causes.

VIOLENCE: HEROES AND MORE ANTIHEROES

Bonnie and Clyde (1967) has been justifiably linked with the countercultural youth film. Its drifting characters are people whose behavior can be viewed in part as a response to larger social injustices within the milieu. But *Bonnie and Clyde* portended more than an innovative commentary on societal disaffection. Arthur Penn's psychologically

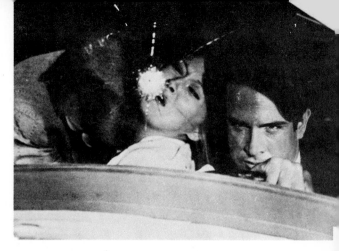

A sense of adventure pervades the early parts of *Bonnie and Clyde* (1967), but as the film progresses the violence turns increasingly graphic and brutal.

based treatment of the violent impulse was constructed with a blend of frolic, horror, and nostalgia that left filmgoers and critics startled and excited.

The action drew on the lives of small-time gangsters during the American Depression, the Barrow gang, a subject treated by filmmakers before: *Gun Crazy* (1949) and *The Bonnie Parker Story* (1958). It was the glamorization of Penn's account and the sentiment generated for his characters that provoked debate about the film's ultimate value. Intimations that society was to blame for the gangster's wayward lives had long existed as a plotting element of the genre; but *Bonnie and Clyde* had been romanticized to an uncommon degree and the violent outbursts treated with farcical abandonment. Lester Flatt and Earl Scruggs' rollicking banjo music on the sound track appeared to belie the horror of the bloodbaths and the deadly chases. Adding to the film's nostalgic tone were soft coloring, evocative filtering, and smart costumes (Faye Dunaway's well-tailored period outfits influenced women's clothing styles during the late sixties).

Penn's folk-hero treatment of societal misfits and his poetic rendering of violence left an indelible mark on developing American cinema. The effort brought focus to a new wave of violence-based motion pictures which in 1967 suddenly seemed to be coming from every direction.

Clint Eastwood

Of more than casual importance was the 1967 arrival from Italy of a trio of Clint Eastwood (1930–   )–Sergio Leone (1921–   ) westerns: *A Fistful of Dollars* (1964), *For a Few Dollars More* (1965), and *The Good, the Bad and the Ugly* (1966). Already internationally successful, these "spaghetti westerns," which Leone produced and in which Eastwood starred

"Dirty Harry," the tainted law-and-order hero.

as an uncompromising, anonymous hero, won American audiences with their tough, hard-hitting display of action.

Eastwood's popularity brought him back to the United States where he teamed with Don Siegel (1912–   ), a seasoned director of action films, for *Coogan's Bluff* (1968). The story offered a violent variation on the western, set primarily in contemporary New York City where Eastwood is an Arizona sheriff tracking an escaped prisoner.

With this entry into American-styled violence, Eastwood launched a series of mythic action thrillers which alternately located him in western and modern settings, always as the loner who unabashedly uses guns to correct injustices.

Don Siegel's *Dirty Harry* (1971) was the first of a trilogy of graphically violent films in which Eastwood portrayed the police officer, Harry Callahan, a law enforcer who, according to advertisements for the film, doesn't "just break cases. He smashes them." Callahan's character is essentially that of the slightly tainted western hero: a mechanical killer on the side of the law who devises his own rules in order to complete a job. Early in *Dirty Harry,* for example, Callahan is accused of shooting his victims in the back (one of many brazen acts which have earned him the nickname "Dirty Harry"). Callahan's bravura is established in a fiery opening scene in which he singlehandedly aborts a bank robbery. Plotting then engages him in the task of tracking down a ruthless murderer, "Scorpio," who is terrorizing the city of San Francisco. Alone, fearlessly, Callahan succeeds.

This mythic pattern is repeated in the two sequels which followed:

Magnum Force (1973) and *The Enforcer* (1976). Psychopathic killers, clandestinely at work in a large urban setting, cannot be suppressed by the police force at large and prompt Callahan's deadly reprisals. The line between the instincts of protagonist and antagonist remains a fine one—an essential requirement of the genre.

Eastwood's role as a hero of moral contradictions extended into western settings in *Joe Kidd* (1972), *High Plains Drifter* (1973), and *The Outlaw Josey Wales* (1976). The visualization of violence in these works is characteristically sensational, the impact of the action sequences a visceral account of human slaughter. In various polls taken during the seventies Eastwood was declared the world's most popular film actor, testimony to the success of his tough, expressionless screen persona.

Sam Peckinpah

Ritualistic treatment of violence characterized the film work of Sam Peckinpah (1926–   ), a director whose vision in *The Wild Bunch* (1969) controversially suggested a legendary, nostalgic interpretation of bandit life. Bloodbaths and human slaughter are offered as the outlaw's final, self-destructive response to a rapidly vanishing era. Set in revolutionary Mexico in 1913, Peckinpah's world seems devoid of human goodness with children as well as adults unperturbed by the brutal violence that surrounds them. An atmospheric rendering of locations via Lucien Ballard's cinematography aids the nostalgic toning. As in *Bonnie and Clyde* violent death is stylized with slow-motion recordings and quick-cut editing. Even so the rampant and graphic bloodlettings reveal the western antihero at an insensate extreme.

Peckinpah's *Straw Dogs* (1971) viewed violence as a condition of

In Peckinpah's *Straw Dogs* (1971) violence becomes a ritual of self-completion.

During the Sicilian sequence of *The Godfather* (1972) Michael (Al Pacino) discovers that it is impossible to hide from the explosive terror of the underworld.

survival and completeness. In the archetypal manner of Conradian novels (e.g., *Victory*), a mathematics teacher (Dustin Hoffman) is drawn out of his quiet isolation in a Cornish village and forced to respond to instinctive urges that begin to surface after the rape of his wife (Susan George). The mathematician's complete reversal from withdrawn gentility to horrific behavior is presented thematically as a passage from innocence to guilt (knowledge) and, thus, personal liberation.

Francis Ford Coppola

Francis Ford Coppola's (1939–   ) screen realization of Mario Puzo's explosive novel *The Godfather* in 1972 placed violence within an epic, romantic framework that made its treatment a commercially palatable boon to Paramount Pictures which was still rebounding from the bleak sixties. In *The Godfather* Coppola mixes family ritual and criminal violence with an equally effective sense of lyric pageantry. An ability to devise dramatic action and to create irony are other notable directorial strengths.

Coppola's cinematic talents are evident, for example, in *The Godfather's* final scene which employs parallel editing to connect a baptismal rite with a "family"–sponsored vendetta occurring elsewhere in the city. "Do you renounce sin?" the priest asks of Michael (Al Pacino), the new "godfather." As he answers "I do," a simultaneous visualization of the bloodletting, ordered by Michael, appears in ironic juxtaposition.

Supporting Coppola's taut direction are Nino Rota's evocative music, Gordon Willis' chiaroscuro images, and a dedicated cast of players headed by Marlon Brando and Pacino. *The Godfather's* romantic view of family life in the underworld drew filmgoers who rarely if ever attended motion pictures and the film broke all box office records. In 1980 it still ranked as one of the five most profitable pictures ever produced.

The Godfather Part Two (1974) continues the Corleone saga through Michael's development from a new young "godfather" into a paranoid American gangster—ruthless and devoid of the family commitments that characterized his father's position as a patriarchal leader of organized crime. Into this modern progression of the narrative, Coppola interweaves a flashback account of the early life of Vito Corleone, the original family don (earlier Brando, now Robert De Niro). The dual treatment provides a dramatic framework for tracing motivational roots of twentieth-century gangsterism. Emerging from the epic romance and pageantry is a brooding, somber view of total character corruption. Coppola received Best Picture Academy Awards for both *The Godfather* and *The Godfather Part Two*.

Antimythic Violence

Not surprisingly, the rapid advancement of graphic violence stirred a public controversy. At the center of the debate was the sympathy engendered for the perpetrators of violent acts—the self-appointed law-and-order enforcers and a whole assortment of likeable, but misguided, lawbreakers. The perennial concern was the relationship of

The Godfather Part Two (1974) revealed in sepia-toned flashbacks the violent rise of Vito Corleone (Robert De Niro) to "godfather" status.

real-life violence to media violence, an issue as old as dramatic performance itself.

In their open treatment of violent material, American filmmakers occasionally veered from the mythic gangster, law-and-order stories into thematic approaches that, while controversial, attempted to examine more objectively the nature of violence and its impulses. Richard Brooks' (1912–   ) *In Cold Blood* (1967) and Martin Scorsese's (1942–   ) *Taxi Driver* (1975), although different in style, made inquiries into violent activity without offering clear-cut resolve.

In Cold Blood presented a journalistically-styled adaptation of Truman Capote's docudrama book about the murders of a Kansas family and the two killers' execution. The story was filmed on location (by Conrad Hall) and used unfamiliar actors (including local residents) to increase authenticity. Brooks' work was both praised and criticized for its objective, unromantic depiction of crime.

Equally controversial was Scorsese's *Taxi Driver,* a violent, grim study of a pathological loner (Robert De Niro) who benignly drives a cab by night but whose mind harbors a growing hostility of the most volatile, dangerous kind. In Paul Schrader's scenario the cab driver is a part of the humdrum life of New York City, a working functionary, and at the same time an individual on the verge of becoming a homicidal killer. At the end of the film the man uses his sharpshooter skills to gun down the inhabitants of a brothel so he can free a runaway teenage girl (Jodie Foster) whom he has taken under his protective wing. It is clear that the hostile release, rewarded by society, is really an innate, psychopathic gesture rather than an act of social benevolence. The film concludes with the disturbing suggestion of future violence from an individual incapable of a normal relationship, a condition further aggravated by the impersonal, big-city environment in which he lives.

Scorsese's study of the violent mind is open-ended, offering neither a solution to the problem nor a moralizing statement about such criminal types. The viewer, however, cannot fail to recognize the presence of such individuals in society or to note the unnerving effectiveness with which the cab driver's personality is dissected.

Taxi Driver offered a striking departure from other contemporary screen treatments of the psychopath, more typically dealt with in the manner of the Dirty Harry trilogy where a heroic figure rises up to suppress societal misfits by pitting violence against violence. The more credible *Taxi Driver* avoids formularized law-and-order conclusiveness, leaving instead a disturbing awareness of the true complexities of dealing with criminal violence.

Scorsese's ability to isolate tough characters in a well-defined social milieu had been demonstrated earlier in *Mean Streets* (1973), an incisive analysis of value struggles within New York's Little Italy.

The tradition of guns and violence in American cinema goes back at

least to *The Great Train Robbery* in 1903 when Porter's half-dozen casual killings in a brief twelve-minute film were considered unduly sensational and shocking. Despite public outcries that were heard then and in more recent times, the American filmmaker's fascination for treating violence on the screen has not diminished.

THE WELL-CRAFTED MELODRAMA, NOSTALGIA, AND COMEDY

While it was assumed by many American producers during the late 1960s that their audience was essentially a young one, there appeared from time to time an occasional, enormously successful big-budget picture which appealed to a broad spectrum of society. The reception of *Lawrence of Arabia* (1962), *Tom Jones* (1963), *Mary Poppins* (1964), *My Fair Lady* (1964), *The Sound of Music* (1965), *Doctor Zhivago* (1965), and the James Bond series suggested that perhaps the mass audience still existed after all. Yet similarly lavish efforts made in the latter half of the decade and aimed for general audiences failed dismally, e.g., *Doctor Doolittle* (1967), *Star* (1967), *Paint Your Wagon* (1969), *Darling Lili* (1969). By 1970 the large-scale escapist film was considered a high-risk commodity.

During the first year of the seventies two successful films of old-style Hollywood fashioning gave hint of things to come: *Love Story* and *Airport*, both released in 1970. *Love Story* was based on Erich Segal's best-selling novel of a doomed love affair between a young couple from different backgrounds (Ali McGraw and Ryan O'Neal).

Airport was a melodramatic account of efforts to land safely a jetliner following a mid-air bomb explosion. Taken from Arthur Hailey's best-selling novel, the film offered a combination of special-effects thrills and a large, diverse cast of characters.

The pivotal importance of these two American films can be verified by the fact that only five motion pictures made prior to their release in 1970 were more successful at the box office: *Gone with the Wind* (1939), *Doctor Zhivago* (1965), *The Sound of Music* (1965), *The Graduate* (1967), and *Butch Cassidy and the Sundance Kid* (1969). Inflated ticket prices were partially responsible for the record-breaking successes of *Airport* and *Love Story,* but only partially. The nature of their content and the wide patronage they received indicated appeals that reached beyond the core youth audience.

Melodrama

Subsequent well-crafted escapist melodramas confirmed that the large-scale film could succeed commercially. *The Poseidon Adventure* (1972) proved to be a widely popular special-effects thriller while once again showing Hollywood's artisans to be unmatched when devoting themselves to the creation of realistic screen make-believe. The film's scenic design called for visualization of a large luxury liner's interior layout, turned upside down after the ship crashes into an underwater iceberg. As in *Airport,* the script presented a diverse group of characters who together comprise a melodramatic tale of broad human interest. Young, old, strong, weak, some romantically inclined, some doomed—the survivors wend their way through the inverted ship toward an escape hatch and possible rescue.

Disaster Films The type of screen fiction represented by *The Poseidon Adventure* found its way into numerous repetitions that soon came to be labeled as "disaster" pictures. In a clear throwback to old studio methods, these films reappropriated action stories, mixed romantic leads with a host of character players, and attempted to impress with their technical virtuosity. Audio-visual sensations underscored the formulaic display of character types chosen to represent all facets and age groups of contemporary society. One studio executive appropriately referred to the trend as the "all-entertainment family package."

The calculated packaging is well illustrated in the *Airport '75* sequel which included in its cast a silent screen star (Gloria Swanson), a popular 1930–1940s screen star (Myrna Loy), a 1950s television star (Sid Caesar), a popular contemporary singer (Helen Reddy), a teenage idol (Linda Blair), a heroic flight attendant (Karen Black), and a *deus ex machina* hero (Charlton Heston).

Karen Black is charged with piloting a disabled jetliner until Heston can be lowered by rope into the cockpit to save both the plane and his faltering relationship with the flight attendant. In the meantime in the cabin: Helen Reddy, disguised as a singing nun, has entertained with her guitar; Gloria Swanson (who ad-libs her own dialogue) has reminisced nostalgically about early film work and airplane rides with Cecil B. De Mille; Sid Caesar has amused as an inebriated buffoon; and discovery of Linda Blair's illness has added urgency to the plane's rescue.

The disaster picture was phenomenally successful in several instances: in the early *Airport* series, *The Poseidon Adventure, Earthquake* (1974), and *The Towering Inferno* (1975). Other efforts attracted large audiences but the margin of profit was considerably less. By the end of the seventies the failure of *Beyond the Poseidon Adventure* (1979) and *The Concorde—Airport '79* (1979) showed the genre in a state of uncertainty.

Monsters Fires, earthquakes, and icebergs were not the only villains conjured up at the time by Hollywood's special-effects artists to impose on the well-being of screen characters. A demon possessed young Linda Blair in William Friedkin's *The Exorcist* (1973) and hidden terror lay beneath the waters in the form of a shark in Steven Spielberg's *Jaws* (1975). Two of the most profitable motion pictures ever made, these films spawned successful sequels and numerous imitations where malevolent beings invade and terrorize the human condition.. Vicious bears (*Grizzly*, 1976), deadly whales (*Orca*, 1977), killer bees (*Swarm*, 1978), and all sorts of demonic spirits (*The Omen*, 1976; *The Amityville Horror*, 1979; *The Fog*, 1980) provoked terror in American audiences, outdrawing at the box office many loftier efforts and proving the horror melodrama one of the most durable mass-appeal stories of the seventies.

The monster melodrama most commonly depersonalized evil by developing terror through subhuman or extraterrestrial forces. A fascinating subcategory of the genre, however, derived well-tailored action/suspense from stories in which an aberrant human mind produces the terror.

Typical of this category were *Two Minute Warning* (1976), *Rollercoaster* (1977), and *Black Sunday* (1977). The common dramatic ingredient is a deranged villain who attempts to vent hostilities in a highly populated public arena (football stadiums, an amusement park). Counterforces discover the potential threat to the unsuspecting crowds and work frantically to locate and intercept the would-be mass killer—succeeding at the last possible moment.

Curiously, the principal villains in both *Rollercoaster* and *Black Sunday* are disturbed Vietnam veterans—left unstable and bitter by their war experiences and seeking to express their anger through public acts of violence. Spectacle, a broad assortment of character types, and climactic, last-minute-rescue crosscutting are other common elements of this type of screen melodrama.

To add aural sensation to its story, *Rollercoaster* included Sensurround, a special-effects sound system introduced by Universal two years earlier in *Earthquake*. The system utilized special speakers, strategically placed throughout the theater auditorium, and low-frequency, infrasonic sound vibrations to create a feeling of physical movement. The device accompanied only selected scenes (earthquake tremors, rollercoaster rides), offering a special-effects novelty of limited dramatic value.

Science Fiction Reemerging in the seventies as mass-appeal, special-effects entertainment was the science-fiction spectacle. The cult popularity of Kubrick's metaphysical *2001: A Space Odyssey* (1968) and the remarkable success of the television series, *Star Trek* (1966–1969), had anticipated the explosive arrival of George Lucas' *Star Wars* in 1977.

A heroic space fantasy of unparalleled crafting, populated by imaginative, well-drawn characters, and thematically offering itself up as a futuristic morality play, *Star Wars* experienced a success that was nothing short of phenomenal. By 1980 it had domestic earnings of nearly $200 million—far above its nearest challenger, *Jaws.* Further, the film's visual magic again reaffirmed, even more vividly than *The Poseidon Adventure,* the American film industry's position as the unrivaled manufacturer of dreams. Thematically significant was the fact that *Star Wars* drew on individual heroics and positive forces in combating evil.

Steven Spielberg's *Close Encounters of the Third Kind,* also released in 1977, brought yet another science-fiction spectacle to the screen with a similarly optimistic point of view. In his visually compelling account of contact with "unidentified flying objects," Spielberg presented the unknown (through a UFO creature) as potentially good and hopeful.

The presentation of clearly drawn lines between good and evil in *Star Wars* and the positive conclusion of *Close Encounters of the Third Kind* added to the broad popular appeal of these two meticulously crafted fairy tales. Their success stimulated a rash of space films, including *Battlestar Galactica* (1978), *Alien* (1979), *Buck Rogers* (1979), *Star Trek* (1979), *The Black Hole* (1979), and the second *Star Wars* episode, *The Empire Strikes Back* (1980).

Superman (1978) extended the popular appeal of the big-budget optical-effects spectacle into the treatment of a mythic comic-book hero. Its reception ($81 million in 1979), not surprisingly, led producers to seek out other comic-strip characters for screen updates (e.g., *Popeye* and *Flash Gordon,* both 1980).

Nostalgia

Love Story's successful display of unabashed sentiment in 1970 was followed by other well-received screen romances, suggesting further change of direction for the American motion pciture. Robert Mulligan's *Summer of '42* (1971) departed from the defeatist attitudes of countercultural heroes of the late sixties for a memory story of growing up during World War II. Employing a blend of humor, scenic atmosphere, lyric

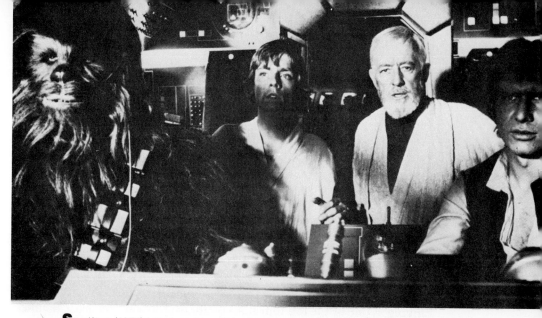

Star Wars (1977) introduced a variety of screen heroes: mechanical, animal, human, and spiritual.

music, and the all-but-forgotten dissolve, Mulligan presented a poetical-ly affective treatment of adolescent love and pain.

George Lucas' *American Graffiti* (1973) recreated a nostalgic milieu for pre-activist youth during the early 1960s. The world depicted is that of recently graduated high school students cruising through small-town America on a summer's evening. The most serious complications pre-sented are an attempt to purchase a bottle of liquor illegally and concern over sweetheart loyalties while separated by college. At the film's end, however, Lucas interjects an epilogue statement about the fate of several male characters in the film—a means of conveying·that the innocent era as visualized was soon ended by social and political realities brought on by involvement in Vietnam.

Adult nostalgia in another prewar period formed the subject of Syndey Pollack's *The Way We Were* (1973). The film begins in the 1930s with Barbra Streisand leading left-wing college activities and Robert Redford portraying a campus athlete with writing aspirations. Mixing romance and personal idealism, the story traces the couple's lives from college days through the patriotic fervor of World War II and into the McCarthy-tense 1950s. Their ill-fated romance interweaves with the country's rapidly changing social moods to evoke a bittersweet memory of lost love and causes. Pollack's film received less than a favorable critical reception, but the palatable blend of romance and social refer-encing was shown to be commercially potent with *The Way We Were*

A scene of underage youths purchasing a bottle of liquor recalls one of the many comic vignettes that comprised *American Graffiti* (1973).

ranking as one of the top four films of 1973. Only *The Exorcist, The Sting,* and *American Graffiti* (in descending order) were more profitable.

The Sting, also starring Redford, helped further verify and reestablish the seemingly sudden market appeal of stylish screen fare. George Roy Hill's treatment of efforts by two con artists (Redford and Paul Newman) to outsmart a racketeer (Robert Shaw) incorporated atmospheric decor, nostalgic color toning, and Scott Joplin's music with charming effect. Its earnings approached $80,000,000 and in 1980 it was still listed among the ten most successful motion pictures ever made.

The impact that the financial returns of these nostalgia-based films had on the progression of American cinema was properly noted in a satirical lament uttered in the mid-seventies by Los Angeles critic-historian Charles Champlin who asked: "O Sting, where is thy death?" Nostalgia as represented in these pivotal films continued throughout the decade. The examples set by *American Graffiti* and *Summer of '42* in treating the young were further represented by such works as *Class of '44* (1973), *The Paper Chase* (1973), *Saturday Night Fever* (1977), *Fraternity Row* (1977), *Animal House* (1978), *Grease* (1978), *Hair* (1978), *Meatballs* (1979), *Breaking Away* (1979), *A Little Romance* (1979), *My Bodyguard* (1980).

Adult nostalgia within specified social settings appeared in *The Great Gatsby* (1974), *The Great Waldo Pepper* (1975), *Gable and Lombard* (1976), *New York, New York* (1977), *The Big Fix* (1978), and *Yanks* (1979).

Efforts to capitalize on the growing appeal of the past resulted in the two-part compilation tribute to Hollywood, *That's Entertainment* (1974 and 1976) and numerous remakes of films from the studio era, including: *The Front Page* (1974); *Farwell, My Lovely* (1975 originally *Murder My Sweet,* 1944); *A Star Is Born* (1976); *Heaven Can Wait* (1978, originally *Here Comes Mr. Jordan*); and *The Champ* (1979).

Comedy

The Sting's triumph as a lighthearted, comic-book-styled treatment of hoodlumism appeared to have ushered the escapist screen comedy forcefully back into the commercial mainstream of American cinema. Throughout the seventies comic material in every imaginable form won the favor of mass audiences, including Mel Brooks' genre-inspired parodies: *Blazing Saddles* (1974), *Young Frankenstein* (1974), *Silent Movie* (1976) and *High Anxiety* (1977); saucy domestic comedies: *For Pete's Sake* (1974), *Shampoo* (1975), *Fun with Dick and Jane* (1977), *The Goodbye Girl* (1978), *Housecalls* (1978), *Same Time Next Year* (1978), *10* (1979), *The Last Married Couple in America* (1980); suspense comedies: *Silver Streak* (1977), *Murder by Death* (1976), *Foul Play* (1978); the irreverent spoof: *Kentucky Fried Movie* (1977), *Animal House* (1978), *The Jerk* (1979), *Airplane!* (1980); black comedy: *The End* (1978).

Social Implications

Together the disaster film, science-fiction spectacle, the horror movie, the nostalgia exercise, and the screen comedy comprised a major portion of American motion-picture output during the seventies. In a country recovering from the political tensions of Vietnam and Watergate, and suddenly confronting economic uncertainty, the filmgoer's mood apparently welcomed opportunities to laugh, to remember a seemingly less complicated past, and to witness on the screen disasters and personal traumas greater than those posed by immediate social and economic realities.

By decade's end the 1970s also had reestablished the common-figure hero—in depressed times an apt, uplooking companion for the escapist genre film. These heroes often took the form of small-time sports figures battling established champions: *Rocky* (1976); *The Bad News Bears* (1976); *Breaking Away* (1979); *Ice Castles* (1978); *Rocky II* (1979).

The mythic, larger-than-life hero was projected through the screen presences of Luke Skywalker, Superman, James Bond, Buck Rogers, Flash Gordon, and Captain Kirk—all individuals able to take control of events and shape their own destinies. These heroes, too, reflected through their mass-appeal reception a society being drawn to screen entertainment with positive, upbeat themes and clear-cut solutions to dramatic problems.

LOOKING AT VIETNAM

Except for a rare action escapade, the Vietnam war, seemingly, did not exist for the American feature filmmaker. In 1968 John Wayne co-directed with Ray Kellogg a screen version of the popular book *The Green Berets*, a heroic account of American Special Forces' activity in Vietnam. Wayne's film adaptation (in which he also starred) offered guerilla warfare as mythic entertainment, emphasizing the action and adventure in Viet Cong-Green Beret encounters.

Another feature film with Vietnam references, *Welcome Home, Soldier Boys* (1972), depicted four Green Beret veterans on a violent rampage as they drive from an army discharge center in Arkansas toward California. On the road the men are shown using and discarding a female hitchhiker, then completely destroying a small New Mexico town. Richard Compton's potentially revealing treatment of the Vietnam veteran as war casualty gave way instead to a display of anarchistic gangsterism.

Direct visualization and analysis of the Vietnam experience were confined almost entirely to television network reportage which brought the war's drama to the public on a nightly basis.

Hearts and Minds

At the tail end of nearly a decade and a half of American involvement in Southeast Asia, the documentary film *Hearts and Minds* (1974, released 1975) opened in selected theaters around the United States. In its limited run the Bert Schneider-Peter Davis study of U.S. participation in Vietnam was seen by only a tiny portion of the public, a consequence of delayed distribution by Columbia Pictures which sponsored the documentary. The film reached theaters just as American withdrawal was underway and it failed to generate any sizable interest among a populace weary of the country's divisive Vietnam experience.

Hearts and Minds represented the first serious effort by American feature filmmakers to come to grips with the social and political realities of the war. The idea for the film had come to Peter Davis in 1972 after he had completed the controversial television documentary *The Selling of the Pentagon*. Davis was inspired to undertake a study of American involvement in Vietnam with the intention of attempting to better understand his country's participation. With Bert Schneider, who like Davis came from an established Hollywood family, the two filmmakers over a year's time gathered documentary-news footage and embarked on filming missions that took them to Vietnam, Washington, and to other locations for interviews with participants in the war.

From the massive collection of acquired footage (more than fifty hours) the Davis-Schneider team arranged an emotionally charged, two-hour presentation that depicted the war's politics and its personal tragedies at home and in Southeast Asia. Employing a crosscutting technique which juxtaposed a clear set of protagonists and antagonists, Davis and Schneider were able to project a forceful political drama.

Scenes from romantic Hollywood war movies were combined with direct interviews and verité-styled location scenes to produce a compilation film which was both evocative and immediate. Shock footage of napalmed children, brutal assassinations, and other war horrors on both sides were incorporated to force the viewer into a human confrontation with the war's toll.

Hearts and Minds' ultimate impact was twofold: in suggesting the enormous loss incurred by the war and in revealing the tragic implications of a philosophy that advocates winning at all costs.

Early Dramatic Efforts

The dramatic feature film began more serious consideration of Vietnam's impact in *Heroes,* released late in 1977, and in three films issued during 1978: Sidney J. Furie's *The Boys in Company C,* Hal Ashby's *Coming Home,* and Michael Cimino's *The Deer Hunter.* All dealt with young soldiers and how military assignment in Vietnam altered their lives.

Heroes' seriocomic script tells the episodic story of a young veteran (Henry Winkler) who is left disturbed, confused, and restless by his war combat experiences. In the film's most touching scene, Winkler, on a flight by bus across the United States, stops for a reunion with an army buddy and discovers that, despite mutual war experiences, the two men on American soil are worlds apart. Unfortunately, most of the principal character's volatile actions in *Heroes* resemble the psychotic, antisocial behavior that made melodramatic antagonists of returned veterans in *Rollercoaster, Black Sunday,* and *Welcome Home, Soldier Boys.*

The Boys in Company C treats the lives of five young Vietnam-based Marines in various stages of war-pressure adjustment, focusing ultimately on their individual responses to a futile war. A low-budget effort with a cast of unknowns, the film received only minimal public and critical attention.

With *Coming Home,* released three years after the war ended, the Vietnam screen drama found a large responsive audience. Aided by the appearance of Jon Voight and Jane Fonda in the principal roles, Ashby's film develops the personal relationship between an embittered paraplegic veteran and the wife of a Marine captain. The complexities of the love story, which begins in a California veteran's hospital where Fonda works as a volunteer, are compounded when the woman's husband (Bruce Dern) also returns from Vietnam emotionally and physically scarred. *Coming Home's* script examines Vietnam in its aftermath, concentrating on the human emotions and growing personal and political consciousness that are a result of exposure to any tragic war. Ashby's candid direction of sensitive scenes and Haskell Wexler's naturalistic cinematography allow the story to escape sentimental treatment.

The Deer Hunter

The Deer Hunter, although widely controversial, received the Academy Award as best motion picture of 1978 (competing with *Coming Home*). A

The Deer Hunter (1978). Following Nick's funeral his friends return to their favorite bar for a toast to the dead soldier.

work which freely mixes cinematic styles, metaphoric imagery, and intense characterizations, Cimino's film presents a haunting account of the personal traumas experienced by three naive and inarticulate men who are cast into Vietnam without emotional preparation and who must return home without moral support.

A critical opening wedding ceremony defines the principal characters' ethnic, small-town backgrounds, and a deer hunt which follows conveys their self-devised rituals of male exercise—acted out on the slopes of snow-covered mountains. Called to Vietnam from their simple existence in the Pennsylvania steel town where they live, the three men (Robert De Niro, Christopher Walken, John Savage) are shown immediately caught up in a terrorizing war whose atrocities (the source of controversy over the film) leave each permanently affected.

The Deer Hunter extends treatment of Vietnam's tragic impact into both personal and community confusion. In the film's final scene, which follows Nick's (Walken) funeral, the dead soldier's hometown friends gather in their favorite bar where, together, in a pathetic effort to convince themselves that Nick's death has some meaning, they sing "God Bless America."

The importance of Cimino's film was in its frank attempt to deal with the lives of simple people who found Vietnam inexplicably devastating. Unlike the principal characters in *Coming Home,* Cimino's people could not even know the release of vented bitterness and political anger.

Apocalypse Now

Francis Ford Coppola's *Apocalypse Now* (1979) moved beyond the theme of political consciousness and personal trauma to an attempt at visualization of the war itself. A desire to convey the absurdities, madness, and moral dilemmas of a guerilla war fought without battle lines and against a largely invisible "enemy" provided the dramatic impetus for the ambitious film. Earlier dramatic films about Vietnam had been located back in the United States, or had only briefly looked on the site of the conflict.

From locations in the Philippine Islands, where the terrain resembles Vietnam's, Coppola worked against great odds (including typhoons) between March 1976 and May 1977 to reconstruct episodes which would suggest the war's horrors.

Apocalypse Now's opening scenes set the tone for the remainder of the sprawling, archetypal story by Coppola and John Milius. Employing a wide-screen format to full advantage, the opening shots reveal the eerie contrast of American helicopters flying in serene formation above the lush beauty of Vietnam's tropical terrain. The lyric effect is shattered when the helicopters dip from the sky and with their napalm and machine guns destroy a Vietnamese village.

The somber ironies of a war waged against the anonymous guerrilla are forcefully conveyed in a scene where five innocent Vietnamese peasants are gunned to death when their riverboat is halted for a search. One of the victims, a woman, triggers the death spray when she naively bends down to lift a puppy from a box and it is feared that she has reached for a grenade or other type of weapon.

In addition to its epic and tragic illustration of Vietnam's madness, *Apocalypse Now* seeks to develop a larger view of human nature by drawing on the plot and structure of Joseph Conrad's classic novel *Heart of Darkness*. Coppola's principal character, an Army captain named Benjamin Willard (Martin Sheen), like Marlowe in Conrad's fiction, is deployed on a mission by riverboat to locate and destroy a man named Kurtz. Kurtz (Marlon Brando) in *Apocalypse Now* is a highly respected army colonel who has seemingly gone mad and is living in a state of tyrannical rule over a colony of army defectors and pagans.

Coppola's intentions, like Conrad's, were to create a mythic, archetypal journey through "the heart of darkness" as Willard's boat proceeds from Saigon to Kurtz' village and beyond. On a literal level the journey permits a passing view of the war with each leg of the trip illustrating a different facet of the Vietnam experience. On a symbolic level, *Apocalypse Now* engages the mythic passage from ignorance to self-awareness (through "darkness" to light). Cast into a state of chaos and anarchy, Willard is able to recognize Kurtz' madness and withdrawal as resulting from knowledge of the civilized world's horrors. The intended dramatic effect is that of catharsis, provoked by movement to the center of humankind's dark nature.

Considerable critical attention was focused on Coppola's success in bringing forth these symbolic ideas. The film's final surrealistic scene, with Willard encountering Kurtz, was considered by many to be at pretentious odds with the spectacular realism of earlier parts. Also confronting Coppola was the difficult task of rendering in dramatic terms Willard's moment of epiphany—a challenge better met by Conrad through the literary advantage of a precisely controlled point of view.

Although unconnected projects, *Coming Home, The Deer Hunter,* and *Apocalypse Now* formed a dramatic triology which together showed American filmmakers striving for a comprehensive interpretation of Vietnam in both personal and general terms.

DIRECTORIAL STYLES

The rapidly changing consumer response to film fare during the sixties and seventies was evident in the prevailing "boom or bust" state of industry economics and in the diversity of cinematic exercises undertaken by major directors working through Hollywood's administrative center. John Avildsen, who had been responsible for the harsh social realism of the antiheroic *Joe* in 1970, was by 1976 interpreting for the screen Sylvester Stallone's upbeat American success story, *Rocky.* John Schlesinger had moved from sensitively rendered studies of unusual personal relationships in *Midnight Cowboy* (1969) and *Sunday, Bloody Sunday* (1971) to the melodramatic suspense thriller *Marathon Man* (1976) and a nostalgia-laden World War II romance *Yanks* (1979).

Increasingly, opportunities for leading directors to supervise inexpensive, personally inspired films diminished after the late sixties as promotion and distribution costs continued to inflate. The "small" film that fell short of being declared a sensation by critics and word-of-mouth response (the latter usually more important than the former), most commonly failed at the box office. These economic lessons, abetted by the erratic conditions of the film industry at large, pressed important directors with reputations for individual expression to also apply their talents to the "well-crafted," mass-appeal property—a role, ironically, much like that played within the old studio system where directorial styles found their outlet in varied assignments.

In more recent times, vital American directors, nevertheless, continued to make important contributions to the growth of film art. A small but impressive group of film artists, many still in their youth, showed through their inspired work that original, provocative expression of enduring quality remains possible within the medium despite its tense conservatism.

Among those directors whose work has evidenced individual creativity and notable achievement are Hal Ashby, Woody Allen, Robert Altman, Mel Brooks, John Cassavetes, Francis Ford Coppola, Milos Forman, Bob Fosse, Sidney Lumet, Paul Mazursky, Martin Ritt, Paul Schrader, Martin Scorsese, Melvin Van Peebles, and Claudia Weill. A sampling of representative films by these selected directors indicates the diversity of content and method in the progress of cinematic art in the United States.

Hal Ashby

Hal Ashby's (1936–   ) outstanding films during the 1970s included *The Last Detail* (1973), *Shampoo* (1975), *Bound for Glory* (1976), *Coming Home* (1978), and *Being There* (1979). All are notable for their keen social observations of American life. *The Last Detail* skillfully and humorously dissects the personality of professional servicemen on special duty, with strong collaborative support from screenwriter Robert Towne *(Chinatown)* and from Jack Nicholson in the principal role of a forthright sailor. In this film as in *Shampoo,* which details a day in the life of a sexually active hairdresser, Ashby explores morality within specifically defined social settings—in the military, and in late-sixties California, respectively. Atmosphere and milieu play critical roles in both of these raucous social comedies.

Bound for Glory, based on the life of folk singer–social activist Woody Guthrie, reevoked a feeling for Depression-era America and the mood of the times which made Guthrie a folk hero. As in *Coming Home,* Ashby's Vietnam-related character study, songs inspired by the era appear liberally on the sound track to frame a drama about emerging personal conviction.

A novel by Jerzy Kozinski provided Ashby the material for *Being There,* a political satire of sophisticated stylization. Through a socially deprived and simple-minded gardener (Peter Sellers), who wins over industrial executives and politicians with homespun pronouncements that are taken as pointed aphorisms, Kozinski's screenplay offers an ironic commentary on gullibility. Ashby's work shows a strong penchant for interpreting screen characters whose lives reveal, often outrageously, well-placed societal concerns.

Woody Allen and Mel Brooks

The foremost directors of resurgent American screen comedy, Woody Allen (1935–   ) and Mel Brooks (1927–   ), frequently write, direct, and act in their films. Their physical presences enhance stylistic and thematic interests, with Allen appearing in satirical comedies as the lovable loser and a zany Brooks functioning in parodies of popular motion-picture genres.

Virgil, the first of Woody Allen's lovable losers, fumbles a bank robbery in *Take the Money and Run* (1969).

Allen In his first effort as director, writer, and actor, *Take the Money and Run* (1969), Allen incorporated a potpourri of comic approaches which suggested the eccentric style of subsequent work: topical one-liners, sight gags, non sequiturs, parodic references to film types (in this case the newsreel and the *cinéma vérité* documentary). The essential Allen character—the born loser who fumbles in life and in love—originates through the creation of Virgil, a nuttily neurotic man who, after marriage, embarks on a career as a bank robber but is shown to be totally inept.

This screen persona continues in comic variations in *Bananas* (1971), *Sleeper* (1973), *Love and Death* (1975), *Annie Hall* (1977), and *Manhattan* (1979) where Allen is, in order, a South American revolutionary, a twentiety-century man brought back to life in the twenty-second century, a reluctant soldier in Russia during the Napoleonic wars, and a comedy writer (in both *Annie Hall* and *Manhattan*).

In the two latter efforts, among his best, Allen's screen character is merged into autobiographically inspired comedies about personal relationships with women. The romance which develops between the twice-divorced Alvy Singer (Allen) and the offbeat Annie Hall (Diane Keaton) reveals Allen looking beyond a flip approach to his comedy and toward introspective analysis and pathos.

Between *Annie Hall* and *Manhattan* Allen wrote and directed (but did not appear in) the noncomic, heavily psychological study of an immobilized American family, *Interiors* (1978). Allen's film focuses primarily on the characters' gestalt rhetoric while offering set design, lighting, and color as references for interior states.

On returning in *Manhattan* to the more compatible seriocomic style of *Annie Hall*, Allen indicated further maturation in the cohesive treatment of self-involved relationships. Again portraying a twice-divorced, insecure writer moving cautiously and introspectively into new alliances, Allen is able to carry over—with humor—interests explored in *Interiors*. Psychiatric jargon and pseudo-intellectual rhetoric consume the world of one partner (Diane Keaton), whose superficiality contrasts sharply with that of Allen's second companion, a 17-year-old school girl (Mariel Hemingway).

Through his affairs with these two women and through disjointed contacts with friends and a former wife (Meryl Streep), a touching slice-of-life view of Allen's city-based existence emerges. The script freely incorporates the expected topical references and pointed quips which are Allen trademarks. Gordon Willis' cinematography returns to a black-and-white format within a structural style which often employs uninterrupted shots to capture the interior and exterior spirit of New York City.

A compulsion toward satirical review of life as a renowned filmmaker and public personality (à la Fellini's *8½*) provoked *Stardust Memories* (1980).

The provocative, personal nature of Allen's films, their consistently high quality, and the rapport they command through a unique and well-defined screen persona (as complete as Chaplin's or Buster Keaton's) have together sustained a remarkable film career of continuing promise.

Brooks Mel Brooks' comic art took shape in *The Producers* (1968) and *The Twelve Chairs* (1970). Drawing on the talents of a group of screen clowns, rather than on a single comic persona as in Woody Allen's case, Brooks sets zanily contrived plots into unrestrained motion for laughs derived from satire, sight gags, slapstick, and farfetched situations. In *The Producers,* Zero Mostel and Gene Wilder scheme to get rich by producing a Broadway musical, "Springtime for Hitler" (with Dick

Pseudo-intellectual rhetoric in an art museum is part of Allen's treatment of city life and love in *Manhattan* (1979).

Shawn portraying a hippie führer). In *The Twelve Chairs* Ron Moody, Dom DeLuise, Frank Langella, and Brooks romp through Czarist Russia looking for a cache of jewels hidden in a chair.

With *Blazing Saddles* (1974) Brooks produced the first of a sequence of screen parodies in which his iconoclastic style and clown teams are engaged in comic updates of well-understood Hollywood genre pictures. In exaggerating the conventions, motifs, and clichès of the western (*Blazing Saddles*), the horror film (*Young Frankenstein,* 1974), the silent comedy (*Silent Movie,* 1976), and the Alfred Hitchcock thriller (*High Anxiety,* 1977), Brooks reveals himself as a comic purist. Clowning, repetitious sight gags, outrageous take-offs (e.g., Marlene Dietrich's Lola-Lola in *Blazing Saddles*), zany chases, and slapstick action form the body of a typical Brooks parody. The free-spirited nature of his comedy results in works that can be superbly entertaining (*Young Frankenstein*) or only moderately so *(High Anxiety).*

During the height of the comedy craze in the seventies, several of Brooks' favorite clowns entered into their own careers as comedy directors, including Gene Wilder and Marty Feldman.

Robert Altman

Like other important filmmakers of his generation (Norman Jewison, John Frankenheimer) Robert Altman (1925–   ) worked extensively during the fifties and sixties as a director-producer of television pro-

Young Dr. Frankenstein (Gene Wilder) helps his monster creation (Peter Boyle) take his first steps.

A political rally, led by country-western musicians and complete with an assassination attempt, brings *Nashville's* (1975) epic character study to a climax.

grams. An early low-budget motion picture, *The Delinquents* (1957), for the most part went unnoticed, and Altman had to wait for *M*A*S*H* (1970), an irreverent antiwar comedy, to establish himself as one of the most innovative, personal directors of the decade.

Altman has varied his directorial style by treating a diverse range of subject matter. From the black-comedy style of *M*A*S*H,* Altman moved to satirical fantasy for *Brewster McCloud* (1970), an account of a young man (Bud Cort) attempting to fly. In *McCabe and Mrs. Miller* (1971) and *Thieves Like Us* (1973), period atmosphere, achieved through impressionistic aural and visual imagery, dominates nonromantic, antithetical genre studies of life on the western frontier and among small-time gangsters in the Depression-stricken South of the 1930s. Altman's interest in these works centers on realistic values rather than nostalgia, emphasizing through his soft-muted imagery and formal editing the pace and quality of existence in the specified environments. Traditional narrative structure and dramatic crescendos are avoided. Experimental consideration of sound emerges as an important component in Altman's treatment of the environments.

In *California Split* (1974) tight, close cinematography and a multilayered sound track with overlapping foreground and background dialogue aid Altman in defining the sensory, schizophrenic world of two hopelessly addicted gamblers (Elliot Gould and George Segal). A willingness to allow his actors to improvise is also evident in the spontaneous treatment of casino life.

Actor collaboration becomes even more critical in the development of *Nashville* (1975), an epic character study set in country-western music's capital. The principal actors (nearly two dozen) contributed to individual characterizations, with Altman's editing rationale then determined by crosscutting from one story to another to sustain the highest possible level of interest. This approach spontaneously depicts character ambitions in the music capital while pulling the film forward to a critical political rally where the American success drive culminates in an explosive final scene.

In *Buffalo Bill and the Indians* (1976), *Three Women* (1977), *A Wedding* (1978), and *Quintet* (1979) Altman continued to explore uncommon material which subverts audience expectations. *Buffalo Bill and the Indians* offers an antimythic view of an accepted American hero; *Three Women* mystically recreates one of Altman's dreams about three characters whose lives eventually merge in common bond; *A Wedding* gave Altman still another opportunity to subvert on screen the myths and rituals of American life by turning a middle-class wedding day into an irreverent, absurd event; *Quintet* created the fantasized world of a tense, futuristic Ice Age.

In defying commercial dictates and refusing to fit his films to calculated audience tastes, Altman has often seemed to intentionally shun popular success. His adherence to eccentric, personal expression has produced a small but dedicated group of followers who consider Altman a great American director. *Popeye* (1980), a screen rendering of the comic-book hero, hinted at a willingness to treat more traditional material.

John Cassavetes

Alternately an actor (*Rosemary's Baby*, 1968) and a film director with a limited body of work, John Cassavetes (1929–   ) has shown a notable ability for innovative approaches in developing screen characterizations. Improvisation and *cinéma vérité* filming methods, first utilized in two independent projects, *Shadows* (1960) and *Too Late Blues* (1961), resulted in sensitive and realistic interpretations of human qualities.

Cassavetes' major feature-length commercial films include *Faces* (1968), *Husbands* (1970), *Minnie and Moskowitz* (1971), *A Woman under the Influence* (1974), *The Killing of a Chinese Bookie* (1975), and *Gloria* (1980). In all these films dramatic interest resides in examining the intimate reactions of common people to personal crises; plot is usually secondary to character analysis, the consequence of a serious actor-turned-director. To achieve his realistic goals, close actor friends (Ben Gazzara, Peter Falk, and Cassavetes' wife, Gena Rowlands) appear as ensemble collaborators.

A Woman under the Influence typifies Cassavetes' "slice of life" concerns, recounting the story of a woman (Rowlands) who during the course of the film undergoes a mental breakdown, rehabilitation, and reunion with her family. Lengthy camera takes, naturalistic sound and lighting, a fluid camera, and intense close-ups lay bare the woman's responses to her illness. Cassavetes remains with the woman's suffering

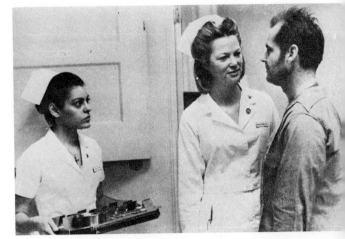

A confrontation between institutional authority (Louise Fletcher) and a spirited rebel (Jack Nicholson). Like *The Cabinet of Dr. Caligari* (1919), *One Flew Over the Cuckoo's Nest* (1975) raised the question: "Who is really mad? The patient or his keeper?"

throughout, refusing causal analysis and conclusive explanations for the crisis other than that noted in the principal character's apparent vulnerability at a particular time in her life.

In *Gloria,* with Rowlands as a former girlfriend of a New York gangster caught in her own underworld crisis, Cassavetes applies his skills in creating realistic characterizations to a more active plot than is usual for his screen exercises. *Gloria* was named co-winner of the Best Picture Award at the 1980 Venice Film Festival.

Milos Forman

Milos Forman (1932–   ) left Czechoslovakia in 1968 after completing *The Fireman's Ball* the year before, and has since worked in the United States where his talents for treating generational differences and character tensions have been effectively utilized in films with American settings.

Taking Off (1971), a generation-gap comedy located in New York, owed much of its inspiration to his Czech-made *Loves of a Blonde* (1965). Forman's established reputation for subtle analysis of human psychology and behavior was evident in the critical reception given *Taking Off* and in the enormously successful adaptation of Ken Kesey's novel, *One Flew over the Cuckoo's Nest* (1975). Aided by Jack Nicholson's brilliant performance as a mental patient doing battle with institutional authority, Forman delineates human impasse with a dark, ironic blend of comedy and tragedy. A film version of the musical *Hair* (1979) had Forman once again interpreting a generation-gap theme, placed within the youth-rebellious Vietnam era. *Ragtime* (1981) offered a stylish, sensitive treatment of E. L. Doctorow's novel.

In all his films, in Czechoslovakia and in the United States, Forman's

In Bob Fosse's films the glitter and glamour of show business settings often stand in ironic juxtaposition to social, political, and personal realities, as in *Cabaret* (1972).

individual achievement has been an ability to treat, with ample doses of humor, the circumstances for humans at odds with their social environment.

Bob Fosse

After directing a traditional-style screen musical *Sweet Charity* (1969), dancer-choreographer Bob Fosse (1927–   ) made a major impression with the innovative rendering of *Cabaret* (1972), and the altogether different, nonmusical, *Lenny* (1974).

Cabaret's screen evolution was by way of the Broadway musical, which had been taken from Christopher Isherwood's *Goodbye to Berlin.* Its conceptual line employs the cabaret as a theatrical device for depicting the decadence and amorality in emerging Nazi Germany, circa 1930. The music hall represents a place of escape for people overwhelmed by events around them; in the opening number the cabaret's Master of Ceremonies offers entertainment as an alternative to life's problems. Following the manner of German musical-theater presentations designed as social commentary, *Cabaret* uses its song-and-dance routines for instructive purposes, commenting on and parodying societal values which allow a Fascist takeover.

Fosse's direction and choreography offer a dynamic, atmospheric rendering of the sardonic musical. Vivid color images, bold camera compositions, and rhythmic montage aid in projecting the cabaret as a surreal, removed world. Fosse's talent for directing actors is also apparent in his successful realization of a script requiring both stylized and naturalistic performances.

An artist whose primary experience comes from the theater, Fosse's film interests consistently fall on the treatment of subject matter within show-business settings. *Lenny,* a screen biography of the offbeat stand-up comedian, Lenny Bruce, proved an intense exercise in character analysis. Fosse avoided the expressionistic devices of the stage production from which *Lenny's* scenario had been taken, employing instead a documentarylike approach (in black and white) that intercuts flashbacks, *cinéma-vérité*-like interviews, and scenes from Bruce's increasingly bolder, drug-ridden nightclub appearances. Together, the reconstruction produces a film experience that has the look of both fact and heightened drama. The directness in cinema styling was ideally suited to recapturing the life of a self-destructive comedian whose theatrical forte was shock and social satire. Together with Dustin Hoffman's totally absorbed performance, Fosse's interpretation reinforces Bruce's cult-hero image.

All That Jazz (1979) continued experimentation with varying film styles in Fosse's semiautobiographical story of a famous choreographer-filmmaker, Joe Gideon (Roy Scheider), whose regard for artistic perfection and women is all-consuming. Combining the abrupt, dynamic images of *Cabaret* with the intense character analysis of *Lenny, All That Jazz* recreates Gideon's self-destructive course in a rhythmic exercise precisely matched to the world of dance and the pace of life set by the principal character. Fosse manages, as in *Cabaret* and *Lenny,* to treat his show-business world in cinematic terms, an achievement which has resulted in considerable praise from critics as well as industry professionals.

Sidney Lumet

Following extensive work as a television director in the early fifties, Sidney Lumet (1924–   ) began a prolific directing career with *Twelve Angry Men* (1957). Notable early achievements included the serious-minded *Long Day's Journey into Night* (1962) and *The Pawnbroker* (1965). In the latter film Lumet examined the life of a spiritually impoverished Nazi concentration camp survivor (Rod Steiger) who, living as a withdrawn pawnbroker, ultimately accepts his responsibility to humankind.

The theme of social commitment and personal morality is a common one in Lumet's best films of the seventies: *Serpico* (1973), *Dog Day Afternoon* (1975), and *Network* (1976). In each of these films the principal character is cast into a morality crisis that forces ethical decisions related to personal or public responsibility: an honest policeman (Al Pacino) in *Serpico* who rebels against casual acceptance of corruption in his profession; a confused bank robber (Pacino) in *Dog Day Afternoon* trapped in a touching public spectacle because of his foolish actions on behalf of a male lover; a television newscaster (Peter Finch) in *Network* who is exploited by the ambitious executives for whom he works.

Lumet's directing in these films is distinguished by an effective

One of the disguises employed by hard-working, honest policeman Pacino) in *Serpico* (1973). New York locations added to the film's real tenor.

combination of realistic location scenes, well-crafted, emotion-filled dramatic segments, strong performances from his actors, and an ability to avoid sensationalism in the treatment of bold subject matter.

Paul Mazursky

Even more consistently than Sidney Lumet, Paul Mazursky (1938–   ) has viewed the world through the issue of personal morality in specific social settings. Beginning with *Bob & Carol & Ted & Alice* (1969) and the autobiographically motivated *Alex in Wonderland* (1970), Mazursky initiated exploration of screen characters reacting to the constantly changing moral climate in America during the latter half of the twentieth century. *Bob & Carol & Ted & Alice* looked satirically at the spouse-exchange fad of the sixties, while *Alex in Wonderland* projected a comic view of the Hollywood way of life through the experiences of a newly arrived filmmaker (Donald Sutherland).

In later works Mazursky's scan of American morality is embodied in: a husband (George Segal) who cheats on his wife (*Blume in Love*, 1973); a 72-year-old widower (Art Carney) discovering the United States while traveling with his cat from New York to California (*Harry and Tonto*, 1974); a young would-be actor (Lenny Baker) adjusting to New York and its environs in the early fifties (*Next Stop, Greenwich Village*, 1976); a surprised divorcee (Jill Clayburgh) after sixteen years of marriage attempting to find a new identity (*An Unmarried Woman*, 1978);

and in three young idealists whose extended *ménage à trois* affair (after Truffaut's *Jules and Jim,* 1961) is nurtured by the liberated lifestyle experiments of Vietnam-era America (*Willy and Phil,* 1980).

A filmmaker with humanistic leanings who frequently draws on personal experience, Mazursky's directorial style strives for an atmospheric, often lyrical evocation of milieu while employing improvisational methods in the development of character action. His subjects come from middle-class backgrounds, and the moral crises in their lives, while viewed earnestly, are invariably presented with an eye to satirical relief.

Martin Ritt

Martin Ritt (1919–   ) turned from the direction of 1950s-styled adaptations of southern literature, e.g., *The Long Hot Summer* (1958), *The Sound and the Fury* (1959), to more intimate studies of the problems faced by average people in the conduct of their lives. During the sixties and seventies, the best of Ritt's films approached, as closely as any other American works of the time, thematic interests associated with neorealism.

In *Hud* (1963) Ritt dissected tensions in a contemporary Texas panhandle family (from Larry McMurtry's novel *Horseman, Pass By*). The conflict between a rebellious son (Paul Newman) and tradition-bound father (Melvyn Douglas) gained in impact from close attention to character, a quality brought to film from Ritt's earlier work as a television director *(Danger)* and actor.

A line-up in a king-sized bed (Elliott Gould, Natalie Wood, Robert Culp, Dyan Cannon) projects an image that is central to Paul Mazursky's film interests: changing morality on the American scene. The characters are *Bob & Carol & Ted & Alice* (1969).

Sounder's (1972) theme of social injustice and personal hardship is reminiscent of Italian neorealism. The father (Paul Winfield) is arrested on a food-theft charge and sent to prison.

Ritt's neorealistic impulse developed more noticeably in *Sounder* (1972), *Conrack* (1974), and *Norma Rae* (1979)—all films located in the southern United States and concerned with the struggles of simple people to improve their lot in life. *Sounder* treats day-to-day problems within a poverty-stricken black family during the American Depression. In a sensitively rendered interpretation of the family's strengths and frustrations, Ritt's work recalls De Sica's *The Bicycle Thief* (1948).

Conrack features Jon Voight as an innovative teacher whose challenge is educationally deprived youngsters on an isolated island off the South Carolina coast. Ritt creates a strong feeling for the environment and its stultifying traditions against which the dedicated teacher must work. Voight's performance and those by amateur child actors uphold the film's strong sense of conviction and naturalism.

Similar qualities distinguished *Norma Rae,* a humanistic account of unionization efforts in a one-industry Alabama town. The struggle to penetrate an ironclad system that is sustained by economic necessity involves a New York labor organizer (Ron Liebman) and a spunky young southern woman (Sally Field). The woman, after conversion to the organizer's point of view, acts as catalyst within the target cotton plant. Ritt manages the story with credible handling of character portraits and location. Refusing to write a scenario that presents the two principal characters in romantic alliance shows remarkable restraint, although personal feelings clearly exist. Ritt's subtle conveyance of these inner, unstated personal tensions adds subtextural enrichment to a film of consistent integrity.

Paul Schrader

The route to directing careers by many successful film-school graduates has been by way of screenwriting. In a system where literary properties increasingly dominate production consideration, enterprising writers with well-established reputations quite logically have sought to interpret their own projects for the screen. Francis Coppola pointed the way, and others who followed include Paul Schrader (1946–   ), scenarist for Scorsese's *Taxi Driver* (1976), Brian De Palma's *Obsession* (1976), Joan Tewkesbury's *Old Boyfriends* (1979), and for *Raging Bull* (1980), also a Scorsese film.

Schrader's self-directed exercises include *Blue Collar* (1978), *Hardcore* (1978), and *American Gigolo* (1980). A native of Michigan, Schrader found inspiration in his home state for the plots of both *Blue Collar* and *Hardcore*. *Blue Collar* examines with frankness and psychological realism the lives of three Detroit automobile assembly-line workers. *Hardcore* has as its principal character a Grand Rapids furniture executive (George C. Scott) whose teenage daughter uses the occasion of a church-sponsored trip to California to run away from home, resettling in the sleazy world of pornographic filmmaking. *American Gigolo* further examines life in a sexual underworld through a fashion-conscious male (Richard Gere) who offers himself for hire to wealthy women in Southern California.

Candor is a major factor in Schrader's work which most commonly focuses on isolated characters whose movements lead to explosive behavior within aggression-provoking environments: the unrelieved landscape of assembly lines and insensitive unions in *Blue Collar;* the sordid, endless neon-lit pleasure establishments in *Hardcore;* the dangerous sex-dominated business world of *American Gigolo.* Schrader has

Three auto assembly-line workers (Yaphet Kotto, Harvey Keitel, Richard Pryor) seek relief from "blue collar" syndrome in a brothel. This scene with its keen sense of psychological realism aids in exposing the frustrations of common workers.

shown a tendency toward detached, passing views of the American landscapes he exposes, particularly in *Hardcore* and *American Gigolo.* Characterizations are minimally developed, resulting in a largely visceral, image-filled discovery of the debased worlds that have captured his attention. The refusal of incisive moral analysis has prompted intense critical reactions, pro and con, to Schrader's early scripts and films.

Martin Scorsese

In addition to *Mean Streets* and *Taxi Driver,* discussed earlier in this chapter, Martin Scorsese was also responsible during the seventies for *Alice Doesn't Live Here Anymore* (1974) and *New York, New York* (1977), efforts which reveal a broader interest in film expression than that represented by his two gritty New York "street" films.

Fashioned as a "road picture" with social relevance to the women's movement of the seventies, *Alice Doesn't Live Here Any More* details a trip across the United States for a 35-year-old widow (Ellen Burstyn) and her 11-year-old-son. Individual scenes are brutally honest in depicting male-female relationships and the demands placed on a mature woman striving for independence. Scorsese incorporates humor and sentiment into the plot, but manages to update the screen romance for contemporary value.

New York, New York paid homage to the studio-made screen musical but was less successful in its blending of romantic and realistic elements than *Alice Doesn't Live Here Any More.*

As with other directors of his generation, Scorsese, also a film-school graduate, reflects in his screen interests a desire to treat material taken from background exposure as well as to apply his studied knowledge of Hollywood traditions to works of generic inspiration.

Melvin Van Peebles

Among the talented black directors to emerge during the sixties and seventies were Ossie Davis (*Cotton Comes to Harlem,* 1970), Gordon Parks (*The Learning Tree,* 1969; *Shaft,* 1971), Sidney Poitier (*Buck and the Preacher,* 1972; *A Piece of the Action,* 1977), and Melvin Van Peebles (1932–   ) who with *The Story of a Three Day Pass* (produced in France in 1967) became the first black American to direct a feature motion picture. Van Peebles adapted this first film from his novel about a black American soldier in France whose weekend love affair with a French woman leads to punitive action on the part of military superiors.

Van Peebles' second film (produced by Columbia Pictures) was a comedy, *The Watermelon Man* (1969), with Godfrey Cambridge and Estelle Parsons. The plot centers on the story of a self-confident insurance salesman (Cambridge) who one day awakens to discover that his skin has changed from white to black. Public and private responses to

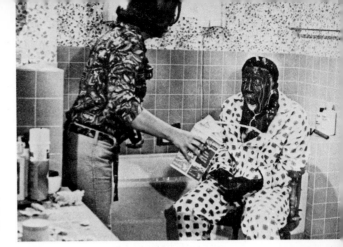

Estelle Parsons in *Water-melon Man* (1969) reacts to Godfrey Cambridge's change of skin color.

the man's new identity provide a humorous yet insightful view of the relationship between color and social status.

For his third film, *Sweet Sweetback's Baadasssss Song* (1971), Van Peebles served as writer, director, star, musical composer, and editor—bringing to the screen a bold indictment of racial injustices. Its hero is an outlaw sex-show performer (Van Peebles) who draws on his male prowess in an escape to Mexico. The film exaggerates both black and white stereotypes for an uncompromising personal statement that was met with both controversy and commercial success.

Van Peebles' emergence as a talented film director, anxious to treat interracial relationships from an individualized point of view, evidenced a vital move toward opening the American screen to self-conceived views of the black experience.

Claudia Weill

After receiving an Academy Award nomination for her documentary study of the first women's delegation to China, *The Other Half of the Sky: A China Memoir* (1975), Claudia Weill (1946–   ) ambitiously undertook the direction of the independently produced *Girlfriends* (1978). The film began as a short dramatic exercise but eventually turned into a feature-length project that was nearly three years in the making and financed solely by grant monies and loans. Weill rose above budgetary limitations ($500,000) to create a remarkably honest portrait of personal growth in a New York City setting.

The film presents an intimate character study of a young aspiring photographer (Melanie Mayron) who one day suddenly finds herself cut loose, alone, in Manhattan when her apartment mate (Anita Skinner) decides to marry. Through a series of telling vignettes, Weill traces the woman's painful movement toward independence and professional

success. A mutual envy that evolves between the young photographer and her married former roommate over opposite lifestyles reveals the self-doubts that often result for the contemporary woman in the face of new options and altering convention. The friendship between the two women matures as they begin to see each other's decision as individually valid.

The film's strengths reside in its deceptively casual, slice-of-life approach. With a blend of humor, simplicity, and spontaneity, Weill constructs an engaging screen experience that avoids the characteristic glamor and romance of many American films.

The unusual promise of *Girlfriends* led to a contract with Warner Brothers and a second feature, *It's My Turn* (1980), a decidedly commercial comedy about a contemporary woman (Jill Clayburgh) seeking to find personal satisfaction in her well-ordered, but not entirely happy, life. In adjusting to a large-scale effort Weill retained her ability to create authentic scenes laced with humor.

The preceding group of filmmakers, working in the United States during the sixties and seventies, represents only a sampling of those notable directors who helped reestablish American cinema as a vital, leading force in the international marketplace. Their importance must be weighed beside others who may be considered equally worthy of assessment, including Peter Bogdanovich, Richard Brooks, Brian De Palma, John Frankenheimer, William Friedkin, George Roy Hill, Norman Jewison, Terrence Malick, Alan Pakula, Sydney Pollack, Michael Ritchie, Steven Spielberg, Peter Yates, and Fred Zinnemann. These directors, too, demonstrate strong craftmanship and flexibility in a complex medium where economics, technology, and audience response constantly challenge artistic expression. The large number of successful feature directors cited in this chapter in itself attests to the continuity of original, spirited, and popular entertainment from American film-makers.

OTHER MODES: ANIMATION, EXPERIMENTAL, AND DOCUMENTARY

Animation

Walt Disney's position in the field of animation was earned through the creation of clever, entertaining narrative exercises which displayed richly detailed movement and visual design. In the early forties a group of animators broke away from the Disney studios to form United Productions of America (UPA). At UPA outstanding screen cartoonists such as Stephen Bosustow, John Hubley, and Bob Cannon developed individual styles which eschewed naturalism in favor of simpler, more graphic expression. Their return to simplicity reasserted the interests of early animators like Emil Cohl in France and Winsor McKay in the United States who, in creating screen characters, had employed simple drawings set against plain backgrounds. Cohl's "Fantoche" (1908) and McKay's "Gertie the Dinosaur" (1909) were also among the first screen cartoon characters to display well-realized personalities.

The trends of UPA led to more sophisticated subject matter that included the delightful screen character "Mr. Magoo," created in 1949 by John Hubley. In 1956 Hubley founded his own company where he produced works which moved American animation into the area of serious social commentary, e.g., *Moonbird* (1960) and *The Hole* (1962).·

The inspiration of UPA artists as well as the influence of work from Zagreb, Yugoslavia and from the Canadian Film Board (most significantly that of Norman McLaren) promoted further experimentation in animation styles.

Even as film "shorts" were gradually disappearing from theater programs in the sixties and seventies, there was evidence of growing interest in the United States in animation among artists and independent producers who saw in the genre opportunities for unique, individualized expression and for the conveyance of ideas.

Mouris, Vinton, Leaf Growing sophistication among American animators is illustrated in the work of Frank Mouris, Will Vinton, and Carolyn Leaf.

Mouris' *Frank Film* (1973) employs a collage technique which animates 11,000 "cut-out" images and incorporates two separate, superimposed sound recordings: a voice-over narration on one, and a list of material objects on the other. The aural-visual combination presents a graphic review of the filmmaker's "life from the beginning to the present and on into the future. . . ." Mouris' innovative work received

Fritz the Cat (1972) continued the trend toward pointed social commentary in film animation that began in the 1940s.

both an Academy Award and the Annécy (France) Festival award, the single most important honor given annually to an animator.

Will Vinton's mode of expression has been in the medium of clay animation, e.g., *Closed Mondays* (1974), *Mountain Music* (1975), *Martin the Cobbler* (1977), *Rip Van Winkle* (1978). With painstaking accuracy Vinton captures physical movement and character nuance. A special technique in *Closed Mondays* and *Mountain Music,* and one common to many contemporary animators, is the instantaneous metamorphosis of image. In *Mountain Music,* for example, the environment springs to rhythmic life as three musicians play a lively folk tune.

In *The Owl Who Married a Goose* (1974) Carolyn Leaf recreates an Eskimo legend through sand animation, another method of shifting line and material substance for kinetic effect.

Additional methods of approach have included video "feedback" animation, photo-animation (kinestasis), object pixilation, and computer-generated abstractions which first received serious attention through the efforts of James and John Whitney (*Lapis,* 1963–1966; *Permutations,* 1967).

Ralph Bakshi Most prominent among American feature-length animators of the seventies was Ralph Bakshi, a bold satirist whose films often integrate social commentary with sexual innuendo and frank language. *Fritz the Cat* (1972) offered an irreverent (X-rated) account of activist America of the late sixties, with cartoon animals representing "easy rider" types, hard hats, Black Panthers, policemen, and other figures associated with the times. *Heavy Traffic* (1973) and *Coonskin* (1975) continued satirical treatment of social ideas, while *Wizards* (1977) presented a futuristic fantasy that pits magic (good) against technology (evil). Bakshi's cutting methods and visual design in the battle sequences of *Wizards* were inspired by Eisenstein's *Alexander Nevsky* (1938). *American Pop* (1981) looked at popular music through a family saga.

Experimental

The standard-bearer for the postwar experimental film movement in the United States was Maya Deren. Her *Meshes of the Afternoon* (1943), a subjective self-study that mixes dream and reality, reasserted the personal, surrealistic possibilities of cinematic expression which had been explored earlier in the European avant-garde (1918–1930). Deren's use of symbolism and abrupt time-space manipulations represented a radical departure from the well-made narrative film and stimulated numerous American filmmakers to follow in the creation of imaginative projections of subjective states.

Leading the Deren trend were Curtis Harrington (*Fragments of Seeking,* 1946) and Kenneth Anger (*Fireworks,* 1947; *Eaux d'Artifice,* 1953). In dreamlike fantasies filled with bold, freely arranged images, these personal visionaries filled their films with references to adolescent sex, politics, social issues, and other introspective preoccupations. Metamorphic imagery figured strongly in Anger's early work which was among the first to examine the subject of homosexuality.

Brakhage As in the European avant-garde, the abstract film emerged as a dominant type. Stan Brakhage (*Desistfilm,* 1954; *Anticipation of the Night,* 1958; *Mothlight,* 1963) achieved prominence as a visual purist whose varied image experiments are projected without sound. *Mothlight,* a good example of Brakhage's interests, was created by placing moth wings between mylar tape and then printing the images as a continuous piece of film. The projected result is a series of abstract designs in motion. Alternating with his abstract films are personal records of Brakhage's immediate world, e.g., *Window Water Baby Moving* (1959), a film which records the birth of his first child.

Others Robert Breer (*Blazes,* 1957; *Fist Fight,* 1964; *Sixty-Nine,* 1968) produces abstractions through a nonlinear flow of images, patterns, and colors. Bruce Conner (*A Movie,* 1958; *Cosmic Ray,* 1961) and Stan Vanderbeek (*Breathdeath,* 1964) are experimentalists who have utilized collage and multimedia methods extensively, most commonly for satiric or black-comedy effect. Vanderbeek's *Breathdeath* makes a mockery of death while Conner's *Cosmic Ray* juxtaposes disparate images (nude girls, firework displays) at a rapid speed. With the help of prisms and distorting mirrors and lenses, Francis Thompson evokes in *New York, New York* (1957) an abstract, whimsical view of the Manhattan environment.

Experiments in electronic animation and structural and minimalist cinema were additional developments within the underground film movement. John Whitney used an analogue computer to generate graphic forms in *Catalog* (1961). *Metanomen* (1966), a graphic creation by Scott Bartlett, derives its images in part from video "feedback" as well as from the computer.

Structural and Minimalist Film Leaders of structural cinema (a film in which a single structural device creates its content) included Bruce Baillie (*Mr. Hayashi,* 1961; *All My Life,* 1966) and Michael Snow (*Wavelength,* 1966–1967). *All My Life* consists of a 360° pan of a landscape and *Wavelength* is composed of a forty-five minute zoom across a room toward a window. In the course of the zoom, the image is varied by changing color temperature, filters, and exposures.

Andy Warhol's single-take immobile camera films (*Sleep,* 1963; *Eat,* 1963; *Empire,* 1964) served to promote interest in minimalist approaches. Minimalist cinema emphasizes simple realism by restricting camera movement, editing, and dialogue—a throwback to the Lumière actualities of the 1890s. In *Necrology* (1970) Standish Lawder presents a somber, uninterrupted twelve minute shot of city people being lifted by an escalator.

Later efforts by independent American filmmakers reveal an assimilation of these various underground methods into fresh, exciting visual experiences. Ken Kobland's *Frame* (1977) combines a matte-process technique with a structural-cinema approach for a fascinating time-space perception. The film's principal image consists of a continuous traveling shot of a row of beach cottages. Into a smaller rectangular frame set over the full-frame shot Kobland inserts varied views of the

Empire (1964), one continuous image of the Empire State Building: an example of minimalist cinema by Andy Warhol.

cottages that reveal what the viewer has just seen on the full screen or what is yet to be seen. The advance-delay inserts appear, variously, in slow motion, normal, and accelerated speeds.

James Benning's award-winning *11 X 14* (1976) presents a superbly realized variation of minimalist methods. Placing his camera onto various scenes of midwest America, Benning allows a single-angle, long-take view of each vignette (there are nearly fifty altogether) to remain on the screen until the mood and rhythms of the environment can be quietly perceived. The effect is that of a "living" photographic album of Americana.

Documentary

With the advent of television, the documentary film in the United States found a more compatible outlet than that provided earlier by theatrical distribution. The need to feed the voracious appetite of the broadcast airwaves and meet the public service demands of the Federal Communications Commission gave new life to the genre.

Network and institutional support underwrote a variety of documentary types, including journalistic: information and analysis (*CBS Reports, NBC White Papers, 60 Minutes*); social: documentaries designed to reveal social problems and to persuade (*Harvest of Shame*, 1960); poetic, educational: documentaries to entertain and teach (*The Real West*, 1961; *The Twentieth Century*, 1957–1964).

Simultaneously, independent documentarists of significance emerged, often producing full-length nonfictional studies with the same personal styling and social perspectives that characterized the underground filmmakers' response to the genre. James Lipscombe, Richard Leacock, D. A. Pennebaker, David and Albert Maysles, and Frederick Wiseman were among those who achieved prominence in the sixties and seventies with documentary films which were characteristically immediate in their treatment of subject matter.

Direct Cinema Drawing on the direct-cinema style seen earlier in the work of George Roquier (*Farrebique*, 1947), Leacock, Pennebaker, Lipscombe, and the Maysles approached their material in a spontaneous manner, avoiding preconceived structuring in order to allow the subject or event to reveal itself. The filmmaker's role was seen as similar to the one played by a reporter: an observer and recorder of what occurs. Hence, the presence of the camera is minimized by wide-angled views and long-take shots. Camera movement and supportive narration are generally avoided. Through scene selection and arrangement the subject is revealed.

The Leacock-Pennebaker documentary *Primary* (1960) gave impetus to the direct-cinema movement. In covering the presidential campaigns of John Kennedy and Hubert Humprhey during the Wisconsin primary, the filmmakers recorded public and private actions of the candidates in a remarkably objective yet intimate manner. The final arrangement of selected scenes demonstrated that the displayed material can present a fascinating account of an event and its participants without the aid of extensive analytical editing.

Among the most successful of the direct cinema applications were Pennebaker's probe of folk singer Bob Dylan on tour, *Don't Look Back* (1966), Leacock's coverage of public reaction to the birth of quintuplets in a small American village, *Happy Mother's Day* (1963), the Maysles' roving view of door-to-door Bible salesmen, *Salesman* (1969), and Ira Wohl's intimate portrait of a middle-aged man whose educational development is that of a child, *Best Boy* (1979).

Wiseman Frederick Wiseman's documentaries incorporate the tactics of direct cinema recording but do not hesitate to set the camera into spontaneous, fluid motion or to pan and zoom freely if necessary to cover a scene. Because his recurring theme is frustration and inadequacy within public service institutions, Wiseman also carefully shapes his material so that positive and negative forces are juxtaposed for heightened effect.

His first film, *Titicut Follies* (1967), exposed inhumane conditions in a Massachusetts mental hospital with such candor a court injunction was sought to prevent public distribution. Other institutional films by Wiseman, all shocking in varying degrees, include: *High School* (1968); *Law and Order* (1969); *Hospital* (1970); *Basic Training* (1971); *Juvenile Court* (1973), *Welfare* (1975), and *Meat* (1976).

The number of documentarists in the United States increased noticeably during the seventies, along with nontheatrical distribution centers needed to meet the high interest of educational and private organizations in the information film. Many of the outstanding independently produced nonfiction films have also been broadcast on the commercial and public broadcasting networks.

EPILOGUE

The future of the cinema has always been and will continue to be plagued by uncertainty. In 1930 producers around the world faced the challenge of newly introduced sound technology and economic depression; in 1950 the American studios anxiously confronted the impact of societal flux, television, and the forced divestment of company-owned theater chains; for producers and exhibitors in 1980 there loomed the impending growth of in-home delivery systems via pay television and video cassettes and discs, potentially a major threat to theatrical consumption of feature films.

In each instance, many doomsayers surfaced to predict the rapid demise and eventual death of cinema. This pessimism and self-doubting are as old as the medium itself; even the sagacious Thomas Edison at first could not see much of a future in the circulation of motion pictures for theatrical consumption.

With each new challenge come adjustment, change, and diverse strategies (often by trial and error) for fully realizing the medium's commercial and cultural potential. To compensate for fluctuation, new technology utilization invariably appears with innovative marketing approaches: in the thirties the addition of Technicolor abetted by double-feature bills; in the fifties wide-screen processes combined with more sensational subject matter; in the seventies new advances in special-effect modes (including Dolby sound) along with the rapid proliferation of self-protective multitheater complexes.

Amidst the confusion and change, somehow, the art of cinema survives. It does so through the diversified, ongoing efforts of film-makers whose creative commitment is inextricably tied to the expressive power of celluloid imagery, as different in stylistic interest as Mel Brooks and Ingmar Bergman, or Stanley Kubrick and Akira Kurosawa. And it also survives through the thousands of extant films that reside in archives around the world, making it possible to enjoy older works for the first time and to revisit others to appreciate them anew.

The art of cinema continues to exist too because of the unique nature of the theatrical film experience. It is impossible to imagine a time when opportunities will cease to exist for the gratification provided by the public, yet anonymous, act of watching a motion picture in a darkened movie house. Only then is the art of cinematic expression made complete for many, many people. To offer such claims, of course, is to close this book on a note of nostalgic wishfulness. Yet others share this view, and none more nostalgically than writer John Updike who has expressed in poetic terms the irrefutable pleasures of the grand old movie house:

> View it, by day, from the back,
> from the parking lot in the rear,
> for from this angle only
> the beautiful brick blankness can be grasped.
> Monumentality
> wears one face in all ages.
>
> No windows intrude real light
> into this temple of shades,
> and the size of it,
> the size of the great rear wall measures
> the breadth of the dreams we have had here.
> It dwarfs the village bank,
> outlooms the town hall,
> and even in its decline
> makes the bright-ceilinged supermarket seem mean.

Stark closet of stealthy rapture,
vast introspective camera
wherein our most daring self-projections
were given familiar names:
stand, stand by your macadam lake
and tell the aeons of our extinction
that we too could house our gods,
could secrete a pyramid
to sight the stars by.

SUGGESTED READINGS

Barsam, Richard Meran. *Non-Fiction Film: A Critical History.* New York: Dutton, 1976.

Curtis, David. *Experimental Cinema.* New York: Universe Books, 1971.

Jacobs, Diane. *Hollywood Renaissance.* New York: Delta, 1977.

Johnson, Robert K. *Francis Ford Coppola.* Boston: Twayne, 1979.

Kass, Judith M. *Robert Altman: American Innovator.* New York: Popular Library, 1978.

Kolker, Robert Phillip. *A Cinema of Loneliness: Penn, Kubrick, Coppola, Scorsese, Altman.* New York: Oxford University Press, 1980.

Sarris, Andrew. *The American Cinema.* New York: Dutton, 1968.

Smith, Julian. *Looking Away: Hollywood and Vietnam.* New York: Scribner, 1975.

Stephenson, Ralph. *The Animated Film.* London: Barnes, 1973.

Youngblood, Gene. *Expanded Cinema.* New York: Dutton, 1970.

GLOSSARY

Ambient sound   Background sound which comes from the location and which adds atmosphere or realism to a film scene.

Angle   The position of the motion-picture camera as it films a scene. The position may be that of a side angle, high angle, low angle, or a straight-on, eye-level view of the scene.

Angle of view   A photographic term which refers to the scope of a shot as determined by choice of lens and camera distance from the subject. The angle of view ranges from a wide angle of view (long shot) to a narrow angle of view (close-up).

Archetype   A literary term, inspired by psychologist Carl Jung, which refers to that element in film, drama, myth, literature, or religion which evokes in the viewer or reader a strong sense of primitive experience. Any image or arrangement of images which activates such primordial responses to literary and dramatic subject matter is referred to as the archetype.

Asynchronous sound   Film sound which, for expressive purposes, is not synchronized with action on the screen.

Available light   Light which comes from existing sources such as daylight or room light and which is used as total or partial illumination in the filming of a motion picture.

Black comedy   A motion picture or a stage play which treats serious subject matter in humorous ways. The tone of the comedy is dark and pessimistic.

Back lighting   One of the lighting elements used in a standard studio lighting scheme, primarily for the purpose of highlighting performers. The light comes from behind the performer, usually from above. When the back light comes from a low position for a romantic effect, it is sometimes referred to as Rembrandt back lighting.

Cameo lighting   (see *Limbo lighting*).

Chiaroscuro lighting   A painting term used frequently to describe a type of motion picture where pictorial representations are rendered with a strong use of lights and darks. In color films light and dark shadings predominate without regard for distinct color values.

Cinematic   A critical term expressing an awareness of that which is peculiar and unique to the film medium. When applied to a specific motion picture, the term indicates that the filmmaker has employed the editing and visual devices, themes, or structural approaches which are especially appropriate to the medium.

Cinéma vérité   A stylistic movement in documentary filmmaking, and a term often applied to a fictional film, where the director, either out of necessity or intentionally, deemphasizes the importance of artistic lighting, exact focus, perfect sound and smooth camera movements. The desired result is a more candid, freer treatment of subject matter.

Closeup   A shot which provides a limited, magnified view of a character or an object in a scene.

Collective story film   A motion picture containing two or more narrative units and arranged so that the separate stories create an expanded treatment of related ideas.

Compilation film   A film created primarily from existing footage that has been reedited around a topical, historical, or visual theme.

Composition   The use of light, color, camera angle, camera movement, and character placement within the film frame for photographic and dramatic expression.

Composition in depth   The arrangement of characters and objects so that the viewer's eye is drawn deep into the film image. This effect is achieved by placing actors and objects in both the foreground and the background areas of the frame composition.

Continuity   The developing and structuring of film segments and ideas so that the events and intended meanings are presented with clarity.

Cover shot   A long view of a film action taken for the purpose of establishing the location and characters within the scene.

Creative geography   A type of editing arrangement where two or more shots taken in different locations suggest spatial unity within a film.

Cut   The splicing together of two pieces of film to maintain continuity of action, to change scenes, or to insert other relevant material into the film narrative.

Deep-focus photography   A motion-picture shot where the immediate foreground images as well as the deepest background images are in sharp focus.

Dialectical film   A film which attempts through its methodology (often the contrast of ideas) to present information for the purposes of intellectual investigation and persuasion. S. M. Eisenstein referred to his dialectical approach in *Potemkin* (1925) as "montage of collision."

Dissolve   The gradual fading out of one shot as another fades in. The dissolve is used primarily as a transitional device to take the story from one location to another, or to indicate a passage of time.

Dolly shot   A moving camera shot in which the camera, mounted on some type of wheeling device, is moved closer to or away from an action during filming.

Double exposure   Two or more images which have been photographed separately but which appear over one another on the same strip of film. Double exposure is achieved by running unprocessed film through the camera twice or by laboratory printing.

Dutch-angle shot   An angled shot in which vertical and horizontal lines within the scene are photographed so that they are in an oblique, tilted relationship with the vertical and horizontal lines of the film frame.

Dynamic cut   A film edit in which a cut from one shot to the next is made abruptly obvious to the viewer.

Epic   A film characterized by its extensive narrative form and heroic qualities. The epic film generally covers a large expanse of time as it follows the continuing adventures of a hero or set of heroes.

Establishing shot   A shot which reveals the location of a film story or scene.

Ethnographic film   A film of an anthropological nature which attempts to describe or visualize the unique social and cultural experiences of one group of people for another.

Expressionism   A stylistic movement in film, drama, painting, and fiction which uses nonrealistic methods in an attempt to suggest psychological mood or inner experiences. Scenic representation is often distorted and darkly somber in visual toning.

Fast film   A film stock which is highly sensitive to light and which allows the photographing of action in lower light levels.

Filter   Most commonly a glass or gelatin element employed to alter the quality of light as it passes to the film emulsion. Filters are used in filmmaking to change color values, increase or decrease contrast, reduce the amount of light hitting the film, and to improve undesirable lighting conditions.

Flashback   A scene or shot in a motion-picture story which presents an event that has occurred prior to the narrative's principal time period.

Flashforward   An editing technique where scenes or shots which occur in a future time are inserted into the developing story-line of a film.

Flat lighting   Lighting within a motion-picture scene which is so evenly diffused that no sense of depth or visual relief is provided.

Flow-of-life film   A term applied to a motion picture where the development of the plot appears to occur in a highly casual, realistic manner.

Fluid camera   A term used to describe the constant movement of the camera during the filming of a motion-picture scene or shot.

Follow boom   A mobile microphone support device which allows the recording of dialogue as characters move about during the filming of a motion-picture scene.

Formalism   An approach to film expression or film analysis which emphasizes the importance of form over content, with the film artist or critic maintaining that it is through cinematic technique that a film's meaning is communicated and understood.

Frame   Each individual photograph that appears on a strip of motion-picture celluloid is referred to as a film frame. To frame a shot means to compose the shot for aesthetic and dramatic purposes.

Freeze-frame   A motion-picture effect which stops (freezes) the motion of the film on a single, repeated frame and allows the chosen image to continue as though it were a still photograph.

Genre   A term for any group of motion pictures which follows similar stylistic, thematic, and structural interests.

Image   The concrete or abstract representation of filmed material as it appears on the screen. In a general sense a film image is the total effect of any photographed material, including its artistic and symbolic qualities.

Impressionism   A style of expression in which the filmmaker seeks to suggest emotions, mood, and sensory effects through a fleeting but vivid use of scenic details.

Intercutting   Editing which moves back and forth between two or more separately developing story elements.

Iris (In-Out)   A laboratory transition effect, occurring when the image moves into a circle which rapidly decreases in size until it disappears. This is an iris in. When a new image appears in a reversal of this process (from small circle to full screen image) this is an iris out.

Jump-cut   The cutting together of two noncontinuous shots within a film scene so that the action appears to jump ahead or back in time.

Kinestasis   A filmmaking technique in which still photographs rather than moving images are used as the source of visual information.

Limbo lighting (Cameo lighting)   A type of motion-picture lighting where light falls only upon the actors in the set area. Space around the actors remains in total darkness.

Long shot   A shot which provides a wide view of a filmed area, enabling the audience to delineate relative proportions with regard to the elements in a scene: their size, shapes, and placement within a visible location.

Long take   The filming of a dramatic action in a single, unbroken shot which, similarly, is edited into the film as a lengthy, uninterrupted shot.

MacGuffin   A term used to describe a plotting device that sets a film intrigue into motion through the curiosity it generates. The MacGuffin may be a missing object, person, or other element of curiosity.

Master shot (scene)   The technique of filming a single, long take of a dramatic action and then repeating the action for closer views. The long-view shot or master scene provides the basic unit of action into which medium and close-up shots can be inserted.

Matched cutting   Cutting on two identical points of action when changing from one shot to another in a scene. A matched cut from a medium shot to a close-up, for example, allows the action to proceed without a noticeable break of continuity.

Matte-screen processing   A laboratory method for combining a foreground action with a separately recorded background scene. A silhouette of the foreground action, called a matte, is produced on high-contrast film and then combined in the optical printer with the background scene.

Medium shot   A shot which in scope falls somewhere between a close-up and a long shot. In a medium shot of a performer, the area of view usually shows the person from the waist up.

Mise-en-scène   A term referring to the total elements in a film shot, including both the performers and the physical setting.

Montage   Another word for film editing—the process of assembling and arranging film shots for a desired effect.

Multi-image shot   A shot in a motion picture which includes two or more separately recorded images within a single frame.

Myth   A type of story, usually of unknown origin and sometimes containing supernatural elements, which has been handed down through a country's literary heritage.

Naturalism   A stylistic approach in literature, drama, or film with an emphasis on stark reality. The environment is a central force in shaping social conditions and the destiny of characters.

Neorealism   A film movement which began in Italy near the end of World War II and characterized by realistic location shooting, stories of common, beleaguered people, and imbued with a strong sense of social consciousness.

Pan   The movement of the camera left or right (horizontally) across a film scene while the camera is mounted on a fixed base.

Parallel development   Switching in a motion picture between two or more separate lines of action which are occurring simultaneously.

Pixilation   A type of animation which employs objects and human beings (rather than hand-drawn images) in a frame-by-frame recording process.

Production values   A trade concept used in reference to the quality of settings, costumes, lighting, and sound within a motion picture.

Realist film   A film which strives for a semblance of actuality and which avoids techniques that suggest artifice or subjective interpretation of screen material.

Rembrandt back lighting   (See *Back lighting*).

Reverse-angle shot   A shot which changes the angle of view so that subject matter is revealed from an opposite direction than that provided by the previous shot. Alternating over-the-shoulder shots in a two-character scene are reverse-angle shots.

Scene   A unit of a motion picture usually composed of a number of interrelated shots that are unified by location, time, or dramatic incident.

Scope (shot)   The angle of view taken in by a motion-picture lens. Shot scope may range from exteme long shot to extreme close-up.

Screwball comedy   A brand of comic film which originated in the 1930s, characterized by a zany, fast-paced, and often irreverent view of domestic or romantic conflicts that ultimately are happily resolved. Witty repartee and unlikely situations are other common qualities of the genre.

Sequence   A unit of film composed of interrelated shots or scenes which together comprise an integral, unified segment of the narrative.

Series films   Motion pictures, usually of feature length, which repeat characters from film to film and employ stories of similar style and type.

Shot   The continuous recording of a film action from the time the camera starts until it stops. The shot is the basic unit of film construction.

Slapstick   Comedy derived from broad, aggressive action, with an emphasis often placed on acts of harmless cruelty.

Soft focus   A photographed image which lacks sharp definition.

Sound track   The optical or magnetic track at the edge of the film which contains music, dialogue, narration, and sound effects.

Spectacle   A film characterized by lavish production design, epic theme, grand scope, and a large cast of screen performers.

Spin-off   A term used to describe a motion picture that is inspired by another film, usually a highly successful and popular work which the spin-off seeks to imitate.

Stop-action (motion) filming   The photographing of an action for trick effect by a break in filming that permits elements in the scene to be changed, added, or deleted before filming of the action is resumed. This stop-action (motion) process permits the effect of a sudden appearance or disappearance of objects or actors when the film is projected.

Structural cinema   A type of experimental film which places its emphasis on sustained or repeated views of filmed material.

Studio picture   A motion picture made principally on a shooting stage rather than on location, and usually characterized by exact technical control of lighting, settings, camera, and sound.

Style   The manner by which a motion-picture idea is expressed so that it effectively reveals the idea as well as the filmmaker's attitude toward the idea.

Subjective-camera shot   A shot which suggests a character's point of view by having the camera assume the character's eye scan or body movements.

Surrealism   A modern movement in painting, sculpture, theater, photography, literature, and film that seeks to express subconscious states through the disparate and illogical arrangement of imagery.

Symbol   An object or image which carries both a literal reality as well as a larger, more abstract meaning.

Synchronous sound   A term referring to the precise coordination of film images with their corresponding sounds.

Tilt   Camera movement up or down (vertically) while filming action with the camera mounted on a fixed base.

Time (motion picture)   A term which refers to the nature and possibilities of a motion picture's temporal elements. If action in a film proceeds in a rigid time continuum, it is referred to as actual time. If the filmmaker, however, uses editing to draw out or shorten a film action, time is extended or compressed.

Tracking shot   A moving camera shot which follows the movements of characters or vehicles. The camera tracks either ahead of, beside, or behind the moving action. Also sometimes referred to as a trucking shot.

Transition   Any one of a number of devices by which a film moves from one scene or sequence to another.

Voice over   The use of film narration, commentary, subjective thought, or dialogue in which the speaker or speakers remain unseen.

Zoom shot   A shot taken with a varifocal-length lens and which either increases or decreases the scope of the shot as the camera is filming.

INDEX